Terror on the Santa Fe Trail

Kit Carson and the Jicarilla Apache

Doug Hocking

TWODOT®

GUILFORD, CONNECTICUT
HELENA, MONTANA

To my Jicarilla friends, Vigils, Velardes, Wanoskias, Vicentis, Munizes, and too many others who have passed from the scene whose names can no longer be spoken. I never knew you well enough and wish I had.

A · TWODOT® · BOOK

An imprint and registered trademark of The Rowman & Littlefield Publishing Group, Inc.
4501 Forbes Blvd., Ste. 200
Lanham, MD 20706
www.rowman.com

Distributed by NATIONAL BOOK NETWORK

British Library Cataloguing in Publication Information available

Library of Congress Cataloging-in-Publication Data available

ISBN 978-1-4930-4179-4 (hardcover)
ISBN 978-1-4930-4180-0 (e-book)

♾™ The paper used in this publication meets the minimum requirements of American National Standard for Information Sciences—Permanence of Paper for Printed Library Materials, ANSI/ NISO Z39.48-1992.

Contents

Acknowledgments

No author writes a book alone, so there are many people to thank.

My wife, Debbie, as always read my day's work and let me know if it was intelligible. At the Donnelly Library at New Mexico Highlands University, in Las Vegas, New Mexico, I got some wonderful help from the librarians Irisha Corral, Loretta Duran, and April Kent, who were in possession of a wonderfully helpful set of records from Fort Union. You'll find many, many quotes from those records herein. The works of Tiller, Bender, Murphy, and others kept me on track so looking into those records of the past, I knew what the authors were talking about. It's a wonderful experience to read the secondary history and then to suddenly see events through the eyes of someone who was there. Debra Chatham, at Sierra Vista Library, as always was a wonderful help getting me books and articles, often letting me have a bit more than library rules allowed.

I need to thank friends among the Jicarilla who have helped with the present work including Veronica Velarde Tiller, Sheldon Nuñez-Velarde, who makes pots in the old way, Vida Vigil-Garcia, tribal historian along with Vernon Petago, and Vida's sister, Claudia Vigil-Muniz. Some of these folks have been friends since childhood and Vernon remembered that I'd dated his cousin. Price Heiner, Carson National Forest archaeologist, was helpful with information about the Cieneguilla battlefield, and Greg Michno provided helpful information and assistance. Bernd Brand went with me to Cieneguilla. We walked a very long way despite an injury to his leg. The folks at the New Mexico State Library, Joy Poole and Amy Schaefer, were absolutely wonderful and let me in to go through records at a time when the library was closed for remodeling. Heather McClure, and Hannah Abelbeck, photo imaging specialist, at the Palace of the Governors Photo Archive were wonderfully helpful devoting a lot of time to finding me pictures and in suggesting others that might be helpful. Bunker de France and Harry Alexander on *Voices of the West* have always been supportive and helped to get the message out. Clay Renick at the Hutchison County Museum, in Borger, Texas, maintains a wonderful museum and was helpful in getting us to the Adobe Walls Battlefield. Lastly, Gene and Rosanna Baker have always been helpful and supportive of my work.

Our friend, Ron Woggon, loves endnotes, so I made sure that there were plenty just for him. I have to thank Chris Enss for introducing me to the wise and instructive Erin Turner, who despite Ron's thoughts encouraged me to reduce the number of endnotes. And last I should thank my helpful friends of the Amigos and Ladies of the West, many of them TwoDot authors, who share a booth with me at the Tucson Festival of Books: Lowell Volk, Carol Markstrom, Bill Markley, Chris Enss, Melody Groves, Vonn McKee, Rod Timanus, and Kellen Cutsforth.

Introduction

In the early nineteenth century, forbidden Santa Fe drew Americans in search of wealth. The United States and Spain disputed the southern boundary of the Louisiana Purchase. Spain said it was the Missouri River while the French claimed they'd sold the Americans everything to the Rio Grande. The Spanish government, fearing American expansionism, imprisoned travelers who made their way across the plains and confiscated their goods. But still the allure was there. St. Louis was closer to Santa Fe than the City of the Holy Faith of St. Francis was to Mexico City.

The economic theory followed by the Spanish and then the Mexicans called for manufactured goods to come from the center while the outer provinces provided raw materials and were denied the tools of manufacture. Outer regions—New Mexico, Texas, and California—remained poor and underdeveloped at the end of a long tether extending back to Mexico City.

On March 15, 1818, General Andrew Jackson invaded Spanish Florida. The United States and Spain came to terms in the Adams-Onis Treaty of 1819, finally ratified by the US Senate in 1821. Spain gave up Florida and agreed that a line roughly following the Arkansas River was its northern boundary. With its American colonies in revolt, Spain wished to ensure that Americans would not lend support to the rebels. The year the Senate ratified the treaty, Mexico won her independence from Spain. Mexico disputed the legality of the treaty. No one knew how the new government would receive American traders.

The United States from the time of independence had been pushing Indian tribes westward across the Mississippi River, establishing a frontier beyond which it did not allow American pioneers to legally settle. The Frontier was a line as real as the boundaries of any state. The Great Plains, a desert where water was scarce, were empty of all but Indians and buffalo. Marauding Indians drove travelers to band together in large caravans. The third of the trail beyond the Arkansas River in Mexican territory on both the Mountain Branch and the Cimarron Cutoff belonged to the Jicarilla Apache.[1]

In 1821, William Becknell took a pack train over the Santa Fe Trail. He was not alone. Thomas James was two weeks behind him, and Hugh Glenn arrived two months later. Their profit, suggested to have been several hundred percent, excited others and the next year wagons rolled across the sea of grass. Merchants were tight-lipped about their affairs. We get some idea of the profit to be made in an 1824 news article, which reported that one caravan took thirty thousand dollars worth of goods to Santa Fe and returned with one hundred eighty thousand dollars in specie, mules, and hides, a 600 percent return on investment.[2] In October 1834, the *Missouri Republican* reported that traders "brought in, as near as can be ascertained, $40,000 in gold, $140,000 in specie, $15,000 worth of beaver, 50 packs of buffalo robes, 12,000 pounds of wool, and 300 head of mules, valued at $10,000."[3] Josiah Gregg in the 1844 edition of *Commerce of the Prairies* provided a table showing steady growth in the trade from fifteen thousand pounds in 1822 to four hundred fifty thousand pounds the last year for which numbers are given. Unfortunately, the figures are in the weight shipped and not in dollars.[4] Moreover, Seymour Connor speculates that Gregg's figures are understated.[5]

More than half of this weight continued on from Santa Fe to Chihuahua. New Mexico was poor, but it was a back door to Mexico. Closure of ports and high tariffs discouraged trade by sea. In Santa Fe officials ignored import restrictions and the correct amount of tariff. Continuing on to Chihuahua gave access to regions of Mexico producing gold and silver. The Jackson Administration of the 1830s did away with the national bank, which led to a high demand for specie. The Santa Fe Trade was an important source.

In 1824, Santa Fe trader Augustus Storrs answered a query from Senator Thomas Hart Benton of Missouri by saying that the items in demand in Santa Fe were "cotton goods, consisting of coarse and fine cambrics, calicoes, domestics, shawls, handkerchiefs, steam-loom shirtings, pelisse cloths, and shawls, crapes, bombazettes, some light articles of cutlery, silk shawls, and looking glasses." To this we might add tools and luxury items as well as canned foods and spirits. In return merchants brought back "Spanish milled dollars, a small amount of gold and silver, in bullion, beaver fur, and some mules."[6] This amounted to so many mules that mules became synonymous with Missouri. Thus Santa Fe, and Chihuahua beyond, became an outlet for the textile mills of New England and a source of much-needed specie.

Missouri was the jumping off point for the fur trade, the Oregon and California Trails, and for the Santa Fe Trail. Its western boundary was the Frontier. It was economically important to the export of textiles and the import of specie. Senator Benton hoped to continue Missouri dominance by putting it on the route of a transcontinental railroad, sending his son-in-law, John Charles Frémont, to search for a route across the Rocky Mountains. Kit Carson accompanied the Pathfinder as scout and guide.

Since independence Mexico had been deeply in debt, borrowing from both the French and British. In 1833, Antonio López de Santa Anna came to power as president. In 1834, he abolished liberal reforms, dissolved the Congress, and instituted a centralist government. In 1835, he abolished the Constitution of 1824 replacing it with the Seven Laws. Since 1821, Mexico had been inviting American citizens into underpopulated Texas to settle and become Mexican citizens. With the abandonment of the constitution in 1835, they revolted. In 1836, they defeated Santa Anna in battle and captured him. The settlement forced upon the Mexican president created a Texas that extended to the Rio Grande, placing Albuquerque, Santa Fe, and Taos within its bounds. The Mexican states San Luis Potosí, Querétaro, Durango, Guanajuato, Michoacán, Yucatán, Jalisco, Nuevo León, Tamaulipas, and Zacatecas rebelled as well. California ejected Santa Anna's appointed governor. In 1837, in New Mexico, rebels literally tore Santa Anna's governor to pieces and replaced him with their own. Eight years later, Texas, having declared herself independent, remained in open warfare with Mexico along the Nueces Strip and at sea, and central government authority was largely overlooked in California and New Mexico. France and England threatened to take land for debt. Texas petitioned the United States for admission as a state and, as the country delayed, then negotiated for recognition by Britain. A new British dependency in Texas would not have been good for the United States, nor would British or French seizure of California.

In 1845, the United States accepted Texas as a state. Mexico refused to negotiate and then, in 1846, "invaded" the United States, crossing into land that was in dispute, and killed American soldiers. President James K. Polk countered by invading Mexico from Texas and across the plains to New Mexico and California. Polk's plan always included annexing New Mexico and California, and he sent General Kearny and the Army of the West to make both part of the United States. New Mexico fell without a fight, and Kearny appointed Santa Fe trader Charles Bent governor. He offered the New Mexicans citizenship, exceeding his authority and anticipating the Treaty of Guadalupe Hidalgo by a year and a half. In 1847, in a brief revolt, Taos rebels slew Governor Bent. Kearny fought two small battles and took California. Kit Carson was with the general and forged a close friendship with Lieutenant John Wynn Davidson.

The war ended in early 1848, while the Missouri Volunteers remained in New Mexico and continued to abuse the population until the end of the year. In 1846, Kearny had established civil government and a territorial

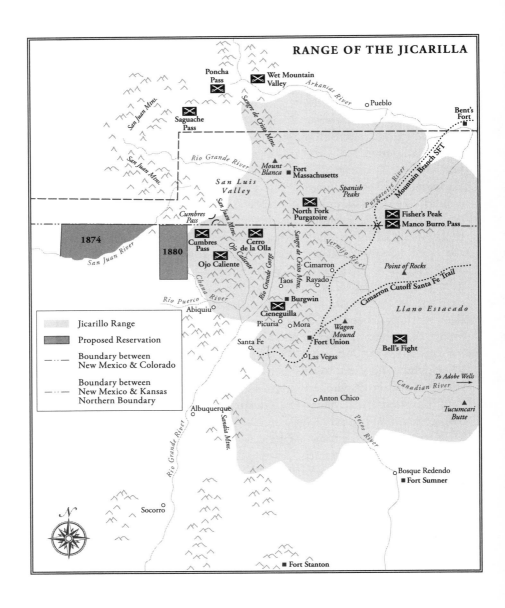

RANGE OF THE JICARILLA

Poncha Pass

Wet Mountain Valley

Arkansas River

Pueblo

Bent's Fort

San Juan Mtns.

Saguache Pass

Sangre de Cristo Mtns.

Rio Grande River

Mount Blanca

Fort Massachusetts

San Luis Valley

Spanish Peaks

Purgatoire River

Mountain Branch SFT

Fisher's Peak

Manco Burro Pass

Cumbres Pass

San Juan Mtns.

North Fork Purgatoire

1874

San Juan River

1880

Cumbres Pass

Cerro de la Olla

Ojo Caliente

Ojo Caliente

Sangre de Cristo Mtns.

Vermijo River

Cimarron

Chama River

Rio Grande Gorge

Taos

Rayado

Point of Rocks

Cimarron Cutoff Santa Fe Trail

Llano Estacado

Rio Puerco

Abiquiu

Burgwin

Cieneguilla

Picuria

Mora

Santa Fe

Wagon Mound

Fort Union

Bell's Fight

Las Vegas

To Adobe Wells

Canadian River

Legend

- Jicarillo Range
- Proposed Reservation
- Boundary between New Mexico & Colorado
- Boundary between New Mexico & Kansas Northern Boundary

Albuquerque

Sandia Mtns.

Anton Chico

Pecos River

Tucumcari Butte

Rio Grande River

Bosque Redendo

Fort Sumner

Socorro

N

Fort Stanton

constitution but Congress did not accept it. It was not until September 1850 that Congress, divided over the issue of slavery, granted territorial status to the newly acquired land. Confusion reigned in civil affairs; there was a territorial governor, then a military governor, and at times both disputed each other's authority. In a gesture worthy of a comic opera, Texas even sent officials to Santa Fe to assume control of her "western county." Sensing the confusion and disorganization, the tribes of the southern plains considered open warfare, and in 1847 and 1848, merchants on the Santa Fe Trail reported that Indians accosted every caravan that traveled the trade route. In June 1848, Jicarilla Apache occupied Raton Pass and for a while closed the Mountain Branch of the trail.

Their range extended from Abiquiu on the Chama River north through the San Juan Mountains to Mount Blanca and east and north across the Sangre de Cristo Mountains to the Arkansas River and Texas Panhandle. Santa Fe trader Josiah Gregg had dismissed them in 1844 as a small and unimportant band. In 1846, Governor Bent estimated that there were only about five hundred Jicarilla Apache, minimizing the threat they posed. He was mistaken as there were more than twice that number, about thirteen hundred Jicarilla in all. Other governors reported that they were the most troublesome tribe of all. It was the Jicarilla who on three occasions closed the Santa Fe Trail.

In May 1848, Kit Carson carried dispatches from General Kearny in California to Washington, DC. He chose to travel by the Old Spanish Trail, which ran across California deserts through southern Utah and Colorado to Taos.[7] Along the way he lost many of his rifles and most of the party's food. In July his bedraggled party confronted Jicarilla Apaches, whom he deemed dangerous. Perhaps he'd heard about the June events near Raton Pass when the Jicarilla closed the trail.

In November 1849, near Point of Rocks, the Jicarilla struck the two wagons of the White Wagon Train, killing the men, and taking Ann White and her baby daughter captive. They had closed the trail again and travelers turned back. While leadership in Santa Fe panicked, Major William Grier sought out Kit Carson as guide and scout. Carson demurred. He knew that his Rayado ranch was in Jicarilla territory. When they came by Carson fed them and gave them a few steers and had no trouble. He ridiculed others like rancher Samuel B. Watrous who refused to bend and suffered numerous raids. The major persuaded Carson to go along in pursuit of Mrs. White and afterward the Jicarilla raided Carson's ranch. In the spring of 1850, though plainsmen thought the group large enough to be safe from Indian attack, the Jicarilla killed an eleven-man mail party at Wagon Mound. Travelers and wagon trains turned back again, and the trail was closed a third time.

The Jicarilla were defeated and sought peace. Governors and superintendents of Indian Affairs negotiated treaties, which the Senate rejected, but the Jicarilla remained at peace. In 1853, Governor William Carr Lane, a lame duck his entire time in office, negotiated a treaty with the Apache and had them start farms. His successor, Governor David Meriwether, repudiated the treaty saying that it would lead to war. The Senate rejected it. The war didn't come until Lieutenant John Davidson attacked a peaceful Jicarilla camp at Cieneguilla. A year and a half of war followed with Kit Carson, by then the Jicarilla Indian agent, recommending a fair and just peace treaty from shortly after the war began. The war continued another year and a half until Governor Meriwether could claim victory and renegotiate Lane's treaty, claiming it as his own.

Many people have never heard of the Jicarilla Apache. After the war of 1854/55, they never again took the field against the United States. They were distant from the "States," and the eastern newspapers didn't as yet have the resources to report on their years of war. The nation soon convulsed in the Civil War and Americans tended to forget what had occurred before the war. The Jicarilla continued to fight for their rights in negotiations and with passive resistance. Unenviably, they wandered, drawing rations at Abiquiu and Cimarron, not allowed to settle, with too little game to hunt, told to stay away from towns. In 1887, the Jicarilla were the last tribe settled on a reservation, but it was one they had chosen.

In 1848, Kit Carson was a potential foe of the Jicarilla. By 1849, he had settled at Rayado and was a neighbor. That year soldiers recruited him to scout against the Apache. The Jicarilla struck back and he struck back harder. That was the mountain man way of warning off those who would depredate against them. In 1854, he became their Indian agent and tried to negotiate a supply of rations to feed them. After Davidson's defeat at Cieneguilla, Carson scouted for the Army and then asked for a peace treaty. The governor refused and the "chastisement" of the Jicarilla continued into the fall of 1855.

Kit Carson can be a difficult man to understand. He was intelligent but illiterate. He spoke his mind bluntly and did not express himself as a diplomat or politician. He didn't seem to understand what people might think seeing his words in writing. We only know him through what others wrote for him. How close they came to his original words and meaning is hard to say. He had been a mountain man and believed in tit-for-tat as a means to deter continued violence between his people and the Indians. Carson realized that whites were depriving the Indians of the wild game they needed to subsist and asked for the government to make reasonable treaties ensuring that they would be able to survive. He understood that Indian depredations were driven by the need to eat but at the same time believed that the Indian should be chastised when he depredated. He expressed this bluntly as "we've got to feed them or exterminate them." This was not a call for genocide. He wanted them fed. It was an expression of reality and the future as he saw it.

He was loyal to friends, and this got him into difficulty when the friends were General Carleton and John Frémont. He came to Lieutenant Davidson's defense at a court of inquiry when two years prior he had decried the lieutenant's acts. He called for a treaty with the Jicarilla, but a year and a half later said they wouldn't abide by it. As much as he stood by friends, perhaps the change of opinion he expressed had more to do with the man who was his enemy, Governor Meriwether. He objected to Governor Meriwether's bureaucratic machinations in making war on a people in order to take personal credit for Governor Lane's treaty. Nothing else in the record explains his complete reversal of opinion on Davidson's blunder and the rejection of a treaty he had called for.

Santa Fe was tethered to the "States" by the 950-mile-long umbilicus that was the Santa Fe Trail. The new territory was unable to support the indigenous population, Indian and Mexican, along with the US troops that had arrived in 1846 and stayed both to protect the claims of the new government and to protect the people from Indians. Since they were positioned on the trail and had closed it before, the most minor depredations of the Jicarilla Apache magnified their threat. Where earlier governors had largely dismissed the Jicarilla, Meriwether was able to believably leverage their menace into "the most dangerous and troublesome tribe of all." After 1855, the Jicarilla Apache depart from the collective consciousness, brought down by the ambitions of a governor and a young lieutenant and the negligence of Congress.

Only one thing happened, and it is up to the historian to tell us what that was. Human motivation is a bundle like a telephone trunk line. The same individual can point to different motivations at different times and express them differently to divergent audiences with equal truth. It makes history interesting. There are different facets of the story the historian can emphasize with equal truth. Differing tellings may be more relevant to different times. In his book about the Jicarilla Apache, *Depredation and Deceit*, Greg Michno emphasized the role of false claims for reparations in generating difficulty with otherwise peaceful tribes. This is a thread that runs through the Indian Wars, though this may not be the most important factor in the story of the Jicarilla.

Recently, Malcolm Ebright explored the role of the Indian agent. Many readers will be familiar with the Hollywood image of the corrupt Indian agent who stole the food and annuities the government had promised to give the Indians in exchange for their land. Ebright noted:

> *William Unrau argues that the unfavorable reputation of Indian agents was often the result of scapegoating—blaming individual Indian agents when it was the system itself that was broken. Unrau challenged other scholars to deepen their analysis of the Indian agent, asking, "Where is the closely argued monograph . . . challenging the devil theory of the Indian Agent?"*[8]

Perhaps the Jicarilla Apache were lucky in their agents. They had many good ones: John Greiner, Kit Carson, Lorenzo Labadie, and Benjamin Thomas. According to Ebright, "an examination of the career of Benjamin Thomas shows that he was neither dishonest nor corrupt, but was instead an effective advocate for the Pueblos [and the Jicarilla], although he was constrained by bureaucratic and political limitations."[9] Unable to promote the Jicarilla Apache desires "Thomas found a way to advocate for the Apaches through a series of letters purportedly from the Jicarilla chief Delgatito Largo, but actually written by Thomas himself."[10] Thus, he defines the good agent as one who advocated for the Indian. The concept seems anachronistic.[11] We can applaud Agent Thomas today, but the standard would have been confusing to many in the nineteenth century when folks were still fighting wild Indians.

In *Depredation and Deceit* historian Greg Michno deals with the law of unintended consequence. In 1796, the United States passed "An Act to Regulate Trade and Intercourse with the Indian Tribes and to Preserve Peace on the Frontiers." It called for punishment of whites who trespassed on Indian lands committing robbery or other crimes against friendly Indians. When Indians invaded an American state or territory committing "murder, violence, or outrage," the citizen could apply to the government for compensation, which would come out of the annual stipend being paid by the government to the Indians. A door was opened to fraud. The act potentially encouraged settlers to exaggerate claims for damage. In 1834, the act was modified. Claims had to be made within three years and there was no cap on the amount to be paid. If the Indian annuities were insufficient, the amount would be drawn from the treasury. "Whites were free to file fraudulent claims and soldiers free to march out to confront Indians and accuse them of depredations, not knowing if the parties they accosted were guilty or innocent."[12] In some years, the people of New Mexico managed to claim more stolen livestock, especially sheep, than there had ever been livestock in the territory.

Whether this led to violence against the Indians is questionable. The military investigated claims at the source and time and again dismissed them. Frequent claimants included Lucien Maxwell and Samuel B. Watrous.[13] The Maxwell Land Grant, the largest in the territory, included much of northeastern New Mexico.[14] In attempting to populate it and while conducting business all through the Jicarilla range, Maxwell was in one of the most exposed positions possible; he was on the frontier. We would expect someone in this position to suffer more depredations from the Indians. Kit Carson partnered with Maxwell in Rayado at the foot of the Sangre de Cristo Range. Carson and Maxwell both gave livestock to the Jicarilla in return for the use of their land. Others have speculated that Maxwell added these gifts to his depredation claims and probably exaggerated them as well, including stock that disappeared which might have been taken by Indians.[15] To Maxwell it would have seemed only fair. These were not the extremely exaggerated claims that seem to have included whole herds of sheep driven to California and sold there to feed the Forty-Niners. In the summer of 1849, emigrant Charles Pancoast met Carson at Rayado and wrote of his handling of stock theft.

He [Kit Carson] spoke of the difficulties he had experienced in maintaining the lonely position he occupied and in protecting his Stock from the Raids of the Utes and other Indians. He had called in the aid of the U.S. Soldiers, and being thoroughly acquainted with the haunts of the Indians, he had punished them so severely that they had found it their best Policy to make their Peace with him. He now enjoyed their Friendship, and often gave them meat; and they no longer molested his Stock, although they continued to steal that of others.[16]

"[A]lthough they continued to steal that of others" seems likely to refer to Samuel Watrous, who ranched at La Junta and was a beef contractor to the army.[17] He was in a very exposed location near Las Vegas, where the Jicarilla came to trade, and Mora, on one of the trails that led over the Sangre de Cristo to Taos, and was hit perhaps more frequently than any other stock grower. His claims, though they may have been exaggerated, appear to have stemmed from real raids. The frequency of depredations against Watrous and his response to them seems to indicate that he did not enjoy the sort of "friendly" relations with the Jicarilla that Kit Carson did.

In 1855, the peak year of raiding, there were only ten incidents attributed to the Jicarilla. This was a year when they were on the run and may not have had time to hunt, and so we may rightly attribute these raids to the presence of the Army. The peak years for conflict between the Army and the Jicarilla were 1849 and 1850, but in those years depredations amounted to two and four respectively and included incidents of murder and mayhem, not just stock raids. For a people often described in these years as starving, this does not appear to be an unusual number of stock raids. Promise of repayment by the US government undoubtedly motivated some claims and encouraged people to exaggerate, but claims often took many years to be settled. Some of Maxwell's claims were not settled for over thirty years and thus after his death. Presumably, only those with deep pockets could pursue them that far. Claims were filed, investigated, and dismissed without much aggravation to the Indians. This would not have been the only motivator to war.

Anthropologist B. Sunday Eiselt has speculated that "[h]istorians and anthropologists have perpetuated a view of the Jicarilla as peripheral players in narratives of the American West . . . the Jicarilla rarely garner a footnote, leaving us with questions and contradictions that limit our understanding of their place in history."[18] She notes that before going on a raid, Jicarilla warriors made themselves invisible by donning white clay. In political affairs they also metaphorically "donned white clay," becoming invisible as they shaped their destiny. Rather than pawns of an uncaring US Congress, she sees the Jicarilla as taking a hand in their own destiny. In her view these Apaches made themselves part of the social fabric that held New Mexican villages together, trading mountain products and pottery for manufactured goods, alcohol, and corn. They slipped into the empty lands between the villages and on the plains and lived between 1856 and 1887 almost invisibly, presenting only a small annoyance to the government.[19]

Micaceous pottery like this was an important trade item in metal-poor New Mexico. The addition of mica as temper ensured even distribution of heat so that the pots would not crack when exposed directly to flame. Pot by Sheldon Nuñez-Velarde. AUTHOR PHOTO

In 1854 and 1855, the governor of New Mexico sent troops to crush the Jicarilla, refusing to offer them a peace treaty despite the plea of Indian agent Kit Carson. Prior to 1855, the Jicarilla posed a significant threat to New Mexico and to commerce on the Santa Fe Trail. After 1855, they became invisible without a reservation, drawing "presents" at various locations and otherwise told to stay away. Between 1855 and 1887, they were without a reservation and unwelcome everywhere, but during that period they twice sent delegations to Washington, DC, asking for consideration. Denied a reservation they were sent to live under control of the Mescalero Apache and shaped their own future by asking the governor if they could become citizens and take up homesteads.

Today the Jicarilla Apache are nearly forgotten, their great victory at Cieneguilla overlooked, occurring before the Civil War when New Mexico was still a far-off land. These were the warriors who were once the Terror of the Santa Fe Trail, foe, friend, and fighting comrades of Kit Carson.

Chapter 1

The first recorded interaction between Kit Carson and the Jicarilla Apache came in the summer of 1848 north of Taos. In June of that year the Jicarilla had closed the Raton Pass on the Mountain Branch of the Santa Fe Trail. News traveled slowly across the mountains and deserts from New Mexico to California, but somehow Kit Carson seemed to know that the usually peaceful Jicarilla might pose a real threat. Lieutenants George Brewerton and Kit Carson had selected an escort of mountain men to assist them in carrying dispatches to Washington, DC.[1,2]

Until their recent introduction the Kit Carson of Brewerton's imagination had been over six feet tall, a modern Hercules in build, with an enormous beard and voice like a roused lion. Brewerton would later write about his experiences with the legendary Carson:

> The real *Kit Carson I found to be a plain, simple, unostentatious man;* rather below the medium height, with brown, curling hair, little or no beard, and a voice as soft and gentle as a woman's. In fact, the hero of a hundred desperate encounters, whose life had been mostly spent amid wildernesses, where the white man is almost unknown, was one of Dame Nature's gentlemen—a sort of article which she gets up occasionally, but nowhere in better style than among the backwoods of America.[3]

Any crossing of the deserts on the Old Spanish Trail was hard. One put up with the stench of mule sweat and unwashed mountaineers who dressed in half-cured hides. The food was bad until it ran out and gnawing hunger replaced it. There were no towns or trading posts where one could restock. If one lost or broke a tool, the traveler did without. Brewerton recalled a day of extreme thirst when he found water deep in a crevice in the rock. His servant had appropriated the lieutenant's tin cup and he found himself dipping water in a human skull. "[R]evolting as it would have been under different circumstances, my strong necessity compelled me to make use of it. So I drank a most grateful draught of water from the bleaching bone, and then sat down to moralize upon the event, and wonder to whom it had belonged, and how its owner died."[4] Dust and grit got into everything: food, bedroll, clothing, and between one's seat and the saddle.

Brewerton's journey with Kit Carson had been particularly hard. In crossing the Grand River, they packed their supplies on rafts.[5] "[B]ut a large raft, which carried the greater share of our provisions, was dashed against a sawyer in the stream, which separated the logs leaving the men to save themselves as they best could."[6, 7] They also lost six rifles and three saddles, as well as much of the

Lieutenant Brewerton rode with Kit Carson from Los Angeles to Taos in 1848 carrying dispatches. They encountered the Jicarilla north of Taos. WIKIMEDIA COMMONS

ammunition. Lacking provisions, ammunition, and short of rifles, they went hungry and were reduced to eating horse meat.[8] They still had hundreds of miles to go before reaching the settlements of northern New Mexico.

The day had begun with promise. Kit Carson's party had descended into the San Luis Valley north of Taos. They were within reach of the settlements and safety but were on the lookout for the rumored bands of Indians who had been harassing caravans. Brewerton wrote that fellow lieutenant Kit Carson detected "Indian sign," that is tracks of many ponies.

> *"Look here," said Kit, as he dismounted from his mule, and stooped to examine the trail. "The Indians have passed across our road since sun-up, and they are a war party too; no sign of lodge poles, and no colt tracks; they are no friends neither: here's a feather that some of them has dropped. We'll have trouble yet, if we don't keep a bright look-out."[9]*

They rode mules that the Apache would find enticing despite their poor condition. A few days' grazing would put some meat back on them. In any event, they were meat for the Apache pot. Kit Carson and his party had but few weapons and little ammunition. Worse, they had nothing to offer as gifts to appease the Indians, not even *pinole* and *atole*, which the Indians prized and were always glad to receive. If the Jicarilla discovered how desperate, starved, and defenseless they were, they stood little chance of survival. Their only hope lay with Kit Carson.

Carson recalled the incident laconically in his autobiography:

About fifty miles out of Taos we met several hundred Utah and Apache Indians. They made demonstrations of hostility, and we retired into the brush, where we permitted only a few of them to approach us. We told them that if they were friends, they should leave us, as we were in a naked and destitute condition and could give them nothing. When they saw we had nothing, they left us. I moved on about ten miles where I met a party of volunteers in pursuit of Apaches. I reached Taos the next day.[10]

Brewerton recalled a much more menacing threat and admitted to more terror than Kit Carson ever would. The lieutenants and their party were somewhat less than dashing in appearance. The Jicarilla would have them beat on this count. The travelers were ragged and filthy. In lieu of hat, lost on the trail, Brewerton had his underwear tied about his head and two of those in the front rank had lost their trousers in the Grand River and now rode to battle without. George Brewerton recalled that toward noon Carson spotted a number of Indians some distance ahead.

[W]e called a halt, and after a moment's consultation, determined to make a charge, and as we seemed pretty equally matched in regard to numbers, to take, if necessary, the offensive line of conduct. With this view, we selected ten of our best men, and having arrayed our forces, came down, so far as determination was concerned in very gallant style, each man with his rifle in his hand, firmly resolved to "do or die."[11]

The charge heralded by bellowing mules came to naught when they discovered the presumed enemy was a party of Mexican traders. The Mexicans warned that there were indeed a large number of Jicarilla Apaches nearby who had defeated and despoiled a party of mountaineers.[12]

The next morning, they proceeded at "daybreak, determined to steal a march upon the enemy." As Brewerton imagined the meal he would savor in Taos after so long in starvation, Kit's voice cut in on his musings: "Look at that Indian village; we have stumbled upon the rascals, after all!" The valley the men entered was narrow, the village over two hundred lodges, and they were hemmed in on either side. By keeping close to the mountain's foot, they hoped to slip by unnoticed. The Apaches espied them and a warrior dashed out to confront Kit and Brewerton in the lead. Kit turned to the lieutenant and told

Kit Carson in 1848 at Washington, DC. He lost a lot of weight during his ride from Los Angeles with Lieutenant Brewerton. His ragtag band faced down the Jicarilla. COURTESY PALACE OF THE GOVERNORS PHOTO ARCHIVES (NMHM/DCA), 134000

him that he would try speaking to the brave in "Eutaw" in hopes the man was from a friendly tribe and not an Apache.[13] "[F]rom his paint and manner I expect it will end in a fight anyway."[14]

The warrior looked on in puzzlement as Carson spoke in Ute. Carson turned and directed his followers to make for a patch of chaparral that would give some cover and prevent the Indians from charging the weary, outnumbered band. Carson ordered Brewerton to fall in behind the Indian and be prepared to shoot him as he followed Carson should the situation warrant. As the party entered the grove, Carson fell back alongside Brewerton and whispered, "Look back, but express no surprise." Brewerton did and saw that now 150 warriors arrayed for battle were following.

Now, boys, dismount, tie up your riding mules; those of you who have guns, get round the caballada, and look out for the Indians; and you who have none, get inside, and hold some of the animals. Take care, Thomas, and shoot down the mule with the mail bags on her pack, if they try to stampede the animals.[15, 16, 17]

The Old Spanish Trail had provided a new terror, hostile Indians. Lieutenant Brewerton scanned the enemy ranks before him. The men in his party were close to starvation, their livestock in poor condition, and some had lost their britches to the river. Now they faced a band of Jicarilla Apache, arrayed for war and painted in white clay for battle. A warrior kicked his horse and galloped straight for Brewerton, brandishing his lance and then pulling it away inches from the young man's pounding chest. The ghastly demon face laughed and turned to threaten another of the bedraggled party. Shrill cries filled the air, as pandemonium was unleashed. Another Apache in full war dress drew his bow and aimed his arrow at the lieutenant's heart.

Brewerton found his party completely surrounded in a scene of confusion and excitement. The Indians screamed their war cries, aimed spears, and drew back their bows. Carson's whole demeanor changed. He looked a different man; "his eye fairly flashed, and his rifle was grasped with all the energy of an iron will."[18]

"There," cried he, addressing the savages, "is our line, cross it if you dare, and we begin to shoot. You ask us to let you in, but you won't come unless you ride over us. You say you are friends, but you don't act like it. No, you don't deceive us so, we know you too well; so stand back, or your lives are in danger."[19]

This was largely a bluff. Their ragtag band was outnumbered five to one and a part of the band lacked weapons. They wouldn't hold out long being critically short of ammunition—only three rounds per man. An Indian rider on a weary foam-specked horse galloped up to his chief with news that brought confusion to the Apache. At their chief's direction they fell back and Carson saw his chance: "Now boys, we have a chance, jump into your saddles, get the loose animals before you, and then handle your rifles, and if these fellows interfere with us we'll make a running fight of it."[20]

Kit Carson avoided a fight, but Brewerton's terror was real and the danger he sensed was real. The new government of New Mexico was in confusion and the Indians of the southern plains sensed that things were not as they had been. Like children testing a substitute teacher they struck. In 1848, every caravan on the Santa Fe Trail faced threats from Indian attack. The Jicarilla were very aggressive. They closed the Mountain Branch where it crossed the Raton Mountains in what is called the Massacre at Manco Burro Pass. Pursued by Missouri Mounted Volunteers, they encountered Kit Carson and continued their flight westward into the San Juan Mountains. There at the Battle at Cumbres Pass, Major Reynolds caught up with the band of Apaches that had stolen cattle in the Taos Valley (Rio Grande River). In that fight, the Missourians reported slaying thirty Indians.[21]

George Brewerton, lieutenant, newspaper columnist, artist, and diarist, was associated with Kit Carson over several months and came to know him well. They were equals as officers, leaders of the party. Brewerton was an easterner and an educated man. He wrote down his observations concerning Carson soon after the events. While Brewerton would write that he believed a braver man had never lived and further speculated that Kit Carson never knew what fear was, he noted that Carson was a cautious man who carefully arranged his bed each night with his saddle as a pillow so that it formed a barricade for his head. His pistols, half-cocked and ready for action, lay above it while his rifle lay beneath his blanket at his side where it would remain dry.[22] He never exposed himself to the glare of the campfire except to light his pipe, thus preserving his night vision and at the same time denying enemies a silhouette. Carson had seen men who thought themselves secure killed in the firelight by enemies veiled in darkness. "No, no boys," Brewerton reported Carson as saying, "hang round the fire if you will, it may do for you if you like it, but I don't want to have a Digger slip an arrow into me, when I can't see him."[23] His careful habits led men to accept him as a leader.

Illiterate Kit Carson can be a difficult man to understand. We know him through the words of others. Sometimes, he took actions that seem harsh or cruel by today's standards. He was a man in the wilderness where there was no law. To survive he had to convince would-be attackers that he was too careful and too dangerous to be dealt with casually.

At the Virgin River in southwestern Utah, where Baptiste Tabeau had been killed in 1844, the mountaineers of the Carson-Brewerton party found their camp watched by a lone Indian. Brewerton thought that the Indian reconnoitered the camp with a view to stealing animals and thought it only caution that Carson allowed two of his men to pursue and slay the interloper.[24] Carson was careful. It had kept him alive through countless perils. It may seem cruel to us in this modern age what then was deemed necessity and occurred in a code shared by mountain man and native.

The Virgin River incident was one of many times when some would say Kit Carson was careless with Indian lives. R. C. Gordon-McCutchan illustrates some of the charges made against Carson. For instance, he cites Clegg and Beebe's *The American West*: "Kit was a notable hater of Indians. Nothing made the day for Carson like killing an Indian or two before breakfast and he did it regularly." It goes without saying that the historical record does not support this. Real incidents come down to those like the one mentioned by Brewerton where years surviving in the mountains left Kit with a brutal sense of justice and caution practiced by both mountain man and Indian. Gordon-McCutchan goes on to note that Kit married two Indian women and his love for his first wife and their daughter was deep and sincere.[25]

At another camp on the trip with Brewerton, becoming nervous of a tribe that had been known to be dangerous in the past, Carson took a hostage. Carson, the hostage, the tribe and even the easterner, Brewerton, understood and accepted the intent behind the act.

[T]he actions of the party were so suspicious that Carson concluded to retain one of their number (a young warrior about eighteen years of age) as a sort of hostage for their good behavior during the night. Our so doing appeared to give much greater uneasiness to the tribe than to the object of their solicitude, who either from a feeling of security, or by a strong exercise of that power of self-control for which the North American Indian is famous, exhibited no signs of timidity, but made himself perfectly at home after his own fashion. Sitting beside us on the ground, he conversed freely with Carson in the low, guttural accents of his native tongue, which he eked out with gestures and figures rudely drawn upon the ground. After partaking of our supper, he stretched himself quietly upon a blanket which we had lent him for his bed, and was about composing himself to sleep. . . .[26]

7

Marc Simmons included the following in an article about Kit:

Tom Tobin declared that "Carson was as clean as a hound's tooth." James F. Rusling, who knew Kit at Fort Garland, Colorado in 1867, spoke of his "honesty, matchless coolness, and courage," adding that "the Indians had no truer friend than Carson."... Those sentiments were echoed by famed Civil War General William Tecumseh Sherman. He said with conviction: "Kit Carson's integrity was simply perfect. The Indians knew it and would trust him any day before they would us, or the president either!"... At the outbreak of the Civil War, a young soldier who met Col. Carson wrote in his memoirs, "The Indians think Kit a god." And later, a New England journalist touring New Mexico a decade after Kit's death stated this in a news story sent home: "Carson was a popular man at Taos Pueblo, and the Indians believed he was a little on the supernatural order."... In his own time, Kit Carson was repeatedly categorized by contemporaries as an Indian lover and a leading defender of Indian rights and advocate of fair treatment.[27]

Carson had lived in the Rio Arriba, northern New Mexico, since the 1820s. He could not have helped but meet the Jicarilla in Taos and elsewhere in that region. He may have learned their language, though after centuries of close contact, many of them spoke Spanish, a language in which Carson was fluent. His relations with the Jicarilla must be carefully evaluated and not understood from a few blunt statements. He treated them fairly and even-handedly, so much so that in 1864 Apache warriors were willing to ride under his leadership against the Comanche.

During the first half of the nineteenth century, the Jicarilla were both over- and underestimated. They lived in close proximity to the settlements and understood the whites better than other Apaches. Near at hand they were taken for granted, although at the slightest sign of hostility that same proximity made them a terrifying threat. They were an enemy within the gates and sitting astride the lines of communication. After a century of fighting with the Comanche, the Jicarilla Apache were depleted in numbers and weakened.[28] The Spanish had invited them to be allies against a mutual foe as the Comanche moved from the Great Basin into Texas. Westward expansion by Texans drove the Comanche and other tribes westward onto Jicarilla range, driving the Jicarilla off their hunting grounds on the *Llano Estacado*, the Staked Plains. They settled into the "commons" of the Mexican and Spanish land grants and the Mexican governors made passing mention of them as being of little consequence. In 1822, a Mexican official wrote:

> *That the Jicarilla nation has always been at peace with us cannot be denied and has rendered us some service, when as auxiliary forces they have joined us to campaign against our enemies, but . . . they acted from necessity in consequence of being a persecuted tribe, timid, despicable and limited in force on account of their small numbers of warriors . . . [noting] the just repugnance the people have, to having at this place such malicious and perverse Indians.*[29]

The relationship between Hispanic culture, including the Spanish and subsequent Mexican nation, and the Jicarilla became part of the fabric of New Mexico. For more than a century, the Hispanic presence ended where Jicarilla and Ute hunting lands began. Starting in about 1750 Spanish settlements appeared on the borders of New Mexico—at Abiquiu on the Chama River, at Taos in the north, and San Miguel on the Great Plains near Santa Fe. The barrier to expansion beyond those areas was the Jicarilla.[30]

Speaking of the eighteenth century, Delores Gunnerson noted:

> *Enemy aggressions brought these Apaches of the Plains [Jicarilla] and the foothills into closer proximity [with the Spanish] before the middle of the 1700s. Attacks by Utes and Comanches forced some of the Jicarillas proper [Olleros] to move at least occasionally into the western canyons of the Sangre de Cristos and the Taos Valley, and finally west of the Rio Grande.*[31]

And eventually there they stayed, weakened, occasionally allied with the Spanish, trading with but often despised and distrusted by the New Mexicans who thought them thieves and beggars but who also feared them. Caught between powerful plains tribes, Cheyenne and Comanche, and the Spanish they allied with the Ute who also hated the Comanche. By the beginning of the nineteenth century, they became usually peaceful outcasts in Mexican territory.

Before the American occupation of New Mexico in 1846, there was a collision between Americans and the Jicarilla Apache that is worth noting. Far from being the peaceful and insignificant tribe the Mexican governors described, the Jicarilla showed themselves willing to attack a large party of Americans. In 1839, the governor of Chihuahua authorized and handsomely paid James Kirker, sometime mountain man and mercenary, to recruit a fifty-man army of mercenaries to fight and exterminate Apaches.[32] This was his second scalp-hunting expedition. Kirker, then at El Paso, recruited men and for reasons unknown headed north toward Taos. Governor Manuel Armijo of New Mexico was not at all happy with Kirker's presence in

James "Don Santiago" Kirker, mountain man, scalp hunter, Apache killer, and in 1840 one of the first Americans to fight Jicarilla. WIKIMEDIA COMMONS

his domain and may have believed the mountain man was there to usurp him in office. On September 4, 1839, as Don Santiago, as Kirker was known, and his army camped at Ranchos de Taos, Jicarilla Apache struck. Matt Field was nearby and preserved the story, writing in the *New Orleans Picayune*.[33, 34]

Jicarilla descended on Kirker's camp and made off with some of the horses. "Mistaking the guerillas to be traders, the robbers did not believe that their victims would dare give them chase."[35] Even as the raiders exited his camp, Kirker had his men mounted and in pursuit. Delayed driving stock, the Apache headed for a ravine that led into the Embudo Mountains. Guessing their intent, Kirker got ahead of them and laid an ambush. Below him in the ravine, Kirker saw 120 warriors. The war party did not suspect its danger until fifty rifles opened fire on them. Twenty are said to have fallen in the first volley. The Jicarilla turned and headed back to Ranchos de Taos to take cover in the plaza and church, all trying at once to force their way into the building and the sanctuary Kirker would not observe. Shots and screams rang out for a half-hour until finally the Apache begged for mercy. Don Santiago allowed the survivors to depart, but they left behind forty of their number and the stolen horses, along with all of their own livestock. Kirker lost two men killed. Matt Field described James Kirker as brave as a lion, a heroic status he would enjoy for some years to come.[36] Meanwhile, Governor Armijo demanded that Kirker return the "stolen" Indian stock. "The perpetrator of these unlawful acts," said Armijo, "must be informed that he needed approval from the government of New Mexico before taking livestock from its Indians."[37] Jicarilla animosity toward Americans increased.

Historian Janet Lecompte wrote that memories of his [Kirker's] scourging were behind retaliation taken after the American occupation from 1846 to 1848. "Weary and hunted Apache, who had lost many hundred of their people to Kirker's gang, began to creep forth seeking revenge against their compatriots of the killer."[38, 39] Kirker's biographer questioned how much influence this defeat might have had:

How accurate her [Lecompte] "many hundred" is and how much the memories of Kirker figured in the provocation of the Jicarillas and the Utes may be over stressed. However, it is certain that the killing of immigrants and the attacks on wagon trains on the Santa Fe Trail were attempts by those Indians to drive Americans and Mexicans from the upper Rio Grande.[40]

The American advance created new problems. The American occupation of New Mexico opened lands previously reserved to the Jicarilla to Mexican and American occupation—the Chama Valley, the San Luis Valley, and the plains as far north as Pueblo. In the south, far across the Llano Estacado, Texans pushed the Comanche westward into traditional Jicarilla buffalo hunting grounds.

Famed plainsman and Santa Fe trader Josiah Gregg wrote that the Jicarilla were not friendly to the newcomers:

The little tribe of Jicarillas also harbored an enmity for the Americans, which, in 1834, broke out into a hostile rencontre.[41] *They had stolen some animals from a gallant young backwoodsman from Missouri, who, with a few comrades, pursued the marauders into the mountains and regained his property; and a fracas ensuing, an Indian or two were killed.*[42]

Gregg also recorded an event he heard about in Taos:

It is also related, that about the same period, three Indians from the northern mountains having been brought as prisoners into Taos, they were peremptorily demanded by the Jicarillas, who were their bitterest enemies; when the Mexican authorities, dreading the resentment of this tribe, quietly complied with the barbarous request, suffering the prisoners to be butchered in cold blood before their very eyes! No wonder, then, that the New Mexicans are so generally warred upon by their savage neighbors.[43]

Josiah Gregg related that both Santa Fe traders and the Mexican government stood in some degree of terror of the Jicarilla Apache.

After the Treaty of Guadalupe Hidalgo in 1848, with the transition from Mexican to United States rule, the method of handling the "Apache problem" changed from one of benign neglect to something more aggressive. At the same time, there was growing fear that the Apache might join with the Mexicans in a common revolt. The Jicarilla Apache numbered around thirteen hundred members between 1846 when the United States took possession of the Southwest and 1887 when they became the last Native American tribe to be settled on a reservation.[44] Even though their numbers were small, the proximity of their range to important travel routes made them a threat. In fact, "[b]y 1850 the Jicarillas comprised the most serious Indian threat to travelers on the Santa Fe Trail through northeastern New Mexico and to frontier settlers in that region."[45]

In 1852, Agent John Greiner wrote:

The northern Apaches—from their location, and their intimate knowledge of the country, have the power of cutting off all communication between us and the states, if they choose,—and as they range through all the northern settlements and hold daily intercourse with the people—they should be made to feel that it is to their interest to, remain at peace.[46, 47]

In 1854, the *Santa Fe Weekly Gazette* reported:

They have watched nearly every train that came into N.M. from the plains, and whenever they had sufficient strength were sure to attack them. For many months at a time, they have had absolute command of the only direct communication with the United States; and travellers [sic] could not pass except under a strong escort of military. . . .[48]

In studying the events of the 1850s to 1880s in the New Mexico Territory, in the Jicarilla we find a once powerful enemy of the United States now largely forgotten.

Chapter 2

In 1846, the news traveled quickly among the Jicarilla that something important was happening on the Arkansas River. The usual summer caravans had yet to appear on the road the *Mangani* (Americans) called the Santa Fe Trail. Consequential events were afoot. Word would have come to the principal men of the tribe from men out hunting and trading.

Chief Chacon emerged from his tepee into the sunrise above Embudo Mountain. From a triangular buckskin pouch the size of his palm he took a pinch of yellow corn pollen and sprinkled it toward the four corners of the Jicarilla Apache world. First, he cast a few grains toward the Sierra Grande east of the Canadian River on the Llano Estacado with a whispered prayer, then he turned toward the Sandia Peak south of Ocate. Next, he sent the pollen toward the Jemez Mountains and Chama River, and finally, he turned toward the north from whence the *N'deh*, the People, had come, Blanca Peak, their sacred mountain, and the sources of what is now known as the Arkansas River.[1] It was a good land and the buffalo had been plentiful in the region east of the Canadian River before the Cheyenne had come south to trade at Bent's Big Lodge[2] on the Arkansas and before the Texans had pushed the Comanche westward. Now the *llano*, the plains, were dangerous due to the presence of their enemies, and game was scarce. Around Chacon the camp was coming to life as women stoked the cooking fires that had been left to smolder overnight. Soon, he could smell the meat of deer and antelope roasting over hot piñon fires. There would be corn cakes and porridge made of *atole* flavored with piñon nut and choke cherry and *pinole* to drink. He would breakfast and then inspect the camp.

The small band of Jicarilla had only been in the area for a few days. They had come from Las Vegas where they had traded for knives and beads that the *Mangani* had brought across the plains from the east. The Americans had come for the first time when Chacon was a young warrior. While out on a buffalo hunt, he and his companions had concealed themselves and watched curiously from a distance as men dressed in skins led heavily laden pack mules across the prairie. The men had bearded faces and hair that ranged from brown to yellow like the sunrise and red like the sunset. They were taller than the *Nakaiyeh* (Mexicans) and each carried a fine rifle.

Every year after that first sighting, Chacon saw the processions of big wagons with white canvas tops marching four abreast along the trail. Huge, powerful oxen pulled the wagons, directed by the drivers who walked along-side them using their tall whips to gently direct the leaders. They brought canvas for tepees and cotton cloth for clothing as well as beads and mirrors for adornment to trade with the Apache.

The Jicarilla Apache had planted beans and squash and some corn near the Embudo Mountain campsite at the mouths of arroyos where the water would flow gently and wet the ground. Each woman had her own plot, and the tribe customarily left the sites unattended from spring through summer during the rainy season.[3] The crop yields, like the rains, were uncertain, but it would be good to have these things to add to their diet. The Jicarilla believed that it was not good to stay in one place, hunt until there was no more game, and be dependent on crops that might not grow. The women would also check gathering sites to see which wild vegetable foods had produced during the year—yucca at the lower elevations, acorns to thicken stews, piñon nuts, choke cherries, and other foods.

On this late July morning in 1846, Chacon strode through the camp. Tall, lean, and darkly tan, his deerskin shirt with long dangling fringes at shoulder and sleeve was richly adorned in lazy-stitch beadwork, creating large patterns in sky blue with white background and red ornamentation. At his throat a fringed triangle painted yellow covered the neck opening of his shirt and identified him as Jicarilla. Close-fitting leggings decorated with more beading covered him below, and his long, cotton breechclout reached to his ankles.[4] The beadwork identified him as a man of wealth and power with industrious wives. In the camp, twelve white canvas tepees faced east toward the sunrise. Almost as soon as it became available, the Jicarilla began using canvas and cotton clothing. Between them on the narrow spur were pine trees and junipers as well as brush *ramadas* (shelters) erected by the women to provide them space out of the sun to work and cook. He gazed down the steep canyon wall into the ravine below. It was good. An enemy would have a hard time attacking this camp. Such a one would have to crawl on hands and knees while gasping for the thin alpine air. He glanced off in the direction of the setting sun and saw the glint off the water of the river the *Nakaiyeh* called

Rio Grande del Norte near a village they called Cieneguilla.

As he walked through the village that morning, Chacon took in a deep breath of the pine-scented air and looked around again at his industrious people. Many of the women were busy making pots. They gathered clay nearby from sources that were family secrets, dried it, and pounded it to powder. They gathered mica and used stones to grind it fine and then mixed this temper with the clay and water, and when the clay was right, they formed it into pots. These they fired into black utility vessels with pleasing shapes that sparkled in the sunlight. The pots were trade items desired by the *Nakaiyeh* who were poor in metals and so had few pots for cooking.[5]

Women also worked at tanning the hides of deer and buffalo while others stripped willow bark with their teeth and wove it into baskets. These were excellent bas-

Apache tepee with young ladies dressed for the Sunrise or Keesda Ceremony
COURTESY PALACE OF THE GOVERNORS PHOTO ARCHIVES (NMHM/DCA), 2076, PHOTOGRAPHER T. HARMON PARKHURST

kets, tightly woven, and beautifully adorned. The women closed their rims with a herringbone weave unknown to other Apache. A tiny path in the pattern reaching from center to rim might be seen as a flaw, though it was intentional and allowed the weaver's spirit to escape.[6] The chief reflected on this. It was a common theme in the Jicarilla understanding of the universe. A man should die in the open lest his spirit be trapped. After death, his name should not be spoken. The things he loved should follow him into a hastily prepared grave—his blanket, his robe and clothing, his weapons, and even his horse. These were all things that might call a spirit back from the other world and trap it on this side. Chacon picked up a basket adorned with stars and terraced diamonds. It was good.

Jicarilla baskets, tightly woven and strong, were in demand as trade items. Jicarilla artist unknown, ca. 1960. AUTHOR PHOTO

A warning from his lookouts made Chacon aware of the riders even as they entered Picuris Canyon.[7] Even at a distance, those approaching had already been identified as Jicarilla. They would ride up the canyon and over the saddle two miles distant into Ojo Caliente Canyon under observation from Chacon's pickets the whole way.[8] At midmorning the riders entered the camp and turned their ponies over to the boys of the village who would care for their steeds. The new arrivals laden with "gifts" were soon surrounded by their wives and the maidens of the camp. The leader strode up to Chacon and the two sat in front of his tepee.

The new arrival was known as Vicenti, a Spanish name, although he had a Jicarilla name known only to his intimates. Long association with Mexicans provided most Jicarilla with a Spanish name and the ability to speak Spanish. He presented Chacon with a fine knife.

Meanwhile, the others distributed gifts of cloth, beads, and mirrors, keeping for themselves bars of lead and barrel hoops.[9]

Vicenti explained to Chacon that near Point of Rocks[10] he had seen a train of only six wagons led by *Nakaiyeh*, Mexicans. This confused him. Usually there were many more *Mangani* than *Nakaiyeh*. Intrigued, Vicenti and his handful of warriors had stopped the wagon train and demanded the "toll," that is, gifts for crossing Jicarilla land in peace.[11] He learned from the Mexicans that there was a great *Mangani* army with many hundreds of warriors gathering at Bent's Fort on the Arkansas River.

This worried Vicenti as he knew the *Mangani* to be very powerful fighters. Unlike the Mexicans who often had only bows and lances, the Americans all seemed to have rifles and revolvers. Poorly armed, the Mexicans tended to run from a fight where the Americans stood fast. Chacon and Vicenti recalled the fight with Don Santiago Kirker six years before.[12]

The Jicarilla were an independent-minded people living in small, scattered groups, and Vicenti's approach to Chacon amounted to a very polite request for a judgment from the chief about how they should respond to this new threat. The chief was respected for his wisdom and his orders were obeyed by consent. If one did not think the chief wise, he attached himself to another. In war, if one accepted an invitation to join a war party, one agreed to accept the orders of the leader. But no one had to accept the invitation. This led to Jicarilla being very polite and careful of one another's feelings. Jicarilla parents even treated their children with great deference.

The two leaders recalled what they had heard about what Kirker had done to Mescalero and Chiricahua Apache and agreed that the Americans were indeed dangerous, but fortunately not all were like Kirker. Gradually, these two and then the other chiefs of the tribe came to an understanding. They would not take sides. The Jicarilla would not interfere in a fight between Mexicans and Americans. If the Mexicans won, they would be so weakened that the Jicarilla would dominate them. If the Americans won, they were rich and good trading partners. The young man departed, satisfied that he had been heard and his opinion considered. Chacon would speak with Huero Mundo and other leaders and the Jicarilla would arrive at consensus. All would have to agree. Anything else would split the tribe.

It was 1846, and that summer life changed profoundly for the Jicarilla. The invaders waiting at Bent's Fort came south into Mexico.

Chapter 3

On July 31, 1846, General Stephen Watts Kearny crossed the Arkansas River near Bent's Old Fort at the head of the Army of the West en route to Santa Fe. The army consisted of five companies of the 1st Regiment of United States Dragoons, two companies of artillery, and two of infantry, as well as the 1st Regiment of Missouri Mounted Volunteers under Colonel Alexander Doniphan. Somewhere behind them came Colonel Sterling Price and the 2nd Regiment of Missouri Mounted Volunteers.

Kearny had sent merchant James Magoffin and Captain Philip St. George Cooke ahead of the Army to negotiate with Governor Manuel Armijo, who had arrayed his two hundred professional soldiers and eighteen hundred or so hastily raised militia armed with bows and arrows at Apache Pass, the last obstacle on the trail before Santa Fe to block the arrival of the Army in the city. Kearny's wagons and cannon came slowly down the trail and over Raton Pass as he waited for word from his emissaries. On the fifteenth of August, Kearny received word from a captured Mexican lieutenant and four lancers that six hundred Mexicans awaited him in a gorge near Las Vegas, New Mexico. The dragoons and Lieutenant William Emory of the Topographical Engineers relished the coming combat, but were disappointed finding no one waiting for them at the gorge. General Kearny sent word to Governor/General Armijo by way of the released lancers: "Say to General Armijo, I shall soon meet him, and I hope it will be as friends."[1]

In Las Vegas, Kearny, who had just been informed that he had been promoted to general, climbed to a flat roof by the plaza.[2] From that height, he announced to the assembled Mexicans that they were now American citizens and that he would protect them from Apaches and Navajos and other wild Indians. The United States was still at war with Mexico. General Kearny had no legal authority to make these people US citizens, nor did he have authority to organize the Territory of New Mexico and appoint Charles Bent as governor. He was however following the intent of his commander in chief, President James Polk.

At about the same time, Governor Armijo looked at his ragtag army dug in at Apache Pass, and pronounced, "This will never do." He promptly dismissed them, sending the militia home while the professional soldiers followed him as he headed for Chihuahua.

On August 19, General Kearny marched into Santa Fe unopposed. The Missouri Volunteers were surprised at the adobe city. To them it had been a sort of Emerald City that delivered immense wealth to Independence, Missouri, in the form of coins, gold, silver, and mules. Looking at the windowless flat-roofed, single-story dwellings, and the dusty

General Stephan Watts Kearny in 1846 made the first "treaty" of peace between the United States and Jicarilla. Ca. 1850. COURTESY PALACE OF THE GOVERNORS PHOTO ARCHIVES (NMHM/DCA), 9939

unpaved street, the disappointed Missourians named it "Mud Town." Kearny declared New Mexico part of the United States and subject to its civil laws.[3] Rio Grande blankets made at Chimayo and mules imported over the Old Spanish Trail from California were all New Mexico had to offer. Poor farmers and shepherds inhabited the Rio Arriba, the land north of Santa Fe. The Rio Abajo, south of the capital, was only slightly better off. Its *ricos* controlled *peons* who tended their sheep and farms. The real wealth flowed up from deep in Mexico from rich gold and silver mines whose owners wanted American goods without paying the high tariffs charged by the government at Mexican ports. Santa Fe was a remote, barely regulated backdoor to Mexican silver, which flowed up the Camino Real.[4]

General Kearny organized a government, appointing Charles Bent governor, and having Colonel Doniphan, a lawyer in civilian life, draft a constitution and laws, known as the Kearny Codes. Kearny made some attempt to win over the people of New Mexico. He had not defeated them in battle, and Armijo had clearly failed them as a leader. Kearny and his officers attended Catholic mass to reassure the people that the US govern-ment would not interfere with the practice of their religion, and there were gala celebrations and fandangos in Kearny's honor. Unrest was brewing, however, as it became clear that the New Mexican *ricos*, the old ruling class, would not be included in the new government. The people feared for their rights and traditions, and the unruly behavior of the Missouri Volunteers gave substance to their discontent.

Lieutenant William Emory went to work building Fort Marcy—its guns aimed at the plaza—on a hill north of the city. Meanwhile, the general set out to keep his promise of protecting the citizenry from the "wild Indians" by visiting several tribes and telling them of his conditions for continued peace. On September 23, 1846, General Kearny met at Abiquiu with a chief of the Jicarillas, probably Chacon. In a long speech he promised the Jicarilla aid and protection if they would settle down to a life of farming and if they committed no depredations. According to a soldier who was present, Chief Chacon responded:

Father, you give good advice for me and my people; but I am old and unable to work, and my tribe are unaccustomed to cultivating the soil for subsistence. The Apaches are poor; they have no clothes to pro-tect them from the cold, and the game is fast disappearing from their hunting grounds. You must, therefore, if you wish us to be peaceable, speak a good word to the Comanches, the Yutas, the Navajos, and the Arapahoes, our enemies, that they will allow us to kill buffalo on the great plains. You are rich—you have a great nation to feed and clothe you—I am poor, and have to crawl on my belly, like a cat, to shoot deer and buffalo for my people. I am not a bad man; I do not rob and steal; I speak truth. The Great Spirit gave me an honest heart and a straight tongue. I have not two tongues that I should speak forked.

My skin is red, my head sunburnt, my eyes are dim with age, and I am a poor Indian, a dog, yet I am not guilty. There is no guilt there [putting his hand on his breast] no! I can look you in the face like a man. In the morning of my days my muscles were strong; my arm was stout; my eye was bright; my mind was clear; but now I am weak, shriveled up with age, yet my heart is big, my tongue is straight. I will take your counsel because I am weak and you are strong.[5]

General Kearny distributed some blankets, butcher knives, beads, mirrors, and other presents for their squaws, and the Jicarilla departed under the promise that they would be good and faithful citizens of the United States.

When messengers reported that Colonel Sterling Price was on the trail nearing Santa Fe with the 2nd Missouri Mounted Volunteer Regiment, General Kearny prepared to depart on the conquest of California. On September 26, General Kearny with five dragoon companies and Emory's Topographical Engineers departed Santa Fe and headed south along the Rio Grande to find a route to California. Kearny left behind Doniphan and his Missouri Volunteers with instructions to await the arrival of Colonel Sterling Price before departing to the south to link up with American forces coming from Texas.

In December 1846, a group of disappointed *ricos* in Santa Fe ineffectively plotted a coup. Bent's government got word and foiled their efforts. In January 1847, Governor Bent heard rumors of unrest in the north. Bent believed that he knew the people and that they were sympathetic to him—after all he was married into an important family at Taos. His spouse, Maria Ignacia Jaramillo, daughter of Don Francisco and Apolonia Vigil Jaramillo, was elder sister to Kit Carson's wife. The Jaramillos and Vigils were two of the most important and respected families in the Rio Arriba. Only the Martínez family was more powerful. In Taos, Padre Antonio José Martínez preached against the Americans and the danger they posed to the people's religion and customs. According to the priest the Bent brothers sold whiskey to the Jicarilla in exchange for livestock stolen from Mexicans. Governor Bent prepared to head north to the scene of pending insurrection. He declined an escort. Friends had told him to remove his family to Santa Fe at once. He responded:

Why should they want to kill me or my family?. . . Have I not been their friend? Have I not supplied them with medicines when they were ill, with food when they were hungry, with clothing when they needed it. . . . Have no fears for me. I will depart with my family in good time.[6]

In Taos, the sheriff arrested a Mexican agitator for sowing unrest along with two Taos Pueblo tribal members held on petty charges. Representatives came to Santa Fe to see Bent, asking that the governor have them released. Bent replied, as he should under American law, that he, as governor, had no authority to release the accused until a court of law tried the men's cases.

The people of Taos took this refusal as, in essence, a guilty verdict. Under Mexican law both the *alcalde* and the governor combined executive, military, and judicial powers. Thus as a governor under Mexican law, Bent would have had the authority to grant an appeal even before the trial. It was the duty of a Mexican governor or *alcalde* to set matters to rights, to achieve justice and tranquility. The Mexican officers did not necessarily have a duty to follow the letter of the law.

The day before Charles Bent arrived, the people of Taos, both Native American led by Tomasito Romero from the Pueblo and Hispanos led by Pablo Montoya, demanded the release of the sheriff's prisoners. David Clary described the mob as "downtrodden people seeth[ing] with resentment at the obnoxious behavior of the occupation troops and at the loss of the society they had always known."[7] The mob, fueled by whiskey and wild talk, attacked the prefect and sheriff. They hacked Prefect Cornelio Vigil to pieces and slew Sheriff Stephen Lee. "U.S. Circuit Attorney James Leal was stripped and tortured for hours in broad daylight, and then thrown, blinded but still breathing into a ditch where he was eaten by hogs." Among those slain were Narciso Beaubien and Pablo Jaramillo.[8] Jaramillo was an in-law to both Kit Carson and Governor Bent.

Catholic priests, among them Padre Antonio José Martínez, who had trained in seminary nineteen of the twenty-three priests then in New Mexico and who was probably the leader of the Penitente secret society, preached against the abuses of the Americans, insults and physical assaults by the troops, the selling of whiskey to *cimarrones*, that is, wild Indians, and the implied threat to the people's Catholicism. When the drunken mob went wild it was Padre Martínez who, at great personal risk, hid Americans and their allies in his home.

That January, Kit Carson was not in Taos. At Socorro in October 1846, General Kearny had pressed the scout into service to guide the Army of the West to California. Carson, hoping for a brief visit with family in Taos, had been en route to Washington with dispatches from John Charles Frémont announcing that California was in American hands. Carson blamed himself for not being home to protect his family and brother-in-law, Bent, when the revolt broke out. He, like Bent, felt he could have prevented it. Throughout the rest of his life, Kit Carson would blame the priest for inspiring the revolt. It is not at all clear that the padre had revolt in mind and certainly not the drunken, mad, murderous shambles that haunted the streets of Taos.

Governor Bent headed north from Santa Fe, arriving in Taos on January 18, 1847. In the early morning of January 19, the horde pounded on his door. "We Want Your Head, Gringo," the mob cried through the closed door of Governor Bent's home as he dug through the adobe wall into the house next door and evacuated his family. The mob of drunken Mexicans and Pueblo Indians took him, and while he was still alive, removed his scalp, pulling a bowstring across his head.

The Taos Rebellion lacked coordination, planning, and the assistance of the old ruling families. Warren Beck wrote:

> *Most writers of New Mexico history contend that the Taos uprising was an outgrowth of the earlier plot at Santa Fe and was carefully planned in advance. Evidence to substantiate this point of view is lacking, and Bancroft is probably correct when he states that "it does not clearly appear that the Taos outbreak had been definitely planned in advance." More than likely, the outbreak at Taos resulted when the ignorant natives listened to the exaggerated charges of Pablo Montoya . . .*[9]

On January 20, 1847, news of the revolt and the death of Charles Bent reached Santa Fe. Believing a force of rebels was approaching the City of the Holy Faith from the Rio Arriba, companies D, K, L, M, and N of the 2nd Regiment of Missouri Volunteers, a company of 1st Dragoons under Captain John Burgwin, and a company of hastily assembled volunteers, many of them mountain men, under Captain Ceran St. Vrain, Bent's old partner, gathered and the force of 479 men started north along the River Road to Taos.

On the 24th, about 20 miles north of Santa Fe, at Santa Cruz de la Cañada, a crossroads, the army halted where the road to Taos divided into the River Road, running west to the Rio Grande at Santa Clara Pueblo, and the Mountain Road ran east into the mountains to Chimayo, Truchas, and Trampas. As St. Vrain's scouts descended from Santa Fe through a desert of sand and stone and peered over the canyon rim into the valley of the Santa Cruz River, they detected the rebels in considerable force around the plaza and entrenched in the hills behind blocking both branches of the highway.[10] In summer, the region would have been lush and green with irrigated fields and large, shading cottonwood trees. In mid-winter the trees' skeletal limbs were veiled in a haze of pinyon smoke from cooking and heating fires.

The village of La Cañada, with its plaza, church, and large, flat-roofed houses on either side of the road, stood atop the river terrace, twenty feet above the valley floor. Behind it to the east only a few yards distant were barren hills of sand and stone dominating the River Road, and atop those hills more than a thousand New Mexicans stood ready to oppose the little American army. Atop the houses of the town, St. Vrain could see *Chimayosos* distinguished by their braided ponytails. Many held guns.

Colonel Price brought up his cannon and bombarded the town, but with little effect. A Missouri battalion charged in order to dislodge the enemy out of one of the large houses from which a "warm fire" was coming. With the rebels removed from the house, the entire force went forward into the plaza. Behind the town, the army continued the charge up the hill while Captain St. Vrain came in from the flank in order to cut the enemy off. Beyond the town, there was brisk fighting in a walled apple orchard, but in a few minutes Colonel Price's force drove off the rebel force, determined to be about fifteen hundred strong. Price's force took possession of the town for the night. In all, the army suffered the loss of two killed and four wounded while the rebels lost thirty-six killed.[11]

The next day, the 25th of January, about four hundred rebels showed themselves on a distant hill and Price went in pursuit north along the River Road. He moved slowly northward through a hostile countryside, scouting possible enemy positions. On the 28th, the army found the enemy in the gorge of the Rio Grande del Norte near La Joya. The steep-sided mesa was topped with a one-hundred-foot-thick layer of black volcanic rock chunks, some of which had broken loose and tumbled down the slope providing excellent cover and concealment. Colonel Price looked north along the River Road. Arroyo Ocale separated La Mesita from the high ridge on his right. The Rio ran around the mesa on the west but steep cliffs manned by sixty or eighty of the enemy barred that path. It seemed the army would have to follow the road. Colonel Price sent Captain Burgwin and his company to locate a way to bypass the "mob" holding the hillside.

Working his way up the slope to the right, Burgwin discovered seven hundred of the enemy posted on both sides of the mountain, "just where the gorge becomes so contracted as scarcely to admit the passage of three men marching abreast."[12] The road was blocked. Captain St. Vrain dismounted his men and started up the steep slope on the left. Flankers went out on the right and left ascending the slopes. Fire erupted from the enemy, but they retired at the approach of Colonel Price's men. Captain Burgwin and the 1st Dragoons broke through the defile, spread out, and captured the town of Embudo. One man was killed and one severely wounded, while the enemy had twenty killed and about sixty wounded. Colonel Price's command continued up the valley from Embudo toward Trampas on the south side of the Embudo Mountains.[13] They would descend on Taos from the mountains to the east.[14]

On February 3, Price's men marched through Don Fernando de Taos continuing north to the Pueblo village.[15] The village consisted of two large, then the largest in North America, apartment blocks five stories high separated by the Taos River. Roughly midway between them on the west was the San Geronimo Church. The rebels took shelter in all three buildings making the central plaza a "kill zone" with interlocking fields of fire.

Colonel Price considered his situation. The church, surrounded by a low wall and graveyard, would have to be taken first, but the approach would be difficult. The rebels could engage his men as they neared the church from that point and both apartment blocks. To the north, south, and west of the church they would be caught in the crossfire. Price called up his artillery intending to flatten the buildings from a safe distance. The colonel would soon learn that artillery had little effect on adobe.[16] The guns fired on the church for two and a half hours until night fell and they ran low on ammunition.[17]

On the 4th, Colonel Price stationed Captain St. Vrain and his mounted volunteer mountain men along with Captain Slack and his men on the eastern side of the pueblo to block any escape by the rebel forces. Price stationed Captain Burgwin and the 1st Dragoons 260 yards west of the church. He then brought up the artillery, intending this time to breech the walls of the adobe buildings. After the battle he wrote: "Lieutenant Dyer established himself with the 6-pounder and two howitzers [300 yards north of the church], while Lieutenant Hassandaubel, of Major Clark's battalion of light artillery, remained with Captain Burgwin, in command of two howitzers. By this arrangement a cross-fire was obtained, sweeping the front and eastern flank of the church."[18] To Colonel Price's disgust the artillery passed half the day pounding the buildings without achieving a significant breech, nothing his troops could assault. Even though there was no opening as yet, he sent Captain Burgwin and his men and Captain McMillen and his soldiers to try the walls of the San Geronimo Church from the west. Captains Angney and Barber of Price's regiment were told to approach the building from the north.

Burgwin's men established themselves under the surrounding wall of the church gaining some cover and covering fire. Through the acrid, eye-tearing smoke of gunfire, stinking of brimstone, the breath of Hell, the captain shouted to his men to bring up the ladders they had made and the axes. They would try chopping through the adobe walls and lighting the roof structure on fire. They had little success, although the roof began to smolder. Burgwin then ordered his men around to the front doors of the church, although this exposed them to more enemy fire from the plaza. Moments later while chopping at the doors, the captain fell gravely wounded. He would die three days later.

Using heavy axes, some of the soldiers had managed to cut small holes through the eastern wall. The men ignited the fuses of artillery shells and, using them like hand grenades, pushed them through the openings doing great execution inside the church. The six-pounder cannon was brought up close and fired at one of the openings until it was a "practicable breach," a space large enough for one or two men to pass through at one time, and then a shell was tossed in followed by the cannon firing three rounds of grape through the hole.

Price's force took possession of the church. The enemy retreated to the eastern apartment building. The men under Slack and St. Vrain drove fifty-one of the rebels from the five-story pueblo. In the open about 150 of the enemy were slain.[19] Price's loss was seven killed and forty-five wounded. The army captured many of the ringleaders, who were subsequently tried for murder and treason.

The American invaders appointed French-Canadian trader and naturalized Mexican citizen Carlos Beaubien as a judge. Beaubien had lost his son Narciso to the rebels. The drunken mob of rebels had murdered the young man in Taos plaza during the initial orgy of violence. He now presided over their trials. Lewis Garrard was witness to at least one of the trials.

After an absence of a few minutes, the jury returned with a verdict of "guilty in the first degree"—five for murder, one for treason. Treason, indeed! What did the poor devil know about his new allegiance? But so it was; and, as the jail was overstocked with others awaiting trial, it was deemed expedient to hasten the execution, and the culprits were sentenced to be hung on the following Friday—hangman's day. When the concluding words "muerto, muerto, muerto"—"dead, dead, dead"—were pronounced by Judge Beaubien in his solemn and impressive manner, the painful stillness that reigned in the courtroom and the subdued grief manifested by a few bystanders were noticed not without an inward sympathy...

Court was in daily session; five more Indians and four Mexicans were sentenced to be hung on the 30th April....[20]

Altogether the court tried fifteen of the prisoners, who when found guilty of murder or treason were hanged. The charge of treason is problematic. The court based it on General Kearny without authority making the people of New Mexico US citizens.

At Mora, at the eastern end of the pass from Taos across the Sangre de Cristo to the plains, there was a brief rising. Missouri Volunteers quickly suppressed it. As recent writers have noted, "[T]he rebellion continued throughout the territory, with numerous bloody raids, skirmishes, and executions until July of 1847."[21] Relations between Missourians and New Mexicans were not good. Although General Kearny had pronounced the people living in New Mexico as American citizens, it wasn't legally so until the Treaty of Guadalupe Hidalgo was ratified in the spring of 1848. Americans—that is, mountain men, Santa Fe traders, US dragoons, and Missouri Volunteers—continued to refer to the *vecinos* (New Mexico residents) as Mexicans.

Judge Charles "Carlos" H. Trotier de Sieur Beaubien who often reported that the Jicarilla would soon join with Mexican rebels. He was the father-in-law of Lucien Maxwell. COURTESY PALACE OF THE GOVERNORS PHOTO ARCHIVES (NMHM/DCA), 8799, PHOTOGRAPHER NICHOLS & HOWARD

The risings had lasting effects for all of the residents of New Mexico. Since the Taos Pueblo were Indians who had risen as rebels, there was real fear on the part of the Americans that other Pueblos and the tribes of Navajos, Utes, and Jicarilla Apaches who surrounded New Mexico might join them in a future revolt. Judge Carlos Beaubien had connections throughout the Rio Arriba. In the years that followed, he repeatedly reported that he heard of surreptitious meetings and of rebellious talk. He told of whispers that Mexicans were approaching the *cimarrones*, the wild and nomadic tribes, for their assistance in revolt. The military would dismiss his claims, although it was probably true that rebellious Mexicans approached tribes like the Jicarilla who were not interested in joining such a revolt. Regardless of the veracity of the rumors, however, the fear was real. In 1847, New Mexico settled into an uneasy peace.

Chapter 4

Having conquered New Mexico in the summer of 1846, General Kearny was ready for the next task of the Army of the West. The Mexican-American War was still raging. General Zachary Taylor was fighting in Mexico. In October 1846, General Kearny departed from Santa Fe to conquer California, leaving, as he thought, Governor Bent and Colonel Price well in control, unaware that an uprising was brewing in Taos. Along the way to California, he would meet Kit Carson returning with news that Mexico's west coast state was already in American hands. He would then press Carson into service as a guide. On the journey ahead, Carson would forge friendships that would affect subsequent events in New Mexico.

On October 6, 1846, Kearny and Carson met south of Socorro on the Rio Grande. Lieutenant Carson, commissioned by John Charles Frémont, brought word that Frémont had already conquered California. Kearny's guides, among them Antoine Leroux, Pauline Weaver, and Carson's old friend, Tom Fitzpatrick, were unfamiliar with the trail ahead.[1,2] There was as yet no established road. The general directed Weaver and Leroux to head back to Santa Fe and meet Colonel Philip St. George Cooke and his battalion of road builders.[3] Kit Carson was deeply troubled by his new orders. He had made a promise to his friend Frémont to carry the dispatches all the way to Washington. That night he prepared to desert in order to carry on with his original instructions, but Tom Fitzpatrick talked him out of it. Carson later said:

> [A]nd then, as Mr. Fitzpatrick was going on with the despatches, and General Kearny seemed to be such a good friend of the colonel's [Frémont], I let him take me back; and I guided him through, but with great hesitation, and had prepared everything to escape in the night before they started and made known my intention to Maxwell, who urged me not to do so.[4]

More than twenty times on the road, General Kearny told me about his being a friend of Colonel Benton and Colonel Fremont and all their family, and that he intended to make Colonel Fremont the governor of California, and all this of his own accord, as we were travelling along or in camp, and without my asking him a word about it.

This statement I make at the request of Senator Benton, but had much rather be examined in a court of justice, face to face with General Kearny, and there tell at once all that I know about General Kearny's battles and conduct in California.[5]

The road ahead was dry and rough without much grazing for livestock, Carson told the general. They'd be in and out of the canyons of the Gila River. It was pack mule country and no place for wagons. Carson became the guide. Of the three hundred dragoons accompanying General Kearny, he sent two hundred back to Santa Fe along with the wagons. Two heavy howitzers were the only wheeled vehicles continuing on to California. Lieutenant John Davidson was in charge of them.[6] Wheels made in higher humidity in the East and Midwest dry and shrink in the arid Southwest. Wheels dependent on tight-fitting wooden parts and bound together by an iron tire become loose and fall apart. Cannon are heavy. Riding on narrow wagon wheels they sink deeply into mud and sand and become difficult to move. Horses pulling them tire rapidly. Worst of all the weight bouncing over stones and ruts breaks axles and spokes. Every day the cannon lagged far behind coming into camp in the late evening and then required repairs.

Kit Carson never warmed to General Kearny, but shared hardships and difficult times—thirst, weary limbs from climbs in and out of canyons, hunger, crossing the Gila as many as nine times a day through frigid water, the journey across the Gila Trail and the Battle of San Pasqual—bonded the others together. Davidson suffered some of the hardest, most backbreaking labor, and Davidson and Carson became friends during the journey. Kit Carson, a backwoodsman with little education, barely able to sign his own name, had a weakness. He was impressed with men of education who came from the wealthy and powerful families of the United States. He was doubly impressed when they warmed to him and treated him as an equal and as a man with important wilderness skills that they lacked.

General Kearny with one hundred men and only a few pack mules to carry supplies left the Rio Grande and crossed the Black Range to the

Santa Rita del Cobre abandoned copper mines. The Apache had driven the Mexican miners away. There they met with Mangas Coloradas, chief of the Bedonkohe Chiricahua.[7] Learning that Kearny intended to fight the Mexicans, he volunteered the friendship of his people to the general, offering to have his people help kill the people of Mexico. Kit Carson with a twinkle in his eye told Lieutenant Emory he wouldn't place much faith in Mangas Coloradas's exaggerated promises of friendship.

Not the least of the Gila Trail's challenges was starvation for man and especially for beast. Grazing was poor to nonexistent. Horses and mules suffered and lost weight until their backbones stuck up and saddles settled down on them until they created open sores. The cannon moved slowly at best and broke axles and spokes almost daily. Lieutenant Davidson arrived in camp late each night, well after sunset and then began repairs, only to rise again long before daylight to begin the new day. On October 21, after two weeks of Carson leading the army through mountain and canyon, Dr. Griffin wrote, "The howitzers have not come up yet, and it is now 8 P.M.—poor Davidson, he has a sweet time of it."[8] Lieutenant Emory noted that every time the guns left the Gila River bottoms, "nearly every part of their running gear [had] broken down and [been] replaced."[9] Finally, the Army of the West emerged into the low desert. "[N]o one observing our cavalry at this moment would form notions favorable to the success of the expedition."[10]

In the desert, they found water in the Gila River, level going, and succor among the Pima Indians who farmed along the river. The Indians fed them and provided grazing for their stock, but warned them of what lay ahead on the way to California. From the villages of the Maricopa, allies of the Pima, they had to make a choice. They would either go hundreds of miles out of their way following the Great Bend of the Gila River or cut across forty miles of waterless desert. After that they would join the river again only to confront the black, broken lava beds of the Sentinel Plain. Water and grazing would be scarce for another 150 miles until they reached the junction of the Gila and Colorado Rivers.

They cut across the Forty Mile Desert and rejoining the Gila River continued on to near its junction with the Colorado. Their food was nearly gone and their stock worn out. Grass was scant. Their tired animals scarcely had the strength to continue the journey. The riding stock of the Army of the West was becoming unusable. Even General Kearny had to switch to riding a mule. He dismounted half of his troops and assigned the riding mules to pack service.

Approaching the Colorado they detected a large camp across the river. They feared it might be one thousand soldiers come from Mexico to retake California. Kearny sent Lieutenant Emory, who had earned the general's respect, with fifteen men to scout the Mexican position. The lieutenant discovered that it was a party of California vaqueros taking horses to the Mexican army in Sonora. Emory confiscated most of the herd, denying their use to the enemy, but soon learned that the horses were wild and not adapted for immediate service.

First the soldiers would have to accustom the stock to saddles, carrying a man, and taking orders from the reins. They had only a few days in which to accomplish this training. So the stock would still be skittish and apt to balk at commands. Training a horse for military service goes well beyond this. It takes months to train a horse to anticipate and follow military commands so it can perform in formation much as the men do when marching. Horses are naturally nervous of anything unfamiliar. Loud noises and the flash of light on steel sabers frighten them. They have to learn to withstand the shock, fury, and flash of battle. There was no time for this.

General Kearny purchased twenty-five half-broken horses and allowed the Californios to take the rest. A quarter of his force was now mounted on half-trained steeds.

From the vaqueros, Kearny learned that California was again in Mexican hands. He would have to fight to retake land. In the winter of 1846, even before the Mexican-American War officially began, Lieutenant John C. Frémont had joined the Bear Flag Revolt of Americans in California against the Mexican government. In July, Commodore John D. Sloat arrived and soon all of California was temporarily under American control. However, becoming angered with overbearing American officials, the Californios revolted and just as quickly all of California except the villages of San Diego and Monterey, hundreds of miles apart, were again in Mexican control.

Ahead of Kearny and his army lay another challenge. To get to the coast and the rest of the forces fighting for California, the Army of the West would have to skirt the southern California sand dune desert by going south. Along the route, there would be no grazing and they would have to dig up to eighteen feet down for water, in the few places they could find it. All of the elements of the desert seemed to conspire against them. The thorns of the chaparral in a sterile land "were a great annoyance to our dismounted and wearied men whose legs were now almost bare." Dr. Griffin described these as "Georgia uniforms."[11] And then as they approached the mountains, they would learn of the fog and rains of California's winter and would also arrive cold and wet. The army would arrive on the coast starving on half-broken, half-starved stock, dressed in rags and tatters of uniforms.

Each man was armed with the Model 1842 smoothbore "horse pistol," the Hall's carbine, and a saber. Double-flapped carbine and pistol cartridge boxes holding thirty to forty paper cartridges, and a case for percussion caps were worn on the soldiers' belts. In rain and fog, even in their protective cases, the cartridges could become wet and useless. The pistol had a range of about twenty-five yards and the carbine, a shortened smoothbore musket, a range of one hundred yards. In theory, the carbine could be loaded and fired on horseback. The military academy taught that sabers were the dragoons' primary weapon. The saber was always ready. Other weapons took time to reload and were unreliable in rain, fog, and wind. Both pistol and musketoon were muzzle loading. The cartridge held a ball and charge of powder. To use a cartridge the soldier reached into his cartridge box and extracted a paper cartridge. Lifting it to his mouth he bit off the end down to the powder. He then dumped the charge and ball down the barrel and forced it home with the ramrod. Then the soldier cocked the hammer. Reaching into his cap pouch, he pulled out a percussion cap, looking like a little top hat a quarter-inch across, and placed it firmly on the nipple under the hammer. When the trigger was squeezed, the hammer descended on the fulminate of mercury cap (like the tip of a self-striking match) and it exploded, igniting the charge in the barrel. The caps were easy to drop, especially if a soldier was excited. The number of caps found by archaeologists and the ratio of dropped to fired caps tells us something of the length of the battle, how long forces stayed in one place, and whether they were calm or panicked.

The Californios, who were excellent horsemen, were armed with lances. Usually a commander used lancers in scouting and in attacking disorganized cavalry and retreating infantry. Combat with organized cavalry who were armed with sabers was considered unequal combat. Usually sabers won the day.[12] Against a single lancer, a dragoon armed with a saber could knock the lance aside and have his way with the horseman, who could not swing his long lance to defend himself. When the lancers had a temporary advantage in numbers as they would at San Pasqual, the dragoon would knock one lance aside only to be pinioned by the lance of a second rider. The lancer did not drive home too deeply for fear that he would have difficulty withdrawing his weapon anchored in flesh. Instead, he pricked his enemy again and again drawing blood, and weakening his foe.

Kit Carson related that around December 3, 1846, General Kearny sent Carson and Lieutenant Davidson along with twenty-five dragoons to intercept a party of Californios headed for Sonora. They succeeded in surprising them and captured some seventy or so horses of which forty were gentle enough for the men to ride.[13] Kearny's command was mounted on horses that were broken to saddle but not trained for war. It would prove his undoing.

On December 3, the Army of the West arrived at Warner's Ranch, a well-known stop on the road to California owned by Jonathan Warner, an expatriate who was being held in San Diego by the US Navy on charges of being a Mexican sympathizer.[14] In his absence, the foreman of the ranch offered to cook dinner for the officers. No sooner had he done so than the hungry dragoons stole it and the officers had to wait while another was prepared. Meanwhile, seven hungry men devoured a full-grown sheep.[15] The famished Army of the West helped itself to such resources as the ranch provided.

On December 5, Kearny continued his march toward San Diego. Ahead a large dust cloud alarmed Emory and the other officers, who feared a force of California cavalry might have been sent to intercept them. As it happened, Admiral Stockton had sent a forty-one-man detachment of marines, sailors, and Bear Flaggers and one cannon under Marine captain Archibald H. Gillespie to meet them.[16, 17] The marine reported that the rebellious Californians had sent Andres Pico and his squadron of mounted lancers to defeat the Army of the West, which, unknown to the Californios had now been augmented to about 150 men. The lancers were bivouacked at the Luiseño Indian village of San Pasqual nine miles away.

Late that night, Kearny dispatched Lieutenant Thomas Hammond and ten dragoons to scout Pico's position. Before Lieutenant Hammond set out, Captain Gillespie offered the services of his "mountain men" to the general's scouting expedition and the general rebuffed him. Apparently, Kearny did not trust the military skills of mountain men, Bear Flaggers, sailors, or marines. The Navy did not train sailors and marines for mounted combat. The Bear Flaggers were a mixed bag of skilled mountain men and California settlers unused to discipline or organized, military combat. They may have been excellent scouts, but the general could not count on them to fight as a cohesive unit.

Lieutenant Hammond returned about 2:00 a.m. on the 6th, the noise of his horsemen having alerted the Californios to the American presence.

Hammond did not gain additional knowledge of the enemy's disposition or numbers.[18] Worse, one of Hammond's men lost a blanket while close to the enemy camp. General Kearny was certain that the actions of Hammond and his dragoons had alerted the Mexican lancers to the presence of the army. Kearny determined, as a result, that they needed to attack rather than allowing the enemy force—probably only about seventy-five lancers—to flee, alert a larger force, or ambush his force farther down the trail. Further, the general was convinced that the enemy was craven and would not stand and fight. Besides, as Kit Carson reported in his autobiography, part of the general's plan was to seize the enemy's horses.

In organizing his force for battle, Kearny further slighted Gillespie by assigning him to guarding the baggage train with his marines and Bear Flaggers. They were fresh and better mounted than Kearny's men, but he did not trust them to perform as a unit. Gillespie in turn painted the dragoons as unfit for combat:

> [The dragoons were] exhausted by their long and arduous march; indeed the whole force, save the officers, presented an appearance of weariness and fatigue rarely, if ever, met with upon any other service. The men were without any exception sadly in want of clothing; that which they wore was ragged and torn, they were almost without shoes; and although we [as seafarers] were constantly accustomed to much privation and suffering, my own men considered their own condition superior to these way worn Soldiers, whose strength and spirits seemed to be entirely gone.[19]

On the morning of December 6, 1846, Kearny attacked in the dark before daylight of a foggy and rainy day with little knowledge of the enemy position or terrain.[20] Through dark canyons choked with stone and brush the dragoons "stealthily" approached the "sleeping enemy." Gillespie remembered:

> The clang of the heavy Dragoon Sabres, echoing amongst the hills upon this cold frosty morning, and reverberating from the mountain top back upon the Valley, seemed like so many alarm bells to give notice of our approach.[21]

Kit Carson recalled the fight:

When we arrived within ten or fifteen miles of their camp, General Kearny sent Lieut. Hammond, and three or four Dragoons, ahead to examine their position. He went, was accidentally discovered, saw the encampment as reported. They were in an Indian village. He then returned to us and gave the information found. The General then determined to attack them. We packed up about one o'clock in the morning and moved on. When within a mile of their camp, we discovered their spies[22] that were out watching the road and our movements. The trot and then the gallop was ordered to pursue the spies. They retreated to their camp.

I was ordered to join Capt. Johnston. He had fifteen men under his command. We were to proceed in advance. Our object was to get the animals belonging to their camp.[23]

Kearny believed he had tactical surprise on his side, even though the enemy knew he was somewhere nearby. He hoped that if he moved quickly, Pico would not yet have organized a defense. Then too, he wanted the fresh horses held by Pico's men. Behind Johnston came the general and his staff, including Emory. Behind them came Captain Benjamin Moore. Carson said:

Captain Moore, having a part of two companies of Dragoons and a party of twenty five volunteers that had come from San Diego, was ordered to attack the main body. They were attacked, only fought about ten or fifteen minutes, then they retreated.[24]

Behind them came Lieutenant Davidson and the three cannon, the carriages of artillery limbers and guns creaking and groaning in the night. The cannon were in bad shape, patched together after months on the trail in difficult conditions, and likely to break down. The Bear Flaggers had cannon as well, liberated from Sutter's Fort and of dubious quality and heritage. Normally the cannon would have come near the head of the column since they were direct-fire weapons that soldiers would not want to fire into the backs of charging infantry or cavalry. They'd have fired first into a massed enemy and the cavalry would have then charged around them. Kearny could not yet see the enemy and thus the guns did not have a target.[25] The general wanted to capture enemy horses and did not want the gunfire to kill them.

Captain Johnston, Kit Carson, and a few dragoons charged ahead becoming badly strung out due to the uneven quality of their mounts. The enemy was already mounted and waiting, red pennants waving from the tips of lances. Behind the charge, the bugle blew "Charge as Foragers!"[26] Instead of charging one tight group against a single point of the enemy's line, the dragoons spread out in pairs, each pair attacking at a different point. The Army of the West began their assault. Already strung out, the scene dissolved into chaos. The horses and mules of Kearny's men reared and plunged and screamed fear and defiance. Sabers and lance tips flashed. Horses untrained for war panicked, veering away from the enemy, and throwing their riders. Remarkably, Pico's men fell back a half a mile under the onslaught, but then reformed.

Carson recalled the enemy's retreat:

When we were within 100 yards of their camp, my horse fell, threw me, and my rifle was broken into two pieces. I came very near being trodden to death. I being in advance, the whole command had to pass over me. I finally saved myself by crawling from under them. I then ran on about 100 yards to where the fight had commenced. A Dragoon had been killed. I took his gun and cartridge box and joined in the melee. Johnston and two or three of the dragoons were then killed. The Californians retreated, pursued by Moore, for about three quarters of a mile. Moore had about 40 men mounted on horses the balance on mules. . . .[27]

Carson, on an untrained horse, which balked while crossing the dry bed of San Bernardo Creek, was thrown. His plains rifle broke at the wrist, the narrow part of the stock behind the trigger where one grips the weapon. He scrambled in the chaos to keep from being trampled. His account continues:

The command in the pursuit got very much scattered. The enemy saw the advantage, wheeled and cut off the forty that were in advance, and out of the forty, killed and wounded thirty-six. Captain Moore among the slain, also Lt. Hammond. Gen. Kearny was severely wounded and nearly every officer of [the] command was wounded.[28]

As the Californios reformed, an *escopeta* (short, flintlock musket) boomed in the semi-dark. Captain Johnston fell from his horse, shot through the head.[29] The officers, who were on better horses than their men, got far ahead of their men, where the enemy lancers found them easy targets. Unwilling to strike deeply and chance their weapons sticking in flesh, leaving them disarmed, the lancers pricked their foe again and again. Wounded officers fell bleeding from multiple wounds.

From across the field, the lancers singled out Kearny, charging just behind Johnston's men. They surrounded the general. They wounded him in the arm and buttocks with multiple swipes from their sharp lances. He went down within sight of his troops. Lieutenant Emory, known at West Point as Bold Emory, saw his commander's peril and hastened to his side. He slashed his way through the crowd killing one Mexican before the Californio could finish the general.[30]

Carson later recalled the plight of Lieutenant Davidson:

Lieut. Davidson, in charge of two Howitzers, came up; before he could do anything every one of his party were killed or wounded, and one piece taken by the enemy.[31] They captured it by lassoing the horse, fastening the lasso to the saddle, and then running off. They got off about 300 yds, and endeavored to fire it at us, but could not. It was impossible for Lieut. Davidson to do anything, having lost all his men, and one piece [of artillery], and was himself lanced several times through the clothing and one passing through [the] cantel [cantle] of his saddle, which if the Californian had not missed his aim he, also wou[l]d be numbered among the slain.

We rallied in a point of rocks near where the advance had been defeated, remained there that night, the reason [being we] dare not move on, and having a number of dead to bury. The dead were buried at the hours of 12 and 1 o'clock that night. Next day we moved on.[32]

Hall's carbines now came into play to good effect. The enemy was held at bay. So many of the senior officers were wounded or killed that Captain Henry Turner temporarily assumed command.[33]

Turner held his position at San Pasqual through the day. He then had Carson take the lead with fifteen men who could still ride and fight, while Turner came along behind struggling to keep the wounded moving. The

Army of the West traveled about seven miles and the wounded suffered at every step. On December 7, the Californians received reinforcements and their numbers increased to 150.

As the Army of the West proceeded toward the coast and San Diego, the Californios would show themselves on every hill but retreat when challenged. Carson recalled:

Late in the evening we [were] still on the march, being within about 400 yards from the water where we intended to camp. They then charged on us, coming in two bodies. We were compelled to retreat about 200 yards, to a hill of rocks that was to our left. After we had gained our position on the hill, the Californians took another hill about 100 yds. still to our left, and then commenced firing. Captains Emery [sic] and Turner took the command of what dragoons we had, charged the enemy on the hill, routed them, giving us full possession of their position; there [we] remained for the night.[34]

Kearny sent messengers to Commodore Stockton in San Diego requesting assistance and wagons to carry the wounded. Help was on the way. Pico captured the returning messengers. There was a prisoner exchange, but Pico only gave one of the messengers to Kearny. Unfortunately, Pico did not exchange the man who knew that help was coming. Carson and Lieutenant Beall crept away at night between the enemy pickets, losing their shoes in the process. They walked to San Diego through rock and cactus barefoot, suffering greatly.

In suffering, despair, battle, and hardship, Lieutenant John Davidson and Kit Carson had become fast friends. In 1850, Davidson would go on to conduct the Bloody Island Massacre of California Pomo Indians. In his fights with the Pomo, he developed a profound disrespect for the fighting qualities of Indians. In 1854, expecting little or no resistance, he engaged in the unprovoked attack on a Jicarilla Apache camp at Cieneguilla. The Apache handed him his head. Initially appalled at what Davidson had done, Carson called the attack unprovoked, but subsequently, at a court of inquiry, he defended his friend.

Chapter 5

Josiah Gregg, Santa Fe trader, wrote in *Commerce of the Prairies* of an enmity between Jicarilla Apache and Americans that dated back to the 1830s. He recalled that a backwoodsman from Missouri with a few comrades had pursued marauding Jicarilla, regained their property, and in the process killed a few of the Indians. The tribe protested to the Mexican governor at Santa Fe:

> *A few days afterward all their warriors visited Santa Fé in a body, and demanded of the authorities there, the delivery of the American offenders to their vengeance. Though the former showed quite a disposition to gratify the savages as far as practicable, they had not helpless creatures to deal with, as in the case of the Indian prisoners already related. The foreigners, seeing their protection devolved upon themselves, prepared for defence, when the savages were fain to depart in peace.*[1]

Publishing in 1844 about the period from 1831 to 1840 when Gregg was active on the Santa Fe Trail, it is unlikely that he was aware of the horrific reputation James Kirker would eventually own. He points to an enmity that was already alive well before 1840 and to a Mexican government that trembled before the Jicarilla and was prepared to bow to their demands. The tribe may have been small, but they brought terror to the Santa Fe Trail. They were not pleased that the Americans fought back and killed their people. Josiah found them worthy of mention.

Danger from the Jicarilla and Ute was a daily expectation for settlers within the Jicarilla territory and travelers through the region in the 1840s. In 1845, Santa Fe trader James Josiah Webb had an encounter with the Jicarilla along the Santa Fe Trail near where Alexander Barclay would build his fort:

We had got to within half a day's ride of Rio Colorado, and passing through a grove of pinones [pinyon pine, piñon] to the open plain and thence a mile or so to the cottonwood timber skirting the Rio Culebra, when all at once Tom stooped in his saddle and looking earnestly towards the timber, called out, "People! Indians!" and turned his mule around, taking the path for the grove which we had just left.[2] We all followed in order, getting our arms in hand ready for use, and soon heard a volley of musketry from the grove behind us, and saw a good many people dodging among the trees; but [they] soon came out and saluted us with another volley and a yell of all sorts of sounds and voices. Tom took another look and commenced laughing.

"They are Mexicans," [he said] "and will have a good laugh at us for running."

We turned and met them, and the first to salute him with a shake of the hand was his brother-in-law. The Ute had run off some stock from Rio Colorado and killed one or two herders, and these men had been out all night in pursuit, but concluded they had gone as far as was prudent, or they had any chance of proceeding safely.[3, 4]

The murder of and disappearance of Mexican herders and stock was a common occurrence. Apparently, neither Jicarilla nor Ute was as peaceful as certain Mexican and American governors described. When life in the mountains and prairies became more settled, when the American army had quelled insurrection in the Rio Arriba, and established order, minor crimes, such as stock stealing, became more evident. Once order was established, Americans would not tolerate stock theft as Mexicans had. Some like Kit Carson and Maxwell understood the Indians, and would make gifts to compensate them for the loss of hunting grounds, thus regulating the extent of their own losses. When Indians raided them, they struck back with considerable force, sending a message: "I'll make gifts in fairness to keep the peace, but steal from me and I will chastise you to the extent of my ability."

In early 1846, before the coming of General Kearny, Jicarilla warriors sat in waiting on River Road along the Rio Grande near Embudo where the steep sides of the canyon made an excellent place of ambush. The young men were clad in cotton breechclouts with buckskin leggings. Their leather shirts had long fringe. Their faces were covered in white clay making them invisible to their enemies.

Despite what Mexican governor Manuel Armijo claimed about the peaceful insignificance of the Jicarilla Apache, a small party of them now lay in wait hoping that a *Nakaiyeh*, a Mexican, would soon come by with something worth stealing. Spying a traveler, their leader would have remarked on their luck. It was a *Mangani*, an American, plodding north leading pack mules whose panniers would be stuffed with good things for trade.

Nonetheless, they hesitated. The American was bound to have weapons and put up a fight. They hid among the dark volcanic rock waiting for a signal to strike. Their faces showed white among the black rocks, but some of the rocks were stained white from long contact with the surrounding soils. With white faces and sun-darkened bodies, the Jicarilla seemed invisible.

At a signal arrows flew. The Missouri trader, Crombeck, wounded in leg and chest, screamed in pain and fell from his riding mule.[5] The long rifle that had rested across the pommel went with him to the ground. Badly hurt, perhaps dying, he nevertheless raised his heavy plains rifle and fired at a white patch on a black rock. It burst into red mist. Infuriated, knowing they'd have time as he reloaded, the remaining white-faced Apache burst from cover. They were surprised as the man pulled out and fired his revolver at them. Revolvers were still new and unfamiliar.

Since the American had slain one of their relatives, the others sought revenge. A few of them held Crombeck down. Another drew his knife and slashed the still living man's belly. The warrior with the knife reached in and pulled out the man's entrails. Crombeck did not live long. Another warrior crushed the Missourian's skull with a rock. Hastily they created a small landslide to cover the dead warrior.[6]

Up until 1847, the Jicarilla Apache contented themselves with minor thefts and the occasional murder of someone who resisted. Once wagon trains crossed the Arkansas River near the modern borders of Kansas, Oklahoma, and New Mexico, they were in the country of the Comanche, Kiowa, and Jicarilla Apache. Blue painted wagons, their white canvas covers like billowing sails, came four abreast pulled by teams of slow-moving oxen across the sea of grass. The drivers walked alongside, their whips reaching higher than the wagon tops, gently touching the backs of the great beasts, talking to them and giving them direction. On the wagons their muzzle-loading rifles were close at hand. Many carried the new revolvers tucked in their belts. Men on horseback preceded the caravan and rode out to its flanks raising dust, alert for Indians. The walking men wiped dust from their eyes and scanned the near horizon. They too were alert to the threat. At a word from the wagon master they would close in tight, four wagons side by side with many in each row. They would become a fortress bristling with the arms of the drivers ready to repel Indians.

Of travel in the year 1847, Santa Fe trader James Josiah Webb wrote:

Every train we met, we were warned to look out for the Indian on a white horse. And after crossing the Arkansas, [we] were more cautious in keeping well together, and [had] scouts far enough in advance to give the train sufficient time to corral and secure the animals and form a line for defense.[7]

As might be expected, 1847 began in confusion. In 1846, the Army of the West had occupied New Mexico and then as the 1847 new year dawned had put down rebellion in the Rio Arriba, particularly Taos, and Mora. The year 1847 started with Charles Bent as governor. After his murder Donaciano Vigil, a native New Mexican, replaced him, remaining in office until October 11, 1848.[8] At the same time, Colonel Sterling Price was the military governor. The overlap of authority was a frustration and confusion to both governors. There was a legislature and a key member, often its president, was Padre Antonio José Martínez of Taos, the most politically powerful man in New Mexico.[9]

Martínez came from one of the wealthiest families of the Rio Arriba. He was the first New Mexican ordained as a priest. In a highly unusual move, the bishop in Mexico authorized the padre to open a seminary and ordain priests. Padre Martínez served in both the Mexican and American legislatures. He preached against American whiskey sellers and hide traders, but favored the American constitution, as he understood it. To him freedom of religion meant that the state would protect the people from the church. So much power in the hands of one man made him a threat to the American leadership.

The mostly illiterate Mexicanos of the legislature passed some interesting laws drawing from local tradition. General Kearny had promised too much when he made them citizens and gave them a constitution and government. It wasn't until the Compromise of 1850 that Congress organized New Mexico as a territory. Thereafter, the president would appoint the governor and New Mexico would be free to organize a constitution and legislature. In the interim, the ability to make laws and the authority of officials remained in question. The Missouri and Illinois volunteers remained in New Mexico mistreating the local populace.

Adding to the confusion, Texas still claimed all of New Mexico east of the Rio Grande and sent representatives to assume control of the government. In 1836, after the Battle of San Jacinto, the Mexican president had promised to withdraw his soldiers beyond the Rio Grande. Santa Fe, Albuquerque, Taos, and Chimayo were on the Texas side of the river. In 1840, the Texans had invaded New Mexico to take possession, albeit with a spectacular lack of success, and they had harried caravans on the Santa Fe Trail attempting to charge import duties.

Where there is confusion, the unscrupulous take advantage. The treatment of surrounding nations, the Indians, became uneven and irregular. Would be Mexican rebels invited tribes to join their revolt. The Indians of the plains, including the Jicarilla, were aware of the confusion and sensed the lack of military strength along the Santa Fe Trail. Some saw an opportunity to sever the trail, others an opportunity for plunder. The Army was in New Mexico, California, and Mexico and not on the plains. The Americans were weak along the trail and all caravans received unwanted attention from Indians.

Of this time Jicarilla Apache historian Veronica Velarde Tiller wrote: "They [the Jicarilla] were considered especially menacing because of their position on the Cimarron Cutoff."[10] Tiller points to the Jicarilla as being in a state of war in the late 1840s and as being willing participants in the Plains Indian uprising.

Civilization was creeping up on New Mexico if only slowly. Order was coming to society gradually. One sign of the change was the printing of the land's first English language newspaper.[11] In September 1847, the paper reported:

We learn that a letter was received a few days ago from Judge Beaubien, stating that the Indians, and disaffected Mexicans connected with them, threatened to commit depredations on the citizens of that place, and that they were in danger of losing their stock. The men of property and character have requested troops to be sent up, and we hear that several companies will go. The Indians are the Apaches or Jicarillas, who have been stealing and murdering individuals and small parties for some time. They must be punished severely, and until it is done, we cannot expect peace and order in that neighborhood.[12]

In 1847, the Jicarilla robbed a party coming to Taos from Pueblo, a settlement near Fountain Creek on the Arkansas River in what is now Colorado, and murdered them. Indian agent Thomas Fitzpatrick reported the murders. He saw a shift in the pattern of Jicarilla raids. They were now aimed at Americans.[13]

The Jicarilla threat had been present for some time. They had been murdering and stealing, attacking small parties. The Mexican governors lacked the resources to do very much about them. The Jicarilla were mobile and faded away into the mountains and prairies when attacked. In the period before American occupation, they did not plant crops extensively or tend herds of sheep like the Navajo. So the official story was that they were not much of a threat. Governor Bent dismissed them as a small tribe, underestimating their strength by more than half. In 1846, at Abiquiu, General Kearny made a peace treaty of sorts with the Jicarilla. The Rebellion of 1847 took up much attention until Judge Carlos Beaubien pointed out the danger that they posed if they chose to join rebellious Mexicans and Pueblo Indians.

The Indians seem to have been taking advantage of unsettled conditions. While the wagon trains were on guard, others seemed to take trouble with the Jicarilla Apache in stride. Englishman Alexander Barclay was conducting business on the Arkansas River near the Rocky Mountains, north of the Mountain Branch of the Santa Fe Trail.

In November 1847, it was cold on the high plains, the world blanketed in fresh snow. The men and their mules stood out as black dots against the white mountains as they approached. The previous day's hunt for lost animals had been unsuccessful. Alexander "Don Alexandro" Barclay shook his head clearing some of the falling snow from his hat. He was not a handsome man, blessed, or cursed, with features that made it difficult to look happy. His scowl was perpetual. He stood tall in a capote made from a Hudson Bay blanket. It kept him warm enough. The new arrivals brought "Taos Lightning" and news from as far away as Mexico City.

That night Barclay wrote in his diary:

November 8th Cold, cloudy, heavy and snowing—sent José Doloris [Dolores] to hunt horses lost on this river below and Fontaine qui Bouille to where the wagons were camped. Returned without them.[14]

November 9th Waters, D'd Burrows, Jno. Hawkins, Benj. Chouteau, Ed. Tharp and others from Taos with Whiskey [and] as usual news. Old Mexico City taken—1,600 Americans & 9,000 Spaniards killed. Apaches on Punie [Poñil Creek?] killed Louisson, Walter, Betts and a Louis—took off Tharp's oxen and goods he had in wagons & Beaubien's and Maxwell's cattle.[15] *Heard also that G. Bent had died at Ft. William.*[16] *José Dolores went today down to Gant's Fort to look for lost horses and slept a short distance up Fontaine qui Bouille on his way up that river hunting them.*[17, 18]

Poñil Creek is about twenty miles north of Cimarron near the Raton Pass. The Beaubien referred to was one of the nine children of Judge Beaubien, and Lucien Maxwell was Beaubein's son-in-law. These names—Barclay, Beaubien, Maxwell—arise again and again in conflict with the Jicarilla. They were the settlers farthest into Apache territory and farthest from the settlements.

Alexander Barclay, a longtime employee of the Bents at Fort William, set out in 1848 to establish Barclay's Fort, an Indian trading post, at the junction of the Mora and Sapello Rivers in New Mexico. From the upper reaches of the Arkansas River where he was living in 1847, he reported the weather and the loss of livestock along with the delivery of whiskey from Taos. Just as casually he reported the death of acquaintances at Poñil Creek. He expressed no surprise that Jicarilla had attacked a party. To Barclay, it was a common occurrence and not a statement made with a gasp, "The Jicarilla are on the warpath!" This is the life to which he was accustomed.

On November 13, 1847, the *Santa Fe Republican* wrote:

Maj. Reynolds[19] *with two companies left Taos in pursuit of the Jicarillas, who have for some time been committing depredations on the frontier. It is hoped they will meet with this lawless set of Indians and give them a chastizing which will restore quiet to the frontier. Major Reynolds has the reputation of being an active and efficient man, and we expect him to reduce to subjection a tribe which richly deserves the epithet of Arabs.*

Since writing the above, we learn the storm forced the Major to return, it being impossible to do anything in such weather.[20]

Major W. W. Reynolds did not make contact with the Jicarilla, and his campaign seems unlikely to have angered them. Thus, the Jicarilla continued to do what they had done for a long time.

One terrifying aspect of many of their raids was that the Jicarilla came in great numbers and attacked large parties usually deemed safe from Indian attack. In 1848, they confronted a large party at Manco Burro Pass and soon after confronted Kit Carson and George Brewerton.[21]

As the Mexican War came to an end, the military began to take note of the depredations occurring within the department. The level of violence is hard to gage. "Frequent" can be anything from once per year to twice per week depending on the speaker or writer and his or her motives. Military governor and departmental commander Colonel Sterling Price issued Order No. 22 on March 27, 1848.

Head Quarters,
9th Military Department,
Santa Fe,
March 27th, 1848
Order No. 22

The Colonel Commanding is deeply pained at the intelligence which he daily receives of the frequent outrages, committed upon the persons and property of the peaceable inhabitants of this Territory by the Navajoes, Apaches and other tribes of Indians, whose incursions are as devastating as they are frequent and daring.

This painful finding, not a little enhanced by the fact that three-fourths of the force remaining in this Department are infantry, and are utterly powerless against the rapid movements of mounted men, who are familiar with every inch of the country; and that, in consequence, his garrisons are compelled to sit still while murder and robbery is committed under their very eyes. . . .

Mexican inhabitants of this Department, be authorized to arm and equip themselves—organize in parties, and hold themselves in readiness to repel all incursions and to recover the property that may have been stolen from them by the Indians. . . .[22]

It is interesting and suggests a high level of real concern that the military governor was willing to allow Mexican inhabitants to "arm and equip" themselves, since they had so recently being involved in insurrection and there were presumably still a few *insurrectos* hiding in the countryside and accosting travelers. When he refers to Apaches, he is almost certainly talking about Jicarillas and Mescaleros. In 1848, the Gadsden Purchase was still six years in the future and the southern boundary of New Mexico was somewhere north of Santa Ana. Much of the Chiricahua and Western Apache country had yet to become part of the United States. They were still distant from populated areas.

A horrible event was about to occur.

Chapter 6

The Apache people shared a language and culture, but they were not organized politically above the extended family. Participation in warfare and raids was voluntary. Some great chiefs exercised influence well beyond their extended family or band. But, that was influence, not political command. Lecompte suggests that in June 1848, the Jicarilla, long seething over the 1839 Kirker campaign of murder and deceit in Chihuahua, possessed the political consciousness to suddenly burst forth in a spectacular and unexpected revenge raid on Americans.[1] It seems far more likely that their actions were inspired by events closer to the Jicarilla homeland, by confusion, abuse, perceived weakness of the Americans, and by both plains tribes and Mexican rebels urging them to war. Scarcely noticed in the war years, in 1848 the war intensified.

In June 1848, the Jicarilla Apache closed the Mountain Branch of Santa Fe Trail at Raton Pass. Traders had long attempted to locate a better route for wagons than the rough road then in use. On June 11, 1846, Charles Bent wrote from Bent's Fort (Fort William):

> *Charly Town & Pedro Luna passed some miles west between what I passed and the old Rattone Road [Raton] the[y] report that, that rout fine and nothing to be done except to cut away some oake brush to make it a perfectly easy route, a plenty of Wood, Watter, and Grass, they reporte that to leave the Animas [Purgatory River] in the morning with Waggons, they can get onto Red River [Canadian] in the eavening, this is almost too good say that it could be crossed in two dayes, it is fine. I shall try and have it explored this summer.*[2]

Towne had, in fact, rediscovered a long-used route across the mountains, Manco Burro Pass, a few miles east of Raton Pass. The Mountain Branch of the Santa Fe Trail certainly offered better water and grazing than the

Bent's Fort on the Mountain Branch of the Santa Fe Trail at the Arkansas River was an Indian trading post, not a military establishment. Barclay's Fort and Adobe Walls were built on the same pattern. Barclay was a former Bent employee. Adobe Walls was built by Kit Carson, then in the Bents' employ. AUTHOR PHOTO

Cimarron Cutoff, but the difficulties of the Raton Pass proved a drawback. The Army of the West lost many of its wagons to the dangerous road. The Charles Towne route through Manco Burro Pass seemed promising, but Bent, overcome by events, never got the chance to examine it. General Kearny soon arrived at his fort on the Arkansas. Two years would pass before Towne tried it again and then out of desperation.

On May 1, 1848, one of the largest wagon trains ever to make the journey from Pueblo south into New Mexico arrived at Raton Pass. Eighteen men, including Alexander Barclay, and wives and children made up the party, bringing with them dogs, chickens, pigs, and other livestock. The Indian trade at Pueblo was down. Business was bad. Perhaps there were just too many traders in a shrinking market. Barclay thought he'd try again in New Mexico. Halfway up the pass eight of Mundy's teamsters traveling on foot met the Barclay party with a report that Ute Indians had surrounded Patrick Mundy's caravan—claiming to be protecting it from Jicarilla Apache. In the night, the teamsters had crept away and escaped. They left Mundy behind, who was unwilling to surrender his goods, certain that they'd be plundered.[3]

On May 13, 1848, the *Santa Fe Republican* proclaimed:

More Indian Depredations —
Narrow escape of a Trader with his wagon—a grand plot to rob and murder Mr. Monday

Some five or six days ago, news was received in Taos, that a trader by the name of Monday, a partner of Waldo, of Jackson county, Mo., was in the vicinity of Red River, surrounded by a large party of Eutaws, who had commenced robbing him of his goods, stock &c, and probably in a few days would kill him unless he received some assistance, for which he called on the citizens of Taos to render him. Mr. Kearney, Quinn, Kirker and others of Taos immediately started to his relief.[4]

In fact, the Ute were holding Mundy, a Santa Fe trader, and plundering his goods. When confronted, they swore they were only protecting him from Jicarilla Apache. Barclay and company turned back and ran into the Ute camp. He mounted his small cannon and aimed it at the Ute, but before he could fire, thirty-one men from Taos galloped up, including Apache killer James Kirker.[5] Soon after the Army of the West had arrived in New Mexico, Kirker had presented himself, offering his services as a scout and guide. In this period, Americans in the territory considered him something of a hero. It is unclear whether any of them were aware of his activities in Chihuahua where he had murdered many Apache. The Jicarilla and Ute probably were aware and undoubtedly recognized him from previous encounters. The Jicarilla had fought him in 1839.

The first recorded meeting Kit Carson and George Brewerton had with the Jicarilla Apache was recounted in an earlier chapter. It occurred in late June or early July 1848 west of the Sangre de Cristo Mountains. The people he met were coming from the vicinity of the Raton and Manco Burro Passes. As then noted, Carson thought if warriors he met were Ute, everything would be all right, but if they were Jicarilla, his party was in for trouble. Kit Carson boldly stared them down. Somehow he was aware that the Jicarilla Apache were at war with the Americans. Weeks earlier Lucien Maxwell had encountered the Jicarilla a few miles away east of the Sangre de Cristo.

On June 4, 1848, Lucien Maxwell wrote to his father-in-law, Judge Carlos Beaubien, that he had departed from Greenhorn on the first of the month with a party of eighteen, sixty horses, and four hundred deerskins. At the foot of Raton Pass, they encountered a large Jicarilla village and turned back. The Indians followed. Near Apache Creek, the Indians caught up, shouting that they were Utes and friendly. Their yells frightened the horses, thirty of which ran off and were captured by the Apaches. There was a small skirmish but the men escaped to Greenhorn.[6] The messenger went by way of the mountain peaks to avoid the Jicarilla.[7]

At Greenhorn on the upper Arkansas River, on June 6, 1848, John Brown sold off what goods he could, settled accounts, and with his wife Luisa, and a babe in arms, John Jr., headed south. He like Maxwell and Barclay planned to move south into New Mexico. Along with him went Archibald Metcalf and Blackhawk, a Delaware Indian. Lucien Maxwell and his manservant Indian George, leading sixty horses and mules packed with deerskins traded from the Utes, made a second attempt to get their property to Taos. Charles Towne and perhaps others went with them. It should have been a large enough party to dissuade Indian attack, since as yet Americans had not realized that the Jicarilla were at war with them.

Seven miles south of town while crossing Apache Creek, scene of Lucien Maxwell's recent skirmish, Jicarilla attacked the train. The warriors cut in between the men, driving off the pack animals. A few of them pursued Luisa. She clutched her four-month-old son tight to her breast, wheeled her horse about, and, leaning low in the saddle, galloped off toward Greenhorn closely followed by whooping Indians. The men of her party screamed to her, "Save yourself! Throw the baby away!"

She clutched tighter still, her arm around the baby's neck. Hooves thundered behind her. She held the baby even tighter. A warrior grabbed at her clothing and a piece tore away. A deep arroyo appeared ahead. The extra weight of the baby would be too much. The horse would founder on the long jump. She hung on whispering a prayer to Spanish angels. The horse leapt. Its forelegs hit firmly but its hind limbs struck low on the bank, which broke away. There was a momentary hesitation but momentum carried them forward. Something popped in John Jr.'s neck.

On smaller ponies, the Jicarilla dared not try the leap. They screamed their rage as Luisa rode away safe to Greenhorn. Beyond the range of their screams, the mother stopped to examine her child. She had wrenched his neck so that ever afterward he carried his head bent forward, a mark of the love of a mother who would not throw her child away.[8]

Meanwhile, the men of the party had taken refuge in the arroyo and successfully fought off the Indians, felling three. The travelers now faced certain vengeance. What had been a raid on property had become the Apache version of war. They would conduct murder raids against those who had slain their kin. Brown and his family along with Metcalf chose to stay in the relative safety of Greenhorn, near Pueblo and a handful of ranches and farms along the Arkansas River.[9]

In Taos, receiving Maxwell's letter, Judge Carlos Beaubien went to the Army for assistance. On June 14, 1848, Captain Samuel A. Boake, with fifty Missouri Mounted Volunteers of Company G, 3rd Regiment guided by mountain man Old Bill Williams, left Taos hunting Apache.[10,11] At the foot of Raton Pass, near the Purgatory River, they came upon a Jicarilla camp and attacked.[12] The two sides exchanged shots but no casualties resulted. The Indians fled and Boake pursued ineffectually eventually giving up the chase because he had become ill. He had captured thirty head of horses, perhaps the recent property of Maxwell. Boake had successfully enraged the Apache without humbling them at all.[13]

Women, children, and tepees in a Jicarilla Apache camp. COURTESY PALACE OF THE GOVERNORS PHOTO ARCHIVES (NMHM/DCA), 21552, PHOTOGRAPHER H. F. ROBINSON

Meanwhile, Lucien Maxwell would continue his attempts to cross the Raton Mountains going south and return to Taos. But first, Lucien headed north to Pueblo with the rest of the original party, which now included Charles Towne, Blackhawk, José Cortez, Andrés Fernández, Faustin Trujillo, and José Carmel. At Pueblo he was joined by Little Beaver, an Indian trapper, and by a man named Piles, who worked for Alexander Barclay, along with two children, six and four years of age, Mary and James Tharp. They were being returned to their grandfather in Taos after the death of their father, killed by Comanche.[14] Maxwell then went east to Bent's Fort. There Elliot Lee, who had survived the Taos Rebellion in 1847, and Peter Joseph de Tevis joined him. Maxwell would try a different route through the mountains avoiding Raton Pass.[15] Some of the original party went with him. Fourteen in all took the road to Manco Burro Pass.

At noon on June 19, 1848, they arrived at the narrow valley at the top of the pass. Steep piñon-covered slopes closed in on all sides of the twisting canyon. They lunched and rested, letting their stock graze a short distance away as they ate their dinner. Suddenly there were Indians galloping by at close quarters. Their war cries echoed from the hard black canyon walls. They took cover as best they might protecting the women and children among them. Men dressed in black broadcloth, Mexicans in serapes, and frontiersmen in beaded buckskin fired as the Indians passed. The air filled with acrid, sulfurous smoke. They scrambled to reload pouring powder from flasks and horns down long barrels and forcing patch and ball after, bringing their weapons to waist height to fit percussion cap under hammer. A minute went by as they feverously worked to be ready for the next assault. Men with Colt revolvers checked that caps were in place on all cylinders while those with single-shot weapons wished they'd spent their cash to better arm themselves. Only then, a minute later, did they realize their shots had no effect. Too far away before the men fired, the Jicarilla had escaped unscathed.

They gathered on the canyon side among rock and trees, making sure front and sides were covered by their fields of fire. Their rear was safe; the black volcanic cliff above made approach impossible. There was nothing to be done about the stock and precious packs. For now, only lives mattered.

Men shouted back and forth from their hidden positions, judging the size of the party that had attacked them. If the Jicarilla were but few, they might escape and even reclaim some of their stock. Time passed and the party began to relax. Maybe the warriors were satisfied with what they had stolen. Long minutes crawled by unbroken by talk. They watched intently for any sign.

One of them sniffed the air and cried out that the Apaches had lighted the grass afire. Another cried out and pointed. The Jicarilla were returning. It was a larger war party than any of them had imagined, perhaps 150 braves. The fire would drive the Maxwell's party from cover.

They held their position a little longer trying to save their baggage, but finally they moved staying together, covering each other with aimed fire. Fighting continued for hours. Occasional shots went out to keep the Apaches back and wary. The Jicarilla, at a disadvantage for range, returned fire with a few muskets and with bow and arrow. The frontiersmen, although heavily outnumbered, knew their business and fired on any warrior who showed himself. The Maxwell party's new position proved disadvantageous, too exposed. They suffered casualties.

As they moved to try for better ground, Blackhawk fell, the wound mortal. The men did their best to look after the children, who were having a difficult time keeping up with the others. The boy and girl fell too far behind and Jicarilla warriors snatched them. Arrows and bullets from the Jicarilla wounded five of the men. Maxwell was hit in the neck. He fainted. Indian George, his servant, broke cover and rushed to the stream returning with a hatful of water. He fed the water to the wounded man.

One of their number reached the conclusion they had all been considering. The only way out was up. They would have to scale the cliffs open and exposed to enemy fire. Elliot made the first move in the open. An Indian ball blew away his middle finger and then a second passed through his thigh, fortunately without breaking the bone.

Ramon Tafoya, Buffalo Calf, Jicarilla warrior of the Red or Llanero Clan, Fred Harvey Company postcard before 1910. COURTESY PALACE OF THE GOVERNORS PHOTO ARCHIVES (NMHM/DCA), 40788

Charles Towne cried out as he was hit. His leg broken, he could no longer proceed under his own power. He begged for someone to carry him. The slope was too steep. No one could drag himself and another up the canyon side. The warriors soon overtook Towne and his cries rapidly ceased. The Jicarilla warriors shot José Carmel through the kidneys, and he too stayed behind to face the Indians on his own. Indian George hoisted Lucien Maxwell on his back and in a feat of devotion and strength carried him up the canyon side.

Nearing the top, George fell wounded. Maxwell, having recovered with blood still seeping from the wound in his neck, fetched water and bound George's wound.

By the time they reached the mountaintop, eight were wounded and the party had been reduced from sixteen to eleven.[16] As night came on they continued until they came to water, then huddled together and tried to sleep. They had left everything behind except their weapons and suffered cruelly from the cold at that high elevation. The next day they moved up higher still and then hid themselves, afraid to move in daylight for fear that the Jicarilla would detect them.

As they stumbled forward in the night, Elliot Lee could not keep up. The wound to his thigh made it difficult to walk. Lee told the others to go on without him. Down below he could see the fires of the Indian village.

Four days after the attack, having gone all that time without food, Lee stumbled on an abandoned Indian camp, its fires still warm. He helped himself to a haunch of antelope left behind. After eating his fill, he filled his shot pouch with meat and stumbled painfully on. He found wagon tracks and stumbled upon friends and was saved after traveling on his own seven days and eighty miles.[17]

Meanwhile, the walking wounded stumbled on toward Taos. They were growing weak from starvation and exhaustion, unable to sleep without blankets during the cold mountain nights. Peter Joseph, unhurt, was urged to go ahead to get help. He made Taos and returned with Major Reynolds, forty soldiers, and Dick (Richens) Wootton as guide.[18] Andrés Fernández died in Taos of his wounds. Three months later American merchants redeemed the Tharp children from the Apache for $160 in trade goods. The girl died shortly afterward of the hardships of her captivity.[19] Four years later, Lucien Maxwell filed a claim for indemnification of depredation over his loss of stock and hides. The courts disallowed the claim saying it had been filed three years after the statute of limitations and because there was no treaty with the Jicarilla at this time.[20]

On June 27, 1848, reporting this misadventure shortly after it occurred, the *Santa Fe Republican* went on to say:

> *We have just been informed by some traders who have just arrived here, that the Indians are constantly attacking the trains as they pass in the vicinity of Wagon Mound, that part of the country being filled with Indians. Mr. B.F. Coons, who has just arrived, informs us that he was attacked in that vicinity and was compelled to leave his carriage to save his life, having only three men with him.*
>
> *We think it advisable to have troops started for that section of the country.*[21]

In late June, Captain Boake returned to Taos with thirty-two head of mules and horses captured from the Jicarilla, as noted above, probably only recently the property of Lucien Maxwell. On August 1, 1848, the *Santa Fe Republican* published notice of his ineffectual return due to illness. The populace believed the Army had to do something to chastise the troublesome Jicarilla, who threatened both the Cimarron Cutoff and the Mountain Branch of the Santa Fe Trail.[22] The two branches of the trail join south of the Raton Pass at Wagon Mound north of the Turkey Mountains, and again at La Junta twenty miles farther south where Barclay built his fort. This was Jicarilla territory and their hostile actions had effectively closed the trail, severing New Mexico from the United States.

On July 18, 1848, Major William W. Reynolds left Taos with 150 soldiers. He intended to pick up the pursuit where Boake had left off. His target was the Jicarilla blocking the Raton Pass. With him went Old Bill Williams,[23] Levin Mitchell,[24] Robert Fisher,[25] and James Kirker as "spies."[26]

In three detachments the Missouri Mounted Volunteers rode across the Sangre de Cristo to the northern gateway to Raton Pass along the Purgatoire River. There they picked up the trail of over four hundred Indians leading back across the mountains to the San Luis Valley north of Taos. The soldiers, sabers clanking, pack mules braying, crossed the Rio Grande and continued the pursuit into the high San Juan Mountains. They climbed through ponderosa and lodgepole pine to barren mountaintops above the treeline and descended into deep valleys lush with streams sprung from mountain snows. The path was arduous, but the trail left by hundreds of Indians was clear. The danger of ambush by so many warriors was real, keeping the men alert and

Cumbres Pass where Jicarilla warriors fought the US Army in 1848. AUTHOR PHOTO

tensions high. Finally, at Cumbres Pass near the headwaters of the south-flowing Chama River, the enemy went to ground.

The Missourians stumbled on a band of Indians. Both sides rushed to their weapons. The Jicarilla fired bow and arrow and trade fusil.[27] The soldiers responded with muskets. The fight was at close quarters. Neither the Jicarilla's nor the Missourians' weapons had a range greater than one hundred yards. The soldiers brought muskets to shoulder and fired, acrid smoke filling the crisp mountain air, but the reloading process was too laborious and by then the outnumbered Apache had flown.

Old Bill signaled for the soldiers to follow him and set off at a rapid pace following the fresh trail. They made contact and scattered other bands as they went. It was a fast-moving, running battle. Finally, the Jicarilla consolidated at the strong position in the pass. Major Reynolds rode back and forth in sight of the enemy, giving direction and encouragement to the men. He had a company dismount to form a base of fire. One man from each squad of four held his and the others' horses, walking them back away from direct fire but near enough if they were needed. The front rank knelt and fired while the second rank reloaded. In this way they were never caught unprepared and unloaded if the enemy should attack.

Heavily forested mountainsides provided the Jicarilla with cover and concealment. The valley floor was grassy and open giving the dragoons room to maneuver. An uphill direct assault against an enemy on such good ground would have cost heavily in casualties. Major Reynolds did not make this mistake.

The major directed the other companies to maneuver around the flanks, while one company held the enemy in position. He searched for any weakness in the Jicarilla defense. In this manner the battle continued for three hours, the Apache unable to escape, and the soldiers unable to overrun their position. Losses on both sides began to mount. Warriors would show themselves and then feign being hit to fool their enemy. The soldiers thought they killed thirty-six Jicarilla. Maybe, but until you hold the ground and count the bodies, unconfirmed "kills" are easy to claim. The soldiers' weapons had an advantage of range over those of their enemy.

Captain Salmon was hit and fell from his horse. Soldiers sprang to his aid dragging him from the line of fire. His wound was not serious. Old Bill was not so lucky. A bullet shattered his elbow. Undeterred he continued to keep his rifle hot during the engagement. Two soldiers died and five more were wounded until, low on ammunition, Major Reynolds broke off the engagement.[28]

If losses to the Jicarilla were as high as thirty-six, this must have been devastating to a tribe of one thousand to thirteen hundred members. Everyone would have lost a close relative. Nonetheless, depredations continued. On September 6, 1848, the *Santa Fe Republican* reported:

> *James H. Quinn, Esq., and Mr. Hicks have just arrived from Taos, who informs us that the Indians in that vicinity still continue their attacks upon the citizens—and running off stock. . . . Mr. Quinn informs us that the citizens of that place stand their guard regularly, and are so organized as to be able, as far as possible, to defend themselves and property, but still it is certain that it is necessary that there should [be] as soon as possible a force sent to garrison that part of the territory.*[29]

Elsewhere in the same edition the newspaper wrote:

A few days since, a young man by the name of Russell was found dead near the foot of Taos mountain. It seems that Mr. R was returning to Taos from this city with another young man, and whilst crossing the mountain, they were attacked by a party of Apaches. Mr. Russell was shot dead on the spot, whilst his companion fortunately made his escape uninjured. They were both discharged volunteers and men of good character. We understand that these Indians are daily committing their depredations in that vicinity, and the citizens of that place are hourly expecting an attack upon their little village. [30]

The August 9, 1848, *Santa Fe Republican* announced that Brevet Lieutenant Colonel John M. Washington, 3rd Regt. US Artillery, had been appointed civil and military governor of New Mexico. That month companies of the 3rd Artillery, 1st and 2nd Dragoons would arrive to replace the regiments from Missouri and Illinois. Lieutenant-Colonel Washington, artillery, was placed in command of a detachment consisting of Graham's squadron (D and E), Troop H, Second Dragoons, three troops from the First Dragoons, and a battery of light artillery (Ringgold). They did not arrive in Santa Fe until October 10.[31] In the interim, on August 27, Special Orders No. 37 placed Major Benjamin L. Beall, 1st US Dragoons, in command of the troops of the 9th Military Department (New Mexico).[32]

Kit Carson returned home in 1848. That winter Carson made two trips with Major Beall in pursuit of Jicarilla Apache and Moache Utes. Kit Carson said of the first expedition: "After surmounting many difficulties and passing through severe hardships, we finally accomplished the object of the expedition and returned to Taos."[33]

The object was to find the Jicarilla in their winter camps. The Jicarilla country in the mountains of northern New Mexico and southern Colorado is bitterly cold in the winter. The snows in the mountain passes are deep. For the Jicarilla it is a time to spend in one's tepee with the sides rolled all the way down, a fire going, and a tepee liner to provide insulation from the cold outside the warm tepee. Thick buffalo robes provide warmth and a place to sit.

As he was making his return to Taos, Carson discovered a small Jicarilla camp. Beall and his dragoons captured two of the men. Carson described the men as chiefs and Beall parleyed with them, receiving in return a promise of better behavior. Kit Carson trusted the Jicarilla to keep their word, as biographer Dunlay notes: "Some sources say this action was on Carson's advice; his apparent satisfaction with the results of the expedition would suggest that he at least approved of the release."[34]

In November 1848, Sergeant Charles Williams met with a band of Jicarilla about sixty miles west of Taos. He held a friendly parley with them as they seemed inclined to peace at this time.[35]

The year ended with Kit Carson home, but soon to go out again with Ben Beall against the Jicarilla. In July, Carson traveling with Brewerton and party had been wary of the Jicarilla, afraid that meeting them would lead to a fight while a meeting with the Ute would not. The "war" with the Jicarilla went back at least as far as 1847 and perhaps further. Carson did not go with Frémont on his winter expedition. Perhaps he had broken with his friend, still troubled by the order to execute two Californios in 1846.[36] General Kearny had Frémont brought before a court-martial in early 1848, and the Pathfinder was found guilty of insubordination and other charges and cashiered from the Army. Although he had been dishonorably discharged, President James K. Polk soon commuted his sentence and reinstated Frémont in the Army. His influential father-in-law, Senator Thomas Hart Benton of Missouri, sent Frémont out on his disastrous 1848 winter expedition. Carson continued to work with the Army, and despite his wariness of the Jicarilla convinced Beall to give them decent treatment. This is the pattern that remains in place through the following years. Carson was ready and willing to chastise the Jicarilla for depredations and to assist the Army in its efforts, but equally ready to insist on decent treatment if they agreed to be peaceful.

Chapter 7

With the end of the Mexican War, the Missouri and Illinois Volunteers had been replaced in the fall of 1848 by regular soldiers of the 1st and 2nd Dragoons, and 3rd Artillery in far smaller numbers, to keep order in the territory. The threat of rebellion had diminished, but danger remained in the form of the Jicarilla and Ute.

Due to the ongoing constitutional crisis over slavery and the claims the new state of Texas had made on New Mexican lands, Congress was unable to organize New Mexico as a territory until the congressmen agreed upon the Compromise of 1850. New Mexico's legislature, courts, laws, and its ownership remained in doubt.

Matters in New Mexico were confused on all fronts. The military governor struggled to keep order. The Jicarilla had been dealt a mighty blow at Cumbres Pass by the Missouri Volunteers, and for the moment they seemed relatively quiet, but the quiet would not last.

In 1849, Kit Carson was home in New Mexico at Taos with his beloved wife, Josefa, and still working occasionally as an Army scout. In February 1849, Kit Carson served as guide for Major Ben Beall, taking two companies of dragoons, about seventy men, to Bent's Fort on the Arkansas River. Bent's Big Lodge, as the mountain men called it, was an adobe castle with two turrets, one in front and one on the opposite rear corner, each surmounting small cannon. The American flag flew atop the gatehouse of the central *zaguan* (entryway). Flanked by rooms on either side, the entry was fifteen feet deep and led into a large central plaza. A trade window on one side of the *zaguan* was for members of tribes who were not trusted in the plaza. The gate remained closed but they could still trade. In the rear was a large corral with a high adobe wall topped with prickly pear cactus to discourage thieves from climbing over. The plaza was ringed with rooms that rose two stories above it. It was an outpost of civilization and trade, placed in an area where wood for heating and cooking fires, grass, and water were readily available.

The Southern Cheyenne and others liked to make their winter camp in the area. Beall hoped for an exchange of captives and the return of Mexicans held by the Cheyenne.

When Carson and Beall arrived at Bent's Fort they found "four nations of Indians, some two thousand souls" camped outside the gates. In addition to the Cheyenne, the tribe into which William Bent had married, there were Arapahos, who had divided from the Cheyenne in the early nineteenth century, Kiowa, and Comanches. It is less likely that Jicarilla and Utes would have been present. Tom Fitzpatrick, the Indian agent who had his headquarters at the fort, was strongly opposed to any attempt to take the captives by military force. The tribes would oppose it, and the force was not large enough to fight them. Kit Carson advised the major that Tom was correct and went on to say, "The Agent, traders, and officers of his command" were all opposed to attempting to take them by force.[1] Beall heeded their counsel and did not reclaim the captives. In subsequent years, this point would come up again in treaty negotiations.

George Bent recalled that Carson worked briefly for his father William, probably in March 1849, building a trading post along the Canadian River on the Llano Estacado that came to be called Adobe Walls.

Early in 1849, the Arapahos had defeated the Ute in a battle on the plains, capturing and destroying Ute livestock and camp equipment. To survive the Utes then began stealing stock from Mexican settlements that were spreading toward the San Luis Valley through the territory shared by the Jicarilla and Ute, and including the Jicarilla's sacred mountain, Mount Blanca, north of Trincheras and Ute Creeks near what is today Fort Garland, Colorado. The Indians attacked exposed settlements, lonely shepherds, and horse and cattle herds. The Utes told the traders that they bargained with that they intended to make reparations later for any depredations.[2] And up to that point, their reputation was such that the traders took note of it. Several bands of the Utes (or Utahs) were allies of the Jicarilla. The two tribes intermarried and often fought side by side. Ouray, the great chief of the Ute, was born to a Jicarilla mother. Their lands were side by side and the Comanche were their mutual enemy.

In March 1849, at Cerro de la Olla, the Ute would suffer a defeat at the hands of the US dragoons. Until then, they had been generally peaceful. This may have been in part because their lands were relatively remote from the settlements, and they had little contact with Americans and Mexicans except for trappers and those plying trade along the Old Spanish Trail. Kit Carson and Brewerton had passed peacefully through their lands and thought themselves safe if the Indians they encountered were Ute and not Jicarilla. The defeat occurred near where Carson had encountered the Jicarilla war party, north of Taos and a few miles west of the Rio Grande. It seems likely that there were at least some Jicarilla among the Ute the dragoons attacked. As Lecompte notes the Utes got little credit for taking the trader Mundy into "protective custody" and later were linked to the Jicarillas at Manco Burro Pass. Nonetheless, this did not destroy the tribe's reputation for peace.[3]

In spite of the offers of reparations in Santa Fe, Lieutenant Joseph H. Whittlesey received his marching orders. He was to take fifty-seven men of Companies A and G, First Regiment of Dragoons, to chastise the guilty Utes. With the assistance of Old Bill Williams, Antoine Leroux, Charles Autobees, and Asa Estes, who served as guides, Whittlesey located a Ute camp not far from Mexican settlements at the 9,475-foot Cerro de la Olla, a bowl-shaped, wooded hill that rose two thousand feet above the surrounding river plain.[4] The Ute, unaccustomed to war with the Americans, were taken by surprise. Lieutenant Whittlesey reported to his commander:

> *I have the honor to report that in obedience to your orders of the 9th I left this post on the 11th inst. to chastise the Eutaws for the depredations they have committed during the past winter (which since their discomfiture on the other side of the mountains by the Arapahoes has become unsupportable).*
>
> *In command of Fifty-seven men of Company A, First Dragoons, strengthened by a detachment of ten men of Company G, First Dragoons and a mountain howitzer (a part of this force being already at the Rio Colorado) on the 13th when about fifteen miles north of the Rio Colorado I perceived a small party on the opposite side of the Del Norte [Rio Grande] which at this point runs through a deep canon.[5]*

Hoping that the Indians hadn't seen his command, the lieutenant struggled to find a passage through the deep gorge and had to have his cannon dissembled, occasioning, as he said, "much delay." He left behind a detachment under Sergeant Batty to handle the cannon, ordering them to follow as soon as they could, and pushed ahead with twenty-three men through a prairie heavy with spring mud, snow, and rocks, fearing all the while that his quarry might detect his approach and escape. Eventually, his trusty scouts saw the smoke of a village on the Cerro de la Olla. Lieutenant Whittlesey continued his report:

> *A half mile or so in front of their village I was met by five men, well mounted, some of their chiefs who asked me what I wanted.*
> *I replied, "I came to fight."*
> *They answered, "It is well," and turned and fled.*[6]

Whittlesey quietly formed the ranks of his men just out of sight of the camp.[7] The bugle sounded, and the mountain men in the lead screamed like Indian warriors. The dragoons charged, pistol in left hand, saber in right, reins in teeth directing their horses with their knees. The horses knew the drill and the commands; their riders had little need to direct them. In line they emerged from the trees into a meadow filled with tepees and cook fires. One hundred or more Ute warriors stood aghast, and then scrambled for weapons and to get their families to safety.[8] Women and naked children ran screaming away from the ravaging horde. Across the meadow the soldiers spread death and havoc, toppling tepees and felling brave men who tried to stand against them. As they reached the far treeline, ten bodies lay bleeding behind them. They turned to strike again.

Whittlesey's report continued:

> *At this moment I wished to have my command advance more cautiously, but my bugler, Otto Akerman of Company A, First Dragoons, having been carried as I suppose by his horse into the midst of the enemy and far in front of the line, I found it impossible for some moments to make myself heard until we reached the edge of the slope.*
> *There I halted, and finding that the enemy so far outnumbered us, and had so greatly the advantage of position, I made a flank movement to the right up the slope intending to turn his left and driving him from his shelter.*
> *I found, however, the snow so deep in the pines that I could scarcely pass it, and the enemy, seeing my movements, met it by a similar one with greatly superior numbers. My men and horses formed for them a fair target while they were completely sheltered from my fire.*[9]

Deep snow kept the dragoons from penetrating into the trees. The long chase had left their horses blown. The lieutenant tried to flank the enemy and the Ute countered his move. The dragoons took a position among the trees, and the officer ordered them to dismount to receive the enemy's charge. It didn't come.

The lieutenant then ordered his men to burn the tepees. A man ran from the trees and a soldier mounted quickly. His horse knocked a Ute warrior flat. The dragoon leapt from his horse and pinned the man. He had a chief's son as his prisoner. Two women and the chief's son became hostages, forced to watch as their village burned.

The lieutenant looked around. As the action slowed, he would have asked for the butcher's bill. A good officer checks on the situation of his men and ammunition each time the action slows. His first sergeant would have responded that Bugler Otto Akerman and Private John Brade had gone down under arrows fired from the woodline. The men had been cut off from their comrades during the flanking movement.[10] Whittlesey recovered the bodies of his men and took the dead soldiers with him, knowing that if he failed to do so the Indians were likely to strip them of clothing and weapons and mutilate them. Whittlesey's men had burned more than fifty lodges and the Ute's possessions, leaving them with little but their weapons and the clothing on their backs.

As they hid in the trees, the Ute recognized the old man who had guided the soldiers. It was Bill Williams.

Later that spring Old Bill Williams returned to the Ute's mountains where he had led Frémont on his disastrous Fourth Expedition. He was looking for the instruments and papers Frémont had cached. They were of high value and Bill would be able to sell them, "compensation" for the disaster he'd helped cause. Ute warriors killed him.[11]

In April 1849, as a result of the ongoing skirmishes with the Ute, Colonel J. M. Washington ordered the establishment of subsidiary posts away from Santa Fe. He ordered a garrison to Las Vegas on the edge of the plains, and he sent Major Ben Beall to establish a post near the confluence of Ute and Trinchera Creeks in the San Luis Valley. This would serve to interdict the Sangre de Cristo Pass, near what is now called La Veta Pass, in southern Colorado, then in use by Ute and Jicarilla as a route to the Great Plains and Arkansas Valley. Captain J. M. Valdez's company of volunteers was put to work building a stockade at the pass. In less than a month, however, the colonel ordered the project abandoned over the protests of Lieutenant Whittlesey, who pointed out that this would expose the "Rio Colorado frontier" to the "full fury" of the Indians.[12, 13]

On the western frontier where Ute, Jicarilla, Navajo, and Comanche came to trade often, bringing in captive slaves (both Native American and stolen Mexicans), Colonel Washington assigned a company of New Mexico Volunteers under Captain John Chapman to the town of Abiquiu on the Chama River west of the Rio Grande. Founded by Mexicanized Pueblo Indians from the Hopi country, by old Spanish dons like the Martínez family whose powerful scion was Padre Antonio José Martínez, and by *genizaros*, Abiquiu's mixed population made for chaotic conditions. The mix was not good, and although many had forgotten their roots, all of the Rio Arriba remembered Abiquiu for its late-eighteenth-century witch trials.

In a letter dated April 10, 1849, Captain John Chapman to Captain Henry B. Judd, the former says that he is trying to get evidence that the prefect of Abiquiu is more friendly to "Eutaws" than to the Americans.[14]

Abiquiu, a *genizaro* settlement that traded with Ute, Jicarilla, Comanche, and Navajo. It was the Ute-Jicarilla Agency for many years and a military outpost.
COURTESY PALACE OF THE GOVERNORS PHOTO ARCHIVES (NMHM/DCA), 13695, PHOTOGRAPHER T. HARMON PARKHURST

Evidence of this was that property of the doomed Frémont expedition had been found among items traded by the Ute in Abiquiu, apparently taken from Bill Williams and Benjamin Kern when they were murdered. Chapman wanted the man taken for court-martial.[15] Captain Judd went to Abiquiu intending to arrest the prefect for being too friendly with the "Yutas" and indifferent to recovering stolen property. After a talk, the man surrendered two stolen horses and escaped arrest and trial.[16] Such miscarriages of justice were frequent and made it difficult for the Army and Indian agents to persuade the Utes and Jicarillas not to seek their own retribution. Abiquiu remained a sore spot. The people of the town cheated and murdered Ute, Navajo, and Jicarilla. They also traded in captive Mexican slaves and hostages of the Indians.

In the spring of 1849, Carson and Lucien Maxwell began the process of settling Maxwell's huge land grant. In the 1830s, Judge Beaubien, Maxwell's father-in-law, and Guadalupe Miranda with the aid of New Mexico governor Manuel Armijo had begun piecing together a huge land grant. It began at the crest of the Sangre de Cristo and ran eastward onto the Llano Estacado. The combined grant extended over 1.7 million acres making them the owners of the largest property in the United States.[17] Carson and Maxwell started a colony at Rayado, about ten miles south of modern Cimarron.

Kit Carson set out on his second try at settled life. Josefa did not join him at Rayado until the winter of 1850/51.[18] In his autobiography, Carson said:

> *In April, Mr. Maxwell and I concluded to make a settlement on the Rayado. We had been leading a roving life long enough and now was the time, if ever, to make a home for ourselves and children. We were getting old and could not expect to remain any length of time able to gain a livelihood as we had been [for] such a number of years. Arrived at Rayado, commenced building and making improvements, and were in a way of becoming prosperous.*[19]

Rayado was a beautiful place. The verdant Sangre de Cristo Mountains, ten thousand feet high, formed the background as grassy, rolling hills stretched out toward a green plain. A stream lined with cottonwood and canyon grape sparkled clear as it flowed by through the plain. The land was rich in game for hunting, and the prairie provided rich grazing for cattle. Carson and Maxwell soon had settlers from Taos working to irrigate and plow the land. The windowless adobe house enclosing its own plaza was not so grand in 1849, nor was the nearby Maxwell home quite the Victorian mansion it is today. Charles Pancoast described Rayado as it was in 1849:

> *On the 26th (July) we crossed a Mountain Ridge and entered a beautiful Valley covered with fine grass, over which hundreds of Horses, Cattle, and Sheep were ranging; and about Sundown we had the pleasure of seeing a Spanish Rancho at the foot of a high Mountain. This was Riadjo, the Rancho of the famous Mountaineer Kit Carson, so long the Scout and Guide of General Fremont. The Ranch House could not be said to be stylish: it was a two-story log affair, surrounded by Adobe walls for purposes of fortification. Inside the walls were several Adobe Houses, and outside a number more, as well as a large corral and several Buildings used as Stables, Slaughter Houses, etc. Carson had about him a dozen or more Americans and Mexicans and about twenty Indians beside a number of Squaws, all to be fed at his Table; and judging from the waste we saw around the place, his Table was of no mean order.*
>
> *Kit himself was "a superior representative of the genuine Rocky Mountain Hunter," clad in a buckskin coat and pants, with moccasins on his feet and a Mexican sombrero on his head, his hair down over his shoulders. At first, though he was hospitable and provided beef for his guests, he had little to say, but, sitting around the travelers' campfire, he opened up.*[20]

Carson spoke to Pancoast of the difficulties of maintaining his lonely position on the frontier. Stock thefts by Jicarilla and Ute were a constant threat. Even though Kit Carson and the Jicarilla treated each other as neighbors, the possibility was always present some young warrior might attempt a stock theft. Moreover, Carson was vigilant from habit and experience and because Mexicans and Americans in his vicinity were being raided. Carson spoke of aid from soldiers and of leading the dragoons to the haunts of the Indians with which he was thoroughly familiar. Carson told the Quaker *"he had punished them so severely that they had found it their best policy to make their peace with him. He now enjoyed their Friendship, and often gave them meat;*

and they no longer molested his stock, although they continued to steal that of others [emphasis added]." Nonetheless, Kit Carson maintained a guard over his cattle by day and a sentinel by night.

Lucien Maxwell's approach to Indian theft was similar. Jicarilla, Ute, and others would often drop by at Rayado expecting to be fed and clothed and provided with gifts of trade goods. These people would have provided the same gifts of hospitality to visitors arriving in their own camps. Expecting hospitality, if they did not receive it, they might understand the rebuff as hostility and resort to theft as they would against any enemy. Maxwell made gifts. He knew the people and their customs. He, like Carson, knew that he was in a sense paying rent for being on their lands. If stock was stolen, Lucien Maxwell would demand that the military chastise the offenders. Where Maxwell differed was that whether stock was stolen or given as a gift, he would make a claim

Lucien Bonaparte Maxwell, former mountain man, friend of Kit Carson, de facto agent for the Jicarilla, and son-in-law of Carlos Beaubien. He owned most of northeastern New Mexico east from the crest of the Sangre de Cristo Mountains. His holdings included much of the Jicarilla range. About 1870. COURTESY PALACE OF THE GOVERNORS PHOTO ARCHIVES (NMHM/ DCA), 50592

against the government for losses through depredation.[21] This was unlikely to have done him much good against the Jicarilla as, until 1851, there was no treaty with them and thus claims for compensation were not allowed, and those that were allowed took years to settle. Nonetheless, he was a frequent claimant.

In May 1849, commander of the 9th Military District (New Mexico) Colonel Washington dispatched Captain John Chapman to find and further punish the Utes. Apparently, they were the same ones Lieutenant Whittlesey

Kit Carson's house at Rayado. Lucien Maxwell's house was nearby as was a building housing a small garrison of soldiers including Sergeant Holbrook, who helped Kit recover stock stolen by the Jicarilla in 1850 after he upset his "neighbors" by leading the army in pursuit to recover Ann White in November 1849. AUTHOR PHOTO

Interior of Kit Carson's sala, or hall, a meeting room at Rayado. AUTHOR PHOTO

had dealt with in March. In the field between the Chama River above Red Wall Canyon and the El Rito River west of the Rio Grande in the San Juan Mountains, an express messenger galloped up to Captain Chapman. He brought a change of instructions. Jicarilla had entered the Valley of Abiquiu and murdered not less than ten of the inhabitants. The captain of volunteers turned his command south and soon interdicted and utterly surprised the Apache, who hadn't expected the "cavalry" to arrive from the north.

With forty hard-riding men behind him, Chapman came upon forty lodges of the enemy the next morning. The camp was peaceful. Fires burned. Breakfast cooked. Piñon smoke was thick in the air. The Apache looked south for pursuit. The Jicarilla greatly outnumbered Chapman's command. Nonetheless, without hesitation and with total surprise he charged through the camp. His sudden charge routed them. The volunteers cut through the ranks of the Apache warriors with revolving pistols and sabers. Behind them blood covered the ground and twenty of the enemy lay dead, wounded, and dying. The engagement was short and sharp. Three of Chapman's men were wounded but still in the saddle. Behind a servant boy lay dead. There was no time for a burial. The Jicarilla had been chastised, but would soon reorganize and envelope his small command. Chapman ordered his men to regroup and continue the march south toward civilization.[22] Colonel Washington reported to headquarters in Washington:

> *From the enclosed report of the affair by the Captain himself, it will be seen that his officers and men conducted themselves gallantly on the occasion, and deserve much credit.*
>
> *The latest account from the Eutaws, received yesterday, represent them as being inclined for peace; and, to effect that purpose, express a willingness to surrender the perpetrators of the murders committed on the inhabitants of this territory within the last two months, and to restore all the captured property. . . .*[23]

Also in May 1849, Sergeant James Bally, 1st Dragoons, with a detachment from Cantonment Burgwin,[24] rode into the Embudo Mountains[25] to the vicinity of Santa Barbara[26] where he met Chief Chacon of the Jicarilla,[27] who told the sergeant that there was a village of sixteen lodges nearby under Chief Flache Vayada.[28] He proceeded to Ojo Sarco, a hot spring, where he found the Indians and called the chiefs and the *alcalde* of Santa Barbara to council. "I informed [the chief] that the Coln. Cmdg at Taos had heard that the Indians were Steeling Horses & Sheep from the Mexicans & that I had been sent to see if it was true."[29] The chief denied the charges. His people were innocent of any crimes. They had taken nothing without paying for it. The chief requested that Sergeant Bally ask the *alcalde* if this were not so. The *alcalde* and other *paisanos* agreed that the Jicarilla had not molested them and had taken nothing without paying for it. The Mexicans were satisfied with the Apaches remaining in the area. However, Sergeant Bally reminded the Indians that their recent treaty called for them to stay away from the settlements, so they could not stay in this part of the country. "They must go to their own people on the Rita[30] or form a settlement by themselves." To the sergeant they seemed willing to comply but uncertain of what to do or where to go. He asked the chiefs to come to Taos to talk to the colonel commanding. The sergeant then proceeded to another nearby location where he found thirty lodges of Indians. He ensured that they had not been molesting the Mexicans, and told them to leave the area and for their chiefs to come to Taos. The chiefs promised they would come.[31]

On June 18, Captain Whittlesey reported a meeting with the chiefs of the Jicarilla in Taos. He took the meeting due to the illness of Colonel Beall. Chief Chacon came "stating that they feared that there would be difficulties on the other side of the Del Norte[32] and that in consequence of their desire for peace, they have crossed to this side to avoid being implicated." Chief Lobo sent word by a Pueblo Indian.[33] At the same time, a party of Apaches were killing and driving off cattle twenty-five miles away in the mountains east of Taos. Beall sent Whittlesey out to look into the matter and pursue the miscreants but learned that they had joined the party of Lobo. The captain was ready to attack Lobo's village when Chino, Lobo's son, came out to confer with him and point out that Lobo had come in under a promise of security to parley with Beall. Lobo agreed to be responsible and to make restitution. Whittlesey thought Lobo sincere in wanting peace and that Chacon wanted to continue depredations.[34]

At mid-year 1849, Colonel Washington turned his attention to protecting northern New Mexico from Jicarilla attacks. Exposed ranches on the eastern slope of the Sangre de Cristo Mountains and north of Taos were apparently suffering regular stock raids.[35]

A report of June 18, 1849, by Lieutenant Whittlesey tells of an expedition against Apaches who were passing through Siengilla (Cieneguilla), very close to where Sergeant Bally met them in May at Ojo Sarco, and committing depredations. Perhaps the Jicarilla passed through the area with supreme disdain for the inhabitants, taking such small things as they chose and daring the owners to try to do something about it. In a tiny village, Jicarilla warriors would have outnumbered the *paisanos*. Confronted by Whittlesey's men, Chief Chino, son of Lobo, principal chief of the tribe, protested that the Jicarilla wanted peace and would make restitution for any livestock taken. They brought in nineteen mules and horses in payment for the settlers' losses.[36] American leadership in Santa Fe was continually conscious of their tenuous position. People complained of stock raids. Traders complained of Indian harassment. Not only was Santa Fe at the end of a lengthy umbilicus, the early summer caravans expected in June had been disrupted. Any hindrance of travel on the Santa Fe Trail was soon felt in the city. On August 8, 1849, the *Santa Fe Republican* printed an apology to its readers:

Since the 9th of last June, we have been unable to publish our journal, as our paper has entirely given out. We expect a supply very soon however, and will resume its publication. We will issue a prospectus in the next issue, and hope that all those wishing to see a paper flourish in Santa Fe will give their immediate support and help the press along.[37]

The Apaches and Utes opposed the penetration of settlers into the San Luis Valley, and the Apaches killed four Mexicans at Costillo (Costilla), north of Taos. The violence and thievery continued as Captain Valdez of the New Mexico Volunteers had a skirmish with the Jicarilla, taking some horses from them. A little farther north near the Sangre de Cristo Pass, an emigrant train being escorted by Lieutenant Alfred Pleasanton lost seventeen horses and mules to the Jicarilla. Whittlesey went on to say:

On the withdrawal of Capt. Valdes' Co. the Rio Colorado frontier will be exposed to the full fury of the Eutaws who no doubt will attack as soon as they can cross the Del Norte. The Apaches can muster 300 warriors, while I can get but 45 men. Colonel Beall asks permission to retain Capt. Valdez in this valley.[38, 39]

In July Brevet Major Steen, 1st Dragoons, encountered a band of Jicarilla forty miles south of Santa Fe, and pursued the enemy much farther south, well into Mescalero territory. This overlap of territory points to a problem in understanding the Apache. They all spoke a mutually intelligible language. Political association and band membership reflected personal influence and loyalties. It was ephemeral and temporary. It could change at any time. In the 1880s, the government confined the Jicarilla on the Mescalero reservation. The Mescalero had a tribal membership of about four hundred compared to over eight hundred for the Jicarilla. The Indian agent chose to use only Mescalero for his police force. The Mescalero were unhappy with the Jicarilla presence, claiming they over-hunted. The Mescalero had already claimed the best lands, and the agent sent the Jicarilla to the less desirable locations on the reservation. The Ollero were unhappy with this arrangement and left the reservation headed north to the Chama River Valley. The Llanero were left behind apparently content to live with the Mescalero. This suggests a preexisting relationship between them and an overlap in band membership.

On July 5, Major Enoch Steen with Lieutenant George H. Thomas, 3rd Artillery, and thirty men of the companies G & H, 1st Dragoons,[40] pursued Apaches who had killed several Mexicans near the Placer Mines forty miles south of Santa Fe.[41] They picked up an Apache trail and within a few hours located the scene of the massacre, discovering the bodies of six Mexicans. The pursuit continued south for the next six days. In the White Mountains at Dog Cañon, they overtook and fought the enemy until nightfall.[42] Steen's men killed five of the Apache, losing three of their own wounded. Steen wrote: "we had eaten our last bread on the 23d isnt., and the horses' feet were without shoes and bleeding. I set out on the morning of the 24th to find Dona Ana, a small Mexican village. . . ."[43] The Sacramento Mountains near the scene of the action were nearby and are the heart of Mescalero country. Nonetheless, the pursued may have been Llanero Jicarilla.

The Ninth Military District (New Mexico) had been hammering the Jicarilla since 1848. The commanders in the field refer to numerous depredations by the Jicarilla, though some may be attributable to Utes and Mescaleros. Michno provides an appendix detailing claims for reparations. Here are the claims against the Jicarilla:

Ruis, Enacio. #2415, 2-15-1849. Apache $501 (horses). Not proven . . .
Martinez, Jose Benito. #5994. 6-12-1849. Jicarilla. $1,735. Filed 7-16-1855 . . .
Pino, Vincente. #2834. 9-10-1849. Jicarilla. $2,790 . . .
Gonzales, Jose Maria. #7012. 12-10-1849. Apache. $108 . . .[44]

Four claims don't seem likely to have excited much interest from the military. Unfortunately, "numerous" can mean anything from two to two hundred. Undoubtedly there were depredations by the Jicarilla. They remain less than completely visible much like many of the actions detailed here which do not appear in the *Chronological List of Actions with Indians*, which only includes actions involving soldiers of the regular army, and not volunteer formations. These latter went underreported by their officers, who were unaccustomed to filing military reports. Some of them, like Kit Carson, were illiterate and others nearly so. The actions participated in by volunteer units seemed to have produced many more casualties among the Indians than those reported by regular formations. The reasons for under- and overreporting enemy deaths range from undisciplined slaughter of a defeated foe to simple braggadocio. West Pointers kept their bragging under finer control.

On August 16, a band of Jicarilla went to Las Vegas, New Mexico, to trade on the heels of a summer of skirmishes and conflicts. They wanted "powder and ball." Captain Henry B. Judd, 3rd Artillery, was the commander of the local detachment at Las Vegas, which also had men at Mora, Barclay's Fort, and Rayado.[45] Judd's attitude to the Jicarilla shows up in his "despatches." He didn't trust the Jicarilla, whom he said had "falsely treated for peace at Taos" the previous year. Judd wrote:

I have the honor to report that a party numbering about forty Apaches (Jicarillas) came to this post today with an evident design of committing depredations, should a chance be presented, as well as to supply themselves with powder and ball they could obtain by barter or otherwise. After forbidding anyone to trade with or entertain them, I held a talk with those who were represented as being their principal men, and from the contradictions, falsehoods and duplicity pervading their own statements I felt convinced that their object was anything but pacific . . .

I therefore determined to seize the party . . . and ordered a command under Lt. Burnside to proceed to their camp half a mile out of town. The Indians were already in the Saddle and prepared for any emergency. . . .[46]

When Judd ordered the merchants to refuse trade, the Jicarilla became unruly. Some accounts suggest that many were drunk on the local *aguardiente.* According to Judd these Indians had come "with an evident design of committing depredations should a chance present [itself]."[47] He claimed that they had, furthermore, been robbing and killing along the frontier. According to Tiller, a Jicarilla Apache herself, the party of forty peaceful Jicarillas had simply come to town to trade, but ended up skirmishing with the troops.[48]

Judd ordered Lieutenant Ambrose Burnside and his artillery company to escort the Jicarilla back to their camp ten miles to the south. The Jicarilla were already in the saddle and prepared to offer Burnside a hostile reception when he arrived. Once at the camp the local judge, Herman Grolman, under Judd's instruction, went forward into leveled lances, muskets, and bows to vainly harangue the Apaches, imploring them to

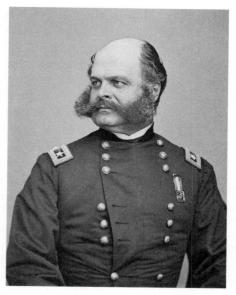

In 1849, Lieutenant Burnside achieved a lopsided victory over Jicarilla who had come to Las Vegas to trade. He was wounded in the throat by a Jicarilla arrow. Burnside went on to command the Union Army of the Potomac in November 1862. WIKIMEDIA COMMONS

forego the lethal consequences of flight and resistance.[49] Judd had ordered Burnside to demand hostages against the good behavior of the Jicarilla, and this demand was included in Grolman's harangue. Seeing that the Jicarilla maintained a hostile stance, Burnside deployed his men in line.[50]

When Burnside's men advanced to within short range, the Jicarilla turned to flee, and then wheeled about to release a flight of missiles from bows and rifles. Burnside called to his men, "Charge as skirmishers!" They drew their sabers and bore down on the camp. Slowed by hills and ravines, they pursued the Apache, who repeatedly turned to fight, and the pursuit briefly disintegrated into hand-to-hand combat. The bloody chase went on for nine miles. In the end, Judd believed that only eight or ten escaped. The fourteen dead lay behind them in the ravines where the Indians had made their stand.[51] The soldiers wounded many more Apache, but there was no way to count them as they fled. The Jicarilla wounded Burnside and his sergeant.[52]

The inequality of casualty counts strongly suggests that the Jicarilla, despite an apparently hostile posturing, were not ready for battle with Burnside. In subsequent parleys and to this day, they persist in claiming that they had only come to trade. It may well be that this was how they thought of the visit to Las Vegas. They came with women and children. Had it been a raid, they had shown on multiple occasions the ability to gather more than one hundred warriors.

During the fight, six Jicarilla (five women and one man) were taken hostage, among them Lobo Blanco's daughter.[53,54] After the skirmish, Captain Judd considered Los Valles south of Las Vegas to be in danger of reprisal and sent Captain P. M. Papin and a company of New Mexico volunteers to defend the area. On September 8, 1849, Papin fought "a brilliant little affair," commanding his forty men in pursuit of the Jicarillas after a raid at a ranch at Chaperito. One of his parties under Sergeant Miller surprised the Indians' camp, and the Apache fled in confusion. The volunteers killed Chief Petrillo and took his horse, lance, and shield, as well as his wife.[55] The attack on the Jicarilla camp, much as Judd had feared, led to increased attacks on the settlements, a hostility made worse because Judd was holding Lobo Blanco's daughter and he was one of the principal chiefs.[56]

The particular Indians at Las Vegas may or may not have been involved in depredations. Some of them probably had been. Had Captain Judd not enforced his edict, the Mexican merchants would probably have conducted trade with them. From the standpoint of the merchants, not trading would have meant loss of income and infuriating the Indians.

Jicarilla chief Chacon, often considered a "peace chief," believed that Judd was aroused over the death of two Mexicans and a theft of cattle at Casa Colorado. Chacon said that the unprovoked attack by the soldiers at Las Vegas and the holding of Lobo Blanco's daughter as a hostage led to an attack almost a year later on the mail party at Wagon Mound, during which the defending frontiersmen slew an Apache leader, Chino.[57]

The Army, especially Captain Judd, remained active against the Jicarilla, harrying them, keeping them on the run. When they couldn't find the Apache, it was because they were being forced to move, making it all the more difficult to hunt and gather and trade. On September 29, 1849, Captain Judd reported from Las Vegas:

An expedition under [was made by] Lt. Burnside against the main camp of the Apaches, to the Gallina Mts., a noted stronghold of the Jicarillas, thence to the Canyon of the Red River, through the Canyon Largo to the Canyon de la Scinta, but was unable to catch up with them. A march of 350 to 400 miles was made.[58]

The Gallina (Turkey) Mountains stand between Barclay's Fort, the future Fort Union, and Wagon Mound. The Red River referred to is the Canadian. Burnside covered a large portion of the Jicarilla country, including areas where they would have hunted buffalo and antelope.

Whether Captain Judd's and Lieutenant Burnside's hostility to the Jicarilla sparked a flame, or if the war of the preceding years was already burning bright matters little. They had won a lopsided victory at Las Vegas. The Jicarilla Apache were about to close the Santa Fe Trail again.

Chapter 8

On September 15, 1849, F. X. Aubry started his caravan, the last of the year, westward from Independence toward Santa Fe. With him was Santa Fe trader James M. White, his wife Ann and baby daughter, as well as her black lady's maid. Aubry's train included ten wagons belonging to the partnership of St. Vrain & McCarty and thirteen belonging to Mr. White. Aubry, the Skimmer of the Plains, who stood all of five foot four inches, was a trusted wagon master who had opened several new trails. In 1848, he had ridden from Santa Fe back to Independence in five and a half days, winning his sobriquet. James White had opened commission and forwarding houses in El Paso and Santa Fe the previous year with headquarters in the latter city. He had been so successful that he decided to bring his family to the City of the Holy Faith of St. Francis.[1]

A traveler on the plains and in the mountains that year described Mrs. Ann Dunn White as "a lady from one of our large cities, tenderly nurtured, highly educated, elegant, and refined."[2] She may have been the first of her kind, a lady from an upper class family who had immigrated to New Mexico to live, other than officers' ladies who may have arrived with the troops. The territory was still an extremely rugged frontier. The Army had not yet seen fit to build officers' quarters and soldiers were still living in rude, windowless adobes and worse, in some places, *jacals*, primitive structures built with wooden poles. Santa Fe lacked sophistication and comfort. Officers and the gentleman merchant class were taught to protect ladies like Ann Dunn White.

The Llano Estacado was lush and green that year and water was plentiful.[3] However, winter came early and the nights were already chilly. The caravan moved slowly across the Great Plains along the Arkansas River, then crossed it heading southwest on the Cimarron Cutoff. Those who plodded along beside the oxen, touching their backs gently with their long whips, spoke softly to their charges giving direction. The wagons, loaded to their canvas tops with merchandise, had no place for the driver to sit. The men were Missouri backwoodsmen, Mexicans, St. Louis and Canadian French, Delaware Indians, and Cajuns from southern swamps clad in rags and buckskin, bright serapes, and straw hats. Out in front rode a tiny, swift-moving man who darted to and fro and far ahead, ever alert. Everyone watched him for signals. In a Dearborn wagon, little more than a flat board on wheels with canvas sides and top and not much in the way of suspension, rode a woman who shivered though she was draped in a buffalo robe. Her lady's maid clutched the woman's child, softly singing to the little one.

They rose early to round up and harness the stock and then ate a light breakfast. At midday they would stop for a more substantial meal, the nooning. They had crossed the Cimarron River that morning. A man on a fine horse dressed in fine, if now dusty, city clothing rode up beside the woman and spoke to her. She nodded and he spurred his horse, riding up to the small man out front. Dismounting he spoke with the wagon master. The nearby teamsters, eating their dinner, heard something unusual. Someone dared to challenge Aubry. None of them would have dared, but this man, dressed in his fine suit, was of the nobility of the trail, a merchant.

The merchant explained to Aubry that his wife was sickly, a gentle-woman, the nights were growing cold, and since they were beyond the danger of Kiowa and Comanche, he wanted to take two of his horse-drawn Dearborns and hurry ahead to Santa Fe, comfort, and safety. Aubry's silence expressed his displeasure. Most men would have backed off, but the merchant, James White, persisted. He would take Ben Bushman, a mulatto, with him and some others as well. His horse-drawn wagons would move much more swiftly than the oxen. His wife and his baby daughter, Virginia, were in danger from the cold. It might snow any day. This prediction proved true. Soon after White and his party moved on ahead, a snowstorm struck and Aubry lost teams and had to cache two wagonloads of goods.[4]

Aubry reminded him that there was still danger from the large war parties of Jicarilla, but White dismissed this.[5] White told the wagon master that he would take Bushman to drive one wagon and a Mexican to drive the other. There were two Germans who had recently joined the caravan who were in a hurry to reach California to look for gold. He thought that would be a large enough party to protect his wife, her lady's maid, and baby Virginia. F. X. Aubry accepted the inevitable, but insisted that he also take William Callaway, an experienced wagon master in his own right who knew the trail, how to find water, and how to deal with Indians.[6]

On October 23, 1849, a cold morning, James White and company parted from the caravan at Cold Spring. François X. Aubry watched White, his wife, and their trail companions pull out from the night's camp. The smaller party was able to move faster than Aubry's caravan, and soon disappeared from sight. He may have sensed that this was the last time he would see any of them alive.[7]

On October 25, in the late morning, James White's little caravan of two Dearborns and a few riders crossed Palo Blanco Creek and pulled off the trail for their nooning. The small party had difficulty bringing the heavily laden wagons across. More hands and more livestock would have been useful. Nonetheless, they crossed and were ready for a rest and a heavy meal.[8]

Unseen atop the low bluffs north of the trail, a Jicarilla hunter watched. He was looking for buffalo, or if none showed themselves, antelope. Most of the tribe had gathered in a camping spot south of Point of Rocks ten miles to the west. The hunter could see dust trails of small parties, almost undoubtedly *Mangani* to raise so much of it, to the east and west of his hill. To the south, he discerned a mounted party approaching. He dismissed them as *Nakaiyeh ciboleros*, Mexican buffalo hunters, men with spears and bows. Far to the east rose the dust of a big caravan one or two days away. He saw opportunity in the heavily laden wagons. The Jicarilla hunter would have considered his next move. The small caravan of rich *Mangani* looked enticing, but the few hunters with him would not be enough to intimidate these heavily armed Americans. He rode back to find his chief, Lobo Blanco.[9]

On the report of the hunter, Lobo gathered fifty of his warriors. Hastily they rode back to the site of the nooning and confronted James White to demand gifts so that the Jicarilla would allow this little band of *Mangani* to cross their land in peace. At the start of summer, Lobo Blanco had promised Lieutenant Whittlesey in Taos that he would remain peaceful, and he might have wondered if they would consider this a violation of the "treaty." They probably wouldn't—such a demand was hardly unusual. Lobo wasn't stealing; he was asking for gifts. Maxwell and Carson and even little wagon chief Aubry made gifts all the time. Still, Lobo Blanco was unhappy about how Captain Judd and Lieutenant Burnside had treated his people at Las Vegas in August. His daughter was still their "guest." James White was not happy about giving up property, but Callaway told him he would have to yield and White was considering what to give them as the women huddled fearfully by the wagons. Ben Bushman stood with his old shotgun protecting the women. The two Germans were inexperienced in Indian affairs. They were at once afraid of the "savages" and indignant at the demand for gifts. One of the Jicarilla poked through a German's pack. Enraged, the German turned and shot him.

With so many Jicarilla present, the whites never got off another shot. Lobo struck down James White and a warrior lanced Callaway. Two of the *Mangani* lay still groaning, barely alive, as the Jicarilla bundled off the two women and the child.

A small party of Mexican *ciboleros* accompanied by a boy of twelve arrived on the scene and gasped in horror at the carnage. Seeing an opportunity, several of them began to rifle through crates, trunks, and wagons. Others went to the aid of the wounded men. Then the band of Jicarilla hunters returned and they circled the frightened Mexicans three times, firing on them, killing several, wounding others. The boy, badly wounded, played dead and watched in horror as the Jicarilla dispatched the two wounded white men and then the remaining *ciboleros*. The Jicarilla went through the camp, taking all they could carry and use, breaking everything else, overturning the light wagons. Baby Virginia's little rocking chair amused the warriors and they did not break it. After they departed, the boy staggered off to the west, dragging himself toward Point of Rocks ten miles away.[10]

Point of Rocks, a popular campsite on the Santa Fe Trail. Near here in 1849, the White Wagon Train was massacred and Ann White taken captive. AUTHOR PHOTO

On October 27, two days after the White caravan was attacked, shortly after night fell, Alexander Barclay came upon the dead bodies and dismounted his horse briefly to investigate. Alarmed, he deemed it best to hurry on and at Point of Rocks hailed the camp of the Honorable Hugh N. Smith and his party. Smith was New Mexico's delegate to Congress.[11] During the night, a gravely wounded Mexican boy staggered into camp to tell his story, and Smith deemed it advisable, the road being unsafe, to turn back to Barclay's Fort and Las Vegas.[12] For the second time, the Jicarilla Apache had closed the Santa Fe Trail.

The next day Barclay wrote in his diary of the scene he had witnessed:

October 28th. Back from U. States with Isaac Adamson, Geo. Simpson & Spencer with his dearborn,[13] myself in barouche[14] and horse— passed dead bodies on road at Point of Rocks, viz., buffalo hunters, night before last, and White's wife and party defeated thereabout between it and Whetstone Branch.

Once at Santa Fe, Don Alejandro Barclay told his story to James Calhoun, the Indian agent. Charles L. Spencer, an American merchant of Santa Fe returning from the United States, was with Barclay at the site of the grisly discovery. Spencer had left his wagons at Cold Spring where White had separated from the Aubry caravan. He saw the dead bodies of James White and five or six of his party. Calhoun reported that Spencer related the following:[15]

They also noticed a baggage wagon upset, and broken into pieces, and what is yet more horrible, some Pueblo Indians were met the ensuing day, who stated they were just from the Camp of the Apaches, and there (saw) an American female and her little daughter supposed to have been the wife and daughter of Mr. White . . .

But it is not to be presumed that these gentlemen remained long enough upon the ground to have ascertained, accurately all the facts the horrible scene might have disclosed. What they saw was by the light of the moon; and that the perpetration was of so recent a moment, as to admonish them that the hot breath of the Indians might be near enough to be scented; they therefore hastened on to Las Vegas and were seventy eight hours without rest . . .

[I]f the two captives are not to be liberated, it is to be hoped they are dead.[16]

The scene must have seemed even more horrible by moonlight in late October. The fate of the lady's maid is totally unknown—Calhoun was referring to Ann and Virginia White. Ann's treatment at the hands of the Jicarilla is open to speculation, but a traveler at the time said:

Setting aside any false delicacy, I will tell you how she was treated, and, understand me, as she, so all white women who fall into the hands of these worse than wild beasts in human shape. They first "passed her over the prairie." That is their jocular way of indicating that she was successively violated by all the Indians present, and there were some twenty.[17]

Kit Carson expressed a similar sentiment.[18]

Barclay was certain that the Jicarilla had made for the canyons of the Red River.[19] Calhoun gave his opinion of the Jicarilla to Commissioner Brown:

They are not considered a numerous band, but they are bold, daring, and adventurous spirits; and they say, they have never encountered the face of a white foe, who did not quail, and attempt to fly from them.[20]

On October 29, news of the massacre reached Santa Fe. F. X. Aubry arrived the next day and sent letters to Las Vegas, Taos, and other communities offering the unheard of sum of one thousand dollars for the return of the captive women. Manuel Alvarez, William Messervy, and Indian agent James Calhoun raised the sum even higher.[21] Calhoun declared himself "entirely destitute of the means necessary to an efficient and prompt action" and said that "a purely military effort, in [his] opinion, can not be successfully made."[22] Colonel John Munroe was moving too slowly to suit Calhoun.[23] Pressure on the colonel began to grow. The public accused him of doing nothing.[24] Meanwhile, Calhoun recruited a Mexican trader, well known to the Apache, to take the message to them that the Indian agent was willing to exchange "such inducements to them as would secure the end," return of the woman and her child. Calhoun described his trader as:

> [K]nowing the Apaches well, their haunts and trails. This man is well known to respectable people here, as a daring, fearless, and withal, a discreet man—I promised to pay him one thousand dollars, and other gratuities, if he succeeds in bringing in to me Mrs. White and her daughter—He goes out quietly, but rapidly, as a trader, and if he finds the objects of his search, will doubtless secure them.[25]

Governor James Silas Calhoun had been agent for the Ute and Jicarilla before becoming governor. He understood their plight. About 1852. COURTESY PALACE OF THE GOVERNORS PHOTO ARCHIVES (NMHM/ DCA), 050460

Colonel Munroe failed to act and may have interfered with efforts to recover the woman and child. An unsubstantiated rumor circulated that negotiations were underway by Captain Judd to exchange his and Lieutenant Burnside's five prisoners for Mrs. White and her child, but, learning of this unauthorized trade, Colonel Munroe refused to allow it to go forward. At Las Vegas, Judd might have found intermediaries among those who routinely traded with the Jicarilla. Weeks later, Colonel Munroe, or perhaps Captain Judd, acting on his own, allowed a mail party with dispatches for Fort Leavenworth to take Lobo Blanco's daughter with them in hopes of making an exchange for Mrs. White. Although Colonel Munroe would eventually send troops from Taos to force Ann White's return, on October 29, 1849, he had his adjutant authorize Major William Grier in Taos to look into the matter:

Major,

Colonel Munroe had received a letter from Judge Beaubien at Taos inclosing a communication from the Alcalde of La de Mora relative to some depredations which are reported to have been committed by a Party of Indians said now to be between Taos to the Mora. If you are not already fully informed upon the subject and it is supposed you are, the Colonel wishes you to collect all information possible relative to it and act accordingly to your judgement with a view of giving full protection to the section of Country under your jurisdiction.

The aforementioned particularly referred to relate to the killing of Mr. White and five other men coming from the States in the neighborhood of the Point of Rocks.[26]

Judge Beaubien led Colonel Munroe to believe that the Jicarilla had already gone west beyond the Canadian (Red) River into the Sangre de Cristo and were west of Mora proceeding over the passes toward Taos. This delayed the military response as it had Grier looking in the wrong place and defending Taos, a city in no danger, while the Jicarilla moved in the opposite direction.

In Taos, Major Grier organized an expedition to cross the mountains toward Mora.[27] He wouldn't find any Jicarilla there and would continue on to the Llano Estacado to rescue Ann White and baby Virginia. He employed Antoine Leroux[28] as chief guide, and Robert Fisher[29] as guide. His expedition would include Company I[30] of the 1st Dragoons and a company of locally recruited spies and guides under Captain Quinn[31] as well as an artillery section. Among those that volunteered were mountain men Jesus Silva, Richens "Uncle Dick" Wootton,[32] and Tom Tobin.[33] James A. Bennett in *Forts and Forays: A Dragoon in New Mexico, 1850–1856* described Major Grier as a "fatherly old man who was designed for a Methodist ministry but whose patriotic spirit exceeded his religious zeal." DeWitt Peters, later Kit Carson's biographer, wrote: "We have the greatest respect for this gentleman and consider him a very able man."[34] Grier's expedition crossed the frigid November Sangre de Cristo Mountains to Rayado, where he attempted to enlist Kit Carson as a guide.

Carson hesitated. He had made an accommodation with the Jicarilla. He fed them when they came by. He gave them a few beeves and they left him alone. Carson was at peace with the Jicarilla. He may have hesitated to join

Grier for other reasons. The major already had Leroux as his senior scout. There might be tension between the two. It seems likely that the dragoon major appealed to Carson's patriotism and sense of chivalry. There was a lady out there on the plains in distress. Both appeals would have touched Carson deeply. DeWitt Peters said:

Kit Carson immediately proffered his services for the expedition. They were accepted, but, much to the surprise of many of the party, instead of being at once placed in the position which his great experience demanded, he was assigned to an inferior position under the command of Leroux. Kit Carson, however, was too good a soldier to exhibit the conduct which the little buzzing talkers so anxiously looked for from their supposed kindling of his jealousy, and quietly took the post assigned him, eager to lend a helping hand, which might even thus be instrumental in saving a valuable life.[35]

If there were jealousies, Kit Carson apparently did his best to avoid them. It was November 9, more than two weeks after the massacre, before the military expedition arrived at the nooning site near Palo Blanco Creek. In the interim, snow had fallen obscuring and obliterating tracks. Kit Carson said:

We marched to where the depredation had been committed, then took their trail. I was the first man that found the camp where the murder had been committed. Found trunks that were broken open, harness cut, etc., everything destroyed that the Indians could not carry with them. We followed them some ten or twelve days. It was the most difficult trail that I ever followed. As they would leave the camps, they, in numbers from one to two, went in different directions, to meet at some appointed place. In nearly every camp we would find some of Mrs. White's clothing, which was the cause of renewed energy on our part to continue the pursuit.[36]

Carson was the first to find the trail and the one who successfully followed it. This surely increased his stature with Major Grier while, perhaps, arousing the jealousy of Antoine Leroux. The subsequent difference of opinion between the two great scouts may have been just that, an honest difference of opinion, although Carson later suggested that there might have been something slightly more sinister afoot.

A large body of Indians, several hundred, dragging travois would have made a significant impression upon the earth.[37] There were many Jicarilla in the band that attacked the Whites. Perhaps half of the tribe was out on the fall hunt, although women and children may have been largely absent. When in fear of pursuit, the Apache scatter like quail, having previously agreed upon a place to meet at the end of the day. These small parties wouldn't have left much trace on the frozen earth. The soil must be soft for the horse to leave a track. Shod horses might leave marks from their steel shoes on rocks, but Indian ponies were unshod. The tracker might look for crushed grass and broken branches, but after a few weeks these signs diminish in visibility. Carson knew the terrain. He knew the places the Jicarilla liked to camp and the kinds of places they liked. He knew what terrain features were likely to produce those camping spots. It was a type of knowledge Carson would have

The Breaks of the Canadian River where Kit Carson and Major Grier pursued the Jicarilla captors of Ann White in 1849. AUTHOR PHOTO

been at a loss to explain apart from saying that it was the most difficult trail he ever followed.

Bits of Ann White's clothing deliberately torn and draped over branches along the way let him know he was on the right trail and that she was still alive. The Canadian River, a slight dip in the prairie at the Rock Crossing where the Santa Fe Trail crosses toward the mountains, within a few miles descends rapidly into a canyon nearly one thousand feet deep. Myriad side canyons provide access to the prairie above and ways for a wily foe to escape undetected. The narrow confines, the twists and turns, provide a plethora of ambush sites. Kit Carson was already more than two weeks behind the Jicarilla. Snow and time and a tribe skilled at concealing their passing faded the trail. If they were to overtake the Apaches, the soldiers would have to move faster than the Jicarilla, leaving their already tired horses—more than a week on the trail from Taos—less time to graze. Carson was confronted with time-wasting blind dead ends.

On November 16, twenty-three days after Apache warriors abducted Ann White and baby Virginia, Carson informed Major Grier that they were close to the Jicarilla camp. They had emerged from the Breaks of the Canadian River onto the level prairie near Tucumcari Butte. Carson put forward a plan. He would lead and when he saw the Indian camp, would signal those behind him to charge. The artillery would roll into position to provide fire, cutting the Apache off from their horse herd and retreat. Carson told the major that they would have to move swiftly once the Indians saw them or it was likely the Jicarilla women would kill Ann White.

Later Carson said that Antoine Leroux countered with a different plan. He proposed that they halt and call the Indians to parley.[38] Dick Wootton was present at the council. He had no great love of Leroux, but nonetheless defended him, blaming Grier for the decision. Kit wanted to charge in and rescue the woman before any ill could befall her; he felt certain, from experience, that they would slay her when attacked. Major Grier, and one presumes Leroux (Carson thought so), thought that a parley would be more appropriate. In any event, Carson thought the soldiers would follow him and was surprised when they didn't.[39]

In the early morning of November 17, 1849, Kit Carson rode ahead of the soldiers, stopping as he came up each hillock before reaching the crest, standing in the stirrups to scan the terrain ahead before exposing himself.[40] He sniffed the air for any hint of smoke from the Jicarilla camp. He tasted the air getting a sense of how close the Apache were and then changed direction to accord with each new bit of information. Carson prodded his horse forward to the next cover—hillock, bush, or tree. He listened for the whinnying of Indian ponies and sniffed the air again all senses alert. Finally, he saw, or perhaps sensed, the crossed poles of a tepee wreathed in the tiniest bit of smoke, dry wood burning, more a mist of heat ripples in the air than smoke. Carson stood in the saddle again and signaled to the soldiers behind him to come into line. He'd wait a few moments allowing the artillery to come into position, wheel about, unhook the limber, and load. The artillerymen had practiced their drill and went through the motions swiftly and smoothly. Now! Before the Apache saw them and could react, he signaled the charge and spurred his horse to a gallop.

A hundred yards on, Carson reined in his horse. Where was the boom of the artillery sending terror through the camp? Where was the thunder of four hundred hooves as the cavalry charged? The prairie was silent! No one was following him. Carson wheeled about, sure that both cavalry and the Apache camp had seen him. He rode up to Major Grier full of anger and fear for the woman. Years later, Carson said:

We finally came in view of the Indian Camp. I was in advance, started for their camp, calling to the men to follow. The comdg. officer ordered a halt, none then would follow me. I was informed that Leroux, the principal guide, told the officer in command to halt, that the Indians wished to have a parley. The Indians, seeing that the troops did not intend to charge on them, they commenced packing up in all haste.[41]

As they stood there, Carson impatiently demanding an immediate charge while the major dithered, thinking a parley best, a shot rang out from enemy camp and a bullet struck the dragoon officer in the chest, knocking him to the ground.[42] Everyone was shaken. They looked around to see on whose shoulders the weight of command would descend. And then, the major moved. Slowly, he rose from the ground. He pulled his heavy buffalo hide gauntlets from inside his tunic where he'd stuffed them. The bullet had pierced coat, tunic, gloves, and shirt and broken the skin. The major pushed his hand inside his shirt and it came away smeared with a single drop of blood. He retched briefly, clearly shaken, then stood straight and announced that a small party would go forward under a flag of truce to parley. Ever the frontier gentleman, Kit Carson excused his disappointment saying, "The gauntlets saved his life, leaving to the service of his country one more gallant officer."[43] Three times Major Grier sent the white flag forward and three times the Apache fired on it.

Finally, the major called the charge. But, it was too late. Carson said:

As soon as he recovered from the shock given him by the ball, he ordered the men to charge, but the order was too late for the desired effect. There was only one Indian in the camp; he, swimming into the river hard by, was shot. In about 200 yards pursuing the Indians, the body of Mrs. White was found, perfectly warm, had not been killed more than five minutes—shot through the heart with an arrow. She evidently knew that some one was coming to her rescue. She did not see us, but it was apparent that she was endeavoring to make her escape when she received the fatal shot.

Kit Carson also said,

I am certain ... that if the Indians had been charged immediately on our arrival, Mrs. White would have been saved. At first, the savages were much confused at our approach, and I do not hesitate to say that she saw us as quick as any one of the redskins did, for it undoubtedly was the all absorbing topic of her mind that her rescue would be attempted by her friends and countrymen. On seeing us coming, she had attempted to run towards us, when she was shot down. ... Yet I cannot ... blame the commanding officer, or the other guide, for the action they took in the affair. They evidently did as they thought best, but I have no doubt that they now can see, that if my advice had been taken, the life of Mrs. White might have been spared for a least a short period.[44]

Crossing the frigid river, the Jicarilla made their escape. The young men of the camp had preserved the horse herd and the Apache rode away on fresh horses. The cavalry pursued, but their horses had come many, many miles and were spent. They could not keep up although they followed for more than six miles. Returning to the Indian camp, they burned its contents. Into the flames went tepee covers and poles, warm winter buffalo robes and blankets, stores of winter food, pinole, atole, cooking ware, horse tack, and winter clothing. The soldiers left the Indians destitute with winter hard upon them. The suffering that would follow is hard to imagine. The soldiers did not find Virginia White in the camp nor her Negro nursemaid. Winter hardship would fall hardest on the elderly and the young. They would die of starvation and the cold.

In the camp a soldier discovered a dime novel that he thought must have belonged to Ann White. The story was about Kit Carson.[45] In the book, Carson rescues maidens and slays Indians by the score. Since the book was about Carson, the young soldier read it in his presence. Carson begged the young man to throw the book on the fire. Carson remarked, "that perhaps Mrs. White, to whom it belonged, knowing he lived not very far off, had prayed to have him make his appearance and assist in freeing her."[46]

As Kit Carson viewed the body of Ann White, he was convinced that she had been ill-treated and was perhaps better off dead. He thought that as emaciated and trail worn she was, and left without shoes, she did not have long to live. A traveler who interviewed him wrote:

"As God would have it," said Kit Carson, who told me of it, "As God would have, she was just dead when we reached her; and perhaps it was as well." Yes it was as well! The poor lady was wasted, emaciated, the victim of a foul disease, and bore the sorrows of a life-long agony on her face; for when a woman captive has not the signal good fortune of being made the mistress of one savage, she becomes the prostitute of the tribe. It might as well be understood that this is the lot awaiting the female made captive by any Indians west of the Mississippi. It is invariable, and the mere statement of outrage and violation is but a meagre indication of such a woman's sad fate.[47]

In requiem Carson said:

She could not possibly have lived long, for the treatment she had received from the Indians was so brutal and horrible that she could possibly last but a short period. Her life, I think, should never be regretted by her friends. She is surely far more happy in heaven, with her God, than among friends of this earth.[48]

93

Perhaps it was so. Kit Carson thought it was. Word never came of the fate of Virginia White. Friends of the Whites continued to offer a reward as did the Thirty-First Congress of the United States in 1850 for her safe return and many people—Indian traders, buffalo hunters, and *ciboleros*—tried to claim it.[49] Over the years, numerous people would claim sightings of Virginia. Pueblo Indians saw her in Jicarilla camps and *Comancheros* saw her in Comanche villages.[50]

James Bennett, sometime private in the 1st Dragoons, recorded an incident in his diary that came while the soldiers were burning the camp:

After dark a noise was heard near our camp. At first we supposed it to be an animal of some kind. 3 or 4 of us made an examination through the willow bushes and found and Indian child which I suppose was about 8 months old. It was strapped to a board as all Indian babies are. I found it. An old gruff soldier stepped up and said, "Let me see that brat." I handed it to him. He picked up a heavy stone, tied it to the board, dashed baby and all into the water, and in a moment no trace of it was left. The Soldier's only comment was, "You're a little fellar now but will make a big Injun bye and bye. I only wish I had more to treat the same way."[51]

This nasty incident did not occur though eastern readers seemed to believe this was how the 1st Dragoons behaved. Bennett wasn't present on this occasion, as he did not arrive in New Mexico until October 1850, eleven months later.

That November of 1849 Don Alexandro Barclay wrote in his diary:

22nd [November] St. Vrain & McCarty's wagons to Las Vegas. Up to this time from the departure of the troops in pursuit of the Apaches who had killed White's party it had been fine weather and the party campt somewhere below on the open prairie the night of the 22nd when it commenced a most desperate and fearfully cold snowstorm which lasted all this day and cleared off in the night of the 23rd.

24th [sic] Doctor [blank] & Williams and a corporal to Fort, expecting to find Major Grier here but in the storm the previous day he had been compelled to make for the Vegas and take it on his back, but did not arrive there till this day. This was the fifth day since they burned the village.

23rd All day looking for Major Grier, of course in vain. Fisher and some others got here this evening.[52]

24th Quinn & party here with all the Apache plunder passing—some of his men slept in the courtyard.

25th Major Grier, Kit Carson & Watkin LaRoux [Joaquin Leroux] from Las Vegas . . .[53]

On the trail, returning from Tucumcari Butte, Kit Carson and Major Grier's force encountered a severe snowstorm. Kit Carson said:

On the return we had the severest snow storm that I ever experienced. Had one man frozen to death. We were trying to make Barclay's fort on the Mora but, on account of the wind, we could not keep our course, but happily learned that in the same storm many of the Indians that we had been pursuing perished. After the storm we went in to Las Vegas.[54]

If Carson thought the storm severe, it must have been something. The suffering in the Jicarilla camp, exposed as they would have been without blankets, buffalo robes, or tepees, must have been horrible. This is one of the cruelest comments Carson ever made. He was angered by what the Apache had done to Ann White and her husband's party. The murder shocked the people of the region, and the death of Ann White was recalled years after it occurred. The events at Manco Burro Pass were also the stuff of legend. In both cases, the Jicarilla temporarily closed the Santa Fe Trail. Hugh Smith turned back until it was certain the trail was safe. Stock stealing was common enough, a monthly or perhaps at times, even weekly occurrence if we consider the whole of New Mexico, but murder was not. The occasional shepherd or lone traveler might disappear, but even that was not common. Large parties

Wagon Mound where in 1850 an eleven-man mail party was slain by Jicarilla warriors. AUTHOR PHOTO

were immune to attack, or so people thought. And when they were disabused of this notion, it struck terror in their hearts.

Sometime in November 1849, before word came in of Ann's death, Captain Judd began negotiations to exchange his Apache prisoners at Las Vegas for those held by the Jicarilla, Ann White and baby Virginia, the lady's maid, and possibly two Mexican girls taken near Wagon Mound. Colonel John Munroe refused to allow the exchange. Judd, either having received belated permission or acting on his own, sent out Sergeant Henry Swartwont with a detachment of twenty men escorting the mail and a party of travelers as far as Lower Cimarron Spring on the Santa Fe Trail.[55] With them went Lobo Blanco's daughter. She was "to negotiate with her people for the release of Mrs. White and such other prisoners as might have been in their hands." At Wagon Mound she was to climb to the top escorted by two troopers to look for signs of her people. Instead the soldiers said, she wept and tried to signal her people. The next morning as two soldiers tried to load her in the mail wagon, something went horribly wrong. She became enraged and tried to kill two of the soldiers with a knife. Failing in her murderous intentions, she went after the livestock and stabbed two mules, killing one.[56] One of the soldiers shot her in the head, killing her instantly and ending her peace mission.[57] The escort returned in the face of the same storm that had met Carson and others. Jicarilla raids continued and intensified into 1850.[58]

Chapter 9

In 1850 there were 1,019 soldiers in New Mexico, up from 665 in 1848, and 708 in 1849, the year of some of the heaviest fighting. There was only one fortification in use. That was Fort Marcy in Santa Fe. The soldiers were located at Albuquerque, Socorro, Abiquiu, Doña Ana, Las Vegas, Rayado, Taos, and Cebolleta.[1] Abiquiu, Las Vegas, Taos, Rayado, and Santa Fe were in Jicarilla country. The military was concentrated in the Jicarilla country as these Apache were the principal threat.

In December 1849, superintendent of Indian Affairs James S. Calhoun and military governor Colonel John Munroe attempted to arrange a peace treaty with the Jicarilla but failed. Hostilities continued and increased in severity. During the winter of 1849–50, Chief Lobo promised to avenge the killing of his daughter and many warriors agreed to help.[2] The Llanero Jicarilla, made destitute by the events at Tucumcari Butte when their camp was burned by Major Grier, robbed of their winter stores, were hungry. In February 1850, a war party drove off what owners claimed was twelve thousand sheep near Santa Fe, killing herders in the process and capturing others, probably to use as drovers so that the Apache would not have to demean themselves by tending sheep.[3] Wanton killing by the Jicarilla had been rare. In the aftermath of the tragic murders of the White Party and Lobo Blanco's daughter, it became a weekly occurrence. In late February, the Jicarilla murdered one traveler and wounded two others on the mail trail near the Pecos River crossing.[4]

On February 27, 1850, fifty-one of the leading citizens of Santa Fe sent a petition to President Zachary Taylor that condemned murders and robberies by warlike tribes and singled out the Jicarillas for their "savage butchery." It decried the events of 1849 as "call[ing] for a vengeance that there is not power enough in this territory to inflict. . . ."[5] The Jicarilla were at war with the United States, which was only slowly, even in Santa Fe, coming to realize that the war had been on for some time. In the last months of 1848, the

Missouri and Illinois Volunteers disbanded and returned home and the local volunteer companies likewise disbanded, so there was "not power enough in the territory" to deal with the threat. As Superintendent Calhoun wrote to the commissioner of Indian Affairs Orlando Brown, "It is my duty to advise you that our Indian troubles are daily increasing and our efficiency as [*sic*] rapidly decreasing . . . this Territory is encircled by wild Indians."[6] It was clear that, despite what Lieutenant Whittlesey had thought about his sincere desire for peace the summer before, Chief Lobo Blanco of the Llanero was the proponent of war, while Chacon of the Ollero led the peace faction.[7] The troubles on the Santa Fe Trail and most of the stock raids occurred on the Llano Estacado in the range of the Llanero. Lobo Blanco was the chief of the Llanero. Although Chacon was haughty and unwilling to accept a bad deal, there were fewer problems west of the Sangre de Cristo and along the Chama River, the range of the Ollero. Chacon sought a workable peace for his people.

Despite the growing evidence that Chacon and the Ollero favored peace, in Taos, the military leadership did not trust Chacon. Some of the earliest and bloodiest conflicts with the Jicarilla had occurred north of Taos, in the San Luis Valley, along the Chama River and in the San Juan Mountains, which was Ollero country. In 1850, inspector general Colonel George McCall conducted a military inspection of the Territory of New Mexico. In his report, he made no distinction between Ollero and Llanero, characterizing the Jicarilla as incorrigible, the most troublesome of all Apaches. He suggested they would "continue to rob and murder our citizens until they [the Jicarilla] are exterminated . . . I know of no means that could be employed to reclaim them."[8]

Kit Carson had returned to his home at Rayado after his role in pursuing the Jicarilla to Tucumcari Butte. The Jicarilla had been frequent visitors to his ranch and had encountered him on many occasions. Before Tucumcari Butte, his ranch had been immune to stock theft due to his good relations with the Jicarilla. During the winter of 1849–50, the Jicarilla took their revenge on him. His stock was no longer safe. Carson told his biographer:

During the winter there was a detachment of ten dragoons commanded by Leigh Holbrook stationed at Rayado. Sometime during the month of March, a party of Indians came and attacked the rancho that was about two miles distant where we had our animals that were gentle kept to graze. There were two men in charge; both were severely wounded. One, however, made his way to the Rayado and gave the report. The Dragoons, three Americans [Robert Fisher and William New], and myself immediately saddled up and proceeded to the Rancho.[9, 10]

It was starving time for the Jicarilla. Every year they suffered after they had depleted their winter supplies and before the grass began to green making game and vegetable food available. The loss of winter supplies to the raids of the Army and other tribes made some years worse than others. Major Grier had spoiled their fall buffalo hunt. The military had burned their tepees, buffalo robes, blankets, and most important, their supplies of winter food. Through the cold and snowy winter, the Apache huddled around their fires unable to hunt effectively, and by March some of them determined to move against the man who had so effectively led the Army to their village.

There were still patches of snow in the shadows at Rayado. The ground was muddy and green shoots of grass were just emerging from their winter sleep. The cottonwoods along the creek, now a rushing mountain stream full of winter melt, were covered in a green mist of budding leaves. The Sangre de Cristo was still covered in snow and chilly winds blew down from the mountains. Sergeant Holbrook worked his men, drilling them for mounted action while allowing them time to repair their clothing and equipment. They'd found a Mexican woman among Carson's settlers to do the laundry, but everything else they had to tend to themselves including repairing their leather tack. They lived in an adobe hut without windows, barely large enough to contain their bunks and gear. It was dark and a little damp with the spring melt but usually warm at night.

Dragoons and mountain men rode through the dusk to the grazing ground. Caring for the wounded Mexican herder and sending him on to Rayado, they picked up the trail at first light and pursued the raiders east toward the sunrise. They rode at the gallop in order to catch their foe and in the process rode four of their own horses to death, leaving those whose horses had fallen behind to their apparent woe at not being able to join the fight.[11]

They rode hard across fields muddy with the spring melt. Driven in a tight pack, Maxwell's and Carson's stolen herd left clear marks in the soft earth, a trail easy to follow even at a gallop. They rode across the prairie and into the canyon of the Red River[12] tight with tall clumps of piñon pine, their crisp scent perfuming the air. They dodged under low-hanging branches and around dense clumps of brush and rock rolled down from the rim, always alert for the enemy ahead and for ambush. Carson saw them first and silently held up his hand gesturing the others to halt and to silence.

Carson relates, "We approached the Indians cautiously and, when close charged them killing five, the other four made their escape."[13] Out from among the trees Carson and Holbrook's men rushed with harsh cries surprising the Jicarilla. Shots rang out from the pistols of mounted men. Then sabers were drawn to hasten the bloody affair. Mountain men halted their horses to fire long rifles at the startled war party, their thick, acrid smoke trapped in the canyon. Surrendering their prize, the Indians, some bloody, disappeared among the trees and side canyons leaving five of their own upon the ground. A soldier leapt from his horse and with his saber cut the scalp from a dead warrior, crying out as he held the bloody trophy aloft. Sergeant Holbrook reported that his men had wounded two of those who escaped.[14] Kit Carson and Sergeant Holbrook recovered all but four of the stolen livestock.

A controversy followed. The sergeant cheerfully reported that his men had taken the scalps of the dead Indians as "a voucher" to prove their kills. This bit of trophy taking conflicted with Army policy and elsewhere had become the subject of a congressional inquiry. Major Grier, in forwarding the sergeant's report, was careful to note that certain Mexican herdsmen had come up and actually done the gruesome deed.[15] Part of Holbrook's report of April 7, 1850, read:

Pursuant to an attack by Apaches on the 6th on the opposite side of the Red River[16] 30 miles from here and an attack on Mr. Maxwell's herders camp, with the assistance of Carson, Fisher and New[ell], we overtook the enemy and killed five Indians. Recovered all the animals but four.[17]

At Headquarters Ninth Military Department in Santa Fe, Colonel John Munroe forwarded the reports to Army headquarters in Washington:

I transmit you herewith a report by Sergeant William C. Holbrook, commanding a party of company "I," 1st Dragoons, stationed at Rayado—being a detachment from the post of Taos—giving an account of a gallant and successful affair in which that detachment was engaged with a marauding party of Apache Indians, the troops having the valuable experience of Mr. Kit Carson and his two associates in conducting the business.[18]

The Jicarilla were out of winter quarters and hungry. The buffalo herds were out of reach until fall. The mountains that once teemed with game had been over-hunted by white, Mexican, and Apache. Where once there had been deer and elk, now there were sheep, horses, mules, and cattle and all were good to eat. The Apaches wanted revenge for what had befallen them at Tucumcari Butte. The injury done to one's own family takes precedence over any harm one may have done to theirs, but empty bellies came first and needed to be filled. If a few Mexican herders got in the way, their lives meant little. This was a season for revenge. On April 20, Indian Agent Calhoun wrote:

Last night the Indians, it is said, made several attacks upon individuals near this place, killed some herders, and drove off Stock. Troops under command of Lt. Burnside, are now mounting for the purpose of enquiring into the facts, and pursuing the Indians.[19]

It would seem that even Lieutenant Burnside, who had been hasty at Las Vegas the previous summer, looked into the truth behind reports before attacking Indian camps. Again and again the record shows troops in the field investigating and dismissing false claims of depredation.

In May 1850, Jicarilla Apache under Chief Lobo sent shock waves up and down the Santa Fe Trail. Mail parties turned back and merchant caravans waited for military escort. The Jicarilla, however briefly, had again closed the trail. Artist Richard H. Kern, whose brother Benjamin had been murdered with Bill Williams the year before, wrote that the events at Wagon Mound were "the most daring murder ever committed by the Indians . . . another such a one will render the road impassable to small parties."[20] The public was shocked because of the size of the party that the Apaches attacked and so completely overwhelmed. Historian Marc Simmons wrote that this was not an isolated episode, but rather formed part of a mini war waged between Jicarilla Apaches and Americans.[21]

The mail from Fort Leavenworth was overdue. No one worried very much. It was spring. Perhaps the Arkansas River was in flood and the wagon had to wait to make a crossing. The government had let a contract to David

Waldo to carry the US Mail on his newly formed stagecoach line. Under the old system, the Army had hired civilian contractors to carry the mail by wagon. Frank Hendrickson and James Clay set out in an Army wagon from Santa Fe in March bound for Fort Leavenworth on the Missouri River in Kansas. On April 18, having delivered the eastbound mail, they set out westbound for Santa Fe accompanied by express rider Thomas E. Branton, making his first journey across the plains. On the trail, they overtook Thomas W. Flournoy, leading a relief train out to rescue the James Brown caravan that had lost its oxen to the terrible snowstorm of November 1849 and been stranded near the crossing of the Arkansas ever since. Flournoy and Moses Goldstein, who had been there all winter, decided to continue on with the mail party. They met an eastbound caravan and Benjamin Shaw, John Duty, John Freeman, John Williams, and a German teamster decided to join them and return to Santa Fe.[22] Perhaps they were invited and even paid as additional guards against increasing Jicarilla activity. One or perhaps two rode in the wagon; the rest were on horses and riding mules. They thought a party of ten men would be safe, even in Jicarilla country.

The Rock Crossing of the Canadian is an easy approach to the river where exposed bedrock makes a firm spot for wagons to ford the river. A short distance to the south, the river drops through vertical rimrock walls into a steep-sided canyon over nine hundred feet deep. On or about May 2, in the early morning at the crossing, Lobo Blanco's warriors were digging pits.[23] In the open flat prairie there was little in the way of cover and concealment for an ambush, so they were creating their own.[24] Before they had finished, the mail party surprised them in the open. Shots were exchanged. Frontiersmen fired muzzle-loading rifles from the saddle along with the new revolving pistols. The Jicarilla returned fire with a few fusils and many bows and arrows.

Henderson whipped up his horses. One of them shouted to the others, "We'll make a stand at Wagon Mound!" Ahead they could just make out the mesa that looked so much like a canvas-covered freight wagon pulled by oxen. To the west, right from this perspective, were the Pilot Knobs.[25] Santa Clara Spring was nearby with good clear water, but it lay in a small canyon where they would be easy prey for the Indians. He steered for the notch between the Mound and the Knobs. The high ground would give his party good fields of fire, making it hard for the Apache to approach without losing men. Their long rifles had better range than anything the Indians carried, and the rapid fire of the revolvers would suppress arrow-fire. The Jicarilla were busy rounding up their horses scattered in the confusion at the ford. With mayhem behind them, the mail party slowed down taking the opportunity to reload their weapons. Wagon Mound was twenty-four miles away. It would be a long ride and they couldn't afford to push their horses to the gallop the whole way, nor could the Apache. It would be a game of hare and hounds. The hounds would approach in small parties at the run encouraging the hare to greater speed while others of their war party followed at a slower pace allowing their ponies some rest. The hares in turn would keep the hounds at bay with pistol fire, going as slow as they dared, saving their horses' strength.

An Apache warrior counted the shots. When the man he followed had fired six times, the warrior urged his pony to greater speed and drew an arrow from his quiver. The man with the pistol had been careless; perhaps he was new to the plains. Drawing alongside as he would with a buffalo, now almost touching, he loosed the arrow, and it went through the man's thigh to be stopped by the heavy leather of the saddle he rode. The Indian was disappointed. He'd hoped his shot would fell the horse. The white man, now in pain, rode on. Another warrior counted shots but mistook shots fired by another frontiersman for those of his quarry. He approached, arrow drawn to his ear, when the pistol almost touching his forehead belched flame that blackened his face. He fell with a small, round hole between his eyes. The game continued all day and another frontiersman received a thigh wound.

The exultant mail party reached Wagon Mound as the sun was setting and went into camp on high ground with cliffs to their back. The Apache would have a hard time approaching. Perhaps they would call it quits. They knew that Barclay's Fort was only about fifteen miles away. They'd be safe there. They tended to their wounded who would ride in the wagon the next day. Half of the men remained on watch while the others slept, but they knew the Jicarilla did not attack by night. Visibility was poor. It had begun to snow.

Just at dusk, a war party of Utes attracted by the noise and dust arrived on the scene. The Utes offered their support to their Jicarilla friends. Lobo Blanco counted close to one hundred warriors in the party with the addition of the Utes.[26]

As day broke, the mail party doused their fire and hitched up the wagon, helping the wounded men into the bed. Clay had just taken the reins and men were just starting to mount their horses when suddenly there were Indians all around them. As Clay gave the wagon mules the whip, shots were fired and arrows flew. A frontiersman fired his rifle, then cracked an approaching warrior's head with the barrel, dropped the weapon, and drew his pistol. A horse threw a man who was trying to mount and had one foot in a stirrup. Flat on his back, he drew his pistol as two warriors descended on him. More shots rang out. The frontiersmen tried to follow the wagon, which was already pulling away from them lurching toward the gap between Wagon Mound and the Pilot Knobs. Briefly the mail party's weapons fire drove the Indians back. The frontiersmen emptied their weapons in haste without thought for future need. Either they survived the moment or there would be no future. Then arrows flew as the men ran and rode after the wagon, unable to reload.

On May 19, the eastbound mail party from Las Vegas stumbled upon the scattered bodies and mail that had lain upon the ground for many days. Returning to Las Vegas, they demanded an escort to Cedar Spring 150 miles to the east, before they would set out again.

Captain Judd sent Lieutenants Ambrose Burnside and Peter W. Plympton to investigate the scene. On May 21, they departed from Las Vegas and arrived at Barclay's Fort, where they enlisted the aid of Alexander Barclay and recruited a group of Mexican laborers to dig graves. They followed the Santa Fe Trail along the eastern slope of the Turkey Mountains to Wagon Mound.

On May 23, Lieutenant Burnside submitted his report:

I arrived at the scene of the murder on the day after I left this place [Las Vegas] and found the remains of Ten persons. . . . The Wagon which Clay and Hendrickson took from this place last March was found about half a mile from the foot of the Wagon Mound with the tongue broken, and a dead mule, still in harness, attached to it. Two of the bodies, in a complete state of putrification, were found in the Wagon, and the remaining eight, very much eaten by the wolves, in its immediate vicinity, the farthest one probably seventy five yards off; one horse and two mules were killed near the Wagon, and two American horses, near the foot of the mound. The ground from these two horses to the Wagon was strewn with arrows, on the road which passed by the foot of the mound, and about a mile from the Wagon we found where the party had encamped. . . .

. . . the two men who were in the Wagon, being wounded each in the left thigh, the most common wound a man receives on horseback, and one that could not have been inflicted whilst they were in the wagon. No signs were discovered of any Indians being killed. The

*attacking party were evidently in great numbers from the large num-
ber of arrows found on the ground; but the best evidence of it is the
small space within which the whole party were killed. So large a party
of Americans have never before been entirely destroyed by the Indians
of that portion of the territory; and in fact ten Americans have here-
tofore been considered comparatively safe in travelling over the road,
with proper care. Mr. Barclay who had been a great deal among the
Eutan Indians, and in fact, traded with them for some time, recognized certain arrows among those left on the ground. . . .*[27]

Burnside's party of Mexicans dug a mass grave and interred the ten men
in it. The wagon was drawn up over the grave and burned in hopes that this
would discourage wolves from digging up the bodies.[28] Chief Chacon later
said that five Apaches and four Utes were killed in the affray.[29]

A few weeks later, Judd sent Burnside out again on escort duty to protect
the mail wagon. On June 12, the lieutenant reported that just beyond Rabbit
Ear Creek near the border of modern New Mexico and the Oklahoma Panhandle he found a blank muster roll wedged between two rocks. On it was
a picture showing how the murders near Wagon Mound were committed.
Believing that the murderers were still in the vicinity, Burnside accompanied
the mail party as far as the Cimarron.[30]

Even as Burnside was seeking after the mail party at Wagon Mound,
Lieutenant James H. Simpson, of the Topographical Engineers,[31] along with
Richard H. Kern, cartographer and artist, were seeking a location for a new
Army post on the plains, one that would guard against Jicarilla depredations.
The military considered the site of Barclay's Fort at La Junta ideal, and the
military attempted to take possession without compensating Barclay. There
was contention between Barclay and the military over possession of his fort.
However, a site about six miles north of La Junta was settled on at a series of
springs known as Holes in the Prairie. This would become Fort Union and its
purpose in the early 1850s was control of the Jicarilla Apache and protection
of the Santa Fe Trail.

On June 26, Major Grier reported that at twelve o'clock, 250 to 300
Indians had attacked the settlement at Rayado. They were, according to the
major, Apaches and Comanches.[32] The Indians drove off all of the stock,
killed a farmer friend of Kit Carson's, Mr. New, as well as another farmer,
a Mexican herder, and bugler Rengel of Company I, 1st Dragoons. Rengel

had wandered off a little distance from the buildings and other soldiers and thus became an easy target.[33] With only twenty-three men at his disposal in Rayado, Major Grier sent to Taos and Las Vegas for all available mounted men to follow the trail of the Jicarilla. Eventually he gathered Companies C and I, 1st Dragoons, and Company K of the 2nd Dragoons as well as ninety civilian volunteers.[34, 35] On July 23, the force left Rayado taking along provisions for thirty days.[36]

In July, the Jicarilla drove off some cattle near Mora that may have belonged to Doyle, Barclay's partner. Doyle was beef contractor for the Army at Las Vegas and was often raided and often filed reports of depredations. On July 17, Auguste Lacome reported encountering 120 lodges of Jicarilla in the Sangre de Cristo Mountains near the Spanish Peaks, northwest of what is now Trinidad, Colorado. It would have been very unusual for that many to gather in July. The Jicarilla usually lived in villages of ten or twelve lodges except during the fall ritual. Reports came in from citizens of Taos who recounted that the Jicarilla were within a day's travel of the town.[37]

Grier's force of 168 armed men on American horses, ponies, and mules headed north up the base of the mountains to the Vermejo River and then followed that stream to its source, bringing their long pack train behind them. His dragoons were clothed in motley, blue woolen uniforms and canvas field clothing. They wore a variety of hats, many of broad-brimmed civilian extraction shielding head and neck from the sun. Only their saddles, tack, and weapons approached uniformity. They carried heavy "wrist breaker" sabers clanking at their sides and musketoons. These shortened, smoothbore muskets had a ring to mount them to the soldier's side and a slide that retained the ramrod so it could not be dropped. Musketoons were designed to be loaded swiftly while on horseback, as rifles or muskets were too long to be handled conveniently from the saddle. Many of the men were also equipped with heavy muzzle-loading "horse pistols." A lucky few had Colt revolvers, which allowed for five shots without reloading.[38] The civilians in the column were dressed in a mix of buckskin, white cotton, and wool with large, sun-shading hats, many of Mexican make and design. They were mountain men, Mexican *ciboleros*, Mexican farmers and shepherds, and Pueblo Indians. The mountain men, clothed in buckskin beaded like Indians, were American backwoodsmen, French Canadians and Metís, and Delaware Indians.

The major turned his column west up the river, crossing the headwaters of the Canadian or Red River high in the Sangre de Cristo. After traveling two days and nights, the force "struck the Indian trail leading over mountains and difficult canyons," and "about 12 on the 25th" came up with and killed or wounded an entire party of Apaches. On that same day, Major Grier's Mexican Spies and Guides, operating ahead of the main body of troops, attacked another small party of Apaches.[39]

The major's main body of troops rode through dense pine forest and open glades and barren fields above the treeline. It was too large a force to move quietly or remain a secret for long. They clanked and swore while their stock neighed and brayed. On July 26, over one hundred miles from Rayado, Grier's men came upon a large Apache camp, 150 lodges, already in motion attempting to escape.[40] In the kind of running fight the dragoons savored, the soldiers killed and wounded several warriors, took sixty head of horses and mules, 150 sheep, and seventy head of cattle. Again the Jicarilla were left destitute, their camp equipment and provisions gone. Six Apaches were killed in the fight along with Sergeant Lewis V. Guthrie.[41] Breaking contact, the Jicarilla fled from the scene.

Major Grier pursued the Apache down the Costilla, westward toward the Rio Grande for ten or twelve miles, but failed to make contact. He crossed mountains and deep canyons to the Moreno trail and followed it southward until it intersected the trail from Taos to Rayado. Back at Rayado he disbanded his civilian volunteers and sent the attached companies of dragoons to their home bases. He had traveled nearly two hundred miles.[42]

In August the Jicarilla stayed well back in the mountains and out on the plains along the Canadian River harvesting and gathering plant foods to replenish their stores. Game was scarce along the Rio Grande due to long overhunting. Short of meat, the Apache did what was necessary, driving off a large number of cattle, mules, and sheep from near Ojo Caliente north of Abiquiu in the San Juan Mountains. On September 30, 1850, Indian Agent Calhoun wrote:

Apaches. These Indians continue their annoyances. About the 1st of this month four of them were surprised and killed on this side of the mountain range between this [Santa Fe] and Taos. A Mr. Maxwell left Santa Fe some three or four days ago, having in his possession merchandise and money, accompanied by two Mexicans, who have returned, and say, on the opposite side of the mountain between this and Taos, they were attacked by Apaches, made good their escape, but suppose Mr. Maxwell was killed, and as a matter of course, his property was carried off by the Apaches. Many other depredations have been reported.[43]

The Mr. Maxwell referred to was probably Lucien, in which case he was not killed. Presumed deaths and depredations did not always happen quite as reported, however. On October 12, 1850, Calhoun wrote:

> *Sir, I avail myself of an opportunity which will offer to-day, or on to-morrow, to say to you, that the report concerning the murder of Mr. Maxwell, of which I advised you on the 30th of last month, was not true—He reached Taos in safety, with his effects, notwithstanding a number of Apache were in his immediate neighborhood.*[44]
>
> *Two Apaches, a man and his wife, are now at this Agency—They were brought to the Head Quarters of this Military Department by order of the Commanding Officer at Abiquiu, and, at the request of Col. Munroe, they are in charge of this Agency.*
>
> *It appears a party of some fifteen or twenty Apaches, men, women, and children, were on their way, from the North East, to Abiquiu, as they represent, to ask permission to reside near that post, and under its protection. Before reaching Abiquiu, near Ojo Caliente, they stopped at a Mexican's house, and asked for something to eat, which was promptly given to them. After they had eaten, the Mexican managed to induce them to wander about his premises, having previously prepared to have executed his bloody purpose, and while thus separated, four of them, one man and three small boys, were murdered upon the spot— One man, a girl, and two boys, are missing. The Mexican ordered his men to fire on the survivors, consisting, principally, of women and children, but they refused to obey the Order—The man who is at this Agency, was not present, having gone a short distance, to report, as chief of the party, to the Prefect of the county, the objects and destina- tion of the Apache party under his command. The Prefect gave them an escort to Abiquiu. A son of the Apache, here, was slain. These Indians will be permitted to reside, for the present, near Abiquiu, and at Col. Munroe's suggestion, I will cause them to be supplied with provisions, to a limited extent. . . .*

The Mexican who caused the murders . . . will be set at liberty upon a mere nominal recognizance. The demoralization of Society here, is such, it would be impolitic, if not altogether impracticable to administer justice in this case. A considerable sum of money has been subscribed to procure a gold medal to be presented to this cold-blooded murderer, and this is done, chiefly, by Americans.[45]

On September 9, 1850, Congress created New Mexico Territory, providing for a civilian governor, a territorial legislature, and the end of military rule. The Compromise of 1850 also put an end to the claim to New Mexico put forward by the state of Texas. On March 3, 1851, Indian Agent James S. Calhoun became governor and superintendent of Indian Affairs. Calhoun would soon be attempting to negotiate a treaty that would end the war with the Jicarilla Apache despite a lack of a workable Indian policy from Washington. In March 1851, on the eve of negotiations with Chacon and Lobo, he wrote:

It is to be regretted that I am without instructions upon this subject. I have a very great aversion to groping my way in the dark; but in the absence of light my soundest discretion must be exercised, [emphasis added] *taking care to avail myself of all the information I may be able to procure, and the advice of intelligent gentlemen.*[46]

Among the issues to be negotiated between Calhoun and the Jicarilla was the matter of Virginia White. The affair of the White Wagon Train had received attention in eastern newspapers and Congress had taken an active interest in the kidnapping. In November the commissioner of Indian Affairs, Luke Lea, wrote from Washington:[47]

Congress having appropriated, Fifteen Hundred dollars for the redemption of the daughter of Mr. & Mrs. J.M. White, now supposed to be in captivity with the Apache Indians, this office is charged with the duty of directing the disbursement of the fund, . . . If as is supposed, the little girl is a captive among the tribe "Apache" proper, or that mixed band termed "Jaccillaras," which for years past, have infested the vicinity of San Fernandez de Taos, the country between it

*and Bent's Fort, and that part of the Santa Fe road which crosses the
Rio Colorado, it is feared that her release will be attended with more
difficulty and danger than if she were in captivity among any other of
the New Mexican Indians....*[48]

Kit Carson had entirely missed out on the Jicarilla raiding his ranch at
Rayado and Major Grier's subsequent expedition against them. On May 5,
he and trapper and trader Tim Goodale had taken fifty head of horses and
mules north to Fort Laramie on the Platte River for sale. At Fort Laramie
the two frontiersmen parted company and Goodale went west to California
while Carson headed south toward Rayado and home. He stopped off at
Greenhorn, on a tributary of the Arkansas River, where he received word
that the Apaches were blocking the road.[49] After convincing a man named
Charles Kinney to accompany him to Taos, Carson crossed the Sangre de
Cristo Pass to the San Luis Valley at Trinchera Creek near modern Fort
Garland and went south along the Rio Grande. By night he hid his animals
in dense brush while he stood watch and slept in a cottonwood tree. At one
point along the journey, he saw a large band of Jicarilla about a half a mile
distant, but they did not detect his party. After returning to Rayado by way of
Taos, Carson discovered that Apaches had run off all of his stock. In late July
or early August 1850, Major Grier had returned from his expedition bringing Carson all of the livestock that had been stolen except those animals the
Jicarilla had eaten.

Carson stayed in Rayado until the fall, when Lieutenant Taylor, 1st
Dragoons, tried to recruit him to apprehend for debts a man named Fox,
a "dismissed dragoon." Carson demurred until the lieutenant revealed his
real intent in pursuing Fox. In addition to debt arising from his dismissal
from the Army, the lieutenant believed Fox was involved in a plot to murder
Elias Brevoort and another merchant, Samuel Weatherhead.[50] Brevoort and
Weatherhead had unwisely hired Fox to head their escort on an eastbound
journey to Kansas City. The merchants carried forty thousand dollars in gold,
and Fox and his men planned to slay them and disappear into Texas with
the loot. Fox chose his accomplices carefully, but one of them became ill and
revealed the plot when he was left behind.

Kit Carson set out on the trail of Fox with ten dragoons. Along the
way he encountered Captain Richard S. Ewell, who was bringing a party of
new recruits out to New Mexico. Ewell joined Carson, bringing with him

twenty-five of the best recruits. They caught up with Fox the day before he intended to spring his plot. They detained Fox and took him back to Taos, where without evidence of an actual crime, he was released and disappeared from history. Brevoort and Weatherhead wished to reward Carson who declined, saying he'd only done what was right. However, in the spring of 1851, Carson received from the merchants a gift of two "splendid silver mounted pistols."[51]

In 1851, Chief Chacon of the Jicarilla was negotiating with Governor Calhoun, seeking a peace treaty to end the years of conflict. Relative calm would follow for several years until the spring of 1854. Kit Carson would spend much of the time at Rayado.

Chapter 10

James Calhoun, Indian agent at Santa Fe, notwithstanding the massacre of the White Wagon Train near Point of Rocks in October 1849, had long desired a treaty of peace with the Jicarilla Apache. In December 1849, he commissioned Cyrus Choice and Colonel Charles Augustus May to seek them out and make a treaty. At the appointed time twelve Indian women armed with bows and arrows arrived and announced that the principal chief was in council with his subordinates. May dismissed the women. The chiefs never arrived.[1]

The first eight months of 1850 were fraught with raids, stock thefts, and murder by the Jicarilla followed by a military expedition that recovered a great many head of stolen livestock and destroyed the winter stores and camp equipment of the band. In the latter part of 1850, for many months, New Mexico was quiet at least as far as the Jicarilla were concerned. The war that had begun soon after the Americans had arrived and had seen the tribe close off traffic on the Santa Fe Trail three times was finally grinding to a halt. The path to peace was not without incident. On January 25, 1851, Jicarillas conducted a raid twenty-five miles from Pecos on the Santa Fe Trail. They drove off several large herds of sheep and other stock from local ranches.[2] Bothersome as it was, this was not war or a revenge raid. It was a hungry people in search of food. Peace was coming.

On February 27, 1851, President Fillmore, a Whig, appointed four agents to assist the superintendent of Indian Affairs, James S. Calhoun, who would not receive news of his appointment until March. On March 3, 1851, Calhoun became the first governor of the new Territory of New Mexico and its ex officio superintendent of Indian Affairs. On April 5, commissioner of Indian Affairs Luke Lea informed the new governor by letter of the appointments. Agents Richard Weightman, Abraham R. Woolley, John Greiner, and Edward H. Wingfield would not arrive until mid-July 1851.[3] John Greiner came to be a valued assistant to an ailing Calhoun, who would die in office in the spring of 1852 while en route to the States. With him went the coffin he had purchased in Santa Fe. He appointed Greiner acting governor in his absence.

Learning of the appointment of the new agents, Calhoun wrote to commissioner of Indian Affairs Lea:

> *Your letter of the 5th and 12th of April last were received on the 24th inst. and I am gratified at the appointment of four Indian Agents for this Territory—If proper laws have been extended over this Territory, and the means are authorized to locate and subsist the Indians for a short period, we can lay the foundations of a quietude unknown to the people of New Mexico.*[4]

A confused, disorganized government within the former Mexican state, squabbling internally, and lacking direction from Washington, did not simplify matters. Between 1846 and 1850, New Mexico had been occupied territory. General Kearny had presumed to declare it a territory and assign it a government. This only led to confusion between a civil government and a military government that could not agree as to the extent of their mutual powers, particularly the power to treat with and make war upon the Indians. Finally, on September 8, the Congressional Compromise of 1850 created the Territory of New Mexico. Colonel John Munroe, the last military governor, remained as military commander of the Ninth Military District. The transition was not an easy one. Colonel Munroe continued to assert himself as if he were still governor and engaged in petty slights, making life difficult for Calhoun. As late as May 24, 1851, Munroe still refused to vacate the governor's offices, writing:

> *Sir,*
>
> *I duly received your letter of the 23d. inst. Requesting that the room now occupied by the Asst. Adjt. Genl. may be vacated for the use of the Legislature at its coming session. The removal of the office at this time would be specially inconvenient and I regret that I cannot accede to your request.*[5,6]

In other words, the outgoing military governor found it inconvenient to move out of the government offices. Organization and civilian government were coming to the new Territory of New Mexico, but coming slowly. Munroe often refused to provide escort for Indian agents and at other times refused to allow these agents to accompany troops in the field. The colonel attempted to make the new civilian government ineffective.

In March 1851, Governor Calhoun asked the military to provide "protection for the inhabitants at the New Placer desir[ing] that the Indians who had been for months located not far from Manzana might be expelled or exterminated."[7] Fortunately, however, Lieutenant J. P. Holliday, who was sent on this errand, failed to follow his orders and did not exterminate the Jicarilla found there. He learned that these Apache had been working with the Mexicans guarding their herds and had just recovered three thousand sheep stolen by Navajos, returning them to their owners. The Jicarilla wanted peace.[8]

On March 31, 1851, Calhoun wrote:

Leut. J.P. Holliday, 2d Dragoons, left Albuquerque on the 18th with forty four men in search of Indians who had committed depredations in the neighborhood of Manzana.[9] He found the camp of the Apaches, near the Smoky mountains, Sixty miles E. of S.E. of Manzana,[10] About two hundred Indians in the camp, Sixty of whom were warriors. The Superior Chief of the Apache East of the Del Norte, Chacon, approached Leut. Holliday, and enquired the object of his visit; declaring at the same time he was for peace, and that his people had committed no depredations of a recent date, and at once agreed to return with the Lieutenant, and he and others are expected here on the 3d of the ensuing month. The Jicarillas and Mescaleros each have a subordinate chief with four warriors, now at the Superintendency. They came in on the 29th inst to ascertain whether I would entertain a proposition for a Treaty of Peace and while engaged in a talk with them, intelligence of Chacon's intention to come in, caused a suspension of our mutual enquiries, and these subordinates will remain here until Chacon's arrival."[11]

The location where Lieutenant Holliday found the two hundred Jicarilla Apache is in the extreme southern part of their range where it overlaps with that of the Mescalero. This reflects a problem always present when dealing with the Apache. The many bands spoke the same language and shared the same or very similar culture. There were no clear political boundaries. The boundaries between bands blurred. Llanero Jicarilla rode with Mescalero who in turn rode to war with Chiricahua. In the 1880s, the Llanero would be relatively content to live on the Mescalero reservation while the Ollero objected strenuously. On July 1, 1852, Colonel Sumner made a treaty with the Apache. Those Apache who signed the treaty were Chiricahuas. It was the only treaty ever ratified by the Senate. Although no Jicarilla Apache signed it, the government included the Jicarilla among those covered by it.

On April 2, 1851, more than a year before Sumner's treaty, the Jicarilla concluded a treaty with Governor Calhoun. Although the Senate never ratified it, this was the treaty the Jicarilla accepted and obeyed. The governor had no direction from Washington as to what he could offer them, but he offered basic terms in a one-sided treaty. The Jicarilla Apache made promises; the government offered nothing in return:

1. The Jicarilla Apache would go where the government told them, build a village, and cultivate the soil.
2. The Jicarilla would abstain from murders and depredations and stay fifty miles away from all settlements. They would deliver up murderers, robbers, and fugitives as well as any captives.
3. The government would be allowed to establish military posts among them and assign traders. The Apache would proceed to Bosque Redondo as a place of trade.
4. If the Apache complied fully, "the said Government will grant them such donations and implements of husbandry, and other gratuities as a proper and sound humanity may demand."[12]

Unfortunately for all, Washington remained unresponsive to Calhoun's pleas for guidance and then for ratification of the 1851 treaty. The government did not approve the treaty with amendments as had been intended, and it did not provide Calhoun with the authority to subsist the Indians nor assign a home where they could farm. The idea behind Calhoun's 1851 treaty was as old as the republic. A democratic republic could only exist if its people were yeomen farmers. All through the nineteenth century government policy toward the Indians was either that they be pushed west beyond the frontier or that they be trained and settled as farmers. New Mexico was beyond the frontier and surrounded by nomadic tribes. The superintendents of Indian Affairs for New Mexico, that is, governors Calhoun, Lane, and Meriwether, attempted to do both by establishing an internal frontier somewhere west of the Rio Grande or east of Bosque Redondo and to settle the Jicarilla on farms along that frontier where they could become peaceful and productive.[13] William Carson expressed the idea as he interpreted the diaries of Governor William Carr Lane (1852–53):

There were two schools of thought about solving the problem. Extremists, deeming it absolutely hopeless, were in favor of cutting the Gordian knot by exterminating all the Indians. But to men who were really familiar with the aborigines and to humanitarians this simple solution was abhorrent. It was their conviction that the way to guarantee so far as was possible the good behavior of the redmen was to placate them with gifts, sometimes including food, and teach them to support themselves by the cultivation of the soil and the raising of stock.[14]

Nonetheless, Calhoun's treaty with the Jicarilla was deeply flawed. Not the least of its defects was that the Senate never ratified it nor did Luke Lea ever provide additional instructions. The treaty said that the Jicarilla must go somewhere to build villages and farm. They agreed to do so, but were never told where they must go, only that they must remain fifty miles away from the settlements. This soon proved unworkable. Chief Chacon wanted to know why, since he was at peace, he was not allowed to come to the settlements to conduct trade. The trade in micaceous pottery and baskets was important to the Jicarilla economy. Months went by filled with Jicarilla sightings and alarms. Investigation showed that there were no depredations, nor were the Apache threatening any. Eventually, mutual consent between the Jicarilla, the Army, and the governor recognized this element of the treaty as a dead letter. The Jicarilla were not in violation. The Apache became white clay invisibly residing among the settlements and along the Canadian River.

The Jicarilla needed to visit the settlements. They needed the trade. Chief Chacon said that it was his opinion that if they could not steal, they must trade or starve:

I and my family are starving to death, we have made peace, we do not want to do harm as you see from our bringing women and children with us, we want to go to the clay bank at San Jose and make vessels to sell so as to procure an honest living, we can't steal and must do something to earn a living.[15]

Toward the end of May, a letter arrived from Washington. On April 12, 1851, Luke Lea wrote to Calhoun advising him that the "Governor of New Mexico, as Ex officio Superintendent of Indian Affairs" was duly designated to negotiate treaties with the Indians in the territory.[16] Calhoun had the authority to negotiate a treaty but was still given no instruction as to what terms he was allowed to offer. The treaty called on them to draw rations at Bosque Redondo, exiling them from their normal range and forcing conflict with the Comanche.

Briefly, the territory was alive with alarmed sightings of Jicarilla near the settlements. Initially, the governor tried to enforce the fifty-mile provision. Calhoun wrote to an officer of the military on April 18, 1851:

Sir:

I understand there are a Band of Apachas [sic] now in lodges within fifteen or twenty miles of Las Vegas in violation of the treaty, as you will remember, made with Chacon and others a few days ago. It is important to ascertain their purposes and for that reason, you are requested to proceed to their encampment at once, first conferring with, and conforming to Lieut. Chapman's views, and ascertain their numbers, designating warriors from others—their precise location—their avowed object, and what band they are. Also glean from them, if possible information concerning Mrs. White's daughter and servant, and the whereabouts of Chacon and others. . . .[17]

The reality was that the Jicarilla were near Anton Chico—one of the places where they traditionally camped to gather micaceous clay and make pots. And there was evidence that Chacon, at least, intended to respect the intent of the agreement.[18] In May, Captain Richard Ewell met with Chacon and various of his chiefs at Mora, northwest of Las Vegas, and was convinced that Chacon and his people were trying to comply with the treaty. On June 14, however, Carlos Beaubien, formerly a circuit judge for the County of Taos, wrote to Governor Calhoun that he believed that the lower classes of people in Taos were conspiring to rebellion together with the Jicarilla and Yutas. In response, Colonel Munroe sent two twelve-pound cannon and sixty artillerymen under Major H. L. Kendrick, 2nd Artillery, to Taos. There, he found that the Yutas and Jicarilla were among the people of Taos "by treaty and passes and safeguards of Military Officers" and that the judge was suffering under a misapprehension.[19] Although this was not the first time Beaubien had raised a false alarm, he was respected and knowledgeable and his suspicions had to be investigated. The military averted a collision with the Jicarilla by investigating circumstances before firing a shot. The peace remained unbroken.

On May 24, 1851, after meeting with Chacon, Captain Ewell wrote that the chief had not been aware that he was to meet Calhoun at Anton Chico and thus had missed their appointment. There was no indication of hostility. Further, as the Jicarilla were among the settlements attempting to trade peacefully, he did not understand the fifty-mile limit clause. Chacon protested that the limit did not make any sense since now his people were at peace.[20]

Between Mexicans, Indians, and Americans, the country was overhunted. There wasn't enough game. The Southern Cheyenne had noticed a decline in the number of buffalo as early as the 1840s. Texans were pushing the Comanche and Kiowa westward into the buffalo hunting grounds of the Ute and Jicarilla. Pushed back into the Sangre de Cristo and San Juan Mountains, the Jicarilla and Ute shared hunting grounds for smaller game with Mexicans and Americans. Military and civilian leaders alike shared the knowledge that they would either have to feed the Indians, at least until they could get their own farms going, or exterminate them because the Indian was starving and would depredate to feed himself. Commissioner Lea and the treaty of 1851 did not provide for feeding the Indians any more than they provided land for farms.

In July 1851, a wary Governor Calhoun wrote: "The homes of the Eastern Apaches [Jicarilla] are in this territory, and these Indians have committed more aggressions—than the combined tribes immediately east of them—and they are as often, and in as great numbers, upon the plains as other tribes."[21]

By the end of August 1851, however, Calhoun's position had softened toward the Jicarilla and he could report that no outrages had been committed by the "Apaches roaming east of the Rio del Norte" since the treaty. In other words, the treaty was a success, and the Jicarilla were behaving even though they were within fifty miles of the settlements. In bureaucratic style he said in one letter that he desperately needed the treaty ratified and needed money and instructions to make it work and in the next told of the great success that was due to his efforts.

In July of 1851, the four new Indian agents arrived along with the new commander of the Ninth Military Department, Colonel Edwin Vose Sumner. Governor Calhoun would find the new commander at least as difficult as outgoing Colonel Munroe; historian Leo Oliva ascribed the hostility of the Jicarillas toward John Munroe as an underlying factor in his replacement.[22] Sumner's inactivity allowed the Jicarilla to remain at peace.

The Department of War was deeply concerned with the high cost of operations in New Mexico. The agricultural output of New Mexico was inadequate to support the troops stationed there. Food and supplies had to be imported over the Santa Fe Trail incurring high costs for transportation. The presence of the military drove up local demand and prices. The new commander arrived with instructions to cut costs.

Failing health led Calhoun to lean more and more on John Greiner, eventually appointing him acting governor as he departed for the States. Calhoun died en route in the spring of 1852. Since the signing of Calhoun's 1851 treaty, the Jicarilla had been peaceful.

On April 21, 1852, Greiner wrote that Chief Lobo Blanco had noticed that he was not getting the same quantity of "presents" being provided to Navajo and Ute. These presents supplemented both diet and the reduction in trade caused by avoiding the settlements. The Navajo and Ute treaties provided annuities above the "gifts" the government allowed the agent to offer when Indians visited. Writing of the visit of Pablo Romero, a trader, who had visited Lobo's village, agent and acting superintendent Greiner said:

He had told Lobo who was complaining about not having received presents, to hold on an[d] they would not be forgotten, and sure enough he heard soon after that the Apache were called to receive presents. He considers Lobo chief of the Apaches a very good man and reliable.[23]

Romero was not alone in considering Lobo Blanco trustworthy and interested in peace. Chief Lobo Blanco and his people lived peacefully on the plains and did not cause problems until the hard winter of 1853/54.

During the summer of 1850, before the subjugation of the Jicarilla and before Calhoun's 1851 treaty, Kit Carson arrived at his ranch along Rayado Creek to learn that his livestock had been rustled by Jicarilla. The excitement over the theft had already subsided. In the fall of that year he met and teamed with Captain Richard S. Ewell to rescue traders Weatherhead and Brevoort on the Santa Fe Trail. Carson then spent the winter at Rayado, staying until March 1851, when he took twelve wagons for Lucien Maxwell to St. Louis for supplies.

In the summer of 1851, returning from the States by way of the Mountain Route and Bent's Fort, a band of Southern Cheyenne pursued Carson. They had a fresh grudge against Americans. An officer had ordered one of their chiefs seized and whipped. Carson had lived with this tribe when he was a hunter at Bent's and had married one of their women, who subsequently divorced him through the traditional expedient of placing his possessions outside the tepee. Kit Carson expected that the Cheyenne he met along the Arkansas River would be friendly. He spoke their language and many of them knew him personally.

However, Colonel Edwin Sumner, coming to New Mexico to assume his post, was ahead of Carson on the trail leading a party of raw recruits, the officer who had offended the Cheyenne, and the four new Indian agents mentioned above. While at Bent's Fort, the officer accused a Cheyenne of taking a ring belonging to his wife and ordered the Indian flogged. [24] Carson's autobiography included a wry account of his meeting with the Indians:

> *I fell in with a village of Cheyenne Indians. They were at the time hostile to the United States, on account of one of the officers of Colonel Sumner's command (that was about ten days march in my advance) having flogged an Indian Chief of their tribe. The cause to me [was] unknown, but I presume courage was oozing from the finger ends of the officer and, as the Indians were in his power, he wished to be relieved of such a commodity.* [25]

The Cheyenne followed Carson's caravan approaching when the wagon train went into camp about twenty miles short of Bent's Fort. He had with him fifteen men, two Americans and thirteen Mexicans. Carson would report later, speaking of the Mexicans, that, "I had a poor opinion of their bravery." [26] After Carson had settled for the night, the Indians came into his camp a few at a time until there were more than twenty of them surrounding the great scout. From behind his back, one brave menaced Carson's head with a tomahawk. Fortunately, one of their number recognized Carson and calmed the situation. Carson ordered the Cheyenne from his camp and had his men take up the march, rifles at the ready. That evening Carson sent an express rider who reached Colonel Sumner, but Sumner chose not to send any aid and the rider continued on to Rayado. As it turned out, the mere sending of the express was enough. The next morning Carson allowed a few of the Cheyenne to enter his camp and he informed them that he had sent for assistance. Carson's autobiography continues:

They departed, examined the road, and [finding] that all I said was true, and he [the express] had advanced so far that they could not over-take him, they concluded to leave me, fearing the arrival of the troops. I am confident I and my party would have been killed by the Cheyennes, for they were a large number around me, if I had not sent forward for assistance, and the only reason they had of attacking me was, as I afterwards learned, the difficulty among them caused by the conduct of an officer of Col. Sumner's command.[27]

At Rayado upon receiving the express, Major Grier sent Lieutenant Johnston and a party of dragoons to Carson's aid. En route to meet the great scout, the lieutenant met with the colonel. Chagrined by a subordinate sending aid from a great distance, Sumner finally decided that he must help Carson and sent Major Carleton and thirty men to travel with the lieutenant. Carson later mused "the conscience of the gallant old Colonel then, I presume, troubled him."

This was the beginning of Carson's friendship with Major (later General) James Henry Carleton, which would endure through the latter's command of the Union forces in New Mexico during the Civil War and which would be strained by the campaign against the Navajo that culminated in their Long Walk and confinement at Bosque Redondo. The frontiersman would later express how grateful he was to Grier, Johnston, and Carleton:

But I am thankful to Carleton and Johnston [for] the kindness they showed me on their arrival and by their anxiety and willingness to punish the Indians that wished to interrupt me. Major Grier, a gentleman and a gallant soldier, is entitled to my warmest gratitude for the promptness [with] which he rendered assistance and cordially showed his capability of performing the high duty to which he was appointed.

Of Sumner, however, he said:

But to the Colonel, I do not consider myself under any obligations; for by his conduct two days previously he showed plainly that by rendering aid to a few American Citizens in the power of Indians, enraged by the conduct of some of his command, was not his wish.[28]

Starting with the incident at Bent's Fort, Sumner's command of the department was off to an inglorious start and while it may seem hardly possible, it only went downhill from there. The new departmental commander came with dire instructions from the secretary of war:

You will use every effort to reduce the enormous expenditures of the Army in New Mexico, particularly in the Quarter Master's and Subsistence Departments—you will scrutinize the administration of these Departments, and will rigidly enforce all regulations having reference to the economy of the service.[29]

Despite the inherently high costs of doing business in New Mexico, Colonel Sumner set out to economize. He ordered his soldiers out of the cities, saving money on rent while transportation costs soared and upkeep exceeded the savings. His soldiers were kept busy building new forts. In the region of the Jicarillas and Utes, he built Cantonment Burgwin near Taos, Fort Massachusetts at the Sangre de Cristo Pass ninety miles north of Taos, and Fort Union north of Las Vegas. He also built Fort Defiance in the Navajo country and others along the then border with Mexico. He withdrew the troops from Las Vegas, Rayado, Albuquerque, Cebolleta, Socorro, Doña Ana, San Elizario, and El Paso. This raised transportation costs and separated the soldiers from the people and places they were there to protect. Fort Union was built on land belonging to Alexander Barclay, which the army eventually paid to purchase. The moves provided the soldiers with a place to farm and raise their own produce as well as places to graze their horses and mules. This might have worked well, except that the soldiers were not proficient farmers and the climate did not cooperate. New Mexico faced a two-year drought. The cost of a bushel of corn to feed the horses doubled and doubled again. Sumner would buy grain for feed, but the horses suffered anyway, becoming useless for field duty.

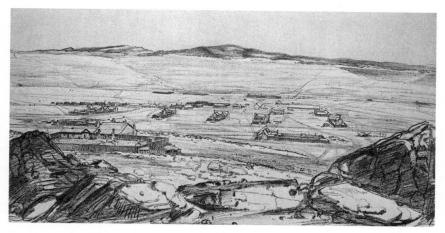

Fort Union, a post on the Santa Fe Trail where the Mountain Branch and the Cimarron Cutoff come together, was founded primarily to control the Jicarilla. Ca. 1859. COURTESY PALACE OF THE GOVERNORS PHOTO ARCHIVES (NMHM/DCA), 14555, ARTIST JOSEPH HEGER

As a result of his construction projects, especially Forts Massachusetts and Union, Spanish culture began to advance again, protected by soldiers; colonists moved onto the plains and north into the San Luis Valley and the Arkansas River Valley. Captain John Pope, a member of the Topographical Engineers, described the phenomenon:

> *The establishment of a military post in Indian country brings with it the inevitable consequence of gradually but certainly driving the Indians to the side opposite the white settlements and, at the same time, of attracting the white to occupy and cultivate the country in its vicinity.*[30]

This advance created new conflicts with the Ute and Jicarilla. Settlers were harassed and the Indians complained to their agents who proved ineffective. The Indians' anger built.

From the start, continuing the tradition begun by his predecessor, Colonel Munroe, Colonel Sumner, known as "Bull," made Governor Calhoun's life miserable. He refused to cooperate with civilian authority or to divulge his plans.[31]

On August 17, 1851, Bull Sumner mounted a 350-man invasion of Navajo country with the intention of chastising this troublesome tribe. Camping in the depths of Canyon de Chelly, a Navajo stronghold, he noted the many fires the Indians kindled along the rim of the declivity indicating their presence on inaccessible heights above his army. He promptly turned his force around and retreated to Santa Fe without a fight. Along the way, the terrain and environment took their toll and he lost over three hundred horses and mules. He reached the conclusion that American horses were ill suited to New Mexico. In future, infantry would lead the way on campaign.[32] During the next two years, military activity was expended on farming and building forts rather than on confronting Indians. He left the department weakened and his successor would have difficulty building its strength. Sumner did not campaign again and the now peaceful Jicarilla remained so throughout his tenure in office.

Sumner requested that four more companies of infantry be sent to New Mexico as dragoons were unsuitable. Congress has always liked infantry. It's less expensive to arm, equip, and train than cavalry. Sumner's economy measures went against conventional military understanding that only cavalry, mounted infantry, and, in a pinch, mounted artillerymen were useful in pursuing Indian raiders. Nonetheless, his recommendation was met with favor by the commanding general, Winfield Scott: "This is a very interesting report. I shall propose, next spring, that we withdraw the cavalry as suggested within. I ought to add that I highly approve the views & measures of Colonel Sumner."

By year's end of 1851, Sumner was proud of his accomplishments, and on January 27, 1852, he wrote:

> *I have the great satisfaction to report the new Posts that have been established in this Territory, are already exercising a favorable influence in our Indian relations. The Utahs, and Jicarilla Apaches, have been perfectly quiet, these tribes are influenced by these Posts, and in order to insure their permanent submission, I intend to put a Post in the Utah country, about eighty miles north of Taos.*[33]

Following his brush with the Cheyenne, in July 1851, Carson returned once more to Rayado and remained there until March of 1852. He and Maxwell supplied the army with hay and other provender at high prices—no doubt the result of drought and increased demand due to the presence of the soldiers. In 1852, during his sojourn, he made a short trapping expedition, going north into the mountains on a hunt with Maxwell and others, trapping, and making "a very good hunt." This was, it seemed, Carson's final goodbye to his old life in the mountains. He returned to Rayado and remained there through the fall and winter. In February 1853, Kit Carson went to the Rio Abajo to purchase sheep on behalf of himself and several partners including Maxwell. In the Abajo were many wealthy *ricos* whose *peons*, debt slaves, tended large herds of sheep. He then went to California with Henry Mercure, John Bernavette, and their employees, followed by Lucien Maxwell and his own herd. Sheep sold for $1 a head in New Mexico, but were worth $5.50 a head in California where the Gold Rush had left meat scarce. On March 1, 1853, President Pierce appointed Kit Carson an Indian agent at Taos to the Ute and Jicarilla Apache. Carson was driving a herd to California and did not learn of it until he was on his way home. He arrived in Taos on December 25, 1853, and assumed his new duties in January 1854.

Throughout his term from March 3, 1851, until his death on May 6, 1852, Governor Calhoun made alternating claims of constant Indian threats and of peace conditions only occasionally punctuated by Navajo raids. The depredation claims show more raids by Navajos in the 1850s than by any other tribe. He complained to Lea that Americans and Mexicans kept trying to excite the Indians "by misrepresentations and outrages upon their rights." He wrote that he knew that settlers exaggerated many of the claims. Although he didn't come out and say it, his own protestations were often as not among them in hyperbole. As Michno says, Calhoun could cry wolf with the best of them.[34] Indian trouble contributed to the economy of New Mexico. Depredation claims had a seldom-realized potential especially when inflated. Soldiers had to be supplied and all in New Mexico seem to have turned their hands to transporting and selling to the military at high markup. Many settled near the posts to relieve soldiers of their income through various recreations. Hog ranching was profitable.[35] The new commander, Sumner, moved the boys out of the cities away from dens of vice only to have the dens relocate.

By November 10, 1851, Bull Sumner was tired of Calhoun's complaints and asked, "Will you please state to me the scenes of desolation that have been recently witnessed in this territory before I reply to your letter of this date?"[36] Undoubtedly, the governor was hearing complaints of Indian activity from many corners. There was money to be made from having the military present in the territory and if depredations diminished there was fear that Congress might reduce the numbers of soldiers. As Sumner wrote, "The truth is the only resource of this country is the government money. All classes depend upon it, from the professional man and trader down to the beggar."[37] Undoubtedly, there were people, like Judge Beaubien, who were honestly concerned after hearing from his contacts among the Indians of "wars and rumors of wars." In many cases the Indians were starving and had good reason to be dissatisfied. Incidents didn't pan out to much. Indians roamed through and among the settlements, trading and occasionally getting drunk and causing disturbances. It never amounted to anything that civilian authority couldn't handle without military intervention.

Throughout 1851, 1852, and 1853, the Jicarilla continued to abide by Calhoun's unratified treaty in all respects except for the fifty-mile rule. By the end of the year 1851, the rule was a dead letter and everyone understood that it was unworkable. The Jicarilla were trying to be peaceful and compliant.

Through the winter and spring of 1852, Calhoun grew increasingly ill, ordered a coffin, and planned a trip back to the States. Colonel Bull Sumner worked on his forts, moved men and supplies from the towns, and did little about chastising Indians. His horses suffered from starvation, and he might have had difficulty mounting a full company of dragoons if he'd had a mind to do so. His 1853 successor in office, General John Garland, would find dragoon mounts in poor condition. Governor Calhoun increasingly relied on Indian Agent John Greiner. Initially, he turned over his duties as superintendent of Indian Affairs to Greiner and ultimately his duties as governor as he departed from Santa Fe. Whether or not this was legal is hard to say. Sumner thought not.

On April 30, 1852, Acting Superintendent Greiner wrote to Commissioner Lea from Santa Fe:

Nearly one hundred Jicarilla Apaches have been at this superintendency this week, being on a moving expedition from Las Truchas to the Rio Pecos. Much trouble was occasioned by their fondness for liquor, and the facility by which they could procure it at the groceries.[38, 39] *These Indians are very poor, very hard to govern, and from their continually roving through the settlements, there is danger to be apprehended from collisions between them and the citizens. The talk held with them at Pecos and the presents there distributed, has [have] produced the most beneficial results, They intend to settle down and manufacture* tinajas

*and baskets to trade with, and
a number of them are beginning
to plant.*[40] *Chacon their head
chief has strongly recommended
them to cultivate the land, and
this year has set them the exam-
ple himself.*[41]

Talk of rebellions and raids
diminished after Calhoun departed.
On June 30, 1852, John Greiner
wrote, "Not a single depredation
has been committed by any of the
Indians in New Mexico for three
months. The 'oldest inhabitant' cannot recollect the time when this
could have been said with truth
before."[42] His diary of that date
reflects that the Mescaleros and
Jicarilla Apache gathered at treaty
talks with the Gila and Mimbres Apaches[43] were "quiet and
contented."

Governor William Carr Lane made
a treaty with the Jicarilla. With his
financial assistance, the Apache started
farms near Abiquiu and Fort Webster.
About 1853. COURTESY PALACE OF THE GOV-
ERNORS PHOTO ARCHIVES (NMHM/DCA), 9999

On July 1, 1852, Greiner wrote in his diary:

*About 50 Indians present, Mescaleros, Jicarillas . . . Treaty made with
Southern Apaches.*

    *Col Sumner assumes to be the head of the department, claims that
[he] is governor by virtue of necessity and by virtue of his office of
governor is sup of Ind. aff. I did not know before that he assumed such
power and questioned his right very strongly.*[44]

From this time until newly appointed governor William Carr Lane
arrived in the fall of 1852 to take office, Greiner found himself at logger-
heads with the colonel. Even after Lane was inaugurated, Sumner remained
resistant to civilian authority.

On July 1, 1852, elevating himself to civil governor and superintendent of Indian Affairs, Colonel Sumner concluded a treaty with the Apache. Its Apache signatories included the Gila and Mimbres Apaches Cuentas Azules, Blancito, Negrito, Capitan Simon, Capitan Vuelta, and Mangus Colorado chiefs, acting on the part of the Apache Nation of Indians, situated and living within the limits of the United States, that is to say, all Apaches. Although a few of them were present, the Jicarilla and Mescalero chiefs did not sign the treaty. Chacon and Lobo Blanco were recognized as the principal chiefs of the Jicarilla, but neither signed. Nonetheless, the US government accepted this as a treaty with all Apaches including the Jicarilla. This is the only treaty applying to the Jicarilla ever ratified by the Senate, and the only treaty under which the government of the United States ever paid reparations for depredations by the Jicarilla.[45]

The treaty promised peace between the United States and the tribes, peace between the tribes, subjection to the authority of the United States, acceptance of US authority to settle disputes between tribes, and between Americans and Indians. It further promised either reservations or the demarcation of an Indian frontier:

> [T]he government of the United States shall at its earliest convenience designate, settle, and adjust their territorial boundaries, and pass and execute in their territory such laws as may be deemed conducive to the prosperity and happiness of said Indians.

The United States also promised to:

> grant to said Indians such donations, presents, and implements, and adopt such other liberal and humane measures as said government may deem meet and proper.[46]

The government of the United States promised no more than to do as it saw fit. It promised land, food, and implements only in principle.

After Calhoun's death, President Millard Fillmore appointed a new territorial governor, William Carr Lane. Shortly thereafter, Fillmore was defeated in the election by Franklin Pierce, a Democrat. Lane knew himself to be a lame duck who would soon be replaced. He arrived on September 9, 1852, and was inaugurated on September 13, an auspicious date commemorated by Colonel Sumner, who took down the American flag that had been flying over the Plaza of Santa Fe in front of the Palace of the Governors since 1846 and refused to return it.

> *Colonel E. V. Sumner, the military commander of the department . . . obviously resentful of the presence of a Civil Government, probably thinking that the authority should have been invested in him, proceeded to do in Lane's case, as he had done in Calhoun's, everything in his power to embarrass and harass him and to interfere with the exercise of his authority. . . .*[47]

Lane had no experience in working for the federal government and no experience in office other than having been the mayor of St. Louis. He became enmeshed in the battle between military and civilian authority, between the Whig Party that appointed him and the Democrats who would soon replace him. Thus when he set out to make treaties with the Indians and to secure the southern border, he far exceeded reasonable expectations of how Washington would receive his treaties.

The Indians, despite Sumner's recent treaty of July 1, 1852, remained an unsettled problem. Although it ratified the treaty, the government had not assigned lands for Indian farms or a frontier, nor had Congress authorized the needed supplies. Starving Apaches came to the settlements to beg for food.

In January 1853, Kittie Bowen, wife of Captain Bowen, wrote that suddenly one day "the garrison was full of Apaches." Fort Union's buildings were *jacal*, upright posts plastered with adobe to fill the spaces between. They were draughty and leaked in wet weather. Their green logs soon crumbled back to the earth. Like most western forts, it lacked a stockade wall. It was a village whose plaza, a parade ground, boasted a flagpole. Officers' quarters were on two sides and barracks on the others. Mrs. Bowen was relieved to learn that the Apache had come to the fort begging for food since they appeared at first to be "the most frightful beings that the sun ever shone upon. Some of their red faces seem to be a foot through the cheeks." Mrs. Bowen served her "guests fine wild turkey, ham, tongue and salad, with ice cream, cakes, jelly and preserves," and "they all enjoyed it very much."[48]

That same month reports came in from Anton Chico on the Pecos River of Jicarillas and Mescaleros starving and begging for food. Indians who came to visit the governor in Santa Fe came seeking gifts including hoes, axes, and sickles. Military officers and frontiersmen like Kit Carson were aware that winter starvation was often the case among tribes deprived of hunting grounds. "We will either have to feed them or exterminate them," was not a statement of a desire to kill them all. It was awareness that the Apache, no matter how peaceable their intent, would fight and steal rather than starve and if they fought or depredated, the government would call on the army to exterminate them. When William Carr Lane learned of the situation, he approached the problems head on.

Governor Lane spent much of his time trying to solve the problem of the "Disputed District." There was an error in the map used to draw up the 1848 Treaty of Guadalupe Hidalgo that ended the Mexican-American War. It showed El Paso in the wrong location although the longitude and latitude were given correctly. Boundary Commissioner John Russell Bartlett agreed to a "compromise" with his Mexican opposite number, which gave away much soil for which the United States had already paid. The disputed area included the "32nd degree corridor," a system of low passes from the Rio Grande to the Colorado, which was the only spot suitable for a railroad south of South Pass in what would become Wyoming. Governor Lane attempted to correct the error.

> [T]he Commission met with bitter opposition from those Americans who envisaged the construction of a railroad to the Pacific through the southwestern corner of New Mexico or what at least had been historically considered a part of the Territory. This area had been claimed by the Mexican state of Chihuahua in 1851, "without producing any authority for this act from the Republic of Mexico and without having obtained the consent of the United States or the Territory of New Mexico"....[49]

Lane did not resolve the difficult problem. While Lane was in the south, he gave instructions to Indian Agent Edward H. Wingfield to have the Chiricahua Apache start farms near Fort Webster.[50] Meanwhile, Dr. Michael Steck, a former Army surgeon who had come west to help the health of his tubercular wife, was working on a similar project at Anton Chico where he met with Mescaleros Josecito, Santa Ana, and Cuentas Azules, and Jicarillas Lobo and San Pablo. Steck also met with Chief Chacon, who expressed a willingness to attempt the cultivation of the soil. Steck convinced Chacon to move his people out of the Sangre de Cristo to the area west of the Rio Grande. In April 1853, while the governor was in the south, Steck made a provisional treaty with the Jicarilla that provided for an Indian frontier twenty miles beyond the settlements. The same agreement was extended to the Chiricahua and soon there were farms at Fort Webster and twenty-five miles west of Abiquiu. Lane agreed, on behalf of the US government, to furnish food for five years and give other aid to all Apaches who would work setting up farms. By May, the local community was applauding Governor Lane. The *Santa Fe Weekly Gazette* sang his praises:

> *Our energetic and go-a-head Governor determined upon his arrival in the Territory, to clear all the country east of the Rio Grande of Indians, and to this end, has opened farms on the Rio Puerco, twenty five miles west of Abiquiu, and on the Mimbres near the Copper Mines.*
>
> *The Jicarillas under Chacon, their old captain, have gone to work with a will. The ground is being plowed up, a large and fine acequia is opened.*[51] *The Indians are planting, and the experiment bids fair to meet the sanguine hopes of the Governor.*[52]

Without waiting for Senate approval, Lane spent between twenty thousand and forty thousand dollars in discretionary funds that would normally have gone toward feeding and making gifts to visiting Indian dignitaries to support the effort to move the Jicarilla and others to farms. He fed approximately a thousand Indians, including 250 Jicarilla who established irrigation ditches and farms along the Rio Puerco. Apart from spending all the money budgeted for the year in the first six months, things were going fairly well. And then the Rio Puerco dried up. No one could remember it ever having done that before. The Jicarilla farming experiment failed.[53]

Governor Lane was a well-meaning, proactive man, who tackled problems head on, seeking workable solutions. Unfortunately, his solutions were not acceptable to Congress, nor to the new president, Franklin Pierce. By the time Lane penned his treaty with the Apache, he knew his days were numbered. He was a Whig, appointed by a Whig, and the new administration would replace him.

Personnel changes were indeed coming. In March 1853, George W. Manypenny replaced Luke Lea as commissioner of Indian Affairs. President

Franklin Pierce appointed David Meriwether as governor of New Mexico Territory and ex officio superintendent of Indian Affairs.[54] Meriwether arranged to have his son-in-law, Captain Edward A. Graves, appointed as an Indian agent to the Jicarilla and Ute at Abiquiu. When Meriwether arrived in Santa Fe on August 8, 1853, Lane had already resigned his position and was campaigning to become the territory's representative in Congress. On July 1, 1853, Colonel Sumner took leave and departed from New Mexico. Colonel Dixon Miles was briefly the department commander until General John Garland arrived on July 20, 1853. On October 31, 1853, the Ninth Military Department became the Department of New Mexico. William Messervy was the territorial secretary and would become acting governor while Lane was on leave in early 1854.

Scarcely had he taken office when Governor Meriwether began blaming everything on his predecessor. On August 31, 1853, as superintendent of Indian Affairs he wrote to Commissioner Manypenny:

Without intending to approve or disapprove of the policy of my predecessor, in causing a portion of the Apache Indians to be removed from the east and settle on the west side of the Rio Grande, where they have been fed at the cost of the government, I would beg leave to suggest that the question now is very different from that originally presented. Many of these Indians have already been removed, under a written contract made with Governor Lane, (a copy of which is herewith enclosed, marked B.) By this contract it is stipulated that the United States will feed these Indians for a given time on certain conditions, which conditions, it must be admitted, have been fully complied with on their part. If, then, the rations stipulated for in the contract be suddenly cut off, it will become difficult if not impossible to assign to them a sufficient reason for this, in their estimation, breach of contract. It then certainly follows that, stimulated by hunger and our supposed bad faith, they will subsist themselves by theft and robbery. Being well convinced in my own mind that such a course would produce this effect, I was induced to instruct our agents to gradually reduce instead of suddenly cutting off their food, until their crops were matured and I could receive instructions from the department.[55]

One way to handle the problem presented by Lane's action might have been to ask the commissioner to go to Congress and have the very reasonable treaty adopted before trouble could begin. Instead he announced that there would be trouble and it would all be the fault of his predecessor, a Whig. He predicted that the Indians would resort to theft and robbery. This prediction proved false. There were no more than 250 Jicarilla under Chief Chacon on the Rio Puerco. It is not clear when they moved away in search of food, but when trouble began, it began east, not west, of the Rio Grande with Lobo Blanco's band.

In September, Jicarillas visiting Fort Union, perhaps members of Lobo's band, were accused of stealing cattle and slaying rancher Juan Silva. Captain Nathaniel C. Macrae, 3rd Infantry, stationed at Fort Union wrote, "When I first heard of the Indian theft, I was rather incredulous." The Jicarilla had been peaceful for several years. At this point, only Meriwether was predicting war. He sent soldiers to investigate and they discovered that there were about five hundred Comanches and Kiowas in the vicinity.[56] The soldiers could not establish that the Jicarilla were responsible when it was far more likely that these untamed raiders of the prairie were to blame.

Juan de Jesus Mares of Taos County claimed that on June 13, 1853, the Jicarilla had relieved him of $2,530 worth of cattle, horses, and other property. Oddly, he did not file his claim until 1855. Although no one seems to have noticed the theft when it was supposed to have occurred in 1853 and although at the very least Mares exaggerated his loss, the government eventually approved it for nine hundred dollars. This was the only claim against the Jicarilla made for the year 1853. It would seem that although Lane and Steck were feeding only a portion of the tribe at Abiquiu, the remainder were abiding by the 1851 treaty made with Calhoun.

Colonel Sumner's false economies in search of frugality had impoverished the department, leaving its soldiers scattered in poorly constructed forts, its livestock crippled, and its transportation costs greater than ever. Although they had been friends, General Garland was soon making complaints about his predecessor.

[H]e has left the Department in an impoverished and crippled condition, wanting in many of the essentials for undertaking a successful enterprise. . . .[H]is economy run into parsimony, the result of which, was the loss of a vast number of horses and mules.[57]

John Garland found his department crippled beyond the ability to act against the Indians. Many of his dragoons had no horses. His stores and granaries were depleted. The horses, mules, and wagons that he had were broken down.

A decision of the Territorial Court in 1852 now came home to roost. The court ruled that there was no "Indian Country" in New Mexico. Since the 1830s, beyond the western boundary of the states and organized territories lay the Indian frontier, beyond which lay Indian country where the Trade and Intercourse Acts applied. Under these acts the federal government sanctioned and licensed traders, who were forbidden from selling whiskey to the Indians. In New Mexico, unlicensed traders and merchants had always sold to the Pueblo Indians and to the nomadic Indians who were on all sides of the settlements. Thus there was no frontier. According to the court, this lack of a defined frontier made the intercourse laws inoperative. Agent Graves, the governor's son-in-law, complained to the Indian service that the Trade and Intercourse Act "becomes a dead letter to all intents." In October, a Jicarilla band under Subchief Tranchaya (Tanchua?) purchased liquor at Mora and, getting drunk, a melee soon broke out during which Tranchaya was slain.[58] The Jicarilla did not take revenge for the murder of their chief. They continued to walk the path of peace.

On August 31, 1853, Graves wrote from the Abiquiu Agency:

The Utahs and northern Jicarilla Apaches have been assigned to this agency. After much labor and fatigue I have succeeded in holding a "talk" with some of the headmen or chiefs of these Indians. I find that a considerable portion of the Jicarilla Apaches have emigrated from the east of the Rio del Norte, . . . and have commenced the cultivation of a farm, which has been very well worked, when it is considered that it has been mainly done by the wild and roving Jicarilla Apaches, who have never been accustomed to look to the cultivation of the soil for a maintenance. These Indians have now from one hundred to one hundred and twenty acres under cultivation, which will yield them, however, but little corn this season, occasioned by the failure of the water in the Rio Puerco, which has prevented irrigation. This stream is now dry for the first time within the recollection of the oldest inhabitants, notwithstanding there has been no unusual drought.

The Jicarilla Apache seem to be on good terms with the United States, or citizens of this Territory, and they seem to be quiet and well disposed; yet I place but little reliance in their promises, or their regards for treaty stipulations, as it is probable that neither would be adhered to any longer than it may appear to them to be to their interest to do so. **Since the annexation of this Territory to the United States they have committed acts of murder, robbery, and other crimes, which, in savage cruelty, stand without a parallel in history,** *as the murders of Mr. and Mrs. White and party attest; to say nothing of the cold-blooded massacre of the mail party in 1850—the bare mention of which makes humanity shudder. Of the many wild tribes of Indians that have infested New Mexico for the last two hundred years, perhaps there are none who have committed so many depredations upon the citizens and property of this Territory as the Jicarilla Apaches.* **They are the most daring, brave, and heartless tribe of Indians who inhabit New Mexico.** . . . *There are about two hundred and fifty Jicarilla Apaches, of all classes, in the vicinity of their farm on the Rio Puerco. When their corn shall be exhausted, which will be very soon, they will be in a destitute condition, both as it regards the means of subsistence and clothing. Their chief pursuits are hunting. The game in their section, as in all other sections of this country, is rapidly diminishing, as I am informed and believe. The government will, I apprehend, have to feed and clothe these Indians to some extent, as this policy has been pursued towards them for some time past; or it is to be feared the alternative of starving or living by plundering and robbing the citizens will be presented. Should this be the case, it requires no sagacity to foretell their action. They can bring from one hundred to one hundred and fifty warriors into the field.*

Chacon, the celebrated chief of the Jicarilla Apaches, is equally pressing and solicitous in regard to presents expected to be made to him and his people. Here the question arises, what kind of an Indian policy is the true one for New Mexico? It is evident, and a fact uncontroverted here, that the Indian policy in New Mexico, as administered up to this time, has resulted in a failure, giving neither protection to life or property.[59]

The "wild" Ollero Jicarilla had been working hard on their farms along the Rio Puerco, which through no fault of their own failed, leaving them hungry. Although these Indians had in the past been the most brave and heartless of any tribe, they had shown their intent to remain at peace and to take up farming. According to Graves, allowing them to take up farming was a false policy that could only result in failure and leave the people of New Mexico in danger. It would appear that the new administration favored a policy of extermination.

By January 1854, the understanding and acceptance of Jicarilla peaceful intentions expressed by Governor Calhoun in 1851 had faded. Assuming office in the fall of 1853, Governor David Meriwether and commander of the Department of New Mexico, General John Garland, would dredge up Lobo Blanco's role in the 1849 White Wagon Train Massacre and abduction of Ann White as well as the chief's presumed role in the 1850 Wagon Mound Massacre.[60] At peace since the summer of 1850, Llanero Lobo Blanco would again become a prime villain even though Governor Meriwether was predicting war with Chacon's Olleros, not with the Llaneros. Historians would promote Meriwether's view by repeating the probably apocryphal accounts from Kit Carson and invented adventures of James Bennett.[61, 62]

Chapter 11

At the beginning of the year 1854, New Mexico was abuzz with rumors of Indian depredations. Some blamed the Jicarilla but investigation by the Army initially showed them innocent. On January 29, 1854, Colonel Philip St. George Cooke, 2nd Dragoons, commanding Fort Union, wrote to General Garland explaining that even as he sent Lieutenant Joseph Maxwell, 3rd Infantry, out to investigate the murder of an American by Indians, James M. Giddings, a respectable citizen, arrived to provide new and more accurate information about the event. The story Cooke had investigated was that one Pedro Gonzales, a buffalo hunter, was the owner of wagons lost to the Apache. While Pedro was away several Jicarilla came into his camp. Pedro's man Salazar and several others killed two Apache and wounded a third who escaped. Soon after Salazar was killed by Indians and the other Mexicans returned home without the drays, warned off by Indians not to come hunting buffalo with wagons but with pack mules only. The Indians were concerned that the Mexicans were taking too many buffalo. Giddings's new information was that the incident had taken place beyond the Arkansas River outside Jicarilla range, and the two white men whose bodies had been found were not killed by Indians but rather by Mexicans who had then been tried by the *alcalde* and let off on some pretext.[1]

The year had begun with a depredation that proved a false alarm, and no records remain of further acts of depredation and violence. Nonetheless, in a report made on March 1, 1854, Colonel Cooke referred to "[r]epeated small depredations, & insults to struggling citizens" without any suggestion of what these might be.[2]

On October 31, 1853, the Department of New Mexico superseded the Ninth Military Department in a revision of the entire military geography of the United States. A colonel, a portion of whose regiment was assigned to the department, usually commanded. Departmental boundaries changed along with the organization of states and territories. In 1853, the Department of

New Mexico included all of New Mexico except that portion west of the 110th degree of longitude, which would be about fifty miles inside modern Arizona.[3] Congress did not create the Arizona Territory out of New Mexico until 1863, partly because the southern boundary of New Mexico was in flux due to disagreements between the United States and Mexico over the meaning of the 1848 Treaty of Guadalupe Hidalgo that ended the Mexican-American War. In practice, the western boundary of the Military Department of New Mexico was ignored when soldiers were in pursuit of Navajos and Apaches. Although it varied from year to year, the department usually had about fifteen hundred men.

The Military Department of New Mexico was in bad shape, short of horses and impoverished by the previous administration. New Mexican horses, though readily available, were considered too small for military service and horses had to be brought from the states, particularly Missouri.[4] The departmental adjutant wrote of the situation, "I am instructed to say that there are no American Horses to be had."[5] The lack of horseflesh was a major hindrance to military campaigns in the region. On March 8, Cooke

Fort Massachusetts is represented here as a model found at Fort Garland, Colorado. The post, twelve miles north of Fort Garland and ninety miles north of Taos, was in New Mexico Territory until the boundary was changed. Its location has been lost three times. Active from 1852 to 1859, a caretaker detail was usually left behind in winter as the post was too difficult to supply. It was used to mount expeditions against the Ute and Jicarilla in 1855. AUTHOR PHOTO

again mentioned the need for horses in his report of a failed pursuit of Indian raiders in February by Lieutenant Bell and two companies of dragoons. "If he [Lieutenant Bell] could have mounted and marched with his whole company, instead of a platoon, his victory would have had more fruit, & he had probably made an end to what is a mere beginning."[6] Eventually, the department would authorize the local purchase of horses.

The parsimony of the previous departmental commander, Colonel Sumner, left Fort Union and other posts short of rations. Cantonment Burgwin, near Taos, was supplied from Fort Union. Crass and Wallsmith, conducting archaeological excavations at Burgwin, noted that "the average U.S. soldier was promised approximately twice as much beef or pork in the army as was consumed, on average, in the general civilian population." They go on to note that "while beef was pound for pound still the predominant meat in the army ration, the soldiers of Cantonment Burgwin ate much more mutton than the average calculated for the army in New Mexico as a whole." The archaeological remnants of rations at the Burgwin site and at Fort Massachusetts suggest that the soldiers were being issued a lot less beef than their official ration allowed.[7]

In early February, Indian raiders, identified as Jicarillas and Utes, took livestock from Samuel Watrous on the Mora River.

Hd. Qrs. Fort Union, N.M.
February 13, 1854

Sir,

You will proceed without delay with thirty three men of your company to Red River, where I have information of a camp of Jicarilla Apaches & Eutaws, some of whom have within three days committed depredations, robbing Mr. Waters of cattle and maltreating his herdsmen[8]—You will take twelve days rations (but only eight of salt meat) & Mr. Tipton will accompany you from Mr. Waters on the Mora, as a guide.[9, 10]

If you find these Indians in camp—or otherwise, your first duty will be to surround them, or cut off their retreat to broken ground: —then, —it appearing that they are a guilty party, —demand the surrender of the actual marauders: if they are delivered or pointed out, have them severely whipped, and take a pony as an indemnity to Mr. Waters: —If they make a plausible excuse, of their inability to surrender the depredators (and time, if necessary may be given them whilst you keep the chief in your power) then seize horses or ponies double the amount in value of the stolen animals.

In case of resistance or insolence or of their being overtaken flying from your pursuit, attack them.

You will of course use your discretion in unforeseen circumstances.

Respectfully &c
P.S. Geo. Cooke[11]
Lt. Col., 2nd Drags.[12]

It is surprising that Colonel Cooke called for such violent action against the Jicarilla, who had been peaceful since the late summer of 1850. The incident was minor. Colonel Cooke considered a single pony adequate reparation as long as the culprits were also flogged. Cooke had learned better than to whip Indians from General Kearny and from Kit Carson. This action was sure to result in increased hostility.

Indian Agent Graves at Abiquiu and Governor Meriwether had both been predicting depredations conducted by Chacon's Ollero Jicarilla on the Rio Puerco west of the Rio Grande; their farms had failed and they were starving at this point. The trouble was supposed to arise from the government cutting off rations. It didn't. The current trouble arose east of the Rio Grande and east of the Sangre de Cristo Mountains among the Llanero Jicarilla. The season had left them hard pressed. Rancher Watrous didn't make gifts to them for the privilege of grazing his stock on Jicarilla land, so they harassed the rancher and his herdsmen.

Meanwhile, on December 25, 1853, Kit Carson returned to Taos and his family. He was returning a rich man, at least as wealthy as he had ever been having made a five-fold profit on the sheep he took to the gold fields, and on the trail from California he had learned that the president had appointed him as an Indian agent. He took office on January 9 as the agent at Taos. Carson's responsibilities included handling government funds, including his travel expenses, expenses for entertaining visiting Indians, and annuities owed to the tribes. The illiterate Kit Carson would have difficulty keeping records and making written reports. He was authorized to hire a translator at government expense, but Carson did not require a translator as he spoke several Indian languages. Instead he hired a succession of clerks, which was not officially authorized but something usually overlooked.

In addition to Carson, there were three other agents in New Mexico but only two of them had contact with the Apache. E. A. Graves at Abiquiu dealt with Jicarillas and Utes while Dr. Steck worked with the Apaches in the south, Mescaleros and Chiricahuas. Indians came to the agents looking for presents and annuities, and to complain of mistreatment by Americans and Mexicans. Chiefs were also expected to come to the agency when summoned to answer for misbehavior by members of their tribe or band. The system had been in place since the frontier had been on the Mississippi River. There were no reservations. Beyond the frontier, Indians roamed at will with the agents attempting to mediate conflict between tribes. At Taos Carson dealt with Taos and Picuris Pueblo Indians and with Ute and Jicarilla.

About the time Kit Carson took office as Indian agent at Taos, the superintendent of Indian Affairs, Governor Meriwether, went on leave. Thus Carson's first reports as agent went to Acting Governor (Territorial Secretary) William Messervy. Upon taking office, David Meriwether had made it plain to all and sundry that no more money would be spent living up to Governor Lane's "contracts." Because Meriwether had been so adamant about Lane's expenditures, Messervy hardly dared to act when Carson approached with evidence that the Jicarilla and Ute were starving. On January 20, 1854, Carson's first report as agent concerned Ute thefts of cattle. He wrote that, "most of the depredations were committed from absolute necessity when in a starving condition." Carson fed the Ute corn and wheat and begged to know from his superiors, "to what extent I may go in supplying their wants, for if the Government will not do something for them to save them from starving, they will be obliged to Steal."[13]

Far from the opinions of those unfamiliar with Kit Carson that he hated Indians, he pled with the government on their behalf, stating that "[h]umanity as well as the plighted faith of our government demands [that the government take a hand in feeding them]." His opinion extended to the Jicarilla who he found to be in a similar starving condition. Though later, when the peace had been breached, he would recognize the necessity to "chastise" the Indians severely before they could be made to respect treaties, Carson felt that both sides needed to live up to their plighted faith and that the US government should act toward the Indians with humanity.[14]

In 1854, of the several depredation claims filed, the government allowed four claims against the Jicarilla under Sumner's Treaty of July 1, 1852. The claimants swore that the depredations had taken place in May, July, August, October, November, and December, but not during the earlier part of the year. In March 1854, soldiers attacked a peaceful Jicarilla village and put the tribe to flight. Thereafter, raiding began anew. Despite starvation and the broken government promises of Governor Lane's unratified treaty of 1853, during the early part of 1854 the Ollero Jicarilla were not raiding. Trouble arose over an incident between the Llanero and Watrous's herdsmen.[15]

On or about February 10, 1854, a group of Jicarilla Apaches visited Watrous's ranch on the Mora and insulted his herdsmen. On February 14, Lieutenant David Bell rode south from Fort Union six miles to the Mora, the cold north wind at his back. He rode through a valley five miles broad framed by piñon-topped hills where snow lay in patches of shade. To his right in the distance visible through ragged clouds glistened the snow-capped Sangre de Cristo. To his left beyond the hills, the southern reach of the Gallina Mountains, were the broad, endless, flat plains of the Llano Estacado. Beside him were his bugler and guidon bearer. The guidon of Company H flapped listlessly in the cold air. Behind them came thirty more men of the company dressed in motley. They wore parts of blue uniforms topped with military caps, Mexican straw hats, or fur. They wore heavy coats in a variety of styles from blanket capote to buffalo. At Watrous's ranch they stopped and Tipton, the rancher's son-in-law, joined them along with a Mexican who would serve as guide. The Mexican showed them the trail of the Llanero.

They went east toward the Canadian River, the haunt of the Llanero Jicarilla. At night, they warmed themselves by fires, their sabers and musketoons clanking by day to announce their presence on the prairie. As they rode they startled deer, antelope, and wild turkey. The prairie was flat, treeless, and brushless, covered in tall grass brown with the season, giving the impression that a man on horseback could be seen twenty miles away. He could be if he was careless, but a man with Indian tracking skill could disappear into the gentle fold of an arroyo. When they came to the Canadian, then called the Red, the land dropped into the abyss of its deep chasm. The ride became difficult as they slid down then climbed up and down through side canyons, always mindful that narrow defiles could conceal an ambush. After a week's hardship, they returned to Fort Union seen by unseen Jicarilla scouts. A scout who knew the Apache's winter camps might have taken them to likely spots. If any cattle had been taken, they should have left a trail even a soldier could follow. Bell was uncertain if any stock had been taken. Maybe this whole frigid ride was about insults offered to Watrous's herdsmen. The lieutenant thought about what Jicarilla insults might include. It probably meant something physical that left bruises. Their colonel thought one pony taken as compensation adequate. Although as anxious for action as any young dragoon lieutenant, Bell was cold and hoped this ride might have put an end to the affair. It didn't.

Despite the seeming lack of villainous activity on the part of the Jicarilla, Colonel Cooke issued new orders on March 1.

> *Head Quarters, Fort Union, N.M.*
> *Sir,*
> *You will proceed tomorrow morning with the efficiently mounted members of C-H 2d Drags, taking fifteen days rations & two days of corn—to make a scout beyond, & down the Canadian river, as far as the "Cinto Mountains" or according to such exigencies as may arise.*
>
> *Repeated small depredations, & insults to struggling citizens are reported—beside the robbery of Mr. Waters, which occasioned your last march, & which you did not succeed in settling with the Indians.*[16, 17]
>
> *Beside the general object of the scout to protect the frontier, you will endeavor to get in your power some important party of these Jicarillas or Utahs & will then compel them to surrender the depredators in Waters' case & any other instances of which you can obtain sufficient information: & have them whipped: & also require the delivery of an equivalent to the losses in ponies.*
> *Respectfully,*
> *Yr. Obdt. Servt.*
> *P.S. Geo. Cooke*
> *Lt. Col. 2d Drags*
>
> *Lt. D. Bell, 2d Drags*
> *Cmdg Co. H*[18]

Lieutenant David Bell was in command of Company H.[19] He could only mount part of his company and had to take members of Company C. He was to take only two days of corn for the horses at a time when spring forage might be scant. The unit was still short of supplies and horses. Colonel Cooke selected Bell from among the officers at Fort Union to lead this mission and made it clear that he was disappointed with the result of the first scout. Cooke reiterated some of the violence of the order that sent Bell out in February. The lieutenant was to whip the depredators, take a Jicarilla leader hostage, and force them to make restitution. This seems severe considering the long period of peace and good behavior. The colonel had effectively told Bell not to come back without having accomplished the mission. Bell would no longer be following a fresh trail, so he was to seize a hostage from the first Jicarillas or Utes that he met. He was not told to investigate, but rather to punish.

On March 2, Lieutenant Bell departed from Fort Union headed north around the Turkey Mountains. Beside him, shivering under his coat, rode Brevet Captain George Sykes, and on the other side Lieutenant Joseph Maxwell, both of the 3rd Infantry, volunteering to serve under Bell's command. Behind them came the bugler and the guidon and thirty men of Companies C and H. North of the Turkey Mountains, the soldiers turned east toward Santa Clara Spring and Wagon Mound, crossing the Canadian River about thirty miles south of the Rock Crossing of the Canadian on the Santa Fe Trail where the canyon was deep.[20] They turned south and rode another fifty miles to the Conchas River.[21] There Lobo Blanco and about thirty of his warriors greeted the noisy cavalcade.[22] Assigning five men to guard the baggage mules, Bell ordered his men into line and moved to parley with the chief.

The lieutenant went forward and, looking down on Lobo, spoke roughly to him in Spanish accusing the Llanero Jicarilla of abusing Watrous's herdsmen.[23] The chief's warriors hearing the rough talk brandished their weapons menacingly. David Bell scanned the horizon nervously. He knew that even seemingly flat terrain could conceal hundreds of warriors. Lobo, a proud Jicarilla, displayed no deference or fear. This bothered the soldier. His men clutched their musketoons.[24]

Lobo Blanco considered his adversary. Even as a child no one had ever spoken to him like this. Children were not scolded or beaten. Adults were entitled to make up their own minds and go their own way. If a leader of a band became overbearing, his followers could easily join a new band. They looked down on Mexicans who were loud and brash, and who beat their children into submission. For all their bluster, Mexicans were subservient, tied to their irrigated fields and unable to easily run from abusive parents or leaders. Since the Mexicans were subservient, the Jicarilla manhandled, mistreated, and laughed at them. Lobo didn't see where his people had done anything wrong, but this lieutenant was behaving in a manner the chief was not accustomed to tolerate. He signaled to his warriors, but there was little need. They knew no one should treat their leader like this.

The chief was bold and defiant, denying the allegations, which he considered to be of no importance in any event. The parley continued at length with each side becoming increasingly tense. Lobo responded haughtily though in even tones. Bell, frustrated, became increasingly loud. The lieutenant demanded that Lobo produce the culprits, so that he could have them flogged. No Jicarilla would ever submit to this. Believing that Lobo Blanco was moving his men into battle formation, Bell reflected on his orders—"take a chief hostage"—"do not fail this time." He signaled to his men to close ranks. He would take Lobo captive.

Lobo, sensing Bell's intentions, sank to one knee and raised his weapon to aim at Bell. The lieutenant leaned forward, spurring his horse so that it knocked the chief sprawling, and he fired his pistol down into the fallen man. The bugler, sensing Bell's danger, fired at Lobo as well, then reeled in the saddle as the chewed bullet of a Jicarilla's fusil took him in the chest. The troopers spurred forward and over the Apaches, firing as they went. Turning their mounts they reloaded in the saddle. At the lieutenant's command, they charged through the Jicarilla line again. They pursued two hundred yards only to discover a deep ravine with steep sides. The soldiers fired a few shots after the Jicarilla, but the range was too great.

Bell knew that entering the ravine was too risky and that Jicarilla reinforcements might be anywhere about. The soldiers withdrew to their original position to tend their wounded and dead. Private William Arnold had been killed in the skirmish, and the bugler and Privates Golden, Steel, and Walker had been wounded—some of them too badly to ride. Glancing around, Bell counted the scattered bodies of five Jicarilla.[25] Lobo Blanco lay nearby pierced by many bullets. When the chief stirred, a dragoon dismounted, picked up a heavy stone, and crushed the Apache's skull.

Near the ravine, a Jicarilla presumed dead raised himself on an elbow and tried to sight his fusil. Seeing this one of the baggage guard with a whoop charged the man, drawing his saber as he went. The trooper split the man's head in twain and in doing so received a shot from the ravine. His head whipped back as his straw hat went flying. Instinctively his horse turned back toward the soldiers. The dead man galloped toward them, blood streaming down his face, falling at the feet of First Sergeant Lawless's mount. Private William Arnold was added to the list of those who had perished.

The casualties reduced the strength of Bell's force, further impeded by the need to care for the wounded. The activity in the ravine indicated that there were Apache reinforcements coming. Bell penciled a quick note and dispatched First Sergeant Lawless, "a famous rider and woodsman," as express rider to Fort Union for assistance at about 2:00 p.m.[26] He required an ambulance and surgeon. Lawless reached the post at about 10:00 p.m., and Post Surgeon John Byrne headed out to the crossing of the Canadian River with an ambulance and ten-man escort mounted on "the best invalid horses."[27] He carried as well verbal orders from Colonel Cooke to Brevet Captain Sykes:

> who with Lt. Maxwell were there present as volunteers, —to call on
> Lt. Bell for a force to protect the large herd of depot cattle, which was
> thought to be in Cañon Largo, on the Canadian. . . .[28]

Sending wounded, dead, and an escort with the surgeon, Lieutenant Bell started out on a new mission. His depleted force arrived at Canyon Largo in time to find the Jicarilla already exacting their first revenge by stealing two hundred cattle from the post contractor grazing them there. Sykes estimated that the Apache had three hundred mounted warriors.[29] A small band of Utes under Chico Velasquez prevented the raiders from stealing the entire herd. A Jicarilla chief had been slain and the Llanero were ready to give up on the broken promises of recent treaties. Most of the Jicarilla and their Ute allies still wanted to maintain the peace.

Years later the Jicarilla recalled the confrontation in which the soldiers killed Lobo Blanco. The story is almost unrecognizable. In 1909, Jicarilla elder Casa Maria, who had been a teenager at the time, recalled the fight, which he probably knew only by word of mouth, this way:

> Long ago, the Jicarilla were camping at Mora. A large band was also
> camping on the Canadian. There were many cattle about there, one
> of which was wearing a bell. This one the Apache killed. They were
> discovered and the American soldiers came, demanding four chiefs.
> The Jicarilla would not give them up. The soldiers rode back and the
> Jicarilla moved their camp to another place. The soldiers came again
> on horseback and demanded four chiefs. Before the fight began, the
> Americans passed about their canteens and drank whisky, becoming
> drunk. They then rode toward the Apache shooting at them. Their fire

was returned, three of the Americans being killed. One Apache had his finger shot off.[30]

On March 8, Colonel Cooke wrote to General Garland saying that he was short horses and men. He could only mount part of one company and speculated that if Lieutenant Bell had had his entire company available, Bell might have made an end to the Jicarilla problem then and there. Bell had followed his instructions with judgment and gallantry and the lieutenant's attack on the Jicarilla was unavoidable.

Again the colonel mentioned numerous depredations by both the Jicarilla and the Ute. These do not appear anywhere else in the record. He found it odd that Chico Velasquez of the Ute came to Bell's protection and aid, since he considered the Jicarilla's Ute allies to be on the warpath and units out of Taos were pursuing one band of Ute. He considered an Indian war to be already upon him and asked if he should meet the threat offensively or defensively, noting in the process that he only had enough men available to serve as escort to mail parties and merchant trains.[31]

Colonel Cooke had sent Bell to pick a fight over depredations and murders not evident in the record of early 1854. But Cooke was steadfast in his version of the facts. A few days later, on March 11, he would refer to Lieutenant Bell's actions as "consequences of numerous petty depredations & warlike tone of these Indians."[32] His actions imply that the colonel was intentionally provoking a war.

On March 12, 1854, Major Nichols wrote to Colonel Cooke on behalf of General Garland:

> I am instructed by the Comdg General to inform you that he has received with lively satisfaction the report of Lieut. Bell, 2d. Drags, giving an account of his triumph over the "Jicarilla Apaches," and will make special report of it to the Comdg. General of the Army. . . .
>
> It is important, at this time, not only to keep open the road by which the mails are carried, but to press these Jicarilla marauders to the last extremity; it is not advisable to patch up a hasty peace with them; talking in the present state of affairs will be of no use. . . .[33]

By March 19, 1854, tensions were escalating. Colonel Cooke wrote from Fort Union that there were believed to be forty-five lodges of Apaches camped three miles from Mora that had arrived five or six days previously "in real or pretended alarm, professing innocence & a desire for peace." He estimated that there might be seventy or eighty men among them.[34] He requested that Major Blake at Cantonment Burgwin send forty-five or fifty mounted troops to watch them since the village of Mora was alarmed at the presence of the Jicarilla.[35]

Lieutenant David Bell wrote from Fort Union about Blake's response to Cooke's request:

> On the evening of the 21st of March Lieut. [John] D[avidson] arrived at Fort Union from Mor[a] where he had left his company, and reported to Col. Cooke for instructions. I was present when he arrived and afterwards during several conversations between him and Col. Cooke in relation to the Indians, their mode of, and ability for war, etc. Col. Cooke and myself occupied the same house and Lt. D. was our guest. He stated that on his way from Cantonment Burgwin to Fort Union, where he had been ordered by Col. Cooke, he met the Apaches in a Cañon between the former place and Mora, that he halted his command and, with Col. Brooks, had a talk with them; he described them as being overwhelmed with fear and protesting that they desired peace, stating also that he had made advantageous dispositions for battle in case they exhibited any signs of insolence or hostility. He also commented upon the miserable quality of their arms, and their mean shrinking deportment, at the same time averring that he was sorry they did not show some signs of hostility, for that if they had he would have "wiped them out." In the same conversation he stated that the number of warriors counted at the time amounted to one hundred and seven.[36]

Bell was offended by Davidson's attitude. He had just fought Lobo Blanco's Llanero and found them cunning warriors. He had achieved a victory and Davidson was, in effect, belittling that fight. But what is most telling in Bell's account was Davidson's desire for an excuse to "wipe them out." In March 1850, Lieutenant John Davidson had participated in the Bloody Island Massacre of Pomo Indians in California.[37] From slaughtering Pomo without any casualties among his own men, Davidson had learned disrespect for Indian fighting capabilities. He had no compunction about slaying women and children and was anxious for combat and dubious glory.

Major Blake thought Davidson was absent at Mora for three days before returning to Cantonment Burgwin.[38] In the remaining days of March, there would be a great deal of traffic over Holman Hill near Mora. Returning to Burgwin, Davidson found that the Apache were no longer at Mora. They had gone westward toward Peñasco and Picuris, an Indian pueblo where they had friends.

General Garland was deeply concerned that the Jicarilla might close the road to Missouri, cutting New Mexico off from civilization. At Colonel Cooke's request, Lieutenant Samuel D. Sturgis came from Albuquerque with sixty dragoons to escort mail and wagon trains on the Santa Fe Trail. In addition to the escort duties, on March 22, Cooke sent Sturgis to the Canadian River to search for stolen cattle. The next day, Lieutenant Bell was sent to the Pecos River on a similar mission. Both failed though somewhat later Sturgis found fourteen of the government contractor's missing cattle taken in the Cañon Largo incident.[39] The Military Department was humming with activity.

Despite the ongoing threat of violence, Major Blake would report that "several of the Indians, one of them their principal chief, the other I think a sub-chief, came into the valley of Taos for the purpose, they stated of going to see the Agent."[40] The chief in question may have been Fleche Rayada, who took Lobo Blanco's place, and the Jicarilla in question were the same forty-five or fifty lodges that had camped near Holman Hill with 107 warriors. Agent Kit Carson wrote to the acting governor of his meeting:

To: Hon. Mr. J. Messervy
Acting Governor and Superintendent of Indian Affairs
Santa Fe, NM

From: Utah Agency
Taos, New Mexico
March 27th, 1854

Sir

I have the honor to report that on the 25th instant I had council with eight Jicarilla Apaches including two of their chiefs at Cantonment Bergwin [sic] and they seem to be friendly and well disposed to all citizens.[41] There are at present about one hundred warriors with their families stationed near Picuris engaged in making earthen vessels. They say they were not engaged in any of the depredations committed on the east side of the mountains and that none of them were engaged in the fight with the Dragoons on Red River, and that they have come over on the west side of the mountains near the settlements, in order to show their friendship and make (ollas) earthen vessels to trade to the Mexicans for provisions, as they are in a starving condition.

I would respectfully recommend the appointment of a special agent to reside among the Jicarilla Apache, and that he be furnished means to procure provisions such as are absolutely necessary for them; and to advise them to desist from committing thefts and robberies. I believe if such a course is pursued the Apaches would soon become quiet and contented. As I said before there are one hundred warriors with their families near Picuris in a starving condition and there is no game in that region by which they can support themselves. The government must either subsist them for the present or allow them to steal.

I am, Sir, Respectfully Your Obedient Servant,
C. Carson[42]

There were more than one thousand Jicarilla Apache. They usually lived in small family groups of forty or fifty people. It was rare for more than that to gather in one place. Alarmed by the hostile actions of the Army, they had gathered in a larger group, "well-disposed to all citizens," in an effort to escape being associated with the band that had confronted Lieutenant Bell and subsequently raided the government beef contractor's herd at Cañon Largo. Agent Carson took their side and defended their intent, imploring the acting governor to feed them.

According to Carson, the Jicarilla claimed not to have been involved in Lieutenant Bell's fight with Lobo. Bell reported that Lobo Blanco had about thirty warriors when they met. So it is likely that none of these people had been involved in that fight. This band of Jicarilla was starving and, if fed, they would remain quiet. If not, they would have to steal to survive. In Taos, Kit Carson met with eight of the Jicarilla, including two chiefs whose people were camped near Peñasco and Picuris.[43] Carson said that these men came along willingly and were not hostages and that there were about one hundred warriors in this group.[44] These then are the same people Davidson encountered at Holman Hill a few days earlier.

Lieutenant Davidson considered the movements of these Jicarilla "suspicious" and sent a party after them. He took two chiefs and another Apache captive.[45] Major Blake thought that the chiefs had better go to Fort Union to Colonel Cooke, and the next morning he set out with the three (or four) Indians, Davidson, and Carson. They remained there for a day or two and talked to Colonel Cooke, who sent them back to Cantonment Burgwin.

Colonel Cooke reported on his visit with the chiefs that Blake had brought to him on March 28:

> *The Apache chiefs, or principal men who came down with Major Blake, are sent back with the bearers of this: —I told them that as long as their band should demean themselves in a friendly & inoffensive manner, they should in no way be held responsible for the band whom we have chastised, and against whom, there are now a squadron of dragoons in the field.*
>
> *And to prevent accidents they must confine themselves to their proper ground, in the vicinity & beyond the valley of Taos; obeying the instructions of their agent.*[46]

At Mora that evening the Jicarilla chiefs, tired of being shuffled about back and forth across the high mountains, quietly parted company with the major.[47] Kit Carson headed for Santa Fe where on March 29, 1854, he was initiated as an Entered Apprentice Freemason. He visited Acting Governor Messervy and got permission to feed the Jicarilla.

Returning to Cantonment Burgwin at three o'clock in the afternoon of the 29th, Major Blake reported that the Indians at the camp near Peñasco were on the move toward the Rio Grande.[48] That evening Blake sent Davidson out to follow and watch the movement of the Apaches, but to avoid if possible bringing on an action and to prevent them from crossing the Rio Grande.[49]

At four o'clock in the afternoon, a column of forty men in blue uniforms and motley outerwear rode west from the log compound known as Cantonment Burgwin. At the head of Company I, 1st Dragoons, rode Lieutenant John Davidson and scout Jesus Silva. Toward dusk they halted at Ranchos de Taos, a church and plaza four miles south of Don Fernando de Taos, to await the arrival of twenty more men and one sergeant from Company F and Asst. Surgeon D. L. Magruder.[50] The combined command set out southward along the Rio Pueblo de Taos to its junction with the Rio del Norte deep in the Rio Grande Gorge. At 11:00 p.m., they stopped for the night at the tiny village called Cieneguilla.[51] Davidson had pushed his troops late into the night concerned that the Jicarilla might cross the del Norte at the Embudo Ford before he could get there.

It was still dark when Sergeants Holbrook and Kent went around kicking bedrolls and waking the men on March 30. The men scrambled to catch and saddle their mounts while one from each squad fetched wood and built fires for coffee and breakfast. At first light, the lieutenant sent Jesus Silva and two men to reconnoiter the Embudo Ford. First Sergeant Holbrook sent a corporal and Private Edward Maher to accompany the scout.[52]

They were soon out of sight of the soldier camp. About two miles down the road, far up the canyon his scouts spotted a haze of smoke from many fires that smudged the sky. Maher was sent to tell the lieutenant.

Davidson, with troops I and F, started down the road Silva had taken toward Embudo. He would block the ford. If they hadn't already, the Apache would never cross and perhaps he'd get his shot at glory by wiping them out as he'd told Colonel Cooke and Lieutenant Bell. Maher arrived riding hard with the report from Silva. The private pointed toward the smoke. Davidson saw it. He pointed, then set out his guidon following him and the column following the guidon. They veered off the road to the left along the old trail between Cieneguilla and Picuris. The clanking horde rode to the drumming of hundreds of hoof beats from the riverside deep into the mountains through piñon pine and juniper into the deep canyon of the Agua Caliente where the first sunlight of day would not break until nearly noon. The trail grew darker as piñon gave way to tall ponderosa pine that hid the narrow strip of blue sky overhead. Davidson sent a corporal and a few men ahead to scout for signs so that they would not be surprised in the canyon bottom.

Corporal Burns was back quickly with a report.[53] Davidson threw up his right arm and the column halted. Looking down at the canyon floor, the sign was unmistakable. Many hooves of unshod ponies had churned the ground. The lieutenant had found his Apaches.[54] The lieutenant spurred his horse forward and the long column began to move again. They rode on in silence, trees closing in, absorbing every sound from the otherwise noisy parade. Taking their cue from the lowering forest, the soldiers spoke in hushed whispers if at all.

The Jicarilla had laid out their camp on a narrow ridge that extended level from the mountain for more than two hundred steps. Sixty tepees were pitched among tall pine trees on a strip of land barely fifty steps wide that dropped off steeply into canyons on both sides. Thin trails of smoke rose from the cook-fires. Two large piles of wood hid "green" pots within ready to be fired. As the sun rose over the mountain, people finished their meager breakfast. Two deer and a sheep bought with money from the black pots they had already fired and sold did not go far among 250 people. That morning the women were already on their knees curing the deer hides and making pottery for sale. Chief Chacon of the Ollero was away from camp and Pacheco was the senior leader present.

When Chief Pacheco heard the approach of Davidson's column and received the report of their arrival from one of his warriors, he ordered the women and children to retreat into the mountains and called his warriors to him. From around the village and up the mountainside, one hundred warriors responded to their chief's call.[55]

As an eerie cry echoed high above the soldiers like an eagle or a Valkyrie, First Sergeant Holbrook turned in the saddle and called out, "Look out, men! That's the war whoop and now we've got to fight. We're in it now!"[56] The sergeant glanced at his watch, an old habit from writing military reports. It was 8:00 a.m.

Farther back in the column, Private Strowbridge heard the strange cry and swiveled his head from side to side, then looked above expecting an attack from the sky. Beside him an old soldier smirked grimly. "Better cap your piece, lad." He turned in his saddle and spoke to those behind as he reached into his pouch for a percussion cap. "Cap your pieces, lads. We're in for it."[57]

Private Maher vividly recalled that in the next few moments as a man dressed like an Indian stepped out on the ridge above and beckoned with his hand, saying in "as good English as I could speak, 'Come on, we are ready for you.'... I had the impression at the time that the man who said come on &c. was a white man."[58] But when Maher turned to the man beside him, Private Null, to ask him to confirm what the man had said Null reported having seen and heard nothing.

At the head of the column, Lieutenant Davidson barked orders to advance up the slope toward the Jicarilla camp, and the soldiers spurred their horses. Any semblance of order soon broke down as they dodged to and fro among the trees and as horses slid backward knocking those beside and behind askew. Lieutenant Davidson gave the order to dismount and the men continued up the hill drawing their mounts by the reins until the horses refused to go any farther. The lieutenant then gave the order to the men to turn their steeds over to the "number fours," the horse holders. Leaving the surgeon behind in charge of a fourth of his command, Davidson divided his men into two platoons led by Sergeants Holbrook and Kent. They advanced as skirmishers, spread out in loose order, and not as a compact force.[59]

On the lieutenant's right, Sergeant Kent ordered his men forward. The two columns advanced soon losing cohesion and sight of each other in the pine forest. The men although in good shape gasped and staggered and stopped to catch breath.[60] Finally, some of the soldiers arrived on level ground crowded with the conical tepees of the Jicarilla. Small fires smoldered here and there. An old couple sat grinning by the entrance to a lodge. No one else was in sight.

Then, somewhere in the camp a shot rang out.[61] A brief flurry of shots followed. Sergeant Kent fell dead at the feet of his men. They raised their weapons and fired at the only targets in sight, the old man and woman sitting peacefully by a tepee. The firing stopped briefly.[62]

From the depths of the canyon, Dr. Magruder's cry was heard. "They're stealing the horses!"

Lieutenant Davidson responded instantly, leading his men down the hillside back to the horse holders. He signaled to the sergeants leading his platoons and noticed that Kent was down. "Leave him. We'll come back for him."[63]

The men tumbled and leapt down the hillside as Apaches fired guns and arrows from hidden positions along their flanks. Beside Bronson a man fell, the feathers of an arrow protruding from his chest, its point from his back. Bronson thought him dead. Beside him another man called out, "Leave him."[64]

In the hollow where they had left the horses, the lieutenant gave instructions while the doctor tended to the wounded. He had his men form a circle around the "number fours" who continued to hold the remaining horses. A horse, stricken by an arrow high in the neck, screamed, reared, and fell dead. There was no place for the horse holders to go where the stock would be entirely safe.

In 1796 a Spanish officer, Cordero, had described Apache tactics saying, "they place ahead of time an ambush in the location most favorable to them. They then send some fast Indians to draw away the people by stealing some animals and cattle; the people go out to pursue them, and they attack them suddenly, making a bloody butchery."[65] There was no sense in which the Jicarilla camp was chosen ground favorable to an ambush and no one led Davidson to leave his horses in a hollow unfavorable to defense. Lieutenant Bell would later write, "This was the most unmilitary as well as the most exposed order possible—it could not be expected that a display of numbers would intimidate the Indians while a large mark was thus presented to their concentrated fire. This is no labored scientific deduction. A non-commissioned officer who would not have appreciated it upon the ground should have been reduced for incapacity."[66]

Far from having been ambushed, Lieutenant Davidson conducted an attack on a peaceful camp on ground and in a manner highly unfavorable to success. The Jicarilla defended themselves. Lieutenant Bell wrote: "[N]ow was to be fulfilled the prediction about 'wiping them out.' It is at least doubtful who fired first—but what matters it? —was not the advance upon the camp in a hostile attitude a bona fide attack? Nobody would doubt it practically if his position was that of the Indians and Lt. D. would have been one

In the Jicarilla camp at Cieneguilla, the terrain drops off steeply on both sides. There is little room for a large camp. AUTHOR PHOTO

of the last to do so. If he had been under the command of almost any officer other than Maj. Blake he would have been tried for disobedience of orders."[67]

Holbrook and the sergeant from F Troop went about calming the men, telling them, "Don't fire until you're sure of your target. Save your ammunition. We've only got what you're carrying." Between them the lieutenant and the remaining sergeants brought the men into order in a poor position. There was a lull broken by the occasional shot or arrow from hidden Indians.

On the upcanyon side there was sudden activity. Indians darted from tree to tree. The soldiers fired and then scrambled to reload in a haze of sulfurous, stinking, eye-burning smoke. The Apaches had charged, moving closer while the soldiers reloaded. And then they disappeared again into hollows in the ground, behind trees.

Suddenly they were darting from tree to tree again. Now and then a triumphant trooper would cry out, "I hit one! Did you see him fall?" In response a dozen musketoons would fire and the smoke would grow thick between the trees further concealing the Apache. Out among the trees and haze, an unscathed warrior would crawl away unseen to a new position. The soldiers thought they had killed many, but only two Apaches died that day.

As attacks came, Davidson moved his men from one side to the other as the need arose. The soldiers moved to aid their comrades, firing while the first group reloaded. Another lull followed and dragged on. Sergeant Holbrook looked at his watch. It had been twenty minutes since the last attack.

A voice called out. "They're over here!" as Indians darted between cover on the downcanyon side. Holbrook called out again, "Steady boys. Don't fire till you have a clear target!" Even though Apache arrows and bullets wounded both men and livestock, the men remained calm. Their fire was disciplined as they'd been taught and as their sergeant now instructed. The doctor moved about to tend the wounded while Sergeant Holbrook crawled to his lieutenant's side.[68]

Time plays games with men in tense situations. Some thought they remained at the horse holders' hollow on the hillside for twenty minutes. Davidson thought he fought there for more than three hours. He was close to panic thinking himself surrounded by three hundred warriors with ammunition running low. He had to get out of this spot. If they ran out of ammunition, they would all die. It is unlikely that the soldiers stayed at this position more than an hour, and they probably did not even stay that long.

Trooper Strowbridge spoke of his lieutenant's courage in this tight spot and of a vocal exchange with the surgeon. Crouched behind cover of fallen trees, Dr. Magruder tended the wounded. He called out to the lieutenant. "Davidson, for God's sake, get down! You're making yourself a target!"

Lieutenant Davidson was calm and in control, standing—not hiding or seeking cover. He was giving his men confidence by exposing himself to enemy fire. "Doctor, I'm doing what my duty demands."[69]

The Indians tried them on all sides. Men thought they saw Apaches fall, but the dead bodies disappeared miraculously. Most of the time the soldiers caught only fleeting glimpses of the Jicarilla surrounding them. Ammunition became a concern. They had only what was in their ammo pouches—forty rounds of musketoon buck and ball, and twenty rounds for the single-shot muzzle-loading horse pistol.

Panic can come on suddenly triggered by any of a hundred things: being splattered with the blood of a man nearby, realizing that you are low on ammunition, having a bullet pass nearby. Davidson looked toward the canyon bottom. He saw a small knoll 150 yards away. His men might be able to defend themselves from this bit of high ground. He ordered his men to make the move. Lieutenant Bell says that he panicked and cried out, "Mount and save yourselves!"[70] Soon after he regained his composure because, although frightened, the men stopped at least briefly at the knoll and, seeing the men in the rear in difficulty, Davidson ran back and directed a rear guard action to slow the enemy while his dragoons escaped to the hill. He and a handful of dragoons charged the Apache and drove them back.[71]

Once the soldiers reached the knoll, Davidson discovered that they were exposed to enemy fire from all sides.[72] Finding the position entirely dominated—there was higher ground within range of Jicarilla weapons all around—the unit continued up the far wall of the canyon.

The historical and archaeological record can take us only so far. Lieutenant Bell, who was not there but who talked to soldiers who were soon after, says Davidson panicked and translated that panic to his men with his order to save themselves. The archaeological record shows that the men were calm at the hollow and dropped very few percussion caps. Thereafter their panic shows as they dropped many more than they fired. Two years later, newly promoted Captain Davidson conducted the court of inquiry into his actions. He selected and questioned the witnesses. Not surprisingly, those selected spoke of his courage. No two of the witnesses gave the same account of events, but that too is not surprising.

His actions were reprehensible not for cowardice alone but for attacking a peaceful Jicarilla camp on ground highly unfavorable to an assault. His

In the Jicarilla camp at Cieneguilla looking toward the ridge where seventeen of Lieutenant Davidson's men died in 1854. AUTHOR PHOTO

misuse of the ground led to the death of twenty-two soldiers. The Jicarilla's acts of self-defense led to a war they did not want and eighteen months of pursuit and battle. The Apache were beaten into the dust over the vainglorious acts of a lieutenant who thought them an easy target.

Half a mile to the north and hundreds of feet above the men on the knoll was a saddle leading to Tierra Amarilla Canyon, the next canyon to the north. Davidson ordered his men up the canyon side. They mounted the wounded on the remaining stock. There were not enough mounts for all. On the open ground of the saddle Davidson thought he would have good fields of fire and the Jicarilla would be unable to approach closely enough to make their weapons effective.

Lieutenant Davidson led his men up the hill. They were a ragtag bunch. Some were mounted on horses, a well man behind one that was wounded holding his fellow in the saddle. Others were on foot, many bleeding clinging to saddle straps hoping the horse would drag them up the hill. Still others tried to drag horses up the slope by the reins. A few clung to their musketoons.

Halfway up the hill, gasping for breath in the thin air, Davidson halted. Dr. Magruder continued to advance up the hill.

The lieutenant called out, "Doctor, stay with the command."

Magruder continued his climb seeming not to notice and some of the men went with him.

The lieutenant called out again, "Halt!" And the two companies came to a halt to catch their breath. The doctor continued on his way.

"Doctor, for God's sake halt!"

The doctor finally paused in his climb.

"Doctor, I lost some of my non-commissioned men and I have no other officers. Will you help me to take charge of these men?"

He nodded that he would.[73]

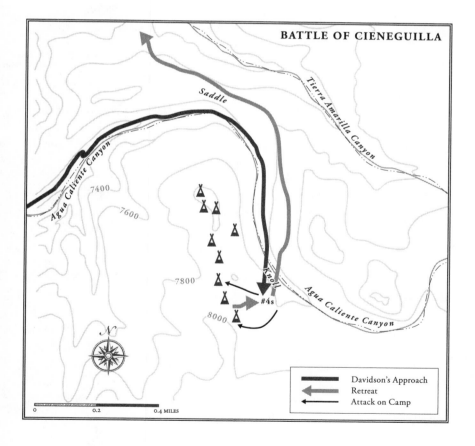

Halting to catch his breath, Lieutenant Davidson noticed that the Apache were also climbing the canyon side to his right and left. They were taking the high ground above the saddle. Starting out again with his men strung out ahead of him and behind as well, struggling to reach the saddle, he pushed on.

Reaching the divide between the two canyons, Davidson looked behind him at Agua Caliente Canyon, ahead another canyon. Later he learned it was called Tierra Amarilla. Away to his left and far below was the Rio Grande. They'd be safe there he hoped. Frustrated by the terrain, perhaps the Jicarilla would depart. His command would only really be safe if they could make it to the River Road three miles away. From there Ranchos de Taos was nearby. They could send for help and for ammunition. On left and right the wooded ridge rose above him. No sooner had they reached the presumed safe haven than the Apache struck.

The Jicarilla came on from all sides. The clear fields of fire offered little advantage. There were too many covered and concealed routes by which the Indians could approach. They were masters of using terrain to conceal themselves. Desperate fighting continued for fifteen minutes. Men and horses fell. The Apache were everywhere. And then there was a lull.

Taking advantage of the pause in the action, Davidson organized his men to move along the ridge toward the River Road. He'd have to defend on all four sides while keeping those too badly wounded to fight safe in the center. This greatly reduced the firepower he could bring to bear on any side. They hadn't gone far before the Jicarilla attacked again.

Strowbridge's horse fell dead almost on top of him. He started to remove saddle and tack from the horse's body as he'd been taught, but his sergeant ordered him to leave it. A soldier saw an Indian leading off one of the dragoons' horses and fired his revolver at him. The Apache followed dodging from tree to tree, cover to cover. The unit would move ahead a few paces, then seek cover, and fire on the Indians. Panicking the soldiers began dropping more percussion caps. Strowbridge saw Private Winter of F Troop rise and fire his revolver at an Indian only to fall dead an instant later.

Private Newhand squatted beside Strowbridge seeking cover behind a tree. A bullet passed through both of his legs as he squatted there.[74] Arrows fell around the soldiers like rain. The ground was covered as if it had snowed arrows. The trees looked like hedgehogs. Lieutenant Davidson was hit but continued in command, ignoring his pain. Strowbridge looked up and saw an arrow protruding from his officer's back. Corporal Dempsey approached the officer and pulled the arrow out.

Strowbridge saw Sergeant Holbrook walking along. "Private, find me a horse. I'm shot and can't go further afoot." Strowbridge did and the sergeant tried three times to mount. He couldn't hoist himself up. As the sergeant turned, the private saw two arrows protruding, one buried nearly to the fletching. Blood flowed freely. The sergeant fell over backwards and died.

In an effort to move faster, the lieutenant called on all who could to mount, taking the wounded with them. One man staggered along holding onto the stirrup of a mounted soldier. He fell and still held on, being dragged until finally he let go. They descended from the ridge and the Apache did not follow.

The soldiers were unaware that the Jicarilla had broken off the pursuit. They only knew that some were out of ammunition and others had but one or two rounds left. They knew another attack could come at any time. Seventeen of their fellows lay dead along the ridge. Twenty-two in all had fallen since they descended from the village. Thirty-six of those who yet lived were wounded.[75] Another Apache assault would take them all.

Behind them were weapons they could not carry, dead men, dead horses, and all of the dragoons' equipment. A few men may have clung to life after their comrades thought them dead. Kit Carson found them with their skulls crushed.

Reaching the road and the river, Davidson sent an express rider to Cantonment Burgwin for wagons and help. The man sent was wounded, in pain, and it was difficult for him to ride. He would bring help to his comrades at Ranchos de Taos. Lieutenant Davidson mounted his men as best he could with the few remaining horses. Wounded men rode double with the very few who weren't wounded. About 11:00 p.m. they arrived at the ranch of George Gould in Ranchos de Taos.

Behind them lay twenty-two dead dragoons. Of those who made it to the ranch at least twenty-three were wounded. Some sources say thirty-six of the remaining thirty-eight were wounded.[76] There can be no doubt that the fight was unnecessary, an unwarranted assault on a peaceful village. It was a debacle for the military, the result of incompetent use of the terrain by Lieutenant Davidson and a brilliantly handled defense by Chief Pacheco. For the next year and a half, the Army—bent on revenge—hounded the Jicarilla until they were no longer an effective fighting force.

The Apache fled across the Rio Grande leaving a rear guard and word that they had lost only two warriors. They disappeared into the San Juan Mountains. Kit Carson, their Indian agent, served as a scout, leading Colonel Cooke to the Jicarilla camp at Ojo Caliente where they fought a battle.

Afterward Carson called for a just treaty to be made with the defeated Indians. Acting Governor Messervy, in his capacity as acting superintendent of Indian Affairs, wanted no part of it. As to the cause of the war, Carson wrote: "The Apaches about Taos were driven to war, by the actions of the officers and troops. . . ."[77]

On April 12, 1854, Carson wrote to Acting Governor Messervy that it "would be best for them to be sent for, and a fair and just treaty made with them. . . ."

The next day Messervy replied:

> [Y]ou will see that war actually exists between the United States and the Jicarilla Apache Indians and that it was commenced by the Indians themselves. I can not under any circumstances make peace with these Indians, much less make overtures to them.[78]

In the summer of 1854, with the war against the Jicarilla raging, Governor David Meriwether, who had been predicting a war with Chacon's people that never came, and who had done nothing to prevent it, now felt vindicated and happy that he could blame it on Governor Lane. He wrote:

> the Utahs are probably the most difficult Indians to manage within the Territory. As for the Jicarillas, no other single band of Indians has committed an equal amount of depredations upon, and caused so much trouble and annoyance to the people of this Territory as the Jicarillas . . . whenever there is any mischief brewing, invariably [the Jicarillas] have a hand in it.[79]

On December 27, 1854, Lieutenant David Bell, who had been reassigned to the just formed First Cavalry Regiment at Fort Leavenworth, wrote a lengthy letter to Lieutenant Williams in New Mexico:

> You speak of Lieut. W. Davidson of your Regt. and his course in relation to his fight etc. Now as Davidson is an officer of your regiment and I am perfectly willing that he should see anything I write about him and if you think proper, I am perfectly willing that you should show him my letter, for I would scorn to say anything behind his back that I would not repeat to himself, and vindicate in the proper

manner. As this is a subject affecting a member of your regiment I will give you my opinion in full, which however you will find to be that of officers at your own post.[80]

He went on at length, describing the battle at Cieneguilla in detail, and accusing Lieutenant Davidson of military incompetence, cowardice in the face of the enemy, and of starting a war with peaceful Indians. A year later, Davidson demanded a court of inquiry. The letter stood alone as the prosecution or accusation. As noted earlier, Davidson conducted his own defense, calling only witnesses of his choosing and asking all the questions. The court was concerned only with the accusation of cowardice and cleared him of that charge. That accusation alone was probably untrue.[81]

Having gotten twenty-two good men killed at a cost to the enemy of only two warriors and having started a war with an otherwise peaceful tribe, Davidson went on to eventually be promoted to general. If anyone in the Jicarilla camp had called down, "Come up if you want a fight," and this is certainly doubtful, could this be considered a gauntlet tossed and a challenge to honor that must be answered? Even in the 1850s, Lieutenant David Bell did not think so.

Major Blake and Lieutenant Davidson were very different in temperament. Blake was not very popular among the men, causing "continuous dissension against [his] capricious and autocratic ways accentuated by drinking on the post."[82] He was an alcoholic and very loose with discipline, especially self-discipline. A little more than a year after Cieneguilla, Blake's battered Company F would riot and mutiny, as Blake tried to settle insubordination with fisticuffs.[83] In June 1856, he would face court-martial. Davidson, on the other hand, who did not drink to excess, was apparently popular with his men, and thought to be a man of courage. He was dedicated to duty and to discipline. Soon after his arrival he leveled charges against Major Blake.[84] Shortly after the fight at Cieneguilla, they were dropped in what Bell believed was a quid pro quo. According to Johnson et al.:

These charges referred to swearing, cursing and abusing noncommissioned officers, allowed half the garrison to be drunk and riotous and unfit for service, taking prolonged absences from the fort under false pretenses, and falsification of records concerning those absences, and all had been leveled against Blake after the time Davidson had arrived at Cantonment Burgwin.[85]

These charges are undoubtedly the ones that Lieutenant Bell referred to in his letter:

Last winter Davidson preferred charges against Major Blake—they were of a very grave nature. A few days after the affair at Cieneguilla the Major made some remark to the effect that D. had done as well as could be expected, when D. instantly offered to withdraw the charges although if true Maj. B. had signed a false certificate etc.[86]

Lieutenant Bell accused Davidson of colluding with Blake, withdrawing the charges against the major. In exchange Major Blake did not prefer charges against Davidson over the debacle. "Davidson acknowledged himself that Maj. could have ruined him with a single word—hence the spirit of mutual concession."

Governor Meriwether and Acting Governor Messervy had systematically failed to provide promised as well as customary gifts to the Jicarilla, believing that it would lead to a war they could blame on former governor Lane. The Apache, although suffering and starving, did not resort to war or major depredations. When Agent Kit Carson saw the Jicarilla in March 1854, they were starving but still peaceful. Colonel Cooke sent Lieutenant Bell out to chastise the Jicarilla excessively over a few cows. This led to a small fight in which Lobo Blanco, formerly thought of as trustworthy and a peace-chief, died. Most of the tribe remained at peace distancing themselves from those who had fought with Bell. Finally, Lieutenant Davidson

Colonel Philip St. George Cooke as commander of the 2nd Dragoons sent Lieutenant David Bell against the Apache and was in command at the Battle of Cieneguilla. A famed Indian fighter, he went on to be a Union general in the Civil War. Carton Studio about 1861. COURTESY PALACE OF THE GOVERNORS PHOTO ARCHIVES (NMHM/DCA), 9854 attacked a peaceful camp where the people were attempting to earn a meager living by making pottery. He attacked incompetently, handing the Jicarilla an overwhelming victory in a very successful defense of their camp. This disgrace led to eighteen months of pursuit and harassment.

As one historian wrote: "The Battle of Cieneguilla marked a high point of Jicarilla resistance, as from that hour the army marked them for doom."[87]

Although it marked a high point in resistance, it was a war they had attempted to avoid. The Apache who camped at Mora attempted to disassociate themselves from the Llaneros who fought Lieutenant Bell. They were Olleros under a different chief. They came over the pass to the Embudo Mountains near Picuris at a site where they collected clay and mica for making pots for sale. Governor Meriwether's anticipation of a war set the military on edge more than any overt action of the Jicarilla.

There was barely room on the ridge for sixty lodges. Both Kit Carson and Lieutenant Davidson had counted about one hundred warriors among them. If we assume one adult warrior per five people, there would have been five hundred people camped along the ridge. That means that more than half of the tribe was somewhere else, perhaps out near the Canadian River where the trouble started.

Three miles from the River Road, they did not lure Lieutenant Davidson into their camp. He chose to attack their camp. They didn't lure him into a favorable spot for an ambush. He blundered into it on his own. The challenge from the camp "come up if you want a fight" is recalled differently either delivered in perfect English, in Spanish, or in broken English. Perhaps there was no challenge, though it really doesn't matter. Davidson violated his orders not to bring on an action.

Lieutenant John Wynn Davidson killed California Indians at the Bloody Island Massacre. In 1854, he attacked a peaceful Jicarilla camp in violation of his orders. The Jicarilla counterattack left twenty-two of his men dead and as many as thirty-six wounded out of the sixty dragoons who rode with him. The one hundred or so Jicarilla warriors who fought him suffered only two casualties. WIKIMEDIA COMMONS

Chapter 12

In 1854, New Mexico Territory was isolated, cut off from the United States by 950 miles of lonely Santa Fe Trail part of which the Jicarilla controlled. Goaded into defending themselves by Lieutenant John Davidson, the Apache were in a war they didn't want, while Governor Meriwether gloated over the vindication of his Indian policy. That policy may be summarized as: My predecessor fed them without authorization from the government, so when I stop feeding them, there will be a war and it will be William Carr Lane's fault. The Jicarilla forded the Rio Grande and disappeared into the San Juan Mountains, a high country not yet populated by whites or Mexicans.

Years later Casa Maria recalled from his childhood the aftermath of the Battle of Cieneguilla:

> *[At Cieneguilla, f]our of the Apache were killed. They took all the arms of the soldiers and the money from their clothes, a large sum. . . . From there the Apache moved to the west side of the Rio Grande. From there they moved to El Rito and afterward to Vallecitos.*[1] *A company composed of Mexicans, Pueblos, and soldiers, followed them, shooting at the Indians who moved their camp without anyone being killed. They camped by Coyote from which place turning back they went to Conejos.*[2]

The news of the battle at Cieneguilla spread like a dust storm through the military posts of New Mexico. At Fort Union, Colonel Cooke anticipated orders from Santa Fe and, pulling together as much of his command as he could, headed to Taos, where a company of militia spies and guides was already being raised in expectation of the army's need:

On the 31st of March 1854, while at Fort Union, I received news from Major Blake, commanding at Camp Burgwin, of a severe action between a detachment of the First Dragoons, under Lieutenant Davidson, and the Apaches, in which the dragoons had "lost from thirty-five to forty dead, and brought in seventeen wounded men." The despatch reached me about nine o'clock in the morning, and by noon of the same day I started with all the troops that could be prudently drawn from the fort, and comprising a detachment of First Dragoons, Lieutenant Sturgis, and Company H of the Second Dragoons, Lieutenant Bell. The entire command had, within sixteen hours, returned from marches of 200 miles, part of the distance through severe snowstorms. Closely following the mounted men came Company D, Second Artillery (serving as riflemen), commanded by Brevet Captain Sykes, Third Infantry.[3]

Kit Carson heard the news while in Santa Fe, where he was being initiated into the Freemasons. He hurried home to Taos. Years later he recorded what occurred in his biography:

On the 4th day of April, 1854, Lieut. Colonel Cooke, 2nd Dragoon, organized a command for the purpose of pursuing the Indians and giving them such chastisement as they deserved. He employed a company of forty Pueblo Indians and Mexicans under command of Mr. James H. Quinn as Captain, and John Mostin, as his Lieutenant.[4, 5] *They were men in every way qualified to perform the service for which they were employed, and that was to proceed some distance in advance of the main body and act as spies and keep the trail of the Indians. I accompanied the march as principal guide.*[6]

Colonel Philip St. George Cooke, 2nd Dragoons, assembled his command rapidly at Fort Union and brought it across the mountains to Taos. Only "efficient" dragoons were mustered for the expedition, meaning that they still had horses that might be able to walk a few more miles. Cooke left Fort Union with ninety-two *beau sabres* and arrived at Taos on April 2 with eighty-eight, the balance having become infantry along the way. In Taos, Cooke waited a day for his foot soldiers to catch up, joined twenty-two men of Company F, 1st Dragoons to his force, and learned that he had accurately anticipated General Garland's orders. In Santa Fe, Garland was aghast. When, at Taos, his orders caught up with Cooke, the general's instructions were to "humble them [the Jicarilla] to the dust."[7]

On April 10, 1854, Acting Governor Messervy made an official proclamation of war against the Jicarilla Apache:

> *Whereas the tribe of Indians, known as the Jicarilla Apaches, have made war upon, and commenced hostilities against the government of the United States; And Whereas, the Executive of their Territory has been informed that divers persons hold constant intercourse with the said tribe of Jicarilla Apaches, in violation of the laws of the United States, and also furnish them with lead, powder, and other means to carry on war, and thereby give aid and assistance to the enemy; Therefore, I, William S. Messervy, acting Governor and Superintendent of Indian Affairs, for the Territory of New Mexico, warn and forbid all persons, either Americans or Mexicans, Pueblo, or other Indians, now at peace with the United States, to hold any communication whatever with said tribe of Indians, directly or indirectly, but to abstain from all intercourse with them. . . .[8]*

Six days earlier, on April 4, shivering with the cold, the long column under Cooke had already headed north out of Don Fernando de Taos. The peaks still glistened white and even on the lower hills the drifts stood three and four feet deep.[9] Twenty Pueblo Indians on foot led the way, followed by Captain James H. Quinn and the fifteen mounted men of the Spies and Guides Company who had been recruited locally. Fearing that the Jicarilla had left a very strong rear guard around the Embudo Ford deep in the Rio Grande Gorge, they went north to Arroyo Hondo.[10] Behind them came Kit Carson and the straight-backed Colonel Cooke, tall in the saddle, every inch a dragoon and a soldier. In all, 110 dragoons drawn from several companies of the 1st Regiment of Dragoons under Lieutenant Sturgis and Company H of the 2nd Regiment under Lieutenant Bell made up the force. Their horses had the appearance of having been ridden hard—the animals were scarcer than ever after the loss of the many mounts at Cieneguilla. Captain Sykes came behind on foot leading the riflemen of Company D, 2nd Artillery. He would walk with his men through the entire campaign. The baggage train followed handled by Mexican "trailers," and behind that Mexican vaqueros chased a herd of cattle. The commissary traveled on the hoof.[11]

The Rio Grande del Norte was frigid with the melting snows of spring. Kit Carson recalled the crossing:

The Del Norte River was high, but it had to be crossed. The bed of the river is full of large rocks and, in crossing, the horses would sometimes be only to their knees in the water and then have to step off of a rock. They would be over their backs and would necessarily have some trouble in ascending the next rock.

I took the lead and finally crossed. The troops then commenced their passage and crossed, meeting with no very serious accident more than two or three dragoons were nearly drowned [in helping] to cross the Infantry. The Dragoon horses had to be recrossed for the purpose of getting them [the infantry] over. It was finally done, I crossing and recrossing the river about twenty times. The command had all crossed.[12]

William Messervy was governor during the many months that David Meriwether was away on a trip to Washington. In 1854, as acting territorial governor, he formally declared war on the Jicarilla. When their agent, Kit Carson, suggested that it was time for a peace treaty, he used the declaration of war as a reason that he couldn't participate in a peace treaty. About 1849. COURTESY PALACE OF THE GOVERNORS PHOTO ARCHIVES (NMHM/DCA), 88121

After making the difficult climb on a narrow track ascending from the gorge, they entered through what Cooke called "a very broken and exceedingly precipitous country." The colonel hoped that by making this difficult approach to gain two days' march "upon [the] intricate and designedly difficult wander-ings" of the Jicarilla.[13] The soldiers crossed many canyons and deep ravines traveling through a waterless and grassless land. Men and horses fell behind. To their shame, more dragoons became infantry, as horses failed. There weren't enough pack animals to support the force, nor was the commissary on the hoof large enough, so the men marched on half rations. Carson recalled the courage of Captain Sykes's converted artillerymen:

> *Captain Sykes, of the Infantry, deserves great praise for his conduct on this march. He was in command of the Infantry. He had a horse with him but on which I do not think he mounted during the campaign. He would wade the streams, through mush ice and snow, often for the distance of ten miles. I really believe that by his conduct the courage of his men was kept up. I could not understand how men were able to undergo such hardships.*[14]

Near Servilleta Carson picked up the trail of their quarry and followed it for two more days through mountain, canyon, and deep snow. On April 8, his "spies" had great difficulty in following the trail until they determined that the Jicarilla had doubled back on them. By mid-morning Carson and the spies were climbing a mountain whose northern slope was covered with snow two and three feet deep. At the top, they located a trail through the snow broken by Apaches and crossed three small canyons. Captain Sykes and his infantry followed close behind.[15]

Quinn, commander of the Spies and Guides, descended into the canyon of the Ojo Caliente and came suddenly upon the Indians, finding himself "not over three hundred yards from them." He charged ahead:

> *Carson had always been ahead with the Spy Company and it being no time to swap knives we charged hard on to the left with the Mexicans and myself to the right with my Pueblos. We took the Camp but the [Jicarilla] having taken possession of the rocks which surrounded the Camp three fourths of a circle returned our fire with spirit.*[16]

Somewhere on the slope behind him, Colonel Cooke looked down on the scene with a keen soldier's eye for terrain. Below him, in a deep chasm, the river twisted around a point of land. The enemy camp stood beside the stream, now a raging torrent in spring flood. "Precipitous crags" in the narrow defile blocked any attempt at a flanking maneuver. The Ojo Caliente behind the camp was "almost forbidden by the torrent, which in several channels amidst trees and thickets, rushe[d] four feet deep over rolling rock." Before the camp stood a field of boulders that had tumbled from above and now blocked access to the Indian village except along its flanks. Jicarilla warriors occupied this boulder field, entertaining Captain Quinn's company with a "warm" fire, buying time for their women and children to escape across the stream.[17]

Sykes and the infantry were close behind Quinn's company and Colonel Cooke ordered them into line as skirmishers to make a frontal assault on the enemy position to take pressure off of the "irregulars." During the fighting that ensued at the mound of rocks on which the Jicarilla held a strong position, the Apache killed one infantryman and wounded another. The air was filled with the war cries of soldiers and Indians and with the screams of fleeing women, children, and horses. Acrid sulfurous smoke filled the

She-Zah Nantan, Ahead of His Story, Jicarilla Apache brave in characteristic costume. About 1874. COURTESY PALACE OF THE GOVERNORS PHOTO ARCHIVES (NMHM/DCA), 40212, PHOTOGRAPHY TIMOTHY H. O'SULLIVAN

air from the fire of many guns. Lieutenant Bell with Company H, 2nd Dragoons, passed by the colonel at the gallop, moving "handsomely to the front, through the fire of the enemy." They took up a position in the angle of the cliffs and mountain and brought down a heavy fire on the enemy from above. There was thunder as musketoon dueled with fusil and the weapons the Jicarilla had captured from Davidson's defeated command. Major Blake then came up with his small squadron of dragoons and dismounted, as the horses were unable to operate on the hill of rocks. The soldier's soldier, Philip St. George Cooke, led them in the charge against the enemy only to find the Apache in retreat, driven off by Bell's fire. With fire coming from above and behind and their women and children in flight from the camp, the Jicarilla had withdrawn. The colonel spied the enemy's horse herd and thought to capture it. He ordered Lieutenant Joseph E. Maxwell to come forward with part of the reserve to seize the enemy's horses. Lieutenant Isaiah Moore, 1st Dragoons, passed down to the riverbank and crossed the river entering the woods and low hills on the far side in pursuit of a fleeing enemy. Colonel Cooke described the action:

After we had passed the flank of the rifles and irregulars, we were fired upon from the trees of the high slope, impracticable for a cavalry charge; —I then dismounted the company, & with Lt. Bell, led a charge on foot; —the enemy did not await it, but dispersed with a dropping fire, while pursued a mile further—in the pine forest—until there was no indication of his presence; and the trail, made in the ravine by the horses & women, was run out. I then turned the skirmishers, with a sweep, & scoured the top of the little mountain, back, toward the original ground; and soon after, having descended, found the other troops, —who had all crowned the hill, —had assembled in the open ravine near the river; Lt. Maxwell was later; —he had penetrated the forest with much boldness, —'though forced to dismount, and had intercepted the retreat of some of the enemy, who abandoned three horses which he captured. I then ordered all to retire to the horses at the Indian camp.[18]

Carson recalled that they pursued the enemy on foot until sunset and then returned to the enemy camp for the night.[19] In the Jicarilla camp, the soldiers found four sabers, two musketoons, fifteen new saddles, and various accouterments that the Apache had taken from Lieutenant Davidson's command. In addition, they captured several of the enemy's rifles, twenty-three horses, their lodges, and great quantities of robes, skins, clothing, implements, and provisions. Cooke fed his horses on the Jicarilla's corn and wheat and burned the rest. Already starving, the Apaches were left bereft of clothing, horses, and shelter.

Captain Quinn reported some of the horror that accompanied the enemy's escape:

> Some Indians were drowned in the stream for I saw some go in whom I did not see on the other side though very close—not thirty yards. The stream is a small one but swollen to a Mountain Torrent. Two Indian horses were drowned in crossing and perhaps more. The Spy Company captured a small child in the pursuit which was humanely taken care of and sent to Taos by Major Blake. . . . I was credibly informed and from what I saw afterward believe the Apaches lost seventeen women and children who losing themselves in the flight perished by exposure by snow and hunger.[20]

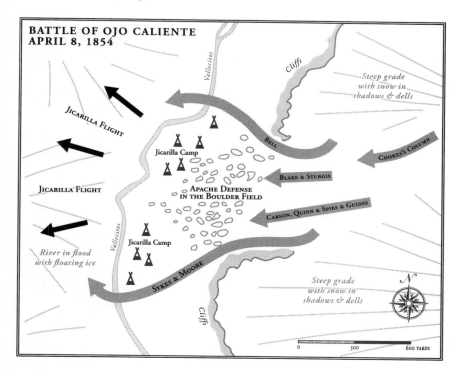

**BATTLE OF OJO CALIENTE
APRIL 8, 1854**

Kit Carson later told Colonel Cooke that five or six of the Apaches had died in the fight and the soldiers had wounded six more. A woman fleeing with a large bundle dropped it as she entered the river and soldiers shot her as she swam, killing her. The bundle contained the baby who would be sent to Taos by Blake.[21] If horses drowned in that torrent, women and children probably did as well.

The Army would pursue the Apache through April, May, June, and July 1854. Unable to rest and unable to hunt, many of the Jicarilla would perish of starvation and exposure. Carson reported:

The morning after the engagement the command started in pursuit of the Indians and followed them for four days through deep snows, and over some of the most rugged, steep and rocky mountains I have ever seen, and finding that the Apaches had separated and gone in different directions, the Col. commanding returned with the Troops to Abiquiien,[22] the nearest settlement, for the purpose of recruiting his animals preparatory to another expedition.[23]

Colonel Cooke reported that Chacon led "77 lodges" of the Jicarilla, that amounting to a force of at least 150 warriors.[24] He noted that all of the enemy's previous camps had been on inaccessible heights except for this one. He concluded that here they had a very strong position with a force greater than his own and thus had intended to bring on a fight and defeat him. Having congratulated himself, he went on to congratulate his officers: [25]

It is scarcely necessary to say that all of the officers exhibited energy and gallantry; and I would thus include Capt. Quinn of the spy company; and Mr. Carson showed his well known activity and boldness. But it would be injustice to pass over the fact that the handsome charge of Lieutenant Bell, —in which the superior instruction and discipline of his company seconded him well, —the fortunate position which he took, penetrating the enemy's line, —had the effect of striking him with panic, & perhaps decided the victory at the first blow. I commend this his second distinguished service under my orders, to the most favorable consideration.[26]

Battlefield at Ojo Caliente. Colonel Cooke came over the ridge where snow was deep in the shadows. Cliffs protected the camp. Jicarilla warriors defended among the rocks at center right. The Vallecitos stream, hidden by trees, was in flood and some Jicarilla drowned. AUTHOR PHOTO

Near Abiquiu soon after the Battle of Ojo Caliente, Major Carleton and a company of 1st Dragoons joined Colonel Cooke. The pursuit continued as they followed the enemy's "horsetracks" through snow two feet deep where the enemy had opened the trail. They were led through forests of aspen and pine prostrated by storm, through bogs where mules sank to their bellies and had to be unpacked. They penetrated the San Juan Mountains to Vallecitos and Canjilon going as far as Las Nutrias.[27] In the valley of the Canjilon, scouts sighted the enemy and Cooke wrote:

On the 11th [April] the indefatigable Quinn, —on the extreme flank of his spies, —caught sight of four of the enemy, on an abrupt hill close to our right, and so gave the alarm that none who saw him doubted they were in force; —I ordered a deployment & disposition for action,

which was performed in an incredibly short time; —the dragoons tak-
ing position at the gallop, and all the troops exhibiting the greatest
alacrity and eagerness; —but the Indians, on foot, escaped like deer,
into the cover of their native fastnesses. . . . the tracks of bare and
diminutive feet left a feeble memorial of its sufferings. . . . Many dead
horses—& some of them had been butchered—marked their retreat;
and signal smokes now, in several directions, and other signs, indi-
cated now that the hard pressed tribe had divided & sought temporary
retreats in the rocky & lofty mountains every where to be seen.[28]

The soldiers turned south following the Rio Chama and pursuing a small
party of Apaches along the Rio Puerco. On April 14, at Abiquiu, Cooke's
force rested—Cooke himself had been suffering from a fever during the entire
campaign. Rest was sorely needed.[29] Thinking the work done, on April 12,
from the Rio Puerco, Carson wrote to Acting Governor Messervy telling
him that the Apache were defeated and it was time to make peace with them:

Having become acquainted with the commencement of the War on the
Apaches about Taos, & accompanied Col. Cooke in his present expedi-
tion, I have to report to you, first, that in my opinion, they were driven
into the war, by the action of the officers & troops in that quarter—
that since they have been attacked, with loss of lives, property, provi-
sions, vigorously pursued through the worst mountains I ever tracked
through, covered with snow:—that their suffering & privations are
now very great, —but that thinking there will be no quarter or mercy
shown them, they will resort to all desperate expedients to escape any
sort of pursuit & they have scattered now in every direction.[30]

Under the circumstances, I will await at Abiquiu, for your con-
sideration of this matter, & decision: —My opinion is that it would be
best for them to be sent for, and a fair & just treaty made with them.
I have no doubt they would be glad to surrender all the government
property which they got possession of, from Lt. Davidson's men.[31]

Messervy, perhaps overcome by the grandiosity of his official declaration
of war against the Jicarilla, responded to Carson:

[Y]ou will see that war actually exists between the United States and the Jicarilla Apache Indians and that it was commenced by the Indians themselves. I can not under any circumstances make peace with these Indians, much less make overtures to them.[32]

On April 14, John Dunn, Carson's able assistant, covering for him at Taos while Carson was in the field, wrote that he had it on good authority that there were sixty lodges of Jicarilla camped in the Raton Mountains and it was they who had fought with Lieutenant Bell along the Canadian River in mid-March. The Olleros, who had not been with Lobo Blanco, had been attacked at Cieneguilla by Lieutenant Davidson.[33]

On April 30, 1854, having received Colonel Cooke's report of the Battle of Ojo Caliente, as the encounter came to be called, General Garland wrote to the commanding general of the Army, Winfield Scott, forwarding the accounts of the fight. In that letter he said:

It is all-important to crush this Band of Pirates. They have too long indulged in murder and plunder to leave a hope of reformation. They do not even pretend to keep good faith in Treaties or promises. Their thorough chastisement will undoubtedly have its effect upon the contiguous Tribes now looking on with deep interest for the result, and will give us assurance of many months of peace.[34]

Those were harsh words for a tribe that had been at peace with the Americans for almost four years and with whom Governor Meriwether, the superintendent of Indian Affairs, knew the United States had not kept faith. His predecessor, Governor Lane, had made promises that the government did not keep. As a result of those failed promises, Lane's successor, Governor Meriwether, had predicted war. Working on his behalf Acting Governor Messervy had declared it.

Colonel Cooke's command rested and recruited at Abiquiu on the Chama River until May 2 when he marched about twenty miles north through the canyons to El Rito. On May 3, he camped at Vallecito. There a fresh company of dragoons, a company of infantry, and forty Mexicans under Captain José Maria Valdez joined him. On May 4 he marched to Los Tusas.[35] The command continued north to the Canejo River where Cooke met with seven Utes who professed great friendship for Americans. They told Cooke that Chacon and the lodges of his immediate family—all afoot—had passed by recently in a starving condition. Among the Utes professing friendship was Blanco, a companion of Chico Velasquez who would be at war with the United States by Christmas.[36]

On May 12, Major William T. H. Brooks brought a relief command out to Rio Colorado to meet Colonel Cooke and his exhausted soldiers.[37] Cooke returned to Taos with part of the command, and Brooks marched against the Indians, going north into the San Luis Valley. He followed what he thought were Jicarilla trails for several days but soon found the country "entirely cut up with trails." He was deep in Ute country and it was impossible to distinguish Ute trails from Jicarilla. On May 15, Brooks gave up the pursuit and returned to Taos.[38]

Christopher "Kit" Carson, seated center, at the Masonic Lodge in Santa Fe with his "brothers" including General James H. Carleton, at Kit's left (right in the photo). 1866. COURTESY PALACE OF THE GOVERNORS PHOTO ARCHIVES (NMHM/DCA), 134000, PHOTO BY NICHOLAS BROWN

Jicarilla elder Casa Maria recalled years later that his band had moved to the east to a place on top of the mountain that might be Fisher's Peak where Major Carleton attacked their camp:

From there they moved eastward to Saikanyediye on top of the mountain. From there they went to the branch of the Arkansas near Pike's Peak and Pueblo. They then moved eastward to a canyon where they mingled with the Ute. They rode down to a place where a Mexican was living, killing all the people that were there. They brought back a scalp and danced with it.[39]

On May 23, 1854, Kit Carson joined Major James Carleton, 1st Dragoons, in pursuit of the Jicarilla.[40] The major led one hundred dragoons and Captain James Quinn's company of irregulars from Taos north into the San Luis Valley to the very slopes of Sierra Blanca, the Jicarilla's sacred peak, and Fort Massachusetts.[41] Carson wrote to Messervy:

Having received information that a party of Jicarilla Apaches, which had been pursued by Major Brooks U.S.A. had crossed the Rio del Norte north of Fort Massachusetts Major Carleton detached Capt. J. H. Quinn with Thirty six volunteers—Mexicans and Pueblo Indians to scour the country and examine the Mosco Pass where it was supposed the Apaches crossed the mountains, and with orders to join him in three days on the Huerfano River.[42]

Carleton and Carson crossed over the Sangre de Cristo Pass to the Huerfano River and the Spanish Peaks. They were soon joined once again by Captain Quinn, who had picked up the trail of thirty Apache lodges, and they followed it toward the southeast and the vicinity of Raton Pass with Quinn and his Pueblo foot soldiers in the lead. Carson wrote:

On the third day after parting we were joined by Capt. Quinn on the Huerfano, who reported that the trail was seen in the Mosco Pass and where Thirty lodges had been encamped about Thirty miles from Fort Massachusetts. The same evening we encamped at one of their stopping places near Maxwell's Pass from which we followed the Trail down on the plain and across the Cucharas to the most northern peak of the Wahatojahs.[43] *Around these peaks the command marched with most astonishing celerity over a very rocky mountainous country, . . .[and] encamped on the Purgatory River. From thence the trail was followed to the vicinity of Fisher's Peak in the Raton Mountains where Major Carleton surprised twenty two lodges of Jicarillas on the evening of the 5th of June—killing a number, and taking all their animals and camp equipage. . . . I have never had the good fortune to travel with a finer command than the officers and troops under Major Carleton, nor never have I seen better marching than was made by them.*[44]

Kit Carson and Major James Carleton had become fast friends, and Carson stood by his friends. When Lieutenant Davidson went before a court of inquiry in 1856, Carson would stand up for him and forget that he had previously said that Davidson had goaded the Jicarilla into war. During that court he would declare the Battle of Cieneguilla an Apache ambush. During the Civil War, Carson would become a colonel of volunteers under General James H. Carleton and on orders from his friend would conduct the round-up of the Navajo and take command of their reservation at Bosque Redondo.

According to Carson as they approached the Raton Mountains they camped for the night, and it was owing to Major Carleton's excellent management that they were able to surprise the Jicarilla the next day. In his autobiography Carson said of the next morning: "I saw a trail that was fresh, informed the Major that, if we met with no accident that the Indians would be found by two o'clock."[45]

Carleton responded, surprised. "Two o'clock? So precise! If we come upon them at two, I will present you with the finest hat to be had in New York City!"[46]

Quinn was sent ahead on foot with three of his Pueblo spies while Carson and Carleton followed close behind. Carson knew that they were bound for an old and favorite Jicarilla camping place, and soon Quinn discovered the horses of the Apache below them on the east side of Fisher's Mesa and about three hundred yards off. Carson crawled forward to a point of rock where he could look down. Below him were twenty-two lodges. He sent a spy who had accompanied him back with the word of the find.[47]

The troops followed, dismounted, marching through brush and timber to keep themselves concealed. The major ordered his men to charge and they descended on the village achieving total surprise. Quinn's report said:

My men were with me, my Pueblos stripped and waiting for the word, the dragoons coming up on the other side single filed when Carson shouted to me to take the ridge over the camp. I ordered my footman to do so and with four of my best mounted men and my twelve indians charged direct for the camp. We shot once and reloaded. . . .[48]

Lieutenant R. Johnston, 1st Dragoons, along with Quinn and three of his men, concealed themselves in the brush. One of these men knew the cry the Apache used when scattered to call the assembly. He gave it now. Two warriors and two squaws soon appeared and the Pueblos shot one and took the others prisoner. The brush was thick and there were many places of concealment. A party of dragoons pursued some of the Indians and their horses. "[Quinn and his men] pursued the [Jicarilla] at full tilt down the mountain and succeeded after a run of about five miles in taking all we had seen but two who dodged us in the bushes."[49] Nothing more could be done. With the Apache scattered, Carleton and his command returned to Taos. Kit Carson wrote to Messervy:

The larger portion of the Jicarilla Apaches it is my opinion, are still on the west side of the Rio del Norte, as we saw no signs of more than Thirty Three lodges that had passed that river; —Twenty two of which were in the fight.[50]

The hat specially made for Kit Carson in New York arrived in Taos sometime later. Inside the band was stamped: "At 2 o'clock, Kit Carson from Major Carleton." Carson proudly pronounced it a fine hat.

On June 28, 1854, word came to Major Nathaniel Macrae, 3rd Infantry, commanding at Fort Union in Colonel Cooke's absence, that Jicarilla Apache raiders had been active near Las Vegas. It was a large party unencumbered by women or children. He sent word to Department Head-quarters in Albuquerque:

Major,

I have the honor to report—that late yesterday I was informed that a party of Jicarilla Apaches had committed depredations in the vicinity of Vegas & then proceeded south. I have every reason to believe this information. The party appears to have been from 25 to 47 in number all mounted—no women.

> *I am Major*
> *Very respectfully*
> *Yr. obdt. Servt*
> *N.C. Macrae*[51]

He then promptly issued orders sending soldiers into the field after what was sure to be a raiding party. Captain George Sykes, 3rd Infantry, was in command of Company D, 2nd Dragoons as well as the squadron and Lieutenant Joseph E. Maxwell, 3rd Infantry, accompanied him commanding Company H, 2nd Dragoons.[52] The regular dragoon officers had been in the field since March and some were still with Carleton, Brooks, and Cooke. Macrae called on two infantry officers to command all of the "efficient" dragoons, that is to say, those that still had horses that were not completely broken down. Macrae ordered his available men into the field and sent the following report to Santa Fe on June 29, 1854:

Sir,

I am informed that Apache Indians have, very recently, committed depredations in the vicinity of Vegas. With all the efficient force of Co. D 2d Dragoons & Lieut. J.E. Maxwell, 3d Infantry, Comdg. 35 soldiers of Co. H. 2d Dragoons you will without any delay proceed in direction of "Watrous" ranche in pursuit of those Indians. Should you be so fortunate as to come up with them, you will treat them as enemies to the U.S. At Watrous ranche you will know whether a guide can be had to accompany you on this scout. Make no delay, however, on this account but proceed after the Indians, continuing the pursuit as long as you may deem it prudent & proper. Hire as many "trailers" & guides as you may deem necessary for the proper execution of this duty. Ten days rations are furnished to your command.

    I am, Sir, Very respectfully

    Yr. Obdt. Servt, N.C. Macrae

    Capt. 3, Inf. Comdg[53]

A band of forty mounted Llanero Jicarilla warriors rode north from Las Vegas driving before them a few head of cattle they had stolen from the Mexicans, a people they did not respect. Poorly armed, the Mexicans were accustomed to cowering and running from the Jicarilla. The Apache were returning to their home in the Sangre de Cristo Mountains where their hungry families waited. On the way, they would visit an old enemy, Samuel Watrous. The man was stingy and would not share his beef with the Apache, even though he grazed cattle on their range. They would be passing very close to the soldiers' fort, but they had just fought them in the Raton Mountains at Fisher's Peak, so they knew them to be far away.[54] Ahead their leader saw

Ranch of Samuel B. Watrous at La Junta near Barclay's Fort and Fort Union. His cattle herds were frequently raided by the Jicarilla and his complaints gave rise to many expeditions against them. About 1885. COURTESY PALACE OF THE GOVERNORS PHOTO ARCHIVES (NMHM/DCA), 11685

the cottonwoods along the stream the Mexicans called Sapello Creek. He laughed. It was well named. Watrous was a toad.

Captain Sykes hadn't sent any scouts ahead of his force, knowing he was safe that close to Fort Union and Barclay's Fort. He planned to hire scouts, guides, and trackers from Watrous or his son-in-law Tipton as Captain Macrae had directed. He wasn't expecting the Jicarilla raiding party, which was last reported heading south away from Sapello Creek. The day was hot; the dust gritted in his teeth and made his ears itch. Already his horse stank of sweat and damp leather. He could feel its backbone as he rode. It hadn't had enough time to properly recruit (rest and recuperate). This would have to be a short scout. He saw a dust cloud up ahead on the other side of Sapello Creek. Watrous must be moving his cows to fresh pasture. The cottonwoods along the stream obscured his view. Sykes was almost in the creek when he realized that the riders ahead of him were the Indians he'd come to find. There wasn't time for a plan. The men would have to react as they and their horses had been trained.

"Sergeant! Bring the men into line! . . . Bugler! Sound the charge!" He glanced over his shoulder. Good. Lieutenant Maxwell had seen his move and brought his men in line. They were charging a little behind his men and to his right.

The soldiers were a little faster than the tired Apache, who had been on the trail for some time. The bugle woke them to the danger before the charge struck them like a sledgehammer on rock. The soldiers hastened and, excited, fired their musketoons wildly. There was no time to reload. They charged into acrid smoke stinking of brimstone, drawing pistols as they rode. Hearts beat fast and bullets went wild. Jicarilla warriors fell. The warriors were quick to recover and bullets and arrows flew among the soldiers. If they took to flight, they knew the soldiers would cut them down. They would have to stand until they slowed the soldiers.

Maxwell exhausted the charges in his pistol and drew his saber. He pointed the tip at a warrior just as he'd been taught at West Point. Deep within the lines of the enemy, Sergeant Smith and Privates Moore and Allen close beside him, the lieutenant bore down on a warrior just drawing his bow. The arrow flew before the saber could arrive and found the lieutenant's heart. He staggered in the saddle as a second arrow found its mark. Then his men were upon the Indian, who fell pierced by lead ball and cut down by saber. Apaches targeted Moore and the sergeant as they stopped to dismount beside the lieutenant.

The fight was soon over. Powder charges had been expended and it would take time to reload. The Indians were now impossible to approach. Their bows were still primed with sharp-tipped arrows. There were Apache dead around the soldiers, and Lieutenant Maxwell lay on the ground.

The Jicarilla rode away driving cattle, glad for their escape but grieving for their lost kinfolk. The soldiers sadly escorted Maxwell's body back to the fort.

Colonel Cooke expressed his regret at the loss of a fine young officer:

Lieutenant Maxwell, at the head of his men, was almost immediately killed by two arrow-wounds. He was in the act of sabring an Indian when shot. Sir, I have no words to express my feelings in making this announcement. A braver, more gallant, and high-toned gentleman and soldier never drew sword.

He had exhausted his revolver not without effect, and fell in the midst of brave men, who avenged his death; for Captain Sykes further reports that the Indian who killed Lieutenant Maxwell was killed by Private Allen; and Sergeant Francis Smith and Private Moore, of H company, Second Dragoons, have arrow-wounds. Both, and more particularly the Sergeant, are entitled to great praise for their daring.[55]

By the end of June 1854, with the Jicarilla scattered and fleeing on all fronts, General Garland considered the campaign finished. It was time to make a treaty of peace with the Jicarilla. He wrote to the general-in-chief, Winfield Scott, at Head Quarters of the Army, New York:

The Jicarilla Apaches have been most thoroughly humbled and beg for peace. They are dispersed in small parties with the exception of one is now hard pressed by about one hundred men under Major Blake and Capt. Ewell 1st Drags. . . .[56]

The Utahs are playing a doubtful game and have to be watched very closely, their sympathies are all with the Jicarilla band of Apaches.[57]

According to Kit Carson, Major Blake and Captain Ewell, although absent through the month of July, did not have any luck in finding the Jicarilla.

On June 30, General Garland posted a second letter to headquarters in the East:

> By request of the Acting Governor of this Territory, Mr. Messervy, I hastened to this place to confer with him about our Indian relations which had become somewhat threatening during my temporary absence at El Paso, so much so as to induce his Excellency to call out some two hundred of the militia of the County of Rio Ariba.[58] These troops succeeded in making prisoners of about 39 Apaches, men, women & children, most of whom have subsequently escaped. Several were however, shot in making the attempt.
>
> The Indians are now driven to such extremity by the regular troops as to have caused his Excellency to dispense with this force, retaining perhaps a Company as minute men.[59]

General Garland retained his confidence during the following months. At the end of July he wrote:

> [T]he Jicarilla Apaches are pretty thoroughly subdued—a party of them recently visited the Acting Govr. and Supt. of Indian Affairs making overtures of peace, promising to establish themselves in a Pueblo and to leave hostages in our hands as a guarantee of their good behavior, but before my return some evil disposed persons induced them to depart abruptly. . . . Major Blake 1st Dragoons made an excursion with a strong party of mounted men to the vicinity of the Utahs but found the news of their depredations and hostility exaggerated. I have now very little expectation of difficulty from that quarter.[60]

Garland remained optimistic regarding the Jicarilla through the remaining months of 1854. He had successfully done almost everything that the military could. He was aware that a band of twenty-five warriors remained somewhere in the mountains, conducting occasional depredations. Most of the tribe was crying for peace.

However, Acting Governor Messervy in Santa Fe was unconvinced. Perhaps he knew the government had nothing to offer the Jicarilla that would maintain the peace for long. He offered starvation or extermination, and given that choice, the Apache would fight and depredate. Calling out over two hundred militia for action in the field was expensive, but as long as it came out of General Garland's budget, it cost the governor nothing. Messervy and upon his return, Meriwether, accurately gauged the mood in Congress as supportive of their strategy. The government was not willing to spend money to feed the Indians while they established themselves as farmers.

In July, a peace delegation from the Jicarilla appeared in Santa Fe but was turned away. That summer the small group of renegade warriors who were conducting minor depredations drifted north to live among the Utes, but never again was the Jicarilla tribe to rise against its conquerors.[61] By the end of September the Indians were entirely peaceful. Nonethe-

Governor David Meriwether repudiated his predecessor's treaty with the Jicarilla and predicted that it would result in war. The war he wanted came but not where or why he predicted. About 1853. COURTESY PALACE OF THE GOVERNORS PHOTO ARCHIVES (NMHM/DCA), 10303, PHOTOGRAPHER B. BILLIAN

less, both Governor Meriwether and General Garland believed the Jicarilla suit for peace evidence of their treachery. At the end of September Garland wrote to his superiors in Washington:

I have the honor to report for the information of the Maj. Genl. Comdg the Army that the Indians within the limits of New Mexico have been remarkably quiet during the past month. The head chief of the Jicarilla Apaches "Chacone" called some short time since upon Govr. Meriwether to beg for peace, but his excellency declined to talk with him upon the subject unless he could bring in his united band. He has now collected one hundred and seven lodges at a point near Abiquiu, on the Chama river; and, as it has caused some uneasiness among the

*inhabitants in that quarter, I have deemed it prudent to order three
companies of Dragoons within striking distance of this treacherous
and degraded band to watch their movements, and if necessary, to
strike the first blow.*[62]

The governor called on Chacon to bring in all of his people. There were
two reasons that this was nearly impossible. Feeding that many people in a
confined area would be difficult as game was scarce. Chacon's people consisted of those who would voluntarily heed his call. In any event, the boundaries between tribes and bands of Apache were far fuzzier than the terms
implied.

Garland's concern over Jicarilla treachery must have sprung from their
demonstrated ability to defend themselves. No one wanted to mention
Davidson's defeat. That was embarrassing, and for the military, the less said
about it the better. When called upon to point to Jicarilla depredations the
answer was either a vague "many" or reference to the events of 1849/50, the
White Wagon Train and the Wagon Mound Mail Party. Undoubtedly there
was deep concern over the Apaches' ability to close the Santa Fe Trail and
over their fighting prowess demonstrated at Cieneguilla. The general may
have honestly thought them treacherous. Perhaps he thought fighting prowess alone could not account for their victory over sixty dragoons.

At the end of 1854, the stories of the Utes and Jicarillas would converge.
The two linguistically unrelated tribes, despite occasional protestations to the
contrary, had long been friends and allies, and intermarriage between the
bands was not uncommon.

On September 30, 1854, a party of Utes visited Kit Carson at Taos to
express their desire for peace. Carson also recorded the grievances of the
delegation, writing, "They complained that they are very poor and game is
very scarce."[63] The Ute's traditional hunting grounds had been shrinking.
The Cheyenne and Comanche denied them the plains and the buffalo hunt.
Mexicans and Americans had crowded into their mountain hunting grounds.
In one instance, a party of Mexicans had slain a Ute, and in retaliation, the
Utes had taken some livestock. The Jicarilla renegades living among the Ute
were still committing depredations from necessity as they were in a very bad
condition. Carson thought they might clean out that part of the country of
its stock.

Making matters worse, in 1852, Garland's predecessor, Colonel Sumner, had ordered the construction of Fort Massachusetts on Ute Creek at the foot of the Sangre de Cristo Pass. Both Jicarilla and Ute used this pass as their gateway to the plains. The fort stood at the northern end of Jicarilla territory on the flanks of their sacred peak, Mount Blanca. With soldiers to protect them, Mexican settlers had moved north from Taos into the San Luis Valley and were placing additional pressure on game while making their herds inviting targets for stock raids.

Nonetheless, the Jicarilla were suing for peace and rising problems suggested it was also time for a council with the Utes. Carson thought it good to call their leaders into council together with the superintendent, Governor Meriwether, and to distribute gifts of blankets, shirts, and such. He spent October gathering the chiefs.

In the interim, in the Sangre de Cristo Mountains, Cheyenne or Arapaho warriors attacked Indian hunters from the Taos and Picuris Pueblos.[64] Governor Meriwether wished to blame the Jicarilla since the attacks took place within their range and beyond that of the Cheyenne. However, Picuris and Taos Indians knew who attacked them; the Picuris had long been friendly with the Jicarilla.[65] This was a sad opening gambit for the council. Meriwether wanted the war to continue. He was coming with nothing to offer that would maintain the peace even though the Jicarilla had agreed to become farmers.

At the council with the chiefs, the Moache Ute demanded horses in payment for the Ute slain by a Mexican for his coat, but Meriwether did not provide horses. He made presents of blankets and capotes including one made from an old blanket. The Ute who received it was insulted and tore it apart. The governor had the Mexican murderer arrested, but he soon escaped and Meriwether did not attempt to have him recaptured and tried.

In his autobiography, Kit Carson pointed to the injustice of having chiefs travel hundreds of miles to receive such presents and so little action and assistance. Worse yet, returning to their camps the chiefs who had received old coats brought smallpox with them. Many of the headmen who attended the council died.[66] Whether it was so or not, old blankets and coats made from them raised questions and the Utes believed them to be the source of the disease.[67] Anger festered and would burst into the flames of war at Christmas in the Ute country.

In all probability, Governor Meriwether was only guilty of insulting the Utes with old blankets and was not responsible for the most heinous deed imaginable. Some writers think it is likely the Ute passed through a village where there was smallpox on their way home. Their route home was due northwest of the Rio Grande where there were as yet no settlements.

In September 1854, General Garland thought the Jicarilla thoroughly defeated. Their chief Chacon, along with their agent, Kit Carson, were suing for peace, while Governor Meriwether with nothing concrete to offer the Indians dithered and offended them. The Ute were away from trails and settlements except for the new ones in the San Luis Valley and had less contact with settlers and the Army. The affair of the blankets sent the Ute to war. Unable to get treaty promises, the Jicarilla joined them. Fort Massachusetts would become the staging area for the military campaigns of 1855.

Chapter 13

In December 1854, there were only three officers at Fort Massachusetts, the post commander Colonel Horace Brooks, 2nd Artillery, Doctor DeWitt Clinton Peters, and Lieutenant Lloyd Beall, 2nd Artillery. Beall and Brooks were not on speaking terms. Beall had been absent from his station for a year without proper leave, and on his return, he was brought before a court-martial, which sentenced him to a year of post confinement and suspension of rank and pay.[1] The artillery was in charge of the post because, during the coldest months, the dragoons withdrew to Cantonment Burgwin. The weather was hard on the horses. The roads were bad, especially when it snowed, and it was difficult to supply. That winter, the doctor wrote of the isolation of his post at Fort Massachusetts:

> *The mountains which surround the post are those laid down on the map as the Cerro Blanco, or white mountains, called so from being always covered with snow.[2] These mountains are a spur of the Rocky Mountains and run through New Mexico, and our post is near the commencement of the Cerro Blanco. The nearest Fort to our north is Laramie which is 800 miles distant. The nearest one to our west is supposed to be 900 miles. To our east Fort Atchinson on the Arkansas, 500 miles. To our south Cantonment Burquin, 110 miles.[3] You see therefore we are quite isolated from the rest of the military world. . . .[4]*

There were a few Mexican communities twenty and thirty miles distant in the San Luis Valley but they offered little. Peters did not hold the

Mexicans in high regard and snatched at any excuse to get away to Taos. In December 1854, he wrote:

I have just returned from Taos, a town about 100 miles from here where I have been to make a flying visit in order to see the sights of the Mexican holydays in honor of Montezuma. Their dances etc. on this occasion are ridiculous they being dressed in ancient costume and performing feats which if attempted in the states would be considered immoral and would send them all to the Penitentiary. I was invited to go to the feast with Kit Carson and we went. The eating (for you can call it nothing else) commenced at about 2 o'c. and lasted about 1 1/2 hours. Nothing but meats of various kinds (vegetables as potatoes etc. being scarce in the country). I asked Kit Carson when it would end and he said whenever you had eaten enough but another member of the party corrected him by saying that whenever beans made their appearance it was time to leave, which was our signal.[5]

Across the mountain passes from Fort Massachusetts, American mountain men and traders had, in the 1840s, established a trading post known as Pueblo. The tiny fort now stood at the mouth of Fountain Creek on the Arkansas River in disrepair with its gate askew. The founders brought along their Mexican and Indian wives and their wives' relations. The Indian trade was poor and the Americans departed leaving behind their Mexican kinfolk. Marcelino Baca built a ranch nearby and built *jacals* for his workmen and their wives. By 1854, the fort was crumbling, but Mexican men still lived there and Mexican families lived at Baca's ranch.

On Christmas Eve 1854, there was a big card game at the fort. Three men from Baca's Ranch attended. The only woman in the fort was Chepita Miera. She had been preparing to leave the fort, and her goods were already packed on Rumaldo Cordova's wagon, which stood outside the gate, for an early morning departure. Accounts vary as to what happened next. The Ute and Jicarilla may have first slain one of the men returning from Baca's. Either they confronted Rumaldo at the gate to the fort trying to gain admittance as friends or, as another account says, by pulling Chepita off the wagon. The warriors soon dispatched him and then slew those in the fort, taking Juan and Felix Sandoval and Chepita captive. Marcelino Baca escaped across the deep snow in the passes to Fort Massachusetts, the nearest military post. There he stayed briefly with Dr. Peters before proceeding to Santa Fe to deliver news of the massacre.

On January 11, 1855, departmental adjutant Major Nichols wrote:

> [O]n the 25th of December last, a body of Indians, known to be Utahs and Jicarilla Apaches, numbering one hundred or more, made an attack on the settlements on the Arkansas river and killed at Pueblo about 18 miles above the mouth of the Huerfano, 14 men, wounded two, carried off one woman and two children, all mexicans—and some two hundred head of stock.[6]

Following the Pueblo Massacre, General Garland had no choice but to mount a major campaign against the Ute and their Jicarilla allies. Any chance of peace was off. But it would be March 1855 before men and supplies could be gathered at Fort Massachusetts for an effort that would extend through the summer.

Meanwhile at Fort Union post commander Colonel Thomas T. Fauntleroy made reports of presumed Jicarilla activity. After the abortive "Old Blanket" council of the fall, the Jicarilla would have returned to their winter camps. On December 10, 1854, Indian raiders, presumed to be Jicarilla, were supposed to have carried off from the vicinity of Las Vegas between four and five hundred head of cattle driving them in the direction of Red River, that is, the Canadian. The colonel sent all forty-seven of his "efficient" dragoons in pursuit. Despite what we learn in song and Hollywood movies, five hundred is a huge number of cattle and difficult to drive. They move slowly and are easily overtaken. The loss of five hundred cattle would have caused a huge stir, spoiling any plans Chief Chacon had for peace. Such a large herd would have exceeded the current needs of the tribe and been beyond what they could care for or hide. Cattle move slowly. The dragoons should have overtaken the herd. There is no report of an action in the *Chronological List*. The patrol appears to have been sent in response to a false report.[7]

The colonel went on to beg that more troops be sent to him, claiming that the settlements in his area—Mora, Rayado, Las Vegas—were threatened by the Jicarilla. Further, he stated that his resources were strained by the need to provide escorts of twenty to twenty-five men for mail parties. It was not clear that the Jicarilla had as yet made a hostile move, but their reputation and the governor's failed treaty council was causing a stir.

On February 9, 1855, even as he gathered men to strike at the Ute and Jicarilla in the San Luis Valley, Fauntleroy claimed to be warring with the Jicarilla on the plains and of having to send four companies of volunteers in pursuit.[8] The colonel was in the process of arming and equipping six companies of volunteers for the San Luis operation, which he would lead. Rudely awakened at 2:00 a.m., he wrote:

I was aroused by the report of several Mexicans, who said that about twenty miles from this place on the waters of the Ocate they were attacked by about eight Indians, and one of their party killed & five or six animals taken off by the enemy. In two hours I had a party of 12 dragoons in the saddle & on pursuit. Having heard various rumors which have been strongly supported by subsequent information that there are more than 50 lodges of the Jicarillas Apaches encamped on Red River about 50 miles from this post, I directed the party that left in the night to confine their operations principally to the collecting of information & to return immediately here if they did not meet with only a small party, which they were ordered only to fight. They have returned this evening just as the mail escort returned & report the death of the man spoken of above & large trails running in direction of Red River. The mail party also reports several facts given them by hunters going to confirm the presence of a very numerous body of Indians in all probability making their way down to join the Indians below. There is every evidence that their families are with them. . . . I have ventured to order two companies of volunteers to take the upper trail on the Ocate & two to strike sufficiently below to meet the party if they are going down & thus by meeting together take them in front & rear. . . . Yesterday morning I rec'd a letter from the neighborhood of Vegas stating the capture & carrying off of a small number of cattle & whilst I write I hear the report that on last night a large amount of stock had been stolen from the same vicinity, & driven towards Canon Largo. It is impossible for me to tell what degree of credit should be attached to many of these rumors but I can not doubt, but that there were many indians in striking distance of the settlements near here.[9]

Rafael Chacon was first sergeant of one of these volunteer companies, having enlisted for six months service. He wrote of the pursuit:

We received our arms at Fort Union (New Mexico) and immediately started in pursuit of the Apaches who had stolen a herd of mares from Don Juan Vigil of La Cueva in the county of Mora. We followed the trail of the Indians through what is now Wagon Mound; they had crossed the Rio Colorado.[10] At Piedra Lumbre they entered the Sierra Grande and recrossed the river at Casa del Aguila, in the neighborhood of what is now Otero in Colfax county. We followed them by the same route and caught up with them in what is Long's Canyon.[11] Then the Indians fled from us, abandoning their camp where they had been making a meal on horse meat. Our own provisions at this time had been exhausted and we ate the meal which the Indians had left. Our horses were also played out and the Indians had escaped with all their horses. . . . We then broke up into small bands to pursue them because they also split into small bands.[12]

It does not appear that this was a large party of Jicarilla. The volunteers and the colonel headed for the San Luis Valley to fight Ute and Jicarillas. It is not clear how many of the Jicarilla were now at war with the United States. There may have been eighty lodges in the north with the Ute. That would account for a little more than half of the tribe. The military was stretched thin fighting in the extreme north of the department in what is today southern Colorado as well as in southern New Mexico. This left the Jicarilla to range in the center, the Canadian River, and Sangre de Cristo Mountains, with very few troops defending them.

In early March 1855, soldiers of Colonel Fauntleroy's command began to arrive at Fort Massachusetts for a campaign of revenge against the Ute and Jicarilla. Companies D and F, 1st Dragoons, came north, along with Company D, 3rd Infantry, joining Company D, 2nd Artillery, under Captain Brooks. The artillery left their cannons behind and would serve as infantry riflemen. There were also four companies of New Mexico volunteers under Colonel Ceran St. Vrain, formerly a partner of the Bent brothers, along with one company of spies.[13] Agent for the Jicarilla and Ute Kit Carson joined the expedition as a senior scout. Colonel Fauntleroy's five hundred soldiers set out from Fort Massachusetts. Surgeon Peters reported some of their hardships en route across the San Luis Valley to the San Juan Mountains:

Fort Massachusetts New Mexico
March 3rd 1855
The snow is also very deep and this adds to our trouble and hardships. Half rations to subsist on if we have to follow the Indians far renders the expedition anything but desirable. In the Southern part of New Mexico another campaign is going on against the Indians in that quarter. . . .[14]

As they proceeded across the San Luis Valley to the Rio Grande and followed it to the mountains, they then turned north "encountering snowstorms and severe cold weather."[15] A large Newfoundland dog that belonged to one of the officers followed their march. It was supposed to have been left behind but got loose and pursued the column. The dog was so friendly that it had soon bonded with many of the soldiers. The animal fell into the waters of a partially frozen stream and was in danger of being swept under the ice. Struggle as it might, it couldn't get up onto the ice nor scale the slippery bank. Finally, a Mexican with a lasso rescued the dog.[16]

On March 19, Kit Carson was in the lead with the quartermaster at his side. He had found a large trail frequently used by the Indians in driving in flocks of sheep and cattle and in going out on raids. The Ute and Jicarilla had recently driven off between eight hundred and one thousand sheep, twenty-five horses and mules, and forty head of cattle from the San Luis Valley settlement at Conejos where sixty or seventy Mexican families had recently invaded the realm of the Jicarilla and Ute.[17] The trail was so well defined that they were able to follow it into the hours of darkness.[18] They followed the Indians into Saguache Pass, a "great natural opening in the mountains that bound, on the west, the valley of San Luis."[19] Carson looked up from the trail to see 150 Jicarilla and Ute warriors painted for war coming downcanyon heading out on a raid.[20] Both sides were equally surprised and drew into line facing each other. The Indians, thinking that this was only a small advance party of soldiers, began to taunt them in Spanish.[21]

"Why do you not attack us? Are you women?"[22]

On command the soldiers threw off their heavy overcoats and attacked. The action was intense. The Jicarilla and Ute led by Ute Chief Blanco scattered when they realized how many were attacking.[23] The soldiers dismounted, as they were better able to use their musketoons from the ground and in order to pursue the Indians into the forest. Dr. Peters established a field hospital, and then remounted and went forward until he found himself in the thick of the fighting. When a Ute warrior charged him. Peters drew his new six-shot pistol and fired and fired again, until the pistol was empty. He then threw the pistol at the unfazed warrior and finally punched him before help arrived.[24] The Indians counterattacked five times pressing the soldiers hard each time. Finally, Captain Smith W. Simpson came up with his command and hit the warriors hard in "an unexpected flanking attack that confused the Indians and put them to flight."[25] In the action, the warriors wounded two soldiers, but suffered the loss of two chiefs and six warriors.

According to First Sergeant Rafael Chacon of St. Vrain's command:

[T]he Indians fought with reckless valor, but in the end they had to abandon the field, leaving their dead, who were buried by order of Colonel Fauntleroy. After the battle was over I was seized by sickness and fell from my horse in a fainting spell. I think this was because I had taken no food that day and as we went along I had kept picking up handfuls of snow and eating it to slack my thirst.[26]

In the night, a soldier sleeping near the middle of the camp and thinking himself still in battle, grabbed his weapon and fired at shadows. He nearly hit a Mexican sentinel who, thinking the camp attacked, returned fire. Soon the whole camp was roused.[27]

General Garland reported the action to Army Headquarters:

I have the honor to report, for the information of the general-in-chief of the army, that Lieutenant Magruder, 1st Dragoons, has just arrived from Colonel Fauntleroy's camp, and brings information of a skirmish between a portion of our troops and the Utah and Apaches, at the Coochetopa Pass; eight of the former were killed, and two dragoons wounded.[28] *After the fight, the Apaches separated from their confederates, were pursued for four days, overtaken, and all of their animals captured. Colonel Fauntleroy, after a hasty refit at Fort Massachusetts, will again take the field in pursuit of the Utahs. The Colonel speaks well of the conduct of the troops, volunteers included.*

Colonel Fauntleroy sent Lieutenant Lloyd Beall, 2nd Artillery, along with the command's wagons, provisions, and pack mules ahead to meet him in the Wet Mountain Valley while he continued in pursuit of the Jicarilla. This was the same Lieutenant Beall who had been brought before a court-martial and was still under suspension. Of necessity, the suspension was overlooked and he became a hero. Between four and five of the dragoons' mounts had to be put down each day. The smaller mounts of the Volunteers were holding up better than those of the Regulars in what can only be described as a winter campaign. With Beall went his company of "infantry" and the "demounted" cavalrymen, 150 in all.[29] Fauntleroy's soldiers set out with a half bushel of corn for each horse and seven days rations on the pack mules. Beall and Fauntleroy would travel by different passes to meet again before the colonel's command ran out of food.

After the fight at Saguache Pass, the Jicarilla and the Ute split up. Fauntleroy pursued the Jicarilla and Kit Carson went with him. The trail led to Poncha Pass and pursuit was swift. Contact was enjoined on March 21. The great scout thought that they were pursuing seventy-five or eighty lodges of Apache now headed down the rugged canyon of the Arkansas. The Indians headed up Beaver Creek and camped. Carson thought they were headed for the Bayou Salade (South Park). The soldiers captured a Jicarilla woman and child along with eight horses. From her they learned that Chief Chacon was leading the Apache ahead of them. Chief Chacon realized that the soldiers were close behind and divided his people into three parties to elude pursuit. Fauntleroy followed the trail of the largest band. Crossing to the south side of the Arkansas, the troops surprised the Jicarilla camp and the colonel ordered an immediate charge. The bugle blew and the confused Apaches scrambled to save themselves and their families.[30]

According to First Sergeant Rafael Chacon, they crossed over the Puerta del Punche (Poncha Pass), and in the Wet Mountain Valley between the Rio Almagre (Fountain Creek) and the Napeste (Arkansas River) they encountered the enemy:[31]

When the Indians started to retreat and to run away I was mounted on a mule, and a lieutenant who seemed somewhat timid kept lagging behind and reining his horse, a very spirited animal that was chafing with excitement. When I saw that he was killing time on purpose I said to him, "Let me have that horse to follow the enemy, or I will kill you." He dismounted and gave me his horse which I mounted and let him have my mule.[32]

Fauntleroy and his men, dragoons and volunteers, routed the enemy, killing several and capturing three, along with most of the Jicarilla's livestock. In the camp they discovered a great deal of mule meat, which Carson pronounced as a sign that the Jicarilla were nearly destitute and in a starving condition. In the night, the three captives escaped. The soldiers were also running low on food and the dragoons' horses were in terrible condition.[33] Rafael Chacon recalled the misery of the volunteer soldiers in this winter campaign:

My Captain every time that he was detailed as officer of the day managed to have me discharge the duties that devolved upon him. One night in the Sierra Mojada (Wet Mountains) while I was going the round of the sentries I became soaking wet, because the camp was located on a meadow which was covered with ice at several places. The ice kept breaking under my feet as I walked along so that when I arrived at the guard quarters I was almost out of breath and my clothes frozen and I chilled. They laid me in the midst of the sleeping soldiers to thaw me out and when my clothes were ready to be taken off they gave me other garments to don while mine were drying.[34]

The command was now distributed to several settlements so that they could obtain forage for their horses. Kit Carson returned to Taos.[35]

After a period of rest and refitting at Fort Massachusetts, Fauntleroy would take the field again on April 23, 1855. Behind him as they rode north toward Poncha Pass was Company D, 1st Dragoons and two companies of Mounted Volunteers, along with the foot soldiers of Company D, 2nd Artillery. Colonel St. Vrain was in command of a separate column that headed east through the Sangre de Cristo Pass toward the Spanish Peaks. Behind him rode Company F, 1st Dragoons commanded by Lieutenant Whittlesey, and two companies of Volunteers under Captains Charles Williams and Francisco Gonzales, whose first sergeant was Rafael Chacon.[36]

On April 28, near Poncha Pass Colonel Fauntleroy and his command marched more than ninety miles in thirty-two hours.[37] Moving fast, they surprised the enemy camp of Utes and Jicarillas, entirely routing them, killing more than forty and capturing six children. The colonel's men also captured all of the Apaches' provisions. On May 10, Surgeon Peters wrote from Fort Massachusetts:

> *Previous to this fight our men had marched 90 miles in 32 hours, waded creeks that were swollen, had eaten but one meal during that time. In fact, for five days, day and night most of the time they were on the march without fires to cook anything over. Yet hardly a complaint was heard, and now they received their reward by accomplishing one of the most effective blows ever struck against any warlike band of Indians. . . .*[38]

General Garland was equally pleased and wrote to Army Headquarters that the people killed on Christmas Day of 1854 had been avenged:

> *On the 31st March last, the operations of Colonel Fauntleroy, 1st Dragoons, against the Jicarilla Apaches and Utahs, which resulted in some small advantage over them. It gives me great satisfaction now to report a triumph over these Indians, seldom if ever equaled in the United States. The Colonel reports in his despatch, herewith annexed, (marked A,) that forty Utahs were killed, in a battle fought with them on the Upper Arkansas, near the Punche Pass. Six children were taken prisoners, thirty-five horses captured, with a number of arms, buffalo-robes, &c., &c., Our loss was one man killed and two wounded. This expedition appears to have been conducted with skill and judgment, and reflects great credit upon Colonel Fauntleroy, his officers and men. The surprise of the Indians at night was of itself a great triumph. These were the Indians who broke up the settlement on the Arkansas, on Christmas day of last year. Their chief is called Blanco. It is gratifying to know that the volunteers participated freely in the fight.*
>
> *On the evening of the 1st and morning of the 2d instant [May], Colonel Fauntleroy reports some skirmishing with the Indians, in which four of them were killed, and some horses and baggage taken.*[39]

The Army had the starving Jicarilla on the run. Colonel St. Vrain discovered Chacon's camp near Rio del Oso and the Huerfano River and in a two-day engagement on April 25 and 26, killed and wounded thirteen Jicarilla.

The Indians forfeited their camp gear. The pursuit continued south and near the Picketwire (Purgatoire) River St. Vrain charged their camp killing one while six women and children became his prisoners. On June 8, his men killed six, and captured twenty-nine horses and six guns.[40]

St. Vrain kept up the pressure as Indians fled south through the Raton Mountains toward the Canadian River and the mountains between Mora and La Joya. In Raton Pass at "the place where the old house of Uncle Dick Wootton was afterwards located" they made contact again. Just below the pass, at Poñil Creek, there was another encounter and they killed several men and captured fifty women and their children. St. Vrain took the captives to Fort Union, and General Garland reported that "Lieutenant Colonel St. Vrain possessed most excellent judgment, and the most perfect reliance can be placed upon his report, which is herewith enclosed."[41]

Richens "Uncle Dick" Wootton, seated left, Ceran St. Vrain, standing, and Jose Maria Valdez. St. Vrain and Wooten were mountain men. Wooten settled at Raton Pass. St. Vrain became a partner of the Bents and a Santa Fe Trader. He served as a colonel of Volunteers against the Jicarilla while Valdez served as a captain and Wooten as a scout. About 1865. COURTESY PALACE OF THE GOVERNORS PHOTO ARCHIVES (NMHM/DCA), HP 2015.11.001

St. Vrain remained active against small parties of Jicarilla who kept up a steady drumbeat of depredations, having been thoroughly despoiled of food, clothing, camp equipment, horses, and the opportunity to hunt. Kit Carson recalled:

On that campaign, the Apache received chastisement for their many depredations that they thought could never have been given them. The commands returned to Taos . . . Fauntleroy did not again take the field. The Volunteers had but a short time to serve, but St. Vrain did not allow them to be idle. He immediately again took the field and kept in pursuit of Indians till a few days before the expiration of service.[42]

In June, General Garland's adjutant wrote to the Volunteer company commander at Abiquiu:

Captain,
Information has been received at these Head Quarters that a party of Jicarilla Apache have recently killed 8 or 10 Mexicans in the mountain district between La Joya, Cantt Burgwin, and the Mora. The Brigr. General Commanding directs that you proceed at once to that section of country, with fifty men of your company, get what information you can in relation to these marauders and punish them to the extent of your ability.

One Lieutenant with the remainder of your company will be left at Abiquiu, as a guard to the depot of supplies at that place.

P.S. It is best that you do not communicate your movement to any of the Mexican population.[43]

And so pursuit continued. According to Kit Carson:

If the Volunteers had continued in the service three months and had been under the command and sole direction of Colonel St. Vrain, there would never again have been need of any troops in this country. The Indians would be entirely subjected and, in all probability, but few of them would be left to be of any trouble.[44]

In March 1855, "A Friend of Truth" wrote to the *Santa Fe Gazette*:

It is true that Governor Meriwether allowed the Indian child to be sold as a slave by one of the agents of his superintendency. It is true that he refused to have stolen property returned by the Utah Indians, known to be in their possession, at the time he was distributing presents among them. It is true that he interfered to prevent a separation of the Indian department from the civil in this Territory, when he knew that unless the separation was made, he must be absent from his civil duties, nearly half the year. It is true that he has taken upon himself the disbursement of public funds, to an extent, that must greatly embarrass his civil duties, or those pertaining to the Indian department. And whatever may be the opinion of the Governor with regard to colonizing the wild Indians, at this time, it is well known that he did not favor that policy for more than twelve months after he came into the Territory, and that he allowed the band under Chacon, the Jicarilla Chief, that had been located, and were successfully cultivating the soil for some time before Governor Lane left the Territory, to disperse and recommence their depredations upon our citizens. That formidable band is now again at open war with us.[45]

The "Friend of Truth" was someone familiar with the inner workings of the superintendency and the treaty councils. Kit Carson might have dictated the letter to the *Gazette*. His hostility for Governor Meriwether was growing and was expressed through opposition to the September 1855 treaty negotiations. Between April 1854, when Carson wanted a fair and just treaty made with the Jicarilla and September 1855, when Governor Meriwether made essentially the same treaty that Lane had with the Ute and Jicarilla, changing only the location of the reservations, Carson changed his opinion of the Jicarilla. They could not be trusted to keep a treaty.

On September 5, 1855, Indian Agent Kit Carson wrote to the editor of the *Santa Fe Gazette*:

Taos, N.M.
Sept. 5th 1855

Dear Sir:
I notice in your Gazette of 1st inst. an article headed "Our Indian Affairs," in which it is stated no Indian depredations have been committed for the last three months, or if any have taken place they were not reported to the proper authorities.
I would request you to read the monthly reports of June, July and August, 1855, which were sent by me to the Superintendent of Indian

Affairs of N.M., and you will find that seventeen persons were killed and one boy captured, and near five hundred head of animals driven off by the Jicarilla Apaches and Comanches. I send the foregoing information so that you may correct the error made in regard to Indians depredations.

Your article of the first instant would cause the public to believe that the Indians on this side of the Rio del Norte are peaceable, which is not the case, for I am informed that they have committed several depredations the present month near Mora and Rayado.

Yours truly,
C. Carson
Indian Agent[46]

Carson was about to attend the treaty conference at Abiquiu with the Jicarilla and Utes. He was definitely raining on Governor Meriwether's parade. We can guess at what Carson was thinking. Meriwether had the war he had wanted. Governor Meriwether, through Acting Governor Messervy, had declared war on the Jicarilla and had won, beating them as no one had before. The war had gone on months after Carson had called for a treaty and then over Meriwether's bungling had gone into a whole new phase that brought in the Utes. In September 1855, Governor Meriwether had won a war and was ready to negotiate a treaty with the Jicarilla. The terms were almost the same as those of Governor Lane's treaty, "the usual provisions," with the difference being that the Jicarilla reservation would be located on the headwaters of the Chama River in the vicinity of modern Tierra Amarilla. And now it was Meriwether's treaty with his name on it, his bureaucratic achievement. This must have rankled with the straightforward frontiersman, Kit Carson.

Ten days after Carson wrote his letter and two days after Governor Meriwether's return from Abiquiu the *Gazette* reported:

Gov. Meriwether, who left town last Saturday for Abiquiu at which place he had appointed to meet the Jicarillas and Muhuache Utahs, returned to Santa Fe Thursday the 13th Inst. There were some five hundred Indians of these two tribes in attendance at the council, with whom treaties were made. They expressed themselves as tired of war, and desirous to live upon friendly terms with the whites; and we most sincery [sic] hope they will keep their promise. The Jicarillas, in particular, were in the most abject condition, and had suffered terribly during the war. The head men of both nations were at the council, and promised to keep their people in subjection. Each tribe has been assigned to a separate region of the country for their future homes, the Jicarillas upon the headwaters of the Chama river, and the Utahs the district they now inhabit. The treaties contain the usual general provisions.[47]

The great difference between Lane's treaty and Meriwether's was that the latter proposed Tierra Amarilla as the site of the reservation. Tierra Amarilla is today the county seat of Rio Arriba County. In 1855, the place name, meaning Yellow Earth, was already in use but the nearest settlement was Abiquiu, forty-five miles to the south. Although the Mexican government made a grant of land to Manuel Martínez in 1832, Ute and Jicarilla made occupation impossible.[48] It was deep in their territory, sixty miles west-northwest of Taos with the Rio Grande Gorge and the San Juan Mountains in between. In 1853, Governor Lane proposed a reservation twenty-five miles west of Abiquiu on the Rio Puerco, a tributary of the Chama River. The distance from settlements proposed in the two treaties was comparable.

Meriwether's 1855 treaty was opposed by political powers in Taos, Judge Beaubien and Padre Antonio José Martínez.[49] Martínez came from one of the most wealthy families in New Mexico. He was a leader of the church, a mentor of priests, the head of a powerful secret society, and a member of the legislature. They composed an open letter to President Pierce and it appeared in the *Santa Fe Weekly Gazette* on May 3, 1856:

1. That Governor Meriwether's treaties of peace appropriating lands to the Utah and Jicarilla Apaches be disapproved, as they conflict with the welfare of our Territory, and her people who did not know that any such treaties had been made until sometime after they were concluded; and for the further reason that our people were not consulted nor were the interests of the Territory secured, and which treaties have met the universal disapproval of the citizens.

2. That land be assigned to the said Utah and Jicarilla Apache Indians to the west of the county of Taos, where there is a great deal of fertile public land, which they can occupy; the climate being very healthy and in every way better suited for the Indians, and where they can live comfortably without injury to our people or the Territory.[50]

The letter does not mention the Manuel Martínez grant; however in 1860, the US Congress confirmed the grant, which included the area around Tierra Amarilla.[51] According to the memorial, forty-five miles from Abiquiu and sixty miles from Taos did not put the Jicarilla far enough away from the settlements. The Jicarilla had lived around Taos, Picuris, Abiquiu, and El Rito since the eighteenth century, in close proximity to the Mexican *paisanos*. Now sixty miles away with a river gorge and mountain range in between was too close. The proposal to put the reservation west of Taos County is also peculiar since at that time Taos County stretched all the way to the western border of New Mexico, then on the Colorado River.[52]

The US Senate did not ratify Meriwether's 1855 treaty. It is unlikely that vacant land grants and the objections of Taos politicos carried much weight. The Congress was deeply divided over slavery and what to do with the territories. But, the Territory of New Mexico was far off and its people did not vote. The Constitution said that all spending bills must originate in the House, while the Senate ratified treaties. Treaties calling for annuities to Indian tribes were in effect spending bills, and this gave the House pretext to object to them. Spending money on far off Indians to protect equally far off non-voting citizens was difficult to justify to one's constituents. Besides, it sounded a lot like paying tribute to haughty pirates of the plains and mountains, and the United States did not pay tribute. The Jicarilla continued without a home drawing "presents" at Abiquiu and Taos, and after 1861, at Lucien Maxwell's ranch in Cimarron.[53]

Kit Carson also spoke of his opposition to the treaty in 1856 while dictating his autobiography:

The Indians were promised certain sums yearly; in case they wished to settle on some stream and commence farming, they had their choice of country. The Superintendent went to Washington with his treaties, which were laid before the Senate, and [are] as yet not confirmed. They should not be. Such treaties were not of a character to suit the people.

*The Apaches are now daily committing depredations. They go unp[un]
ished and, in my opinion, ere long they may again commence hostilities. The other tribes with whom the treaties were made I think will
comply with their demands, and will not again be hostile if the Government does not stop their supplies of provisions during such times as
they cannot hunt.*[54]

There don't seem to have been many depredations. The record is lacking
in campaigns and pursuits, but minor incidents breed and grow when one is
making a point.

Carson also provided his view of the successful management of the Indians. It was similar to what many believed in the nineteenth century:

*I can say that this country [New Mexico] will always remain in its
impoverished state as long as them mountain Indians are permitted to
run at large, and the only remedy is [to] compel them to live in settlements, cultivate the soil, and learn to gain their maintenance independent of the general government.*[55]

Mountain Indians would include both Jicarilla and Ute. In 1855, Kit
Carson's attitude toward the Jicarilla seemed to change from wanting a just
treaty, that would have included the provisions named above, to a position
that there could never be peace with the Jicarilla; they could not be trusted.
This seems at odds with both his and their behavior. He remained as their
agent until 1861 when the Civil War came to New Mexico. The Jicarilla for
their part remained peaceful and also took the Union side in the war.

The apparent change of heart is puzzling. It may be that Carson was upset
after having the Jicarilla so close to a treaty at Abiquiu in late 1854, when
they took the warpath with the Ute and massacred the people of Pueblo. He
may have felt that this was a breach of his trust. On the other hand, Carson
and Governor Meriwether did not get along.

In his excellent work *Kit Carson and the Indians*, Thomas Dunlay
expressed the opinion that this opposition to a treaty applied to a small
group of Jicarilla warriors who continued minor depredations. Carson made
a "hard-line" statement that the Jicarilla should be entirely defeated and only
a few of them left to be of any trouble. It sounds like he was an Indian hater
and an advocate of genocide, but we know from numerous other statements

that this was not the case. According to Dunlay, he was referring to Indians who had been actively engaged in hostilities and had massacred the people of Pueblo. There was a recurring cycle of such events.[56]

Supporting Dunlay's position that the small group still in the field was the issue is the statement from Kit Carson that:

The Apaches did not all come in at the time of the treaty. They were committing depredations. The fact was reported to the Superintendent but would [not] be believed. Treaty should not have been made with the Apaches. No faith can be placed in their promises.[57]

Nonetheless, Carson continued to favor the prospects for continued peace with the Ute over similar prospects with the Jicarilla, who might at any time become a problem committing further depredations. The Ute were rather remote from civilization in the Sangre de Cristo and San Juan Mountains and San Luis Valley. At the time, the valley was the only real friction point for the Ute, while the Jicarilla were at Abiquiu, Taos, Picuris, Mora, Rayado, and Las Vegas and along the Santa Fe Trail. There were regular incidents brought on by contact with Mexicans who stole from the Apaches who in turn stole from Mexicans. They bought whiskey from the Mexicans, got drunk, and raised hell in town.

Dunlay wrote that Carson distrusted the Jicarilla because he must have been aware that they had no united leadership who could enforce observance of any peace treaty.[58] This does not explain the change of attitude between 1854 and 1856. Writing of the 1795 Mescalero Apache uprising, Mark Santiago quoted from Antonio Cordero, one of the Spanish officers who fought them, that the Apaches were "jealous of their liberty and independence," and noted that "every family head in his own camp considers himself a sovereign in his district."[59] This might equally be said of the Jicarilla and of the Ute, in whom Carson did apparently place his trust. According to Dunlay, "Beyond that was the Jicarilla belief that they had a right to whatever grew on their land, granted to them by the supernatural powers, including the livestock and crops that Anglo and Hispanic ranchers thought belonged to them—a difference in viewpoint not easily reconciled."[60] It seems likely that this point of view was also shared by the Ute and indeed by all mountain and plains Indians. The point is perfectly valid and stands at the core of many disputes between white and Indian, but does not distinguish the two tribes from one another. In this context it is unsatisfying since Carson differentiated the Ute and Jicarilla although the explanation applies almost equally to either.

Kit Carson's opposition to the governor was as important as any other factor. David Meriwether was a consummate bureaucrat able to blame his mistakes on his predecessor while taking credit for others' successes. Rather than appeal for financial support for Lane's treaty, which would have been unpopular with Congress and his superiors and if successful would have brought credit to Lane, he chose a course he believed would lead to war. It was a war he could blame on Lane. When the war came, it was caused by Lieutenant Davidson's aggression rather than the failure of Lane's treaty.[61] Nonetheless, Meriwether's administration formally declared war and pursued it beyond the point at which their agent, Kit Carson, after the Battle of Ojo Caliente, said it was time to make a treaty. This would have troubled the straightforward frontiersman. Carson was not alone in his assessment of the governor. We've seen above what "A Friend of Truth" had written to the newspapers. Meriwether had said that Lane's treaty could not work and would cause a war. He got the war and ended it with a treaty in most respects identical to Lane's treaty, except that now it was Meriwether's achievement. Kit Carson was feeding Meriwether's words back to him. Meriwether opposed Lane's treaty and now he was claiming it as his own. Kit Carson was in effect saying, "But you said it wouldn't work."

Fauntleroy and St. Vrain beat the Jicarilla to the dust. The Jicarilla Apache never again warred against the United States and waited until 1887 before they were granted a reservation of their own. There were abortive attempts to confine them with the Mescalero and with the Navajo at Bosque Redondo, but most of the time they wandered, unwelcome in the settlements, drawing meager rations where they were bidden. The Jicarilla never were a problem again. The same cannot be said of the Ute. In later years, when miners invaded their lands, the Ute went to war.

Chapter 14

Lieutenant Davidson's misdeeds did not go unnoticed, although retribution took a while arriving and played out unsuccessfully.

Recently promoted Captain Davidson led the court of inquiry into his own misconduct. He selected and called the witnesses and asked most of the questions. Bell's letter accusing Davidson of cowardice before the enemy, attacking a peaceful camp, and incompetence as a combat commander was the only evidence against him. The outcome was predictable. The court consisted of the following officers: Colonel B. L. E. Bonneville, Major James Carleton, Major William Grier, and the recorder was Lieutenant Henry Clitz.[1] On the third day, Davidson called Kit Carson, who inspected the battlefield that day after the battle as a respected scout, to testify. It should be recalled that in April 1854, Kit Carson had written that "officers" had goaded the Jicarilla into war.

> *Question by Capt Davidson: What is the . . . difference of conduct . . . in Indians generally, towards troops, when they have the advantage in position and numbers, and when they do not have it?*
> *Answer: There is a great difference, an Indian when he sees he has the advantage, probably then the greatest coward is the greatest Brave. They never give any quarter, or at least, I never have known any instance of it.*[2]

At the end of the day at Cieneguilla, Davidson was wounded, twenty-two of his men lay dead, and most of the rest were wounded. Davidson's command was out of ammunition. The Jicarilla broke contact when they could easily have completely destroyed the command. Carson hedges his statement by saying "or at least, I never have known any instance of it."

Question by Capt. Davidson: Would a command of fifty men, good troops, well posted, be disadvantageous to one hundred & seven Indians, and account for their shrinking deportment toward troops, supposing in this case, the troops have the advantage?

Answer: If the troops had the advantage of position the Indians would shrink and be humble, but if the Indians had the advantage they would not. The Indians well know, for instance, that if both parties are on foot, and in broken country, they have the advantage over troops.[3]

Davidson was attempting to show that there were more than 107 warriors fighting against him. Carson didn't help him. According to Kit Carson, if the Apache had the advantage of terrain, they would stand and fight. Davidson then began to insert larger numbers of Indians into his questions, trying to get Carson to agree that there were a great many more warriors than 107 at Cieneguilla. The captain now changed tack to bring in the Utes he had reported as being present.

Question by Capt. Davidson: Were you out with Col. Fauntleroy, in any of his recent expeditions against Utah Indians?

Answer: Yes sir. I was.

Question by Capt. Davidson: Do you know of any arms, saddles or equipments, being captured from the Utahs, which belonged to my command at Cieneguilla?

Answer: I saw many arms in the hands of the Utahs, I have no doubt that were captured at Cieneguilla.

Question by Capt. Davidson: Do you think it a fair inference, then, that the Utahs or a small portion of them were at Cieneguilla?

Answer: The inference is certainly a fair one, there might have been but it has always been my opinion, that there were no Utahs in the fight.[4]

Kit Carson was trying to help his friend but was unwilling to lie for him, saying instead that there might have been Utes in the fight but he didn't think so. Without them, even if all the Jicarilla had been present at once, they wouldn't have had three hundred warriors. Questioning went on to cover the Battle of Ojo Caliente at which Carson was present. He thought there might have been 150 to 200 warriors present at that latter battle but is careful to note that Chacon had joined the camp with additional lodges bringing the total number of warriors at Cieneguilla back down to the 107 warriors Davidson himself had counted at Mora.

Captain Davidson richly deserved punishment for violation of his orders, for attacking a peaceful Jicarilla camp, and for tactical incompetence, but it was more convenient for everyone to make him a hero. Testimony dragged on through fourteen days. Toward the end it became clear that the court's principal interest devolved on the accusations of cowardice made by Lieutenant Bell.

Davidson may have had a momentary lapse of courage, but he carefully chose the witnesses he called so no hint of such a lapse went before the court. The court was willing to disregard Davidson's violation of orders not to bring on an action and to accept Davidson's claim that his attack on a peaceful camp was somehow an Apache ambush. And so, Captain Davidson remained the hero of the Battle of Cieneguilla, and the war that followed was blamed on Governor Lane's mishandling of the Jicarilla.

⁓

Governor Meriwether claimed to have won that war and to have made a treaty with the Apache that would bring lasting peace. As long as David Meriwether remained superintendent of Indian Affairs, the New Mexicans and the Jicarilla enjoyed a mutually hostile relationship. In June of 1857, the offices of governor and superintendent of Indian Affairs were separated and James Collins assumed the latter office.[5]

The Jicarilla came to the agency to voice their complaints against Americans and Mexicans, to answer to the agent for complaints against themselves, and to receive presents of food, clothing, blankets, and tools. Increasingly, food was important, as game within their range was overhunted. They were in competition with American and Mexican hunters and with the Comanche, Kiowa, and Cheyenne for buffalo. As Carson said, he was daily visited by Indians between 1855 and 1861, when he resigned as agent to accept a commission as a colonel in the New Mexico Volunteers to fight invading Texans.

During their joint tenures, Kit Carson and Meriwether remained hostile. Illiterate, Carson needed a clerk to keep his accounts and write his reports. He did not need an interpreter since he spoke Ute and Spanish, which most of the Jicarillas spoke from long association, and he knew Plains Indian sign language. But, the regulations allowed him to pay an interpreter and not a clerk. Carson tried to pay his clerk as an interpreter, but Meriwether rejected his vouchers. The bureaucrat saw this as a way to force Carson from office. There may have been an earlier more direct attempt that failed. The governor frequently sent back Carson's reports as unacceptable. In the end, despite disagreements over expenses and vouchers, Meriwether was never able to show that Carson had misspent government funds. Marshall D. Moody, who looked into Carson's tenure as agent, rated him a good agent, one of the best, who understood the Indians the government placed in his charge.[6]

A confusing story arises from Meriwether's autobiography. It speaks to the open hostility between the frontiersman and the bureaucrat. The details are difficult to reconcile and so we are uncertain of the year. The event may have occurred during the September 1855 treaty negotiations at Abiquiu or a year later at a meeting between the governor and the Jicarilla and Ute chiefs. There was a major altercation between Carson and Meriwether. Kit Carson and the dragoon officer involved, Richard Ewell, don't mention the event in any manner that is recognizably related to the Meriwether account. Carson would have been embarrassed by the events and may not have spoken of them as a result. There are a number of elements in the governor's account that seem entirely improbable.

In 1856, Carson talked about the meeting at Abiquiu between the governor and the Indians:

I frequently visit the Indians, speak to them of the advantages of peace, and use my influence with them to keep them satisfied with the proceedings of those placed in power over them. I attended September 4th, 1856, at the assembly of Indians at Abiquiu held by the Superintendent [Meriwether] for the purpose of giving them presents. They appeared to be content, then there was a disturbance the next day. A Tabauachi Utah tore up the blanket given him. It was old, had been worn, and he was dissatisfied. He wished to kill the Superintendent but was hindered by the other Indians.[7]

The governor also mentioned a Ute who wanted to kill him, but otherwise it bears resemblance to the 1854 meeting that started the war with the Ute. Meriwether might still have been handing out used blankets despite his experience. Carson was there for the opening day of the conference but in a subsequent letter to Meriwether indicates that he had departed before this incident occurred.[8] Nonetheless, it would still have been a recent memory when recorded.

In Meriwether's account, he met with the Ute and Jicarilla in council on the Chama River, taking along an escort of dragoons under the command of Captain Richard Ewell, 1st Dragoons, and a herd of sheep for the Indians to eat. Carson arrived on the second day with Chief Blanco of the Ute.[9] The governor notes that Blanco was a forbidding figure with only one eye and much scarred by smallpox. Meriwether says he turned the sheep over to Carson with instruction to issue ten or fifteen each day to the Indians. The frontiersman ignored these instructions and handed over all of the sheep at once. The governor goes on to say that on learning this he lectured Carson "in a mild manner for his disobedience of orders." Supposedly, Carson then mounted a "highhorse" and told Meriwether that he was agent for these Indians and would dispose of the sheep in any manner he thought proper.

Soon after, there was an alarm among the Indians. Young men rode in at the gallop with the disturbing news that a Navajo war party was attacking. The Ute and Jicarilla, after two years of war, believed themselves betrayed to their old enemies and blamed the governor. Meriwether called it "such a scene of confusion as I never witnessed in my life." Each Indian ran for his horse and mounted as they formed for battle to defend themselves. They brandished lances, bows, and rifles, giving forth the war whoop. One of the Ute cried out that they had been betrayed and should kill the betrayer, Governor Meriwether. The Ute suspected that they had been lured to their death. Kit Carson understood their speech and the danger. The Ute were convinced that Navajo were coming in cahoots with the governor to destroy them. In the midst of the panicked Indians, the governor walked about speaking kind words to calm them.

Carson, who understood what the Ute were saying, called out to Meriwether to follow him. He then took cover under the bank of the river. The governor ignored his entreaties telling Carson that they must show themselves to be bold and unafraid to calm the Indians. Carson warned the governor that the Indians intended to kill him. Meriwether claimed he had never seen such a display of cowardice when courage was called for.

According to Meriwether, Carson then became very abusive. "Governor, you're a damn fool to risk your life in this manner." The governor then told Carson that he was suspended as Indian agent, to which Carson replied impudently that he had been appointed by the president of the United States, an appointment equal to the governor's own, and that the governor had no authority to replace him. According to the governor, Carson became even more boisterous and abusive and Meriwether was obliged to call for assistance from the dragoon officer, Captain Ewell, whom he ordered to place Carson under arrest.

According to Meriwether, all of this occurred while the Jicarilla and Ute were galloping about, screaming war cries, brandishing weapons, and, as Carson would have known, threatening to kill the whites. In the governor's account, Ewell did not have his soldiers take a defensive posture to protect the governor. Instead, they busied themselves with arresting the ferocious former Indian agent.[10] Governor Meriwether said that he preferred charges against Kit Carson:

> the first specification of which was disobedience of orders; the second, insubordination; the third, disrespectful conduct towards a superior officer; and the last was cowardice, in the presence of the Indians.

The Navajo attack was a false alarm. Learning this, the Indians calmed down and negotiations resumed.[11] Carson, in the governor's account, wrote a letter of apology and the governor dropped the charges and reinstated the Indian agent.[12]

In 1864, during the campaign against the Comanche, Carson, after conferring with his Ute and Jicarilla scouts, but not his subordinate officers, ordered a withdrawal from the Battle of Adobe Walls. Some of those subordinates were not happy with the decision and perhaps even thought him cowardly. Caution had kept Carson alive through years in the mountains and many fights with Indians. If Kit Carson took cover during the excitement at Abiquiu, it was through caution because he understood what was being said. If events transpired in any manner remotely as the governor wrote they did, Carson, able to understand what the Indians were saying, and understanding the danger, would have at least given the governor the wisest council possible.

In his autobiography Carson was critical of Governor Meriwether although, still serving under him as agent, he had to hold his criticism in check:

I cannot see how the Superintendent can expect Indians to depart sat-isfied that he had called to see him from a distance of two or three hundred miles, compelled to go several days without anything to eat, unless they have carried it with them. They are given a meal by the Superintendent, then the presents are given. Some get a blanket; those that get none are given a knife or hatchet or some vermillion, a piece of red or blue cloth, some sugar, and perhaps a few more trinkets. They could more than earn the quantity they receive in one day's hunt, if left in their country. They could procure skins and furs and traders could furnish the same articles to them and they would be saved the neces-sity of coming such a distance, thereby not causing their animals to be fatigued and themselves to have to travel without food. If presents are given them it should be taken to their country. They should not be allowed to come into the settlements, for every visit an Indian makes to a town, it is of more or less injury to him.[13]

In June 1857, the government separated the offices of superintendent of Indian Affairs and territorial governor. James Collins became the new superintendent and Kit Carson vented some of his dissatisfaction with Collins's predecessor. Carson expressed his views of what should be done with his charges. They were conventional and very much in line with official government policy of the time. He thought that the Ute and Jicarilla should be established in "pueblos" as far as possible from the settlements.[14] He thought the two tribes should be separated by at least five miles, guarded by the military to protect them from raiding and raiders, and that farmers and "mechanics" should be brought in to teach them.[15] He thought that once they were settled and farming to support themselves, missionaries might be brought in to teach them the "laws and rules of Christianity." As Kit Carson expressed it:

Have no Mexicans to live near the Pueblos, for most of our difficul-ties is caused by them. They steal from the Indians, and the Indians know no law but that of retaliation, and from such acts commence hostilities with the Indian tribes and the United States, and as long as they remain near the Mexican settlements they will be furnished liquor, and the Jicarilla Apaches being notorios [sic] for drinking, will be always in difficulty with the citizens of the Territory."[16]

Throughout his service as Indian agent, Carson did not lose sight of the safety of frontier settlers. He had been on the frontier since his youth and was in sympathy with those so like himself. He did discriminate among tribes on the basis of their perceived degree of hostility to whites, but as time wore on, he would increasingly lay a larger and larger share of the blame on the settlers.[17]

In 1861, Kit Carson resigned as Indian agent in order to accept an appointment to defend New Mexico. He had filled the position with honor, honesty, and had shown concern for the interests of his charges. He left a mystery in his opposition to a treaty with the Jicarilla and his apparent change of heart during 1855.

The Jicarilla never went to war against the United States again, and Carson would call on them as allies against other enemies. They were beaten but not bowed. The Apache would continue to shape their own future despite government opposition and neglect.

Chapter 15

Understanding Kit Carson is not easy. We hear his voice only through others who wrote his words down, adding their own interpretations. Many statements attributed to him conflict. Most show him as a friend to Indians and to the Jicarilla Apache. It is important to evaluate not only his words but his actions as well to understand what he was trying to tell us and who he was. During the Civil War, he served under his friend General James Henry Carleton. Some have described Colonel Carson as an Indian hater and others have heavily criticized his actions at that time. Beyond dime novel descriptions, his true record shows a man worthy of praise. In 1864, the Jicarilla sent out their last war party at Carson's side and as his advisors.

In 1861, Carson resigned his position as Indian agent to accept a commission as a colonel of New Mexico Volunteers. In February 1862, Confederate general Henry Hopkins Sibley, formerly a 2nd Dragoon captain serving in New Mexico, attacked with two regiments of Texans and soon learned that native New Mexicans hated and feared Texans much more than they disliked the Union. Carson played an important role as a regimental commander at Valverde. Sibley captured the fords and went north leaving Fort Craig and its supplies unconquered in his rear. He left behind his wounded, unable to transport them, and went on to capture Albuquerque and Santa Fe. In March 1862, at Glorieta Pass, he was stopped by the Colorado Volunteers in what is called the Gettysburg of the West. Sibley's broken army limped back to Texas.[1]

The Texans held Mesilla on the southern emigrant trail and the Overland Mail.[2, 3] In March, a reinforced company under Captain Sherod Hunter captured Tucson. The southern road to the Pacific was closed to the Union.[4] Colonel James Carleton, Carson's old friend who had bought the scout a hat in admiration, was recruiting a brigade of volunteers in California. Carleton faced a challenge: he had to transport twenty-five hundred men across the deserts of New Mexico, which then included Arizona, 550 miles to the Rio

Grande. His men would have to cross one or two companies at a time so as not to put too much strain on resources of grass and water. Carleton planned carefully. He stockpiled supplies at abandoned Overland Mail stations only to have small parties of Rebels capture and burn them. This delayed his move.

Meanwhile, in 1861, the Jicarilla-Ute agency was transferred from Taos and Abiquiu to Lucien Maxwell's ranch at Cimarron. The reasons for the move remain unclear. Superintendent of Indian Affairs James Collins said that "Kit Carson, and a number of wealthy citizens of Taos, also all the prominent citizens of this [the Cimarron] side of the Taos Mountain," suggested the move. At the time, Carson denied having made such a recommendation but later admitted that he might have recommended it as a temporary expedient.[5] Judge Beaubien and Padre Martínez, both wealthy residents of Taos, would certainly have been glad to see the Jicarilla gone from that city. The only prominent citizen of Cimarron was Lucien Maxwell. The Maxwell land grant extended eastward from the crest of the Sangre de Cristo Mountains out onto the Llano Estacado, including 1,714,765 acres, more or less. He was the largest landowner in the United States and ruled his grant like a medieval fiefdom. He brought in settlers giving them land on handshake deals where they owed him payment as a share of their crops and herds. He was the law and the *patron*. He also was the only one who really benefitted financially by having the agency on his land. For many years to come he would provide grain, flour from his mill, and beef and sheep to the agency for distribution to the Indians. Moreover the Ute and Jicarilla trusted him more than anyone except Kit Carson.[6] Naturally, feeling his herds threatened by the proximity of the Jicarilla, Samuel Watrous complained.

The agency and the Jicarilla settled in along Poñil Creek, fifteen miles north of Cimarron. This seems to have been a peaceful, happy time for them. An informant told Morris Opler about his childhood in Cimarron:

According to one Indian, nearly three-fourths of the tribesmen living along the Cimarron had farms. "In my boyhood," a tribal elder explained, "the people depended quite a bit on agriculture. The wild foods were not certain. You might go several years without having a good crop of berries. Those who were not lazy," he continued, "and took care of their fields ate every day and had plenty." Their principal crop was corn, although they also raised beans, pumpkins, tobacco, and melons.[7]

The government of the Union fretted over relations with Indian tribes during the Civil War. Rumors circulated that agents were attempting to get the Indians to rise and join the Confederacy. Agents of the Confederacy did try to enlist the aid of some tribes, and there were tribes that fought alongside the Confederates. Nomadic tribes often hostile to the settlers surrounded New Mexico with its population clustered in a string of settlements along the Rio Grande. The territory was incapable of producing enough food to feed both its civilian and military population. It was dependent on a long umbilicus, the Santa Fe Trail, threatened by Jicarilla Apache, Cheyenne, Arapaho, Comanche, and Kiowa. In the south, Cochise and his father-in-law, Mangas Coloradas, and the Chiricahua Apache were on the warpath and since the departure of the soldiers, in control of the territory. Only in July 1862 did the California Column begin to win it back. Meanwhile, Navajo, Mescalero, Comanche, and Kiowa raided at will.

Thus, the Ute and Jicarilla, with their agency at Cimarron, were astride the trail and held the balance of power. The two tribes refused to have anything to do with the "Texians except to fight them if they came into this part of New Mexico to interfere with citizens." Both remained friendly throughout the war and, in 1864, supported Colonel Carson in his fight at Adobe Walls.[8]

General Carleton, beset on all sides, had the troops of the California Column and the New Mexico Volunteers at his disposal. He took on the hostile tribes one at a time, starting with the Mescalero Apache, cousins of the Jicarilla. Colonel Christopher Carson was one of the officers assigned to Fort Stanton and the Mescalero campaign. As an officer in the dragoons, Carleton had visited what seemed to him to be a paradise on the plains. It was well watered by the Pecos River and the land was green and fertile. It could become an agricultural haven. Along with Kit Carson and many in the government, he believed that peace could only be achieved with the nomadic tribes if they settled in villages and took up farming. Further, to separate them from white man's vices, particularly whiskey and thieving predators, they must live on reservations at least fifty miles from the settlements. A place he had seen on the Pecos River offered all of this and had the added benefit of being far out on the plains where the Indians could serve as a buffer between the settlements and the Kiowa and Comanche.

Now all that was needed was to force the tribes currently raiding into submission and send them to live at Bosque Redondo. He had the soldiers to achieve his goal. They were hard-fighting frontiersmen. Some of the New Mexicans nursed feuds with the Indians that went back hundreds of years.

Others were scoundrels from the gold fields. Few of his officers were trained professionals from West Point. Some of those recently granted commissions would prove weak on discipline and would have trouble reining in their soldiers' baser instincts. James Graydon was one recently elevated to a captaincy.

On April 21, 1859, the *Weekly Arizonian*, the newspaper at Tubac, reported: "The difficulty between Messrs. Graydon and Burr, which caused an exchange of shots between the parties a few days since, has been satisfactorily adjusted by the interference of friends."[9]

Captain James "Paddy" Graydon rode into Tucson in November 1856, as a sergeant in Troop G, 1st Dragoons, commanded by Captain Richard Ewell. Troop G was one of four companies under Major Enoch Steen arriving to take possession of the Gadsden Purchase. The unit established itself at Fort Buchanan where Paddy took his discharge.[10] The adventurous Irishman established the U.S. Boundary Hotel, known as Casa Blanca, three miles from post. It was a place where soldiers could enjoy recreation not found at the sutler's store—whiskey, women, and gambling. Sarah Bowman, nicknamed the Great Western, who managed the establishment, was reputed to be the best madam in Arizona.[11] Paddy liked excitement and volunteered for every adventure that came along—manhunts, posses, Indian campaigns, gunfights.[12] In July 1861, when the army pulled the soldiers at Forts Buchanan and Breckenridge back to the Rio Grande to defend against invading Texans, Paddy went with the troops. In New Mexico, the governor granted him a captain's commission in the New Mexico Volunteers. By late 1862, he commanded a company under Colonel Kit Carson at Fort Stanton in the Sacramento Mountains.[13] Graydon's behavior and General Carleton's response to it highlight the difference between the seemingly genocidal intent of the general's October 12, 1862, order and how he intended his officers to behave.[14] Carleton's order read:

All Indian men of that tribe [Mescalero Apache] are to be killed whenever and wherever you can find them. The women and children will not be harmed, but you will take them prisoners, and feed them at Fort Stanton until you receive other instruction about them. If the Indians send in a flag and desire to treat for peace, say to the bearer that when the people of New Mexico were attacked by the Texans, the Mescaleros broke their treaty of peace, and murdered innocent people, and ran off their stock; that now our hands are untied, and you have been sent to

punish them; that if they beg for peace, their chiefs and twenty of their
principal men must come to Santa Fe to have a talk here; but tell them
fairly and frankly that you will keep after their people and slay them
until you receive orders to desist from these headquarters. . . .[15]

In October 1862, at Anton Chico, Captain Paddy Graydon met with Lorenzo Labadie, agent for the Mescalero Apache. Labadie informed him that the Mescalero, despite recent depredations, were eager for peace and he would likely encounter them in the Gallinas Mountains. While returning to Fort Stanton, Captain Paddy Graydon and his company camped at Gallinas Spring.[16] The next morning, Manuelito, chief of a large band of the Mescalero, rode up with eleven warriors. The chief said he wanted peace and rations. Graydon distributed flour, beef, and sugar to the Indians.

Two of Graydon's men went out hunting and did not return. Concluding that they had probably deserted, he went in pursuit toward the nearest settlement. En route he encountered Major Arthur Morrison and Company I, 1st New Mexico Cavalry. As they had not seen his men, Graydon now presumed the Mescalero had killed them. Paddy told Morrison about his meeting with Manuelito and the major replied that he was under orders to respect no Indians whatsoever and would shoot the first one he saw. Graydon replied that the chief was peaceful and on his way to Santa Fe to see the general.

Graydon went back to Gallinas Springs and there met Manuelito and another chief, José Pino, along with thirty-one warriors and several women. Manuelito demanded whiskey and when refused drew his pistol. Paddy called for his men to open fire. Eleven Indians died and Graydon captured two small children. His men captured the Indians' horses and these were distributed as prizes of war.[17]

Within hours Major Morrison arrived at the site of the "Gallinas Massacre." To the major it was clear that Graydon had lied to Manuelito, deceiving the Indians by going into their camp and giving them liquor and when they were drunk, shooting them down. At Fort Stanton, both Graydon and Morrison wrote lengthy reports. The Gallinas Massacre became a major topic of discussion.

Shortly thereafter, Colonel Kit Carson arrived at the post, which had been occupied for a time by the Confederates and burned when they departed. Carson's men were forced to live in tents. Soon after, Dr. John Marmaduke Whitlock, of Las Vegas, arrived as post surgeon. Hearing the story of the massacre, the doctor, a friend of Carson's, referred to Graydon as a murderer and thief.

About 9:00 p.m. on November 4, 1862, Graydon burst in on a card game at the officers' room in the sutler's store demanding to know if Whitlock had referred to him as an assassinating cowardly son of a B____. Whitlock replied that while he couldn't recollect the words exactly, that was what he meant to say. Graydon was back and forth several times angrily demanding satisfaction. The doctor calmly put him off "until tomorrow."

In the early morning of November 5, Graydon confronted the surgeon initially in a seemingly friendly manner and then, increasingly angrily until finally Paddy Graydon proclaimed, "if you come to this post again and insult an officer, I will horsewhip you. I am an officer and you are a pimp that follows the army!" Graydon pursued. The doctor backed off and finally drew his revolver and fired on Paddy. Graydon returned fire. Only yards apart, neither was hit. Paddy took cover behind a wagon while Whitlock crouched behind a Sibley tent. Firing continued until Captain Graydon clutched his chest and cried out, "The son of a b____ has killed me." The surgeon grabbed his side. He retreated to the sutler's store.

Lieutenant Morris, double-barreled shotgun in hand, arrived on the scene with about thirty of Graydon's devoted men. Asked to help quell the violence, Morris replied, "No, we are going to kill the son of a b____!" Whitlock emerged from the store trying to make his way to the protection of Colonel Carson. Graydon's men shot the doctor to pieces.

Carson had the Long Roll sounded and assembled all of the soldiers on the fort in a hollow square around Graydon's men, who were then disarmed. Graydon was taken to the hospital. He was expected to recover. In Santa Fe, General Carleton had the reports of the massacre and of this latest incident. He ordered Carson to give Graydon the opportunity to resign his commission and if he refused to send him to Santa Fe under guard. Several of Graydon's men, including Lieutenant Morris, were sent in chains under guard for trial. On November 8, before he could receive word of his impending disgrace, Graydon died unexpectedly.[18]

On November 23, 1862, Lorenzo Labadie, Indian agent, and General Carleton met in Santa Fe with Cadete, one of the chiefs of the Mescalero Apache, who said:

> *You are stronger than we. We have fought you so long as we had rifles and powder; but your weapons are better than ours. Give us like weapons and turn us loose, we will fight you again; but we are worn*

out; we have no more heart; we have no provisions, no means to live; your troops are everywhere; our springs and water-holes are either occupied or overlooked by your young men. You have driven us from our last and best stronghold, and we have no more heart. Do with us as may seem good to you, but do not forget we are men and braves.[19]

Colonel Carson endeavored to be a good commander and to treat the Indians, even the Mescalero, with an even hand. He did not attempt to exterminate them as Carleton's order seemed to imply. The men and officers under his command, men like Paddy Graydon, posed difficulties. Carson did his best to control them and to punish misbehavior to the point of calling out his entire command to surround Graydon's men.

By November 5, 1862, work had begun on Fort Sumner at Bosque Redondo and Carleton sent the Mescaleros thither to become farmers. Carleton gave Colonel Carson a new assignment. He would corral the Navajo and send them to Bosque Redondo as well. The assignment was unwelcome. Carson was ill and wanted to spend some time in Taos with his growing family. As a soldier he had no choice.

The initial reports from Bosque Redondo were positive. In early 1864, the Indian Department decided to have the Jicarilla move from Cimarron where neighbors, particularly Watrous, were complaining of minor depredations, to the Bosque. The department ordered agent Levi J. Keithly to stop issuing presents to the Apaches at Maxwell's ranch. The government would allow the Jicarilla to move "voluntarily" to Bosque Redondo where presents would be issued. It's not clear if any went or if going, stayed without receiving presents.[20] In 1865, the policy was suspended and the Jicarilla remained at Cimarron.[21]

In September 1863, the superintendent of Indian Affairs for New Mexico Territory, Dr. Michael Steck, reported that the Navajos had not been at peace with the whites in the seventeen years since the territory had become a US possession. There had been military campaigns and the Navajo had submitted to six treaties and had broken them before the papers could be filed.[22] As with the Jicarilla and Ute, at least part of the problem was that the authority of the various headmen seldom extended beyond their immediate family. Congress seldom ratified the treaties or kept the promises made by the men in the field.

Unlike the Jicarilla and Ute, the Navajo were successful agriculturalists and herdsmen. It does not appear they were raiding to stave off starvation. The Utes and New Mexicans raided the Navajo for slaves and the Navajo returned the favor. This had been going on for generations with the slave market centered on Abiquiu. Any campaign in which New Mexicans and Ute participated alongside US soldiers was apt to include slave taking unless the commander was concerned, alert, and forceful in prohibiting the practice. Navajo headmen were content to sign treaties. Their young men needed to raid for property, wealth, and particularly sheep to set themselves up, get wives, and become wealthy. The headmen had their wealth.

Some have blamed Kit Carson for the fiasco at Bosque Redondo and for the Navajos' Long Walk to the extent that he has gotten a reputation as an Indian hater. Those assessing blame have seldom been historians who have studied the events. We have seen that he dealt fairly with the Jicarilla and Ute and stood up for them, attempting to get them fair treatment. It therefore becomes important to look at his role as soldier and in the Navajo campaign to access whether he was at fault and nursed some otherwise hidden hatred of Indians.

In 1868, Commissioner N. G. Taylor of the Indian Bureau wrote that the United States had conducted four campaigns against the Navajo and three of these had failed to bring either success or glory. In the fourth, the Indians succumbed to the superior strategy of the renowned Kit Carson, and were compelled by hunger to surrender.[23] It wasn't an assignment that Colonel Carson wanted, but as a soldier he was obliged to do as commanded.

During the Civil War, General William T. Sherman practiced total war. This does not imply the killing of civilians, women, and children. That sort of horror became prominent in the warfare of the first half of the twentieth century. Sherman attacked the enemy's ability to make war by destroying communications, transportation, and manufacturing. Native Americans may have been practicing something similar by stealing each other's horses and taking women as captives and slaves. After the Civil War, American soldiers routinely killed Indian ponies and buffalo. Long before this, soldiers attacked Indian camps, destroying tepees, buffalo robes, blankets, weapons, cookware, and food stores, forcing Indian compliance with government wishes through starvation and exposure to the elements. The warfare that Kit Carson took to the Navajo was nothing new nor was it reserved solely for Indians.

On September 6, 1863, General Carleton wrote to Army Headquarters regarding the Navajo:

One set of families may make promises, but the other set will not heed them. They understand the direct application of force as a law. If its application be removed, that moment they become lawless. This has been tried over and over, and over again, and at great expense. The purpose now is never to relax the application of force with a people that can no more be trusted than you can trust the wolves that run through their mountains; but, to take them out of their country, educate the children, so that they will grow up with new ideas; for, on a reservation, "until they can raise enough to be self-sustaining you can feed them cheaper than you can fight them."[24]

Captain Asa B. Carey, Kit Carson's quartermaster on the expedition, recalled the instructions General Carleton gave the command:

[W]ear the Indians out by capture of their herds of sheep and ponies (they had no other live stock), the destruction of their fields of corn, beans, pumpkins, etc.; the covering by occupancy by small detachments of troops, of all water supply, which in the end would result in acceptance by them of General Carleton's terms.[25]

Kit Carson didn't invent the style of warfare; Carleton's instructions described it. The general's intent was also clear that once the Navajo surrendered they should be fed and treated humanely. Carson executed his instructions efficiently, burning crops, destroying homes, and capturing sheep and ponies. He destroyed resources and reduced the Navajo to starvation and poverty, but both casualties and captures were low while Colonel Carson was in command. The soldiers reduced a lot of property to ash, though Canyon de Chelly with walls nine hundred feet high remained.[26] It was the Navajos' last and greatest stronghold. It had always protected them before. Ever cautious, Colonel Kit Carson was reluctant to enter the canyon. In December 1863, Carleton ordered him to proceed:

You will have the men carry their blankets and, if necessary, three or four days' rations in haversacks. The army of the Potomac carries eight days' rations in haversacks. Unless some fatigue and privations are encountered by your troops the Indians will get the best of you.[27]

Colonel Carson sent Captain Albert Pfeiffer to block exodus from the eastern end of the canyon while he and the main body proceeded to the western entrance. Snow delayed the approach of Carson's force. Arriving at the west end, Carson patrolled the rim on both sides seeking some sign of Pfeiffer, which he did not discover. The captain exceeding his orders proceeded down the length of the canyon to his colonel's position at the west entrance. Pfeiffer and company became the first to traverse the canyon in wartime. This feat alarmed the Navajo. On January 24, 1864, Colonel Carson wrote:

They [the Navajo] declare that owing to the operations of my command they are in a complete state of starvation, and that many of their women and children have already died from this cause. They also state that they would have come in long since, but that they believed it was a War of Extermination, and that they were agreeably surprised and delighted to learn the contrary from an old captive whom I had sent back to them for this purpose.[28]

On January 23, he wrote about the operation in Canyon de Chelly:

[H]aving accomplished an undertaking never before successful in wartime—that of passing through the Canon de Chelly from east to west, and this without having had a single casualty in his [Pfeiffer's Company H] command. He killed three Indians (two men) and brought in ninety prisoners (women and children). He found two bodies of Indians frozen to death in the canyon. . . . [Carson needed his soldiers to go back through the canyon and clear it of the enemy] This command of seventy-five men, I conferred upon Capt. Carey at his own request, he being desirous of passing through this stupendous canyon. I sent the party to return through the canyon from west to east, that all the peach orchards, of which there were many, should be destroyed, as well as the dwellings of the Indians. I sent a competent person with the command to make some sketches of the canyon, which, with a written description of the canyon by Capt. Carey . . . I respectfully enclose.[29]

Within the canyon were two or three thousand peach trees, the pride of the Navajo nation. Although he never entered Canyon de Chelly, Kit Carson ordered them cut down. Winter weather made this a difficult task and the execution was delayed until spring when Carson was long gone.[30] It is a mere quibble to say Kit Carson didn't have the peach orchards cut down. He ordered it, and it would have been done if the trees hadn't been frozen and impossible to cut. At the same time, in total war, it was a perfectly reasonable thing to do.

Colonel Carson wrote to his commander asking for permission to go on leave and visit his family. Carleton rejected his request until such time as Carson could escort as far as Santa Fe the first two hundred captive Navajo en route to Bosque Redondo. The first week of February 1864, Carson departed the Navajo country with the first convoy of 253 captives and escorted them without incident as far as the Rio Grande.[31] He then continued on to his waiting family in Santa Fe.

Defeated, the Navajo now began to flood in surrendering to the army; eventually on April 10, 1864, Carson wrote to his commander concerning the prisoners:

> *I would respectfully suggest to you the propriety, and good policy of, giving to the Indians while at Forts Canby and Wingate, and while en route to Bosque Redondo, a sufficiency to eat. It is while here, and en route that we must convince them by our treatment of them of the kind intentions of the Government toward them, otherwise I fear that they will lose confidence in our promises, and desert also. As suspicion enters so largely into the composition of the Indian character, the greatest possible care must be taken not to awaken it by acts contrary to our promises. I think one pound of Beef, or of flour, Wheat, or Corn, is entirely too small an allowance for an able bodied Indian for one day.[32]*

General Carleton was anxious that his soldiers treat the Navajo well in defeat. He wanted them to settle down to farm and to cease being a drain on the resources of the territory. He ordered his men to treat them with "Christian kindness." The goal, he said, was to transport them to Bosque Redondo as swiftly and safely as possible in the hope that soldiers would never have to fight them again. He warned that if the guards mistreated them, the Navajos would desert and return to their own country, beginning the wars anew. They were now "protégés of the United States—a people who, having given up their country, should be provided for by a powerful and Christian nation."[33]

The Navajo proceeded in small groups, a few hundred at a time, under armed escort. There were far more of them than expected, which put a strain on transportation and food. In any event, as Carson noted, the ration was insufficient. Carleton lacked the resources to provide more. Where commanders of the march were weak, the soldiers, both ruffians from the California gold fields and New Mexicans long at war with the Navajo, may have abused the Indians. The record indicates a significantly higher number in captivity at Forts Wingate and Canby than eventually arrived at Bosque Redondo. But records for individual parties on the march show them arriving with very few losses. The discrepancy is not easily explained, though the kind of disciplinary problems Colonel Carson experienced with the likes of Paddy Graydon suggest that abuse of Indians could have been a genuine problem. In any event, Carson was no longer in command. He had departed with the first 253 and was constantly calling for humane treatment.

Carson asked for the job of Indian agent at Bosque Redondo, and in May the government appointed him. Initially, things went well. The Navajo respected Kit Carson, and they knew how to farm. There were some differences of opinion over the types of homes they should build. They put in crops of wheat, sorghum, rice, and turnips, but mostly corn.[34] As in the past, Kit Carson was a benevolent and fair-minded agent and the Navajo stood in awe of him. However, he found himself pleading for supplies, which were not forthcoming. He had to request cooperation from the captain commanding Fort Sumner. This was galling as he was a colonel and he soon came to believe that the job of agent was more appropriate for a junior officer.[35] He begged to be relieved and was gone by September.

By midsummer the crops were tall in the fields. And then, an army of worms struck and reduced the corn to nothing. Carleton lacked the resources to completely offset this disaster. There were other complaints about the reservation on the Pecos. The river water was alkaline and produced unfortunate effects on the digestion. The land was unfamiliar, flat, and lacking in character. It wasn't like Navajo country. The Mescalero weren't friendly. Carleton's dream did not match the reality.

Kit Carson was gone, on to other pursuits. Comanche and their Kiowa allies had attacked a party on the Santa Fe Trail. The general could not tolerate this threat to his command, as this was the link to supplies and civilization. A joint operation with troops from Colorado was envisioned, converging columns, but the troops in Colorado were busy with the Cheyenne. On November 29, 1864, Colonel John Chivington commanding Colorado volunteers attacked a friendly Cheyenne camp at Sand Creek. There was no hope of quickly obtaining peace. Chivington was a bad commander over even worse ninety-day volunteers—the dregs of Denver's gutters—and he engendered mistrust in the Indians.

The general's acceptance of Carson's proposal to use Ute and Jicarilla auxiliaries against the pillaging plains tribes was not without opposition. Dr. Michael Steck, superintendent of Indian Affairs, thought using one tribe against another "a grave error and dangerous policy," especially since the Comanche had been at peace with the people of New Mexico. Comancheros were New Mexicans who traded manufactured goods, including weapons and ammunition, for buffalo robes. Here, too, was a reminder of how dangerous the Jicarilla had been and might be again. Their natural range included a significant portion of the Santa Fe Trail. In the spring of 1865, the New Mexico legislature wrote to Congress about the exposed and dangerous condition along the Santa Fe Trail and of the hostility of the Comanche and Kiowa. They recommended a treaty of peace with these tribes.[36] In the past, Indian tribesmen and American soldiers had paid for such treaties in blood. Any hostile tribe on the trail was a terror to New Mexico.

General Carleton attacked the Kiowa and Comanche with his finest weapon, Kit Carson. Colonel Carson set out on the Llano Estacado to a place he knew well, one established by his old employers. The Bent Brothers, Charles, William, and George, and their partner, Ceran St. Vrain, were first and foremost Indian traders. They built Fort William, Bent's Old Fort, on the Arkansas River in 1832, to trade with the Southern Cheyenne. William married Owl Woman, the daughter of a Cheyenne chief, and lived at Fort William. His half-Cheyenne son, George, was named for the brother who died at age thirty-three in October 1847. William's son was born in 1843, educated at Westport, Missouri, and joined the Missouri State Guard, a Confederate organization, in 1861, serving Colonel Green's cavalry regiment until captured at the siege of Corinth. Family connections got him released on parole.[37]

In old age, George recalled the events of his life. His father and uncles wanted to expand trade with the Comanche and Kiowa. In 1845, competing with the Comancheros, William Bent built a new trading fort on the Canadian River.[38, 39] Three different nations claimed possession of the Llano Estacado before 1846. In 1836, Sam Houston signed a "treaty" with Santa

Anna under which the latter agreed to withdraw his armies beyond the Rio Grande. Albuquerque, Santa Fe, and Taos are all on the Texas side of the river. Texas attempted to extend her claim several times, including raiding caravans on the Santa Fe Trail, without success. Mexico claimed that everything north to the Missouri River belonged to her but in practice didn't try to extend her reach beyond the Arkansas or onto the Llano. The Comanche and Kiowa nations ruled the land. The fort on the Canadian was not successful and William Bent abandoned it.

After the United States took possession of the land in 1848, Indian Agent Thomas Fitzpatrick, known to the Indians as Broken Hand, called the tribes together at Big Timbers, the site of Fort William, Bent's Fort, including Comanche, Kiowa, Cheyenne, Arapaho, Ute, and Jicarilla Apache. The tribes promised peace. On the strength of this Big Timbers Treaty, William Bent thought he'd try his luck again by reopening Adobe Fort on the Canadian. Kit Carson led the party, which included Lucien Maxwell, Robert Smith, and others, along with two Mexicans to do the cooking and mind the herd. In trade, Carson acquired a large herd of horses and mules. Jicarilla Apache killed the Mexican herder and made off with all but a handful of animals corralled inside the post. The project was abandoned and the fort allowed to deteriorate until only Adobe Walls remained on a low hill beside the river.[40]

In October and November 1864, Colonel Carson gathered his forces at Fort Bascom.[41] At the Cimarron Agency he attempted to recruit one hundred Ute and Jicarilla warriors. For the Jicarilla, it would be their last great war party, and a fight against their ancient foe, the Comanche. Carson changed his request for forces several times. Carleton was unable to provide much more than three hundred soldiers. The three-year enlistments of the men in the California Column had begun to expire.[42] Carson departed Fort Bascom with fourteen officers, 321 enlisted men, and seventy-five Indian scouts. With Colonel Carson, commanded by Major William McCleave went two and a half companies of the First California Volunteer Cavalry, two companies of the First New Mexico Volunteer Cavalry, along with one company of California Volunteer Infantry under Lieutenant Colonel Francisco Abreu, and a battery of two mountain howitzers under Lieutenant George Pettis.[43, 44] Many years later, Jicarilla elder Casa Maria recalled the adventure:

It was at Cimarron also that they started off with Gidi (Kit Carson) after the enemy. There were Ute, Apache, soldiers, and Mexicans. Four different nations went with him after the enemy. They went down the Canadian River to HweLdibade (Mexican name?) where they found the enemy. There were many tipis there. At evening, when they were approaching the camp of the enemy, men were sent out to observe. There their camp was lying some way off. The party moved on until nearly day when they saw the campfires. The horsemen, leaving the others, rode forward. There were two camps of the enemy, one above the other. All the Apache rode together and commenced to fight. They drove them from the upper camp and pursued them to the lower camp where they fought with them. Taking away their horses they fought with them until night. Many of the soldiers were killed. One Apache was killed and one was wounded in the foot. A spent ball entered his foot but did not pass through it. Another Apache received an arrow under his arm through his clothing. Many of the enemy were killed and all their tents and goods were brought home on wagons. The enemy drove them away from their lower camp. They came back to Cimarron where they danced until they were tired.[45]

Lieutenant Colonel Francisco P. Abreu of the New Mexico Volunteers received word from recently returned Mexican Comancheros that about three thousand Kiowa and Comanche were camped for the winter at North Palo Duro Creek two hundred miles northeast of Fort Bascom.[46] By November 4, the troops had assembled at Fort Bascom and the quartermaster had received his supplies in a train of twenty-seven wagons and an ambulance. "[T]he morning of the sixth of November found the command ready to stretch out, the horses having all been well shod, and after some difficulty in crossing the Canadian river, to the north side, the expedition was well on the war path before noon. . . ."[47]

A whole new generation of Jicarilla warriors had taken their elders' place since the last big war party almost ten years before. Issued rifles at Fort Union, they could hardly contain their excitement. They would win war honors and earn pay which when they returned home would make them important men, respected, and better able to find desirable wives. They would be attacking their most hated enemy, one that had denied them access to buffalo herds and thus to food. All the way out from Fort Bascom they sang and danced through the nights, much to Lieutenant Pettis's chagrin as the singing denied him sleep, building up their medicine, their war power:

The Indians with our command, on every night after making camp, being now on the war path, indulged in their war dance, which, although new to most of us, became almost intolerable, it being kept up each night until nearly daybreak, and until we became accustomed to their groans and howlings incident to the dance, it was impossible to sleep.[48]

They marched in good weather, finding ample water at their camps. Cautious, Colonel Kit Carson kept scouts well out on his flanks and to his front. On November 24th, after a short march of eighteen miles, they went into camp in the early afternoon. As the soldiers attended to camp chores, caring for horses, and building fires to cook dinner:

[W]e were surprised to see our Indians, who were lying around the camp, some gambling, some sleeping, and others waiting for something to eat from the soldiers' mess, spring to their feet, as if one man, and gaze intently to the eastward, talking in their own language quite excitedly. Upon questioning Colonel Carson, why this tumult among our Indians, he informed us that the two scouts that he had dispatched that morning, had found the Comanches, and were now returning to report the particulars. Although the returning scouts were at least two miles distant, and, mounted on their ponies, were hardly discernible, yet the quick, sharp eye of our Indians made them out without difficulty.[49]

The returning scouts rode through the camp without speaking to anyone, refusing to answer questions. Without looking right or left, they proceeded directly to Colonel Carson and made their report.[50] They had located the large camps of Kiowa and Comanche. Kit Carson put his plan in motion. Under Colonel Abreu, infantry, dismounted cavalry, and the wagon train would remain in camp coming up with the rest of the command the next day. They would be too slow and too noisy and might give away the command's presence to the enemy. The cavalry, the artillery, and the Indian scouts would go forward under strict orders to neither speak nor smoke since either might betray their presence. This night there would be no war dance. Colonel Carson forbad it.[51]

It would be a long, cold night for the soldiers. The Jicarilla and Ute pulled their buffalo robes around their bodies and drew their legs up inside until, to Lieutenant Pettis, they resembled so many tepees on horseback.[52] Carson rode out in front with Pettis at his side accompanied by the Indian scouts in no particular order, behind them came one half of the cavalry, then the artillery, and finally the rest of the cavalry. They rode through tall cane grass below the riverbanks, six and eight feet tall. At times Carson and Pettis, although riding side by side, lost sight of each other. As the bluff beside the river became less restrictive to their movement, Carson led the troops up out of the sandy bed into the river bottoms.

Kiowa pickets spotted them almost immediately.

"Bene-aca! Bene-aca!" they cried. "Come here! Come here!" Apparently, the Kiowa had mistaken them for friendly Comancheros and were calling them in to trade. Then again, it may have been a challenge, an invitation to a fight. Ever alert, Carson ordered Major McCleave along with Company B, First California Cavalry, and Captain Deus of the New Mexico Cavalry after them. Soon shots were heard which rapidly multiplied into the thousands.

Pettis recalled:

> *Our Indians, who had been riding leisurely along, at the first cry charged into a clump of chapparel [sic] which was near by, and in a moment, as it seemed, came riding out again, completely divested of buffalo robes and all their clothing, with their bodies covered with war paint, and war feathers in abundance, and giving a war-whoop they dashed wildly into the river towards the enemy. . . . Carson gave orders for us [the artillery and remaining cavalry] to move down on our side of the river, he being satisfied that the village would be found within a short distance.*[53]

Many arroyos and creeks are tributary to the Canadian. Pettis and his heavy howitzers had difficulty crossing them but pressed on. Ahead of them the sounds of battle grew more distant. In a meadow they found their Ute and Jicarilla allies busy cutting out their own personal groups of ponies and ignoring the battle. In fairness, this is part of how Carson had agreed to compensate them. The Comanche camp and their horses were miles far-ther downstream. Carson was in contact with the Kiowa, the camp of Chief Dohäsan still two miles ahead.

Early in the morning of November 25, Major McCleave's engagement was short and sharp. He had struck the Kiowa camp and a few seasoned warriors conducted the defense while women and children and the white captives the Kiowa held were hastened away to hiding in the canyon north of the camp. Among the seven captives were the wife and two children of a ser-geant of Colorado Volunteers killed a month before in Kansas. They would not be rescued that day. Most of the Indian men were away on the warpath. Although the attack had come as a complete surprise, the chief handled the defense skillfully.

In later years, Mrs. Goombi, one of the captives who lived out her life among the Kiowa, recalled: "Once when I was a child, our Kiowa camp was raided by the Ute Indians who were led by the white scout, Kit Carson. My parents hid me safely in the brush next to the camp, and I escaped any harm."[54]

Doctor Courtright, the surgeon with the US troops recalled: "In the fight at the Indian village I saw the arrows flying in all directions, and could scarcely distinguish our own Indians from those of the enemy."[55]

Chief Dohäson hurried away downriver to alert the Comanche and bring assistance. Having seen the women and children to safety, the Kiowa warriors now headed downstream four miles to Adobe Walls, Bent's old trading post. McCleave and the cavalry were close behind them. By the time the soldiers arrived, Comanche reinforcements were already close by. The major had his men dismount and fan out as skirmishers. Instead of having the fourth man hold horses, he was able to corral his livestock within the Adobe Walls, thus freeing up another quarter of his men to join in a fight in which they were heavily outnumbered.

Carson, hearing the sounds of battle, was anxious to join in, convinced that it would be over quickly. He did not know of the enormous number of Indians opposing him. He threw his greatcoat into a bush encouraging Pettis's sweating men to do the same. Pettis declined. Carson never saw that coat again.

Dr. Cortright set up the medical station within the Adobe Walls while Pettis brought his howitzers to a spot farther along the ridge. As soon as the howitzers came up, Colonel Carson yelled, "Pettis, throw a few shell into that crowd over thar," and Pettis responded, "Battery, halt! Section right—load with shell—LOAD!"[56] Out to their front about two hundred

Kiowa and Comanche were riding back and forth firing under the necks of their horses. Behind them, urging them on, were fourteen hundred more warriors. The cannon fired. The Comanche, unfamiliar with cannon, stood tall in their stirrups and considered the excitement until the shells exploded among them. They turned their mounts and headed toward their villages at a dead run.

Carson moved his soldiers, and howitzers, to better positions spread out as skirmishers. He knew the enemy would return. He stationed his men along a small, extended ridge giving them a slight advantage in detecting approaching enemies. He anchored his flanks in the bluffs on his left and the open river bottom on his right. It was terrain through which the enemy would be exposed to his fire or through which the Comanche would have difficulty approaching. He turned his line at the ends to refuse his flanks. If the enemy were to approach from a flank, his entire line would be exposed to each projectile. Carson kept the Indians at bay with the long-range fire of his cannon skillfully employed. Only with difficulty and courage could enemy warriors approach close enough for their fire to be effective against Carson's men. When the Comanche and Kiowa returned, they rained down fire on the soldiers from a distance, now cautious of the big guns, careful not to bunch up, and keeping well away from his lines. The fire of the howitzers kept the Indians from massing and overwhelming the soldiers. With the horses corralled instead of held, and with only a single line to defend, cannon holding the enemy at bay, the mathematics of war worked in Colonel Carson's favor. Even though greatly outnumbered, the number of weapons in range of his own did not much exceed the number of his weapons in range of the enemy. His four hundred soldiers and Indian scouts were equal to the one thousand Kiowa and Comanche warriors in their camp of 350 lodges two miles distant.[57]

Over the noise of battle, rifle fire, war whoops, shot, and shell, Colonel Carson relayed his commands through his bugler. Somewhere a hidden Indian bugler responded by blowing the counter order. If Carson ordered the *advance*, the Indian blew *retreat*. Pettis recalled:

So he kept it up all the day, blowing shrill and clearly as our very best buglers. Carson insisted that it was a white man, but I have never received any information to corroborate this opinion. All I know is, that he would answer our signals each time they were sounded, to the infinite merriment of our men, who would respond with shouts of laughter each time he sounded his horn.[58]

The enemy kept coming, more arriving all the time. Colonel Carson saw some of them slipping around his flank beyond the range of his weapons. They rode west toward the Kiowa village to protect the robes and winter supplies the soldiers had left behind, intending to burn them later. If enough of them moved to the west behind him, withdrawal might become impossible. Colonel Carson might lose the village he had come to burn. Moreover, somewhere to his west Colonel Francisco Abreu with seventy-five foot soldiers was approaching with the supply wagons. They might be overwhelmed, leaving Carson and his men without food, shelter, and supplies, including ammunition.

Carson consulted his Jicarilla and Ute scouts, but not his subordinate officers. The Indian scouts agreed. It was time to withdraw. At half-past three in the afternoon of November 25, Colonel Carson prepared his men for the withdrawal. His officers objected. They'd taken one village. They could take another. They had cannon.

Carson was about to undertake the most difficult of all military maneuvers, a withdrawal under fire. Carson called in the "fours," the fourth man from each squad who would hold and lead the horses. This reduced his firepower by one-fourth. He formed a hollow square with the "fours," horses, doctor, and the wounded in the center. The remaining three-quarters of his men spread out as skirmishers. Captain Fritz and Company B, First California Volunteer Cavalry, protected the right flank. Captain Gilbert Tapley Witham, and Company M, First California Cavalry, along with part of Captain Charles Deus's company were on the left. Captain Joseph Berney, Company D, First New Mexico Cavalry, was in the rear along with Lieutenant Sullivan Heath, Company K, First California Cavalry, and the remainder of Captain Deus's company, along with Pettis's howitzers. McCleave was in the vanguard with Carson and the scouts.[59] Perhaps one-third of Carson's firepower was in the rear of this formation, a huge step down from all, while one-sixth was on each flank.

When the Kiowa and Comanche recognized that the soldiers were headed back to the captured Kiowa camp, they realized the threat to their lodges, camp equipment, and winter food. This spurred them into action, and they stepped up their attacks. Realizing that direct assault was devastating to their own ranks, they worked out a scheme to screen their attack. Where modern armies would employ smoke, Kit Carson's Indian enemies lit the grass afire and advanced within a few yards of the troops.

One New Mexican soldier found himself face to face with a Comanche whose weapon was leveled in his direction. The Indian fired and missed. The New Mexican didn't and he stopped long enough to relieve the Comanche of his scalp, the only one taken that day. Later the Jicarilla and Ute scouts bought it from him and danced with it every night on the way back to Fort Bascom.

Colonel Carson, recognizing the danger the grass burning posed, ordered the grass ahead of his force ignited. Once the brief fires went out, he ordered his men across the burned ground and they moved on to higher ground. The howitzers again deterred the massed charges of the enemy. As they advanced on the Kiowa village, they found it occupied by a small force of Kiowa attempting to rescue their supplies. Using an embankment for cover as if it were a trench, the soldiers fired into the camp. Then the howitzers came up.

Pettis stopped at the base of a hill on the side out of view of the enemy. The crew loaded a cannon, then pushed it up the hill until the muzzle was over the crest. From a prone position, the gunner activated the primer without exposing himself to enemy fire. The recoil pushed the gun back on its trail and down the hill, where the crew reloaded out of sight of the enemy to repeat the process. After a fierce exchange of fire, the howitzer and the troops drove the enemy out of the village.

The troops selected the best buffalo robes to keep them warm on the ride back to New Mexico. While the others stood guard in the gathering dusk, about half of the troops set about their task of destruction, dragging tepees together, piling food and other supplies on top and letting the whole burn. In the conflagration went meat, berries, buffalo robes, and even Chief Dohäsan's buggy and spring wagon given to him a few years prior to this by a military unit in Kansas. Carson reported 150 lodges demolished.

In his report to General Carleton, Colonel Kit Carson noted that many of the items destroyed were trade items—powder, lead, percussion caps— which had been used to fire on his men. The enemy had acquired these illegally from Comancheros.

His men hadn't slept in two days and had eaten very little. The enemy was still close by after the fall of darkness as Carson continued his march to the west, now seeking Colonel Abreu and the wagons. Three hours later, exiting the creek bottoms, the tired troops spotted campfires off to their right. They approached cautiously, knowing the enemy was near, afraid that it might be still another enemy village. "Halt! Who comes there?" They had found Abreu's camp. The colonel had picked an excellent defensive site on a hill and they settled in for the remainder of the night.

Early the next morning, November 26, Carson had the bugler sound reveille before dawn as a precaution against attack. The colonel had little choice but to lay over a day, allowing his men to rest and eat, and his livestock to recover. The soldiers cleaned their weapons, cared for their horses, and repaired their equipment. As the sun burned away the night's chill, Kiowa and Comanche warriors appeared on a hill two miles distant. The Jicarilla and Ute scouts rode out to meet them. The two bands exchanged a few shots. The enemy knew to keep out of range of the howitzers. Soon the Comanche and Kiowa disappeared from sight.

Carson's officers wanted to pursue and attack the enemy camp they had discovered. The colonel considered the condition of his men, equipment, and especially of his livestock, and then ordered the command to begin the march home. They set out early on the morning of November 27. All the way home, the scalp taken was the bane of the troopers as the scouts sang and danced with it each night.

During the battle, the enemy warriors shot one California trooper, and then lanced him. Nonetheless he survived. The Indians slew two soldiers and wounded five, although Pettis recalled twenty-one soldiers with wounds. It is possible that minor wounds didn't go into the formal reports. One Jicarilla warrior died in combat. Colonel Carson estimated that his men had killed sixty of the enemy. Each time a warrior fell, the Kiowa and Comanche had been quick to retrieve the body. The Kiowa say that only five fell that day. Carson's figure seems closer to the truth although soldiers have always overestimated enemy dead rather spectacularly. Kit Carson was calm and experienced, not given to speculation.[60] Moreover, there were enough unmistakable deaths to account for more than five Indians. There was one scalped in close combat. A howitzer shell went through the horse of another before exploding and sending him flying. Canister is devastating in its effect on massed troops.

Colonel Kit Carson was not defeated. He had destroyed an enemy village and discovered in the process proof that New Mexico could no longer tolerate the Comancheros. Carson discerned that the enemy force was larger than he could handle with his few men. He was outnumbered at least five to one. Placing great trust in former Jicarilla enemies, he took his scouts' advice and broke contact. He managed what Lieutenant Davidson could not at Cieneguilla; he preserved his command with few losses. He successfully executed the most difficult of all military maneuvers. As George Bent noted:

> But for the coolness and skill of Carson and his Indian scouts the retreat would have become a rout and few would have escaped.[61]

Kit Carson said that if it had not been for his howitzers, few would have been left to tell the tale. [62]

Epilogue: The Forgotten Warriors

On March 13, 1865, the army honored Kit Carson by brevetting him a brigadier general and appointing him commandant of Fort Garland, which was in the heart of the country of his friends the Ute. In November of 1867, his First Regiment of New Mexico Volunteer Cavalry mustered out of the Army, and Carson rode down to Santa Fe and was formally discharged. After he was mustered out, Carson took up ranching at Boggsville near Bent's Fort on the Arkansas River. On April 27, 1868, his beloved wife, Josefa, passed away from complications of the birth of their eighth child. Her death was a serious blow to the bold mountain man. On May 23, at the age of fifty-eight, Kit Carson passed away, a victim of an aneurysm acquired as a result of injuries years before.[1] The Carsons were buried at Boggsville and later reinterred at Taos where they lie today.

Kit Carson had been a good and faithful, honest Indian agent. His friend Tom Tobin said of him, "Carson was as clean as a hound's tooth." And James F. Rusling, who knew Carson at Fort Garland, spoke of his "honesty, matchless coolness, and courage ... the Indians had no truer friend than Carson." General William Tecumseh Sherman said, "Kit Carson's integrity was simply perfect. The Indians knew it and would trust him any day before they would us, or the president either!" One of his soldiers said that "The Indians think Kit a god." Another recalled that "Carson was a popular man at Taos Pueblo, and the Indians believed he was a little on the supernatural order." With his passing, the Jicarilla Apache lost one of their finest advocates.

Historian Marc Simmons, who has a deep understanding of Christopher Carson, wrote: "In his own time, Kit Carson was repeatedly categorized by contemporaries as an Indian lover and a leading defender of Indian rights and advocate of fair treatment."[2]

Lieutenant Davidson and Governor Meriwether, both seeking to advance their own careers, had victimized the Jicarilla Apache, but it would be wrong to think of the tribe as victims. The Jicarilla continued to shape their own destiny even after they were denied a treaty and thus were relegated to drawing rations at Lucien Maxwell's ranch, and they continued to pose a threat to American and Mexican settlers in the region. Furthermore, they had learned that banding together with the Ute and operating with central political will would help them in their struggles against the whites. In June 1868, Major General George Getty, commanding the District of New Mexico, wrote "should an outbreak occur, it will involve the entire Ute tribe and, also, Jicarilla Apache, who are associated with them."[3]

In the first half of the nineteenth century, Indians were pushed back across a "frontier." This frontier was the Mississippi River for a while, then the western border of Missouri. Many of the early negotiations with the Jicarilla attempted to use this frontier, hence the people of Taos wanted the Jicarilla to move west of the western boundary of Taos County. As this became unrealistic, the reservation system came into being. Many of these were created by Executive Order. What can be created by Executive Order can be undone the same way as the Jicarilla found to their chagrin.

Between 1855 and 1887, they wandered without a reservation or a frontier, drawing gifts, not annuities, from various agencies. For many years the tribe has two stories. Some of the Olleros settled against government instruction at Cañon del Oso on the Chama River, drawing gifts at the Abiquiu agency along with the Ute, and later at the Tierra Amarilla sub-agency farther north on the Chama River. Other Olleros, most of the Llaneros, and some of the Ute settled at the Cimarron Agency on Poñil Creek.

At Cimarron the Jicarilla had known Lucien Maxwell for a very long time. He understood them and they trusted him, so that he was able to exert some influence over them when no one else could. He, not their agent, was the man really in control at Cimarron. Maxwell leased the government 1,280 acres on Poñil Creek, where the agency constructed a residence for the agent, an Indian school, and offices.[4] During 1862, the chiefs of both tribes, Ute and Jicarilla, met with Agent William Frederick Milton Arny. They made it clear to him that unless the government provided meat, they would have no alternative but to steal to feed their families.[5] Maxwell was close at hand, happy to sell beef and flour from his mill to the government. The Llanero Jicarilla farmed successfully along the creek and, if Casa Maria's recollections are indicative, the Apache were content. In September 1867, Major Charles McClure reported feeding eight hundred Jicarilla and six hundred Ute. A census of Indian tribes found that there were 1045 Jicarillas. A "renegade" band of forty Ollero warriors and thirty-nine lodges, more than two hundred people, were encamped at Cañon del Oso, on the Chama River between the Rio Grande and Abiquiu.[6] They were renegade only in that the government did not wish them to be there.

Maxwell's Mill in Cimarron where the Jicarilla and Ute drew rations in the 1860s and 70s. AUTHOR PHOTO

That October, agents Arny, Dennison, and Ward visited the Jicarillas on Cañon del Oso (Bear Creek). The agents told the Jicarilla that the government desired them to leave that location and move to Cimarron. The Jicarilla told the agents that they had been born, raised, and lived their whole lives at Cañon del Oso, and some years before, the commander of the army, Colonel Stephen Watts Kearny, had told them they should live on this side of the Rio Grande and be protected by the government.[7] Further, when they had moved to Cimarron on the order of their agent five years before, they learned they were not wanted there either. It was only logical for them to stay where they were living peacefully and providing most of their own support.[8] Their attachment to the Chama River Valley and its tributaries was strong and would come up time and again as they shaped their future.

Ration day at Cimarron. The Jicarilla ride in among the cattle and kill them as if they were buffalo, leaving the women to butcher them. Lucien Maxwell's house is in the center background. About 1860. COURTESY PALACE OF THE GOVERNORS PHOTO ARCHIVES (NMHM/DCA), 8957

The Ollero were happy at Cañon del Oso in their home country while the Llanero were content at Cimarron. Their neighbors at Cimarron reported the Llanero as troublesome. Watrous was especially vocal. The Jicarillas were reported stealing sheep, horses, cattle, and even little children. The rumors proved false.[9] On June 29, 1868, the commander at Fort Union responded to General Getty concerning a rumor of an imminent outbreak:

> *Captain Wm. Hawley, 3d Cavalry reports that no trouble or dissatisfaction exist with the Utes or Apache Indians at Maxwells. The entire Ute tribe is down on the Red River some two hundred miles hunting.*
>
> *The Apache are encamped within two miles of Captain Hawley's Company at the Cimarron.*
>
> *The origin of the report that they were moving west probably arrives [derives?] from their moving into their present village some Indians thought to be a small stealing party of Navajo Indians having run off some stock on the Cimarron, and the Apache being the only tribe known in the vicinity were accused of theft. They immediately moved their whole tribe in to be searched which was done but no stolen property was found. Captain Hawley reports them as well disposed and anxious to maintain friendly relations with the whites.[10]*

Complaints such as these, even false ones, made life difficult and set the government looking for yet another place to put the Jicarilla away from the settlements, away from the Santa Fe Trail. The buffalo herds on the Llano Estacado diminished rapidly after the Civil War, and as buffalo and other game diminished, the need for supplemental meat from the government became ever more important to the Jicarilla. In the summer of 1867, Colonel Henry Inman, a guest of Maxwell's, was witness to the delivery of beef to the Jicarilla and Ute:

> *The cattle, as wild as those from the Texas prairies, were driven by his herders into an immense enclosed field, and there turned loose to be slaughtered by the savages. . . . The squaws, a hundred of them, were sitting on the ground, their knives in hand ready for the labour, which is the fate of their sex in all savage tribes, while their lords' portion of the impending business was to end with the more manly efforts of the chase. Suddenly a great cloud of dust rose on the trail from the mountains, and on came the maddened animals, fairly shaking the earth with their mighty tread. As soon as the gate was closed behind them, and uttering a characteristic yell that was blood-curdling in its ferocity, the Indians charged upon the now doubly frightened herd, and commenced to discharge their rifles, regardless of the presence of anyone but themselves. . . . In less than twenty minutes the last beef had fallen; and the warriors, inflated with the pride of their achievement, rode silently out of the field, leaving the squaws to cut up and carry away the meat to their lodges, more than three miles distant, which they soon accomplished, to the last quivering morsel.*[11]

Resources grew more scarce in 1869, when mines in the Sangre de Cristo began producing gold. Lucien Maxwell's grant ran from the "crest" of the Sangre de Cristo and although some would dispute his ownership, the gold was coming from his property. The range in the area of the gold strike has an eastern and western crest with a long valley in between. The gold strike was in the valley. The descriptions of huge Spanish and Mexican land grants were vague at best. American settlers showed little respect for properties lacking a house and fence defended by guns. The influx of miners to an area between the headwaters of Poñil and Cimarron Creeks put increased pressure on game resources and created occasions for often unfriendly contacts between the Apaches and the miners and their hunters.[12] The complaints about the Jicarilla continued but perhaps the greatest of them came when, on July 23, 1870, Maxwell sold his huge land grant to English investors. The investors wanted the Indians gone so that they could subdivide the land. For their part, the Indians opposed the sale. The investors registered complaints about both Indians and miners who were impeding sales. The government would have to find the Jicarilla a new home. Maxwell was no longer available as a trusted intermediary. In fact, the Jicarilla became upset when they learned of his plan to sell. "Several of the chiefs threatened Lucien's life if he left and said they would fight to prevent the transfer. 'If he sold the country, they would kill him.'"[13] More than once Maxwell went into hiding or had his family hole up at his stone mill. In 1870, the government stopped issuing rations at Cimarron in an attempt to force the Jicarilla there to move. There was almost an uprising and rations were restored. The Jicarilla remained at Cimarron until 1876.

In March 1871, Colonel J. Irvin Gregg, commanding the District of New Mexico, wrote "I have thought it prudent to retain at Fort Union one mounted troop for the present, in view of possible difficulty with the Utes and Jicarilla Apaches in the vicinity of Maxwell's."[14] In 1872, the situation in Cimarron became less tense. The Jicarilla had a successful hunt on the plains, rations were coming more regularly, and Elizabethtown, the mining camp in the Sangre de Cristo that had created problems, was slowly depopulated as mines played out.[15]

Olleros, whom the government called renegades, were still living at Abiquiu.[16] They were on their way to self-sufficiency as settled farmers. The agent reported that the Jicarilla were furnishing half of their own subsistence by raising corn, wheat, and vegetables and by making and selling pottery and baskets, but the government thought it preferable that Washington should not be responsible for the remaining half of the Jicarilla subsistence[17] There was pressure on them to join the Llaneros somewhere out of sight and mind on the Llano Estacado.

A solution seemed to present itself. In August 1868, Ollero chiefs Huero Mundo, Vicenti, and Pantaleon had met at Abiquiu with the Indian agent to discuss possible plans to consolidate the Olleros, not all of whom were at Cañon del Oso near Abiquiu, with the Ute in Colorado to increase efficiency and save on costs. The Ute drew annuities at Abiquiu and lived farther north. On September 1, 1872, the government established an agency at

Tierra Amarilla closer to the Ute homeland. It was a sub-agency of Abiquiu and both Ute and Ollero Jicarilla used it.[18] Some of the people from Cañon del Oso moved north to the new sub-agency. An agreement was reached that reservations for the Jicarilla and Ute might be established in the area. The Olleros were nearing an agreement for a reservation near their homeland.

After the Ute and Jicarilla had been subdued in 1855, American and Mexican settlers first came to the Tierra Amarilla Grant. In the early 1860s, they were only a handful. In 1866, the army established Camp Plummer at Las Nutrias within the grant to protect the settlers.[19] These settlers and the stockmen that settled in the area, once the army made it safe, would be a thorn in the Jicarilla side for many years to come, appropriating Indian lands and stock. Because the grant was still mostly vacant, the land to the west seemed a likely spot for a reservation for the Jicarilla.

Meanwhile in June 1873, Superintendent L. Edwin Dudley met in council with the Llanero chiefs, San Pablo, José Largo, and 376 of their followers in the vicinity of Cimarron. He proposed moving the Jicarilla hundreds of miles south to the Mescalero reservation near Fort Stanton. But the Llanero were unwilling to make a decision until they consulted the Ollero at Tierra Amarilla.[20]

When consulted, Chief Huero Mundo of the Ollero did not want to become a "joint tenant" with the Mescalero Apache. He talked to his half-brother, Chief Ouray of the Ute, who suggested that they make a trip to Washington, DC, to see President Grant. In 1873, Huerito Mundo, son of Huero Mundo, accompanied his uncle, Ouray, and a Ute delegation to Washington where the Ute were working out a dispute over rogue miners on their lands.[21]

On December 10, 1873, Agent Dolan met at Tierra Amarilla with both the Ollero and the Llanero and for the first time they agreed with each other and the agent's proposal. If they surrendered all land claims, which arguably included most of northeastern New Mexico and southwestern Colorado, they would receive the San Juan reservation, ten thousand dollars over a five-year period in annuities, and an additional three thousand dollars for education over ten years. That's when it was discovered that the San Juan Mountains were rich in ore, and no move to the new land was made.[22] The Executive Order was cancelled.

The 1868 agreement concerning a reservation near Tierra Amarilla and further discussion in Washington led in 1874 to a proposal for the San Juan reservation west of Tierra Amarilla land grant that would not intrude on the grant. During this meeting, President Grant promised to Huerito Mundo a reservation west of the Mexican grant. The president made it official with an Executive Order in 1874. The southeastern corner would be at a point where the San Juan River entered New Mexico. The boundary would then follow the course of the river to the eastern boundary of the Navajo reservation. The boundary would then go north to the Colorado line and back to the point of beginning. This was referred to as the San Juan reservation. The Executive Order was countermanded before the Jicarilla ever moved to the location. But it was not forgotten and would hold a place in future negotiations.

On September 14, 1875, the Mescalero agent secured the permission of that tribe to bring the Jicarilla to the Sacramento Mountains near Fort Stanton, the Mescalero reservation, where the Jicarilla would be joint-tenants. In May 1876, the Jicarilla objected. Huerito Mundo recalled his talk with President Grant, objecting that when he went to Washington in 1873, the president had told him that the San Juan reservation would always be the Jicarilla Apache home. He added, if the president could not keep this promise, there was no reason to believe that he would ever keep any other promise.[23] The government then proposed a reservation adjoining the Tierra Amarilla Grant on the west, east of the San Juan reservation. New Mexicans resisted having the reservation near Tierra Amarilla. In April 1876, Colonel Edward Hatch, commanding the 9th Cavalry and the District of New Mexico wrote:

I have the honor to invite attention of the General Commanding the Department, to the intention of the Indian Bureau to remove the Jicarilla Apaches from the Cimarron Agency to Tierra Amarilla, and would respectfully request that the Jicarillas and Band, now at Tierra Amarilla, be removed to the Apache Reservation near Fort Stanton.[24]

The reasons favoring removal to Fort Stanton Reservation are obvious: Tierra Amarilla is no longer a fine game Country and lies in the tract of immigration to the San Juan Country, and is near enough to that region to be included in the settlements that will naturally spring up where there is a lot of valuable land capable of being irrigated.

The same reasons that decide the necessity of removing these Indians from the vicinity of Cimarron, will soon be produced in the Tierra Amarilla Country, that is; the settlement of the Country by raisers of sheep and cattle. The wool interests will soon absorb all the land suitable in northern New Mexico.

The Indian now defiant in Tierra Amarilla District, assuming justly, that the land is his, is now in the habit of ordering the Settler out of the Country, and has recently threatened if they do not go peaceably, he will begin hostilities. The attempt may be made, when the Government will be put to great expense to crush out the hostile Indian, and to a great additional expense to protect the Indian from the Whites, for so rapidly is the Country filling up, and with a population who are not inclined to recognize any rights pertaining to the Indian, there remains not a question as to the result. That the Apaches should be moved from Cimarron is important, but to take him to Tierra Amarilla, will be followed by retracing the ground on his way to Fort Stanton, which must be eventually his Reservation.

For the above reasons I advise that the Band of Apaches now at Tierra Amarilla and Cimarron be removed to the Reservation at Fort Stanton.[25]

One branch of the Old Spanish Trail ran from Abiquiu along the Chama River through the proposed Tierra Amarilla reservation by way of La Jara Canyon and the Navajo River and thus to the agricultural area around Farmington and the mineral-rich mountains above Durango. Minerals, sheep-grazing country, and irrigable agricultural lands were all on Colonel Hatch's mind when he proposed the Cimarron Jicarilla be brought to the Mescalero reservation and that the Tierra Amarilla Agency Olleros be removed to there as well. The Jicarilla were willing to fight for their land and were already driving settlers away. In the late 1870s with other Apaches on the warpath an uprising seemed entirely possible. The war would be expensive and the government was unwilling to rein in settlers.

In 1878, now General Hatch summed up the real problem:

I have the honor to report that an officer and Detachment were sent to the late Jicarilla Apache Reservation on the San Juan to look into the troubles represented by the petitioners of Delegate Romero referred from your Headquarters. . . . The Whites seem determined to have all that is good of the Country set aside for the Utes [and Jicarilla].[26]

In July 1876, the Cimarron Agency was abolished. Sam A. Russell, agent at Tierra Amarilla, wrote of the Jicarilla:

The Jicarilla Apache Indian has no home. As a people they have no country that they can call their own. No incentive to improvement has even been placed before them; they are left to roam over a section of mountainous country of uncertain ownership, or it may be included in a Mexican land grant.[27]

In 1878, he would repeat a similar sentiment with the problem still unresolved:

They have been left by a paternal government without a home and compelled to become wanderers, by being driven from place to place when they have attempted to locate and cultivate soil. They have, through me, been for almost four years begging for a home, a place where they could farm and have schools for their children. It has thus far been denied them.[28]

The Jicarilla resisted leaving their homes. In December 1877, Agent Benjamin H. Thomas of the Pueblo Agency wrote that it was no more possible to move the Jicarillas "than a flock of wild turkeys."[29] At Cimarron, San Pablo and his band were told to start the walk to Mescalero, but many slipped away to Abiquiu. In October 1878, only San Pablo and thirty-two people arrived at Fort Stanton as ordered. As San Pablo and his people, initially most of the four hundred or so Llanero from the Cimarron area, started south as ordered, there was an exchange of letters and telegrams. General Hatch wrote:

The Jicarilla Apaches from Cimarron are now moving to the Mescalero Agency near Fort Stanton and it is the desire of the Indian Department that the selection of the place for the encampment be made by the Commanding Officer at Fort Stanton . . .

You will also notify the Agent referred to, that it would be advisable to have ten days rations for 300 Indians ready for them on their arrival. . . .[30]

Next he sent orders to Lieutenant Rucker, 9th Cavalry, at Fort Union, commanding him to "Proceed with your detachment when assignment is completed to Rayado nine miles south Cimarron to clean up Jicarilla Apaches. You should camp there at least five days. . . ."[31] Apparently Hatch believed those wily Apache might not be fully complying with orders. The next missive instructed Lieutenant Rucker to trust no one. "General Hatch directs that you see for yourself that there are no Jicarilla Apaches at Cimarron and trust no one. Watkins Inspector says there are."[32]

After he arrived, San Pablo and his people didn't want to leave the safety of Fort Stanton. The Lincoln County War was on and the local cowboys robbed them of all their horses. Jicarilla near Abiquiu hearing about this disaster used it as an excuse not to depart for Mescalero. Hatch's adjutant wrote:

Comdg Officer Fort Stanton reports that San Pablo, Chief, Band of Jicarilla Apaches encamped near Post is Uneasy about absence and non-arrival of balance of his band and says if allowed to go up and see them he thinks he could induce them to come up and join him there. . . .[33]

In 1879, General Hatch had a new problem:

It is reported that Bands of . . . Jicarilla Apaches have returned to the vicinity of their old homes and are now committing depredations, killing cattle and threatening the Citizens with violence if they do not comply with requests of the Indians. This information comes from the Governor of New Mexico.[34]

After having one of his captains investigate, the district commander found that there were real problems:

The Jicarilla Apaches I found camped on the Chama, from the Mouth to Tierra Amarilla, in bands. They have no Reservation and go pretty much as they please anywhere. The Cimarron region is their favorite locality. I found there about 500, who are supposed to now belong to the Reservation at Fort Stanton. San Pablo and Band, sent there, were robbed by Texans of all their Stock, and left that Reservation. Nothing can induce them to return but force. It will require at least

four good companies of Cavalry to gather them and compel them to go.
They are in what may be considered a starving condition, subsist prin-
cipally by living on stolen Cattle, this will eventually lead to trouble.
An Indian some time ago was killed by a herder, and in retaliation the
herder was killed.[35]

Short of war, the Jicarilla were practicing passive resistance before
Gandhi thought of it. With their account transferred to Fort Stanton and
the Mescalero reservation, they were cut off from government support and
supplemental rations but they managed to subsist. They also defended their
claim to the lands west of the Chama River. In 1879, Huero Mundo and
his son Huerito again visited his half-brother Ouray of the Ute who recommended another visit to Washington. By January 1, 1880, permission for
the trip was granted and San Pablo, Juan Julian, Santiago Largo, Huerito
Mundo, and Augustin Vigil[36] made the trip to discuss the location of a new
reservation. They wanted the land west of Tierra Amarilla, which was not
part of the Mexican Land Grant and on which there were only four or five
settlers. Officials of the government thought they might buy these folks out
inexpensively. In 1887, this would cause problems. The reservation proposed
in 1880 was not occupied until then, and fraudulent settlers moved in hoping
their illegitimate claims—the land was not open to homesteading—would
lead to the government buying them out. On September 21, 1880, President
Rutherford B. Hayes issued an Executive Order creating the Tierra Amarilla
reservation with headquarters at Amargo.[37] The Apache were told to make
the move in October 1881.[38]

On July 19, 1881, Acting Governor M. B. Ritch wrote the secretary of
the interior requesting that the Tierra Amarilla reservation be returned to
public domain and opened to settlement.[39] Opposition from cattlemen, sheep
herders, and the people of the Tierra Amarilla Grant was causing problems.
The Jicarilla were in limbo again. They continued to live along the Chama
River and made trips to the plains to hunt. When they were seen at Taos,
Mora, and Wagon Mound, there were complaints. Delayed in moving to the
new reservation, the Jicarilla went hunting, creating a stir at Fort Union:

I have the honor to report that there are about forty Jicarilla Apache
Indians under [Chino] encamped at the Northern end of the Turkey
Mts about 8 miles from the Post.[40] *Capt. Shoemaker informs me that*

one of them applied to him for a permit to go to the buffalo country, stating that they had authority to leave their reservation for hunting purposes, but no papers were shown to that effect, and therefore request information as to what action I shall take in the matter....[41]

The Apache had the proper papers, but their presence still created a stir:

Referring to my letter of the 3rd inst. I have the honor to report that yesterday most of the Indians came to the Post and asked for rations, stating that they were hungry, and as I had not heard of their having committed any depredations I issued to them two (2) days rations for twenty (20) Indians.

This band is under Santiago Largo—not Chino as reported in my letter of 3rd inst.—who informed me that they had their families with them, and who has a pass a copy of which I herewith enclose.[42]

With notable exceptions covered in previous chapters, the military usually checked and investigated all incidents before taking action. In many cases, the Army would be the best friend the Jicarilla had and a proponent of their interests. Often military leaders provide us with the clearest possible explanations of events.

By 1882, Colonel Ranald Slidell Mackenzie was the new district commander at Santa Fe. Mackenzie wrote:[43]

It seems that Congress has, for some cause, failed to provide any funds for the subsistence of the Mescalero Apaches, and the same is true with regard to the Jicarilla Apaches, for whom Mr. Thomas is Agent....

Troops cannot be employed to hold Indians as prisoners and starve them.[44]

San Pablo and his people were seen near Taos and then at Wagon Mound. Mackenzie instructed the commander at Fort Union:

Ascertain the whereabouts of Jicarilla Apaches, reported in that vicinity, assure them that no harm will be done them, disarm them and bring them to Union as Prisoners of War.... Do not put them in the Guard house unless insubordinate, but place them under guard at Post.[45]

Captain George Brady had difficulty complying with his orders and wrote, "Indians have split up into small parties and taken to the Mountains. Authority requested to hire guides as I do not know the country."[46] It is surprising how much trouble a tiny band out hunting could cause. One week later, Colonel Mackenzie wrote:

Have twelve men, eighteen squaws, ten children, forty eight ponies. Before turned back San Pablo with the main portion of the band was striking for his Reservation as fast as he could go.[47]

There were more complaints about the Jicarilla near the headwaters of the Chama River and at Amargo. Colonel Mackenzie wrote:

Referring to communication from the Sub-agency at Amargo, N.M. dated May 11, 1883, enclosing petition of the citizens of Pagosa Springs, for troops to be sent to that place to return the Jiccarilla Apaches who are setting fire to the grass and standing timber, slaughtering game etc., to their Reservation, the General commanding the District directs as to say that, if the Indians are firing the country as the enclosed reports show, steps should have been taken at once to stop it.[48]

It was well to forward the papers but action should also have been taken. General Stanley will soon reach [Fort] Lewis, and this matter can be held until his arrival for such action as he deems necessary to take.[49] *The District Commander is aware that the Reservation of these Indians is so situated that it is almost uninhabitable during winter and that the Indians are harmless and obedient, but they must not be allowed to do damage to the country.*[50]

The Tierra Amarilla reservation west of the Tierra Amarilla Land Grant has one flowing river, the Navajo, at its northern extremity. The canyon is narrow providing little opportunity for irrigation or agriculture. The elevation in the northern part of the reservation is around eight thousand feet, making the growing season very short and hard frost possible even in July.[51]

The countryside is beautiful and there are a number of lakes. Mackenzie was right to call the area uninhabitable in winter. If the reservation had in its final form included the banks of the Chama River, irrigation might have been possible. Mescalero agent W. H. H. Llewellyn visited the Amargo reservation and concluded "except for a narrow strip of land near the Navajo River, the reservation was barren and sterile, and could not support man or beast."[52] Nonetheless, the Jicarilla guided their path toward the reservation where they were, in 1887, finally allowed to settle. In the meantime, the Jicarilla would suffer what Tiller calls their "Long Walk" or "Trail of Tears."[53]

On July 13, 1883, the commissioner of Indian Affairs authorized five thousand dollars to move the Jicarillas to Mescalero. Mackenzie's adjutant wrote to the commander at Fort Lewis:[54]

The Brigadier General commanding the District, directs that, on receipt of application from Agent Llewellyn, you send to the Jicarilla Agency, a detachment of one commissioned officer and twenty enlisted men of the 9th Cavalry, to act as escort to the Jicarillas enroute to the Mescalero Agency. . . .[55]

The Jicarilla, especially the Ollero, were unhappy with the orders to move to Mescalero. The government had made promises, the San Juan reservation and then the Tierra Amarilla reservation, and had without reason, as far as the Jicarilla could see, broken those promises. This led to dissension within the tribe as they wanted to know "who agreed to this?" Trouble broke out and the commander at Fort Lewis wrote to Colonel Mackenzie:

Rucker's Troop leaves here this morning. Agent Llewellyn spent yesterday here. He received a dispatch from his Sub-Agent saying the Jicarillas had a great row yesterday, pointing guns at each other. One fourth of the tribe declare they will not move. Llewellyn goes to Amargo this morning and will advise.

Llewellyn also wrote to Mackenzie:

I have just returned from Fort Lewis. On yesterday there was great danger of a fight between the Indians of the Agency. All quiet to-day. Llewellyn.[56]

On August 20, the tribe began the forty-seven-day trek of over five hundred miles. Along the way, six would die. Passing through a Mexican village they contracted smallpox, which led to panic. Mescalero was managed by Major Llewellyn with the assistance of the chief of tribal police, Captain Thomas Branigan. The captain already had a police force of Mescalero Apaches, and he refused to hire any Jicarilla. He believed that being related to the Mescalero would work better with each other than outsider Jicarilla might. For some reason the Jicarilla found this eminently unfair. So too was the division of land. The Mescalero had already claimed the best, most arable land and Llewellyn settled the Jicarilla at infertile Rio Tularosa, Three Rivers, and Carrizo Creek. There were 462 Mescaleros and 721 Jicarilla on the reservation.[57] The Mescalero Apache accused the more numerous Jicarilla of over-hunting the mountains. Neither side was happy with the arrangement, and the Jicarilla felt that the Mescalero got everything and they got nothing. In late 1884, Llewellyn departed as agent. His replacement, Fletcher J. Cowart, arrived in November 1885. Jicarilla were already leaving in small groups, seeking to control their own future.[58]

Adding to the problems at Mescalero, the US Congress was having difficulty keeping up with its commitment to its Indian wards. The commander in Santa Fe wrote to the commander at Fort Stanton saying, "The Secretary of War authorizes the issue of rations from Army stores to the Mescaleros and Jicarillos until their regular supplies arrive."[59] The military came through again, doing a better job of caring for the Indians than the rest of the government.[60]

The Ollero developed an interesting plan. The Jicarilla Apache, they thought, might return to their home country and take up homesteads in severalty, that is, abandoning official tribal relations and acting as other settlers did. The commander of Fort Stanton wrote to Santa Fe:

Agent Cowart telephones that a party of Jacarilla Indians numbering twenty three exclusive of women and children left reservation four days ago followed later by Augustine Pelarde, Augustine Pedilo and another Indian name unknown—Placito had charge of first party they left Reservation without obtaining permission from the Agent. . . . The Agent requests me to ascertain for him if these Indians are on their old Reservation and if they are to have the leaders arrested and the Indians sent back.[61, 62, 63]

The next day, having already seen the Jicarilla as they passed through Santa Fe, Colonel Bradley replied, "Chief Augustine with party of Jicarillas is here on the way to Abicu [Abiquiu] to select lands for location."[64] The Ollero chiefs had made it known that they would give up their claim to a reservation and become settlers on their own land.

The Indian agent took the children of the Jicarilla away from them and held them at two boarding schools on the Mescalero reservation. Distances from the Jicarilla camps made it impractical for the children to come in for classes each day and so they had to board. In most cases the separation was not voluntary. The children were effectively under guard at school so that the parents wouldn't take them back. The Fort Stanton commander reported the first "raid" to his commander in Santa Fe:

Letter from Agent Cowart received last night reports that Augustine, Pidal and Pelarde returned to Agency on 23rd; while school children were out playing stole such as belonged to their camp. . . .[65, 66, 67]

The military District of New Mexico began reporting to Arizona. The evacuation of the Mescalero reservation was growing. General Nelson Miles, recently back from deporting Geronimo, became involved:

[A]scertain the whereabouts of the Jicarilla Indians, there should be one hundred and forty accounted for, forty of these men. Investigate the causes of their leaving reservation, their present purposes, whether they intend to take up land in severalty under the Act of Congress and discontinue the tribal relation.[68]

The Jicarilla returned for the rest of their children and made a daring, silent raid in the middle of the night, managing to depart without waking the guards:

Agent Cowart reports a party of Jicarillas having left Agency last night after taking children from school. They are of same band as those who went to Santa Fe about two months ago.[69]

By November of 1886, Colonel Benjamin H. Grierson, commander of the 10th Cavalry Regiment, was now also commander of the District of New

Mexico. Grierson was sympathetic to the Jicarilla. He noted their predicament at the Fort Stanton reservation "where the Mescaleros have gotten everything and they nothing." After the Jicarilla kidnapped their own children from the boarding school and headed north, he wrote:[70,71]

The Indians who left the reservation the night of the sixteenth instant are probably on their way to join those who left agency some time ago, and are now quietly located from twenty five to thirty miles north of Santa Fe.

General Miles had an interview with a large party of these so called Jicarillas Apaches on the thirteenth instant and heard all they had to say, and after full investigation took such action as he thought judicious. . . .

These Indians say they do not want to remain at the Mescalero Agency, where the Mescaleros have gotten everything and they nothing, and if they have to starve and freeze to death, they prefer to do so elsewhere. Surely no depredations need be apprehended from Indians, principally women and children who run away from an Agency during a violent snow storm. These Indians are similar in habits to the Pueblos and were self supporting long ago, and now want to take up land, go to work and become so again and I judge it will be to the interest of the Government to permit them to do so. . . .[72]

The Jicarillas who had broken out of Mescalero stopped in Santa Fe to see Governor Ross before proceeding on to Abiquiu. Grierson confirmed the substance of that meeting:

Velarde with two other Indians arrived here to place their children at the Romena [Santa Fe] Indian School upon the request of the Superintendent thereof. These Indians were here some time ago, and were assured by Governor Ross that they had a right to come here and take up land. . . . They ask for no supplies from the military authorities and claim that they are able to support themselves.[73]

The Jicarilla weren't asking for a reservation, for annuities, for rations, or for presents. They intended to be self-sustaining, asking only if it was permissible for them to exercise the same rights as citizens. Governor Ross assured them that they could. The Dawes Act (Allotment Act) of 1887 set up a path to private ownership of land and US citizenship for American Indians.[74,75] Unfortunately, although this was the direction Senator Henry Dawes intended, it turned out to be the road not taken. Unscrupulous people used the act to defraud Indians of their land. The Jicarilla as it turned out were lucky and their reservation remained whole.

Colonel Grierson wrote a long letter explaining Jicarilla circumstances:

In regard to the efforts and progress being made with a view to the final settlement of the "Jicarillas" upon lands in severalty and matter connected therewith which have come to my knowledge and under my supervision.

In order that the matter may be more clearly understood I deem it proper to state that the "Jicarillas," although restless and inclined to roam, have for over twenty years been harmless and peaceably inclined, and during much of that time engaged in work making pottery, baskets, etc., to gain a sustenance, and to a certain extent have been self supporting. Their habits are similar to the "Pueblos" with whom they have maintained friendly relations. They have lived mostly in the northern part of this territory and there they greatly desired to remain, but influences were brought to bear upon the Government by those who wished to eventually gain possession of the Jicarilla reservation, which in due time caused the forcible removal of these Indians to the Mescalero Agency. They were told that everything good and suitable for their wants and necessities would be found there, and that ample supplies would be furnished them, but in fact they were scantily provided with food and clothing and soon became virtually servants or peons for their more fortunate neighbors or rulers, the "Mescaleros," who occupied all the most desirable lands within the reservation.

Their murmurs and discontents were from time to time allayed by oft repeated promises of redress of wrongs. They bore all their trouble with commendable patience which could not be found among more civilized people. They had been told that they should return again in a few years to their old reservation, if the Mescalero Agency proved unsatisfactory. They wished to be taken back, or anywhere, away from the Mescalero Agency; but their desires were unheeded, while in fact the same influences were set to work in the meantime to open up to settlement their reservation which they positively assert they never gave up willingly or for any such purpose. Finally in a fit of frenzy or desperation a part of the band fled from the Agency to seek homes in the vicinity of their old friends the "Pueblos." Arriving at Santa Fe they laid their complaints and grievances before the Chief Executive of New Mexico, and Governor Ross, after full investigation of all the circumstances bearing upon the case informed them that they were under the law, entitled to the privilege of taking up lands within the territory as homes for their people, and assured them of his willingness to assist them in doing so. But these poor Indians had left the Mescalero Agency without permission of the Agent who quickly applied for, and obtained, troops to take the field in pursuit of the runaways to force them to return. Fortunately for the Indians and the Government the Department Commander, General Miles, although engaged in closing up his successful campaign against hostile Indians had gained a correct knowledge of the condition and peaceable disposition of the "Jicarillas" and promptly ordered the troops on more important duty, and took such measures as would bring together the escaped Indians, and subsequently, on the 13th of November 1886, met them at Santa Fe, N.M. (the date upon which I assumed command of this District) and after a full investigation, made in my presence, took such action as he deemed advisable and which was in full accord with the present policy of the Government. He authorized the runaway "Jicarillas" to remain in the vicinity of the "Pueblos" north of Santa Fe, assuring the Indians that he would bring the subject before the proper officers of the Government with a view of obtaining for them the necessary authority to secure homes for their people in severalty. . . .

A few days after General Miles left Santa Fe, information was received that another party of "Jicarillas" numbering over one hundred had left the Mescalero Agency to join those who had previously gone away. . . .

The tillable lands within the boundaries referred to were found occupied by Mexicans who had for a long time resided thereon and,

although they had failed to comply with the laws in regard to entries
of those lands it was deemed injudicious and unjust to attempt their
removal. . . . Upon further consultation I advised the setting aside of
so much of the old Jicarilla reservation and available lands adjoining
as might be required as homes for these Indians. Agent Welton at once
ascertained that the reservation although recently surveyed, had not as
yet been opened up for settlement, . . .[76]

The government allowed them to return to tribal lands on the Tierra
Amarilla reservation. The Interior Department had not opened the 1880 reservation to settlement or made it part of the public domain. On February 11,
1887, President Grover Cleveland ordered the reservation set aside for the
Jicarilla. On April 25, five hundred Jicarilla, the remainder of the tribe, along
with two thousand head of livestock began the trek north to their home.[77]
Indian agent Welton found that some Mexicans were occupying lands on
the reservation. They had built pens and shanties to give the false impression that they had settled homesteads. They occupied all of the arable land.
Welton informed them that their claims were illegal and would not be recognized. They were trespassing on the reservations since the land had never
been opened to settlement. Some remained in hopes that the government
would be forced to buy them out.[78]

The headquarters at Amargo was moved a few miles west to Dulce Station on the Denver Rio Grande Railroad, which had been built to access
lumber camps in northern New Mexico. The effort to remove fraudulent
settlers continued for some time. Some returned over and over after being
expelled. In October 1887, Colonel Grierson wrote:

In order to carry out the directions of the War and Interior Departments as conveyed through orders to the District Commander, and
request of Special Agent H.S. Welton of the Interior Department, you
will proceed with your command to the Jicarilla Indian Reservation
in the northern part of New Mexico and take a post at Burns ranch,
recently occupied by a Mr. Roberts, at a point between Dulce Station
on the D&RGRR and Canon La Jara.

From this point you will use your detachment in the most effective manner possible by frequent patrols, to prevent the return on the Jicarilla Reservation of the recently expelled fraudulent settlers, intruders and stock and drive there from all stock you may find not belonging to bona fide settlers.[79]

In May of 1888, fraudulent settlers were still causing problems. There were also legitimate settlers, apparently those with claims that dated to before 1880, when an Executive Order set the land aside for the Jicarilla. They would have to be bought out. In the meantime, many of them exceeded the use of what was rightfully theirs and infringed on Jicarilla rights. Colonel Grierson wrote:

I have recently been informed that a number of the ejected settlers have returned to the reservation and have planted or are now planting, crops thereon and that in some instances they have ordered the Indians

In 1868, advised by their Ute friends, relatives, and allies, the Jicarilla sent three Apache, Huero Mundo, standing at left, Vicenti, standing fourth from left, and Panteleon, seated at far left, in company with the Ute delegation to visit the president in Washington, DC. COURTESY PALACE OF THE GOVERNORS PHOTO ARCHIVES (NMHM/DCA), 45814, PHOTOGRAPHER NICHOLAS BROWN *off their claims. I have also learned that several of the "bona fide" set-tlers who were permitted to remain on the reservation, have on sev-eral occasions interfered with and committed depredations against the Indians, therefore on the 22d instant I deemed it necessary to order a small detachment of Infantry and Cavalry from Fort Union to the Agency near Dulce Station to again remove any of the fraudulent settlers who may have returned or any other intruders, trespassers or their stock that may be found on the reservation and to compel the "bona fide" settlers to confine themselves and their stock to the limits of their recognized claims, and also to protect the Indians and prevent any further encroachments upon their lands.*[80]

In 1887, the Jicarilla Apache had arrived finally at their reservation home. They no longer had to wander unwelcome in the settlements on lands where invaders had used up their critical resources. They were left to struggle with trespassers on their land and were lucky to escape the allotments of the Dawes Act. The land they had selected was not arable. Learning of this, President Teddy Roosevelt doubled the size of their reservation so they would have southern land at lower elevation where herds could graze in winter. In the early twentieth century, Congress and the Executive Branch nearly starved

Jicarilla family at Fort Union. About 1875. COURTESY PALACE OF THE GOVERNORS PHOTO ARCHIVES (NMHM/DCA), 37178, PHOTOGRAPHER JAMES N. FURLONG

them to death through neglect. They had to seek permission to cut their own timber to acquire money to buy livestock. And then, they had to get permission to spend their money, permission that was ten years in coming, while rations were cut. Given the chance in the 1920s, they proved excellent stockmen. Veronica Velarde Tiller has done an excellent job of telling that story.

The Jicarilla won a great battle at Cieneguilla against a vainglorious lieutenant only to suffer two years of chastisement and pursuit. A governor started a war he could blame on his predecessor so he could make the same treaty that had been in place when he arrived and thus take credit for both the war and the peace. The Senate rejected the treaty, leaving a people who were trying to accept a new way of life without a

Christopher "Kit" Carson about 1858, while he was Indian agent for the Ute and Jicarilla. COURTESY PALACE OF THE GOVERNORS PHOTO ARCHIVES (NMHM/DCA), 009824, PHOTOGRAPHER T. MCEWEN

home. Pounded into the dust, they rose again showing themselves successful farmers when given the chance. They took control and shaped their own future, laying claim to lands along the Rio Chama and eventually forcing the government to allow them a home there.

Kit Carson had been their enemy, their wary neighbor, a scout against them, their agent, and finally their friend who rode with them against their ancient enemies the Kiowa and Comanche. The Jicarilla Apache had closed the Santa Fe Trail three times, terrorizing the people of New Mexico with the threat of being cut off from commerce, communication, and supply from the United States. Having defeated the army in battle, the Jicarilla, in a surprising twist, eventually found friends among its leaders, Mackenzie and Grierson, and in Governor Ross, who understood their plight and gave assistance.

APPENDIX A:
POSTS AND FORTS OF THE JICARILLA COUNTRY

Fort, camp, post, cantonment. In military parlance, the operation of a **fort** was paid for from the budget of the Department of the Army, while the operation of a **camp** was paid for from the regimental budget, e.g., 1st Regiment of Dragoons, 2nd Regiment of Dragoons, 7th Infantry, 3rd Artillery. A **post** is a place where soldiers are assigned duty, and thus, is at least in theory temporary and may include facilities leased from civilians. A **cantonment** is the portion of a post where buildings are located, such as barracks. In civilian and infantry parlance, a **fort** is a place to fight from and defend. For cavalry, including dragoons, forts tend to be open without exterior walls with large parade grounds, a place to live and graze livestock, not a fortification. For civilians, a **fort** may also refer to a private trading post such as Bent's Fort and Barclay's Fort.

Abiquiu (April 1849 to October 1851). Abiquiu is on the Chama River about fifteen miles northwest of the confluence of the Chama with the Rio Grande. Throughout the eighteenth and most of the nineteenth centuries, Abiquiu was the frontier of Spanish culture. Its Indian heritage and location on the frontier made it an important trading center for Comanche, Navajo, Ute, and Jicarilla Apache, who often brought in Paiute and Mexican captives and stolen property to exchange. In the 1840s and 1850s an Army detachment lived in rented buildings and Abiquiu served as a base of operations against the Ute and Jicarilla. This was also the location where several treaties were negotiated and the site of the Ute-Jicarilla Indian Agency. In early 1853, the Jicarilla reservation was near here on the Rio Puerco, and it would be a site that they returned to in hopes of once again having it as their reservation. It is between Cañon del Oso and Tierra Amarilla on the Chama River.

Adobe Walls. This was a civilian trading post first established by Bent, St. Vrain and Company, probably in 1848 in the buffalo hunting country on the Canadian River in the Llano Estacado north of modern Amarillo, Texas. It was close to the wintering grounds of the Kiowa and Comanche. There are actually two locations. The trading post was a smaller version of Bent's Fort, and it was soon abandoned. Thus all that was left standing were roofless adobe walls. In 1864, Colonel Kit Carson and army sheltered here during the First Battle of Adobe Walls, a fight with Comanche and Kiowa. Later, traders in buffalo hides established a new trading center about one mile to the west of the first, and this was the location of the Second Battle of Adobe Walls in 1874. The site of the second battle is open to the public; make inquiries at the Hutchinson County Museum in Borger, Texas.

Bent's Fort, Bent's Old Fort, Bent's Big Lodge, Fort William (1832 to 1850). Bent's Fort on the Arkansas River was built as a trading post in 1832 by William and Charles Bent and their partner Ceran St. Vrain. It was the last outpost in the United States on the Mountain Branch of the Santa Fe Trail before the trail crossed into Mexico. The Bents agreed to trade with the Cheyenne at Big Timbers on the Arkansas if they would move south to that location, and those who did became the Southern Cheyenne. William married Owl Woman, the daughter of a chief. It is near modern La Junta, Colorado, and is today a National Historic Park.

Barclay's Fort, Fort Barclay (1849 to ca. 1853). Englishman Alexander Barclay had been a mountain man and factor, i.e., manager, for Bent, St. Vrain and Company. In 1848, he decided to start his own business at La Junta (i.e., the joining together), at the confluence of the Sapello Creek and the Mora River, which is also where the Cimarron Cutoff and the Mountain Branch of the Santa Fe Trail came together north of Las Vegas, New Mexico. The Army established Fort Union six miles to the north after unsuccessfully trying to take the fort away from Barclay. On February 21, 1853, Barclay's partner Joseph Doyle sold the fort at auction to Samuel B. Watrous. Doyle was a beef supplier to the military and a constant source of complaints of cattle stolen by the Jicarilla.

Cantonment Burgwin (August 1852 to May 1860). The Army built the cantonment, actually a partially enclosed wooden stockade with some adobe buildings, something rare in the Southwest, eleven miles south of Taos at the northern foot of the Embudo Mountains. It was named in honor of Captain John Henry Burgwin, who fell during the Taos Rebellion of 1847. The Army intended to get the soldiers away from the corruption of the people of Taos and to save money on rent. It was an important base of operations against the

Jicarilla and Ute. Today it is owned by Southern Methodist University and is used as a research center.

Fort Bascom (August 1863 to December 1870). The fort was built on the right bank (south side) of the Canadian River nine miles north of modern Tucumcari and named in honor of a Civil War hero, Captain George N. Bascom, who died defending Valverde in 1862 (see *Black Legend: George Bascom, Cochise and the Start of the Apache Wars*). In 1864, Colonel Kit Carson launched his campaign against the Comanche and Kiowa from this post. In 1849, Carson pursued Jicarilla Apaches to this vicinity in an effort to recover Ann White and her baby daughter.

Fort Garland (June 24, 1858, to November 30, 1883). The Army established Fort Garland near the confluence of Ute and Trincheras Creeks in what was then Taos County, New Mexico Territory. Today the fort is at the base of La Veta Pass in the San Luis Valley of southern Colorado. The post replaced Fort Massachusetts. Fort Garland is administered as a Colorado State Museum.

Fort Lewis (1878 to 1891). The first Fort Lewis was at Pagosa Springs, Colorado, about forty miles north of Dulce, New Mexico (1878 to 1879). The second Fort Lewis was near Durango, Colorado (1880 to 1891).

Fort Lowell (Camp Plummer) (November 6, 1866, to July 27, 1869). The Army built the post three miles south of Tierra Amarilla to protect settlers on the Tierra Amarilla Land Grant from the Jicarilla. In 1887, the Jicarilla Apache Reservation with headquarters at Dulce was established west of Tierra Amarilla.

Fort Marcy (August 1846 to 1867). On the hill north of the Plaza of Santa Fe one can see the remains of earthen fortifications. Officers' quarters, a hospital, and other buildings were located between the hill and the Palace of the Governors on the Plaza. In 1846, at the order of General Stephen Watts Kearny, Lieutenant William Emory started work on the fort, whose guns faced the city. In the late 1840s and early 1850s, the fort was the Headquarters of the Ninth Military District (New Mexico). The Palace of the Governors is a state museum and the remains of the fort are now known as Fort Marcy Park.

Fort Massachusetts (June 22, 1852, to June 24, 1858). The Army established the post, an enclosed wooden stockade, ninety miles north of Taos on Ute Creek, to control the Sangre de Cristo Pass and the Ute and Jicarilla Apache in the San Luis Valley. When it was built it was in Taos County, New Mexico. Today it is in southern Colorado twelve miles north of Fort Garland, which replaced Massachusetts in 1858. The fort was intended to protect travelers and the settlements around Taos. However, settlers pushed north into the San Luis Valley, angering the Ute and Jicarilla. The elevation was close to nine thousand feet and the area very cold in the winter. Most years the garrison was evacuated to Cantonment Burgwin and only a caretaker element left behind. It was difficult to supply the post, one of the most remote in the United States. In 1855, this became a base of operations against the Ute and Jicarilla.

Fort Stanton (March 1855 to August 1896). The fort is nine miles west of Lincoln, New Mexico, the town made famous by Billy the Kid. It is in the heart of Mescalero Apache country in the Sacramento Mountains of southeastern New Mexico. In the early 1880s, the Jicarilla were located at the nearby Mescalero Reservation. Fort Stanton is a state historic park.

Fort Sumner (November 1862 to June 1869). From 1863 to 1868, Fort Sumner controlled the Bosque Redondo Reservation for the Navajo, Mescalero, and Jicarilla. After the Army moved out, Lucien Maxwell took over the site and his son Pete maintained it as a ranch. It was here that Billy the Kid had his picture taken and was killed by Pat Garrett. General James Carleton selected this site on the fertile Pecos River Valley because it was promising for agriculture, more than fifty miles from the closest settlement, and located between Comanche-Kiowa country and settled New Mexico. He hoped that the Navajo, Jicarilla, and Mescalero would serve as a buffer between the wild Indians of the Llano Estacado and the settled areas along the Rio Grande. By 1864, there were nine thousand Indians living on farms scattered twenty-five miles along the river. Poor weather, plagues of insects, lack of seeds and farm implements, and the animosity between the tribes led to agricultural failure. When the Indians were starving, Carleton lacked supplies of food to send to them. Fort Sumner is a National Historic Park.

Fort Union (July 1851 to April 1891). The post was named for the union of the states, the trails, and the rivers. It was established on the Santa Fe Trail alongside the Turkey (Gallina) Mountains six miles north of Barclay's Fort at the Holes in the Prairie, a set of springs. It became the most important supply depot in the Southwest and was at times the headquarters of the Ninth Military District (New Mexico). The post was built with a dual purpose: (1) To get the soldiers away from the towns, saving money on rent and (2) To control the Jicarilla Apache. Today the fort is a National Monument.

La Joya (1846 to 1852). Soldiers were posted at Velarde between Taos and Santa Cruz to control an important ford over the Rio Grande del Norte.

Post at Albuquerque (November 17, 1846, to August 23, 1867). This post served as a garrison for troops and a quartermaster supply depot. The buildings were rented from Sophia Carleton, the wife of Major James Carleton, later general and commander of Union Forces in New Mexico. The buildings were burned during the Civil War to keep them from falling into Confederate hands.

Post at Don Fernando de Taos (1847 to 1852). In 1849, Sergeant Bally referred to this post as Cantonment Burgwin. Don Fernando de Taos is the community we think of today as Taos. Several miles to the south is the community of Ranchos de Taos and to the north the Taos Pueblo, a multi-storied Indian village. The Army maintained a garrison there after the Taos Rebellion killed Governor Charles Bent. Initially the soldiers were ill-behaved Missouri and Illinois Volunteers who treated the *paisanos* and Indians abominably. Initially the post was maintained to control the local populace. Later it became a base of operations against the Ute and Jicarilla.

Post at Galisteo (November 1851 to January 1852). Galisteo is southeast of Santa Fe. Companies F and I of the 1st Dragoons were quartered here to take advantage of grazing.

Post at Las Vegas (February 1848 to July 1851). *Las Vegas*, the Meadows, about forty-five miles east of Santa Fe, was an important camping spot on the Santa Fe Trail, a final stopping point where livestock could be recruited before the final uphill push through Glorieta Pass to Santa Fe. In 1835, Mexicans established a town at this point. Since it was out on the frontier, it had to be protected from the Jicarilla Apache. The soldiers were housed in rented quarters. It was here in 1849 that Lieutenant Ambrose Burnside confronted and slew Jicarilla who came to trade.

Post at Rayado (May 1850 to August 1851). Rayado is about twelve miles south of Cimarron at the foot of the Sangre de Cristo Mountains. In 1848, Kit Carson and Lucien Maxwell established a community at Rayado. Both built homes here. Companies G and I of the 1st Dragoons used rented buildings as barracks. It was an important base of operations against the Comanches, Ute, and Jicarilla Apaches. Today the location is owned by the Boy Scouts of America and is administered as a museum.

Appendix B: Treaties with the Jicarilla

This list begins with General Kearny's "Treaty" of 1846, which was not a treaty as described in the US Constitution. The Constitution specifies that a representative of the Executive Branch of the government who has been given specific direction as to the terms he can offer negotiates a treaty; the treaty then goes to the Senate for ratification. Stephen Watts Kearny's directions from President James K. Polk must have been vague at best. Kearny, before a treaty with Mexico had been ratified, offered New Mexicans citizenship and organized the conquered lands as a territory with civilian governor and legislature. He had authority for neither. Likewise, soldiers, sometimes as low in rank as sergeant, negotiated "treaties" with various "wild" tribes. The terms were simple: (1) don't depredate, (2) stay back fifty miles from the settlements, and (3) live on lands where we tell you your people can live. In return the United States will: (1) stop killing you, and (2) make occasional gifts to you. These were not the sort of formal treaties upon which claims for reparations could be made.

Later treaties typically offered: (1) defined reservation lands, (2) farming implements, (3) training in farming, and (4) food and gifts until the Indians' farms could support them, usually a period of three to five years. The Indians promised to give up lands and to stop depredating and to keep their people under control. Many treaties called on the Indians to stop warring with other tribes while the United States in turn promised to defend them. Many of these "treaties" existed only as Executive Orders, which could be annulled by a subsequent order. These executive order "treaties" posed a second problem in that Congress had not yet approved the budgetary expenditures they implied and often delayed or refused action.

On the other hand, Congress often refused to consider ratification of formal treaties. The Executive Branch and the Senate were in effect committing funds from the Treasury, but all bills for budgetary items under the Constitution had to start in the House. After 1850, Congress was loath to make treaties with Indians. Perhaps this was just an excuse in a Congress deeply divided over sectional issues. If the Executive Branch made promises and the Indians made promises, but the Senate failed to ratify and live up to the promises made while the Indians kept theirs, in Apache eyes the United States was violating the treaty.

The Army and many of the Indian agents recognized a major problem. White encroachment was depleting game and the Indians were being asked to abandon their hunting lands. They would starve. Rather than starve, they would fight and depredate. So, both the Army and agents often agreed: "We must feed them or exterminate them." Official policy, agreed upon by those closest to the situation, was that the Indians had to learn to farm in order to feed themselves and get off the government dole. To do that, they had to have a reservation. There was a horrible economic unreality in this. Farms had to be near cities where the farmer could sell his produce. The alternative was subsistence farming, a horrible fate. The farmer was left without money to buy anything, and in years of poor crops, he and his family would starve. Perpetual poverty was the best he could hope for.

During much of the time after 1855, the Jicarilla Apache faced a fate perhaps even worse. They were the last Indians to get a reservation. They were assigned to an agency—at Cimarron, Abiquiu, Tierra Amarilla, or at Taos—where they went to draw gifts and, if they were lucky, rations. They were otherwise left to wander landless. Attempts were made to put them on a reservation at Bosque Redondo with Navajo and Mescalero who were hostile to each other, and at the Mescalero Reservation where they were unwelcome outsiders, although their population was almost double that of the Mescalero who controlled the reservation.

TREATY WITH GENERAL KEARNY
SEPTEMBER 23, 1846

September 23 [1846] the chief of one branch of the Apaches with about thirty of his tribe, came to hold a "grand council" with the governor general. The general made a long speech to them through an interpreter, encouraging them to industry and peaceful pursuits, and particularly to the cultivation of the soil, as the surest and best mode of procuring an honorable subsistence; "that they must desist from all robberies and the committing of all crimes against the laws of the territory; that if they did not he would send his soldiers among them and destroy them from the earth; but if they would be peaceable toward their white brethren he would protect and defend them as he would the New Mexicans, and make them all brothers to the white people and citizens of the same Republic, and children of the same father, the President, at Washington City."

To all these things the venerable sachem replied in a spirit worthy of his tribe, setting forth the wishes of his people in a strain of bold, commanding eloquence, which has ever characterized the aboriginal orator. He said:

"Father, you give good advice for me and my people; but I am old and unable to work, and my tribe are unaccustomed to cultivating the soil for subsistence. The Apaches are poor; they have no clothes to protect them from the cold, and the game is fast disappearing from their hunting grounds. You must, therefore, if you wish us to be peaceable, speak a good word to the Comanches, the Yutas, the Navajos, and the Arapahoes, our enemies, that they will allow us to kill buffalo on the great plains. You are rich— you have a great nation to feed and clothe you—I am poor, and have to crawl on my belly, like a cat, to shoot deer and buffalo for my people. I am not a bad man. I do not rob and steal; I speak truth. The Great Spirit gave me an honest heart and a straight tongue. I have not two tongues that I should speak forked.

"My skin is red, my head sunburnt, my eyes are dim with age, and I am a poor Indian, a dog, yet I am not guilty. There is no guilt there [putting his hand on his breast] no! I can look you in the face like a man. In the morning of my days my muscles were strong; my arm was stout; my eye was bright; my mind was clear; but now I am weak, shriveled up with age, yet my heart is big, my tongue is straight. I will take your counsel because I am weak and you are strong."

The general then gave them some blankets, butcher knives, beads, mirrors, and other presents for their squaws, and they departed under the promise that they would be good and faithful citizens of the United States.[1]

CHACON/MUNROE TREATY

APRIL 2, 1851

TREATY WITH THE APACHE INDIANS EAST OF THE RIO DEL NORTE*

It is agreed by the contracting parties; that is to say James S. Calhoun, Governor and Superintendent of Indian Affairs in the Territory of New Mexico, and John Munroe Brevet Colonel of the United States Army, commanding the Ninth Military Department; on the part of the Government of the United States, and Francisco Chacon, Lobo, Guero and Josecito, Head Chief and Captains on the part of the Apache tribe of Indians east of the Rio del

Author cannot find any indication that this treaty was ever ratified by the Senate.

Norte, that the following acknowledgements, declarations and stipulations shall be binding upon the contracting parties, in all times to come. Provided; the Government of the United States shall approve the following terms:

Art. 1st. The said Apache Indians do hereby declare their unconditional submission to the Government of the United States, and will remove to, and confine themselves to such lands and limits as said Government may assign for their use, and build thereon Pueblos, and cultivate the soil for their support, or occupy said limits, and conform to all rules, laws and orders that said Government may prescribe for their observance.

Art. 2nd. The said Indians pledge their identity as a tribe, and their personal existence, individually, to abstain from all murders, and depredations, not go roam within Fifty miles of the settlements, or the established highways of the people of New Mexico, or the roads leading to the United States; unless under such rules and regulations as the Governor and Superintendent of Indian Affairs may prescribe, and unless the aforesaid Government shall assign them limits nearer to said settlements and highways' that they will deliver up all murderers, robbers and fugitives from justice, all captives whether Americans, Mexicans, or other, and stolen property that may be with them, or in their possession, by or before the First day of August next, and will at all times, use their utmost exertions to check and chastise all disturbers of the public tranquility, and will never afford an Asylum, countenance of protection in any shape to murderers, robbers or other wicked persons; but will secure all such persons and all stolen property that they may be able to seize, whether of Americans, Mexicans or others, and deliver the same at the earliest possible day to the appropriate authorities of the Government of the United States.

Art. 3rd. Should this Treaty be approved by the Government of the United States, it is understood and agreed that the said Government shall establish such Military Posts and trading points, as they may select, and in the mean time, duly licensed Traders, shall be permitted to proceed to Bosque Redondo and such other places as the Governor of this Territory may designate, for the purpose of trading with the aforesaid Apaches, and such traders shall not be authorized to offer their merchandise for sale at any other places.

Art. 4th. It is distinctly understood that all laws and regulations emanating from the Government of the United States assigned for the Government of trade, and intercourse with the various Indian tribes within the jurisdiction of said States, are valid, and to be enforced in the country or district of the aforesaid Apaches.

Art. 5th. Finally, it is agreed upon the part of the Government of the United States, should the aforesaid Apaches comply, fairly and fully, with the foregoing stipulations, upon their part; the said Government will grant to them such donation and implement of husbandry, and other gratuities as a proper and sound humanity may demand, and as may be deemed meet and prudent by said Government.

In faith thereof we, the undersigned have signed this Treaty and afixed thereunto our Seals in the City of Santa Fe, this Second day of April, in the year of our Lord, One thousand Eight hundred and fifty one.

John Munroe (HS)
Major 2d Reg Arty, Bt. Col U.S. Army
Commanding Department[2]

James S. Calhoun (HS)
Governor and Superintendent
of Indian Affairs

TREATY WITH THE APACHE
JULY 1, 1852*

Articles of a treaty made and entered into at Santa Fe, New Mexico, on the first day of July in the year of our Lord one thousand eight hundred and fifty-two, by and between Col. E. V. Sumner, U.S.A., commanding the 9th Department and in charge of the executive office of New Mexico, and John Greiner, Indian agent in and for the Territory of New Mexico, and acting superintendent of Indian affairs of said Territory, representing the United States, and Cuentas Azules, Blancito, Negrito, Capitan Simon, Capitan Vuelta, and Mangus Colorado, chiefs, acting on the part of the Apache Nation of Indians, situate and living within the limits of the United States.

Art. 1st. Said nation or tribe of Indians through their authorized Chiefs aforesaid do hereby acknowledge and declare that they are lawfully and exclusively under the laws, jurisdiction, and government of the United States of America, and to its power and authority they do hereby submit.

Art. 2nd. From and after the signing of this Treaty hostilities between the contracting parties shall forever cease, and perpetual peace and amity shall forever exist between said Indians and the Government and people of

The US Senate ratified this treaty. There were about fifty Indians present including Mescaleros, Jicarillas, Acoma Pueblo Indians, and Pueblo Indians. Only southern Apaches (mostly Chiricahuas) signed. However, the government recognized this as a treaty with the Jicarilla Apache.

the United States; the said nation, or tribe of Indians, hereby binding themselves most solemnly never to associate with or give countenance or aid to any tribe or band of Indians, or other persons or powers, who may be at any time at war or enmity with the government or people of said United States.

Art. 3rd. Said nation, or tribe of Indians, do hereby bind themselves for all future time to treat honestly and humanely all citizens of the United States, with whom they have intercourse, as well as all persons and powers, at peace with the said United States, who may be lawfully among them, or with whom they may have any lawful intercourse.

Art. 4th. All said nation, or tribe of Indians, hereby bind themselves to refer all cases of aggression against themselves or their property and territory, to the government of the United States for adjustment, and to conform in all things to the laws, rules, and regulations of said government in regard to the Indian tribes.

Art. 5th. Said nation, or tribe of Indians, do hereby bind themselves for all future time to desist and refrain from making any "incursions within the Territory of Mexico" of a hostile or predatory character; and that they will for the future refrain from taking and conveying into captivity any of the people or citizens of Mexico, or the animals or property of the people or government of Mexico; and that they will, as soon as possible after the signing of this treaty, surrender to their agent all captives now in their possession.

Art. 6th. Should any citizen of the United States, or other person or persons subject to the laws of the United States, murder, rob, or otherwise maltreat any Apache Indian or Indians, he or they shall be arrested and tried, and upon conviction, shall be subject to all the penalties provided by law for the protection of the persons and property of the people of the said States.

Art. 7th. The people of the United States of America shall have free and safe passage through the territory of the aforesaid Indians, under such rules and regulations as may be adopted by authority of the said States.

Art. 8th. In order to preserve tranquility and to afford protection to all the people and interests of the contracting parties, the government of the United States of America will establish such military posts and agencies, and authorize such trading houses at such times and places as the said government may designate.

Art. 9th. Relying confidently upon the justice and the liberality of the aforesaid government, and anxious to remove every possible cause that might disturb their peace and quiet, it is agreed by the aforesaid Apache's [*sic*] that the government of the United States shall at its earliest convenience designate, settle, and adjust their territorial boundaries, and pass and execute in their territory such laws as may be deemed conducive to the prosperity and happiness of said Indians.

Art. 10th. For and in consideration of the faithful performance of all the stipulations herein contained, by the said Apache's Indians, the government of the United States will grant to said Indians such donations, presents, and implements, and adopt such other liberal and humane measures as said government may deem meet and proper.

Art. 11th. This Treaty shall be binding upon the contracting parties from and after the signing of the same, subject only to such modifications and amendments as may be adopted by the government of the United States; and, finally, this treaty is to receive a liberal construction, at all times and in all places, to the end that the said Apache Indians shall not be held responsible for the conduct of others, and that the government of the United States shall so legislate and act as to secure the permanent prosperity and happiness of said Indians.

In faith whereof we the undersigned have signed this Treaty, and affixed thereunto our seals, at the City of Santa Fe, this the first day of July in the year of our Lord one thousand eight hundred and fifty-two.

John Greiner, (SEAL.)
Act. Supt. Indian Affairs, New Mexico
Witnesses:
F. A. Cunningham
Paymaster, U.S.A.
J. C. McFerran
1st Lt. 3d Inf. Act. Ast. Adj. Gen.
Caleb Sherman
Fred. Saynton
Chas. McDougall
Surgeon, U.S.A.
S. M. Baird
Witness to the signing of Mangus Colorado:
John Pope,
Bvt. Capt. T. E.[3]

E. V. Summer, (SEAL.)
Bvt. Col. U.S.A.
commanding Ninth Department
In charge of Executive Office of
New Mexico.
Capitan Vuelta, his x mark
(SEAL.)
Cuentas Azules, his x mark
(SEAL.)
Blancito, his x mark (SEAL.)
Negrito, his x mark (SEAL.)
Capitan Simon, his x mark
(SEAL.)
Mangus Colorado, his x mark
(SEAL.)

Apache Nation Treaty Conferences:
Tuesday June 29, 1852
Mescaleros and Jicarillas all here yet drawn 210 rations for 35 Indians six days. Soldiers rations not enough for Indians

Treaty signed:
Santa Fe, July 1st, 1852.

LANE'S TREATY*
APRIL 1853[4]

In April 1853, Governor and Superintendent of Indian Affairs William Carr Lane made provisional treaties with some Apaches, agreeing to furnish food for five years and give other aid to all who would work. Without waiting for the Senate's approval, Lane spent between twenty thousand and forty thousand dollars on the project. He fed about one thousand natives on farms at Abiquiu and Fort Webster, but the experiment proved a failure. With suspension of the rations, the Apaches became bolder than ever.[5]

Articles of a provisional compact, made at Fort Webster on the Rio Mimbres, the seventh day of April A.D. Eighteen hundred and fifty-three by William Carr Lane, Gov of the Ter. of N. M. & Supt. of Ind. Affairs, on behalf of the United States; and Ponce, Jose Nuevo, Cuchillo Negro, Josecito, Sargento, Vunte Riales, Pinon, Delgadito Largo, Hecho, Vitorio, Placera, Carrasero, and Chiefs, or Captains of Bands, of the Rio Mimbres & Rio Gila Apache Indians; on behalf of their respective Bands.

Art. 1st. Said Confederate Indians, solemnly agree and promise, henceforth to abandon their wandering & predatory modes of life; and to locate themselves, in permanent camps, & commence the cultivation of the Earth, for a subsistence; and as soon as possible, to build for themselves Dwelling houses, and to raise Flocks and Herds.

Art. 2d. They also agree to make Laws; to prevent their people from doing any manner of Evil; & faithfully to execute their Laws. They promise here after, never to resort to the ancient custom of Retaliation, for any Injuries which they may suffer. Nor will they ever attempt, to right their own wrongs,

Although this copy was signed at Fort Webster, the terms are almost identical to the treaty signed by the Jicarilla at Abiquiu.

in any case whatever; but in all instances, will apply to the proper authority, for a redress of their grievances; and will abide all decisions thus made.

Art. 3d. They promise to choose, in their own manner, their chiefs for each Band; one for Captain and the other for second captain, who shall be the organs of communication with their respective Bands, and who shall be charged with the execution of the Law, & be held responsible, for the conduct of the people of their respective Bands.

Art. 4th. It is earnestly recommended, that all the aforesaid Bands, under this Compact, shall after their own manner choose a Council of aged & experienced Chiefs; and a head chief, or Indians of all the aforesaid Bands; who shall have authority, to speak, for all the Bands. And whose further duty it shall be to oblige all the captains of Bands to perform their respective duties, & to render impartial justice, to all their people. And in case any captain should fail to do his duty, to punish him for his misdeeds; & to remove him from office, if he shall merit such an extreme punishment.

Art. 5th. Said confederated Bands, invite the Indians of the Bands of Mangas-Coloradas, Gilans, Delgadito, Hecho, Vitoria & Placero; (who are now absent on the Rio Gila) to join this compact. And they agree to admit the Mescaleros, and all the other Bands, of the great Apache Tribe of Indians, who now roam, on the east side of the Rio Grande, & who may migrate & settle upon the waters of the north side of the Gila; into this Confederacy, upon terms of brotherhood & equality.

Art. 6th. The United States promises and agrees, to supply all the Bands, that may join honestly & faithfully in this Compact, & live according to its stipulations; with Food, to consist of corn & Beef with salt; during the current year, & the year 1854 and also promises to give them a reasonable amount of Food, (of which the agent shall be the judge), for three years thereafter; so that by proper industry, temperance and economy on the part of the Indians themselves, there shall always be an abundant supply of food, for all of them.

Art. 7th. During the year 1854, the U.S. (at the discretion of its agents) shall supply the Bands, which may be aforestated under this Compact, with a certain number of Brood Mares & a few Cows, sheep & goats; and will for five years, from this Date, supply them with an experienced Farmer, to teach them how to till the Earth; and will also furnish them with implements of husbandry; and a Blacksmith & Blacksmith's tools; iron & steel; & some Carpenters tools. But the U.S. does not agree to furnish the Indians with clothing or Blankets; the Apaches must supply these articles themselves, by their own industry.

Art. 8th. All the Indians, who are associated under this compact, & who remain faithful to all its stipulations; shall be defended by the U.S. against all their Enemies. But if any lawless members of these Bands shall hereafter invade the Territories of the Mexican Republic; (the U.S. being at peace with that Republic), the Troops of the U.S. will intercept the return of the Marauding party, & permit the Mexicans to exterminate the Robbers.

Art. 9th. If unhappily an Indian should commit a Murder, upon a White person, the Murderer shall suffer death at the hands of the Indians themselves, or at the hands of the Whites, as the Indians may prefer. And if a white man should commit a Murder, upon an Indian, the white murderer shall be delivered up to the Indians Agent or to the officer in command of the nearest Military post, so that he may suffer the same penalty at the hands of the whites, according to their laws.

Art. 10th. No Individual belonging to any of the Bands hereby associated, shall be allowed to go into the white settlements, except by permission of the agent; and all Indians, who may violate this provision shall receive adequate punishment. And if any Indians shall go upon the desert, which is called La Jornada del Muerte, he shall suffer death, or such other punishment, as the chiefs may order, & the agent shall approve.

Art. 11th. All property which may be stolen hereafter from either the Whites or Indians, shall be mutually given up; & the Thieves, in either case shall be adequately & promptly punished.

All traders & other persons, who may introduce ardent spirits into the Indian Country, shall be immediately apprehended, & delivered to the nearest Indian Agent, together with his stock of liquors; and the agent shall compensate the Indians, who may make the capture & surrender, for their trouble, in the transaction.

No Indian of the Confederation, shall hereafter take any captives; & if they should now have captives, they must be immediately delivered up, to the agent, without any ransom.

The chiefs shall forbid their men and women from frequenting Military posts; & from indulging in Drunkenness, & all other vices; under suitable penalties.

Art. 12th. The Bands who are parties to this Compact, shall be left free to choose where they will make their permanent settlements; **provided**, the place which they may select, may not be East of this post. And if they should locate themselves upon lands, upon which a Valid grant has not been made, by the Spanish or Mexican governments; the U.S. shall make; to each Band, which may number one hundred souls, or more; a Grant of a Township, of 36 sections; & shall cause the grant to be located, so as to include the settlement of the Band.

Art. 13th. This provisional compact is made subject to the approval, or disapproval, of the Government of the U.S.; and shall have no validity, until it shall be approved, & fully ratified by authority of the U.S.

In Testimony whereof said parties to this Compact, hereto set their hands & seals, this day & year as above written.

Witness:

E. Steen

Capt. & Bvt. Maj U.S.A.

Comdg. Fort Webster

Phil. E. Norris

Bvt. 2 Lt 2 Dragoons

E.H. Wingfield, Agent

John Ward Ind. Interpreter

for the Ind. Dept.

F. Flecher, Interpreter

C. Sherman, Ind Trader

Alex. Duvall

Suttler Fort Webster

Henry Grandjean

Mejl. A. Otero

Private Secretary

Wm. Carr Lane - Seal

Gov & Sup Ind Aff.

Terr N. Mex.

The mark of Ponce   X Seal

The mark of Jose Nuevo   X Seal

" " " Cuchillo Negro   X Seal

" " " Josecito   X Seal

" " " Sargento   X Seal

" " " Vernte riales   X Seal

" " " Pinon   X Seal

" " " Delgadito Largo   X Seal

" " " Hecho   Seal

" " " Victorio   Seal

" " " Placera   Seal

" " " Carrasero   X Seal

MERIWETHER TREATY*
SEPTEMBER 12, 1855[6]

Articles of Agreement and Convention made and concluded, in Abiquiu in the Territory of New Mexico this 12th day of September 1855, by David Meriwether, sole commissioner duly appointed for that purpose, on the part of the United States, and the undersigned chiefs, Captains and head men of

Author cannot find any indication that this treaty was ever ratified by the Senate.

the Jicarilla band of the Apache tribe or nation of Indians; they being thereto duly authorized, and acting for, and in behalf of said band.

Art. 1st. Peace, friendship and amity shall forever, hereafter exist between the United States of America and the Jicarilla Apaches, and this convention and every article and Stipulation thereof, shall be perpetual, and observed and performed in good faith.

Art. 2nd. The Jicarilla Apaches hereby covenant, and agree, that **peaceful relations shall be maintained amongst themselves, and all other bands, tribes and nations of Indians within the United States, and that they will abstain from committing hostilities, or depredations,** in future, and cultivate good will and friendship.

Art. 3rd. The Jicarilla Apaches hereby cede and forever relinquish, to the United States, all title, or claim whatsoever, which they have to lands within the Territory of New Mexico except so much as is herein after reserved to them; and the Jicarilla Apaches further agree and bind themselves to remove to, and settle on the lands herein reserved to them, within one year after the ratification of this treaty, without any cost or charge to the United States whatever for their removal, and that they will cultivate the soil and raise flocks and herds for a subsistence, and **that the president of the United States may withhold the annuities herein stipulated to be paid, or any part thereof, whenever the Jicarillas shall violate, fail or refuse to comply with any provision of this instrument,** or to cultivate the soil in good faith.

Art. 4th. The United States agree to set apart and withhold from sale, for the use of the Jicarillas, for their permanent homes, and hereby guarantee to them the possession and enjoyment of a tract of country within the Territory of New Mexico, to be bounded as follows Vis: Beginning on the north side of the Chama river, at the south of the Saboya Creek - and thence up the said Creek to its source - thence westwardly with the summit of the range of Mountains which said Creek heads to the range of Mountains that divides the waters of the Chama from those of the San Juan - thence southwardly with said last named range of mountains to the spur thereof which divides the waters of Chama from those of the Rio Puerco which empties into the Rio Grande - thence along said dividing spur of said mountains Eastwardly to the head water of the arroyo of the Puerto de Abajo - thence down said river to the beginning - It being understood by the parties that the foregoing boundary is to include all the waters of the Chama river above the mouth of the Saboya Creek.

Art. 5th. The United States is hereby authorized to define the boundaries of the reserved tract, when it may be necessary by actual survey or otherwise, and the president may, from time to time, at his discretion, cause the whole or any part thereof to be surveyed, and may assign to each head of a family, or single person, over twenty one years of age, twenty acres of land for his or her separate use and benefit, and each family of three and less than five persons, forty acres of land, and to each family of five or more person sixty acres, and he may at his discretion, as fast as the occupants become capable of transacting their own affairs, issue patents therefore to such occupants, with such restrictions of the power of alienation, as he may see fit to impose; and he may also, at his discretion, make rules and regulations respecting the disposition of the lands, in case of the death of the head of a family or a single person occupying the same, or in case of its abandonment by them, and he may also assign other lands in exchange for mineral lands, if any such are found on the tract herein set apart; and he may also make such changes in the boundary of such reserved tract as shall be necessary to prevent interference with any vested rights. All necessary roads, high ways and rail roads, the line of which may run through the reserved tract, shall have the right of way through the same, compensation being made therefor, as in other cases; but the president may grant the right of way to any such roads free of charge, and establish such military posts as he may think proper.

Art. 6th. In consideration of, and full payment for the country ceded, and the removal of Jicarilla Apaches, the United States agree to pay to them the following sums without interest, to wit; The United States will, during the years 1856, 1857 and 1858 pay to the Jicarillas Three thousand dollars each year, during the year 1859, and the two next succeeding years thereafter the sum of Two - Thousand dollars each year; and during the year 1862 and the next succeeding twenty years thereafter the sum of One thousand dollars each year. All of which several sums of money shall be paid to the Jicarillas or expended for their use and benefit, under the direction of the president of the United States who may, from time to time, determine at his discretion what proportion of the annual payments in this article provided for, if any, shall be paid to them in money, and what proportion shall be applied to, and expended for their moral improvement and education, for such beneficial objects as in his judgment will be calculated to advance them in civilization, for building, opening farms, breaking lands, providing stock, agricultural implements, sees &c, for employing farmers to teach the Indians to cultivate the soil, for clothing, provision and merchandise, for iron steel, arms and ammunition, for mechanics and tools, and for medical purposes.

Art. 7th. The annuities of the Indians are not to be taken to pay the debts of individuals, but satisfaction for depredations committed by them, shall be made by the Indians in such manner as the president may direct; nor shall any part of the annuities stipulated be paid, ever be applied by the chiefs or head men, to the payment of tribal debts or obligations to traders or other persons.

Art. 8th. No spirituous liquors shall be made, sold or used, on any of the lands herein set apart for the residence of the Indians; and the sale of the same shall be prohibited in the country hereby ceded, until otherwise ordered by the president.

Art. 9th. The laws now in force, or which may hereafter be enacted by Congress for the regulation of trade and intercourse with the Indian tribes, shall continue and be in force in the country set apart for the Jicarillas; and such portions of said laws as prohibit the introduction, manufacture, use of, and traffick in ardent spirits in the Indian country, shall continue and be in force in all the country ceded, until otherwise provided by law.

Art. 10th. The Jicarillas do further agree and bind themselves, to make restitution or satisfaction for any injuries done by them or any individual of their band to the people of the United States, and to surrender to the proper authorities of the United States when demanded, any individual or individuals who may commit depredations, to be punished according to law. And if any citizens of the United States shall, at any time, commit depredations upon the Indians the Jicarillas agree that they will not take private satisfaction or revenge themselves, but instead thereof, they will make complaint to the proper Indian Agent for redress, and the said Indians do further agree to refrain from all warlike incursions into the Mexican provinces, and from committing depredations upon the inhabitants thereof.

Art. 11th. This treaty shall be obligatory upon the contracting parties as soon as the same shall be ratified by the president and Senate of the United States.

In testimony whereof, the said David Meriwether, Commissioner as aforesaid, and the undersigned Chiefs, Captains and head men of the said band of Jicarilla Apache Indians, have hereunto set their hands and seals, at the place and on the day and year herein before written.

D Meriwether

Com on the part of the United States

Witnesses present –
Richard L. Ewell
Captain 1st Dragoons
Saml. Ellison
Translator
Lorenzo Labadi
Indian Agent

Guero Lobo
San Pablo
Jose Chavez
Oso
Guero Mudo [Guero Mundo]
Jose Chiquito
Marianito
Carmito
Pantalson [Pantaleon]
Miguelito
Jose Ortiz
Vicente
Montera Blanca

TREATY BETWEEN THE ARAPAHO, CHEYENNE, AND APACHE, AND THE MUAHUACHE UTE, JICARILLA APACHE, AND PUEBLO OF TAOS
JANUARY 22, 1858[7]

Utah Agency, Taos, N. Mexico

On this twenty second day of January A.D. Eighteen Hundred and fifty-eight, in council appeared Guatanamo, an Indian of the Arapahoe tribe, who stated that he was sent to this place by the Arapahos, Cheyenne and Apache Indians for the purpose of making a treaty of peace with the Muahuache Utahs, Jicarilla Apaches and the Pueblos of Taos. In council the Muahuaches were represented by War Chief Ancatash and Jose Maria, the Jicarillas by War Chiefs [blank space] and Pueblos by Warchiefs Jose Maria Cordova and Antonio Jose Suaso.

After due deliberation the representatives of the aforesaid bands have this day entered into a permanent treaty of peace and friendship. Parties may pass and repass through the country of each without molestation if on a peaceable mission. The whites are to be treated as friends, and on no terms whatever shall the bands for whom we are representative join any nation or people at war with the United States. We pledge our aid in quieting any disturbance that may arise between Indians, within the boundaries of our country, and the United States. The enemies of the United States to be considered our enemies.

Witness our hands this 22d day of January A.D. 1858.

Ancatash	his X mark	Guatanamo	his X mark
Jos. Maria	his X mark	Jos. Maria Cordova	his X mark
		Antonio Jos. Suaso	his X mark

Signed and acknowledged
In presence of C. Carson
Indian Agent

CONVENTION WITH THE JICARILLA APACHE
DECEMBER 10, 1873

Articles of Convention made and concluded on the 10th day of December, in the year of our Lord one thousand eight hundred and seventy-three, by and between Thomas A. Dolan on behalf of the United States, and the undersigned chiefs, head-men, and braves representing the Jicarilla Apaches:

Witnesseth: That whereas the Jicarilla Apache now living in the vicinity of Cimarron, Tierra Amarilla and Abiquiu in the Territory of New Mexico, claim and live upon lands ceded to certain parties by grants of the Government of Mexico, prior to the ceding of said Territory to the United States (said grants having been approved by the Congress of the United States) and in consequence the said Jicarilla Apaches have no place on which they can take up land and settle as permanent homes, which they greatly desire to do; Now, therefore, I, Thomas A. Dolan, acting under instructions from the Commissioner of Indian Affairs dated November 15, 1873, on behalf of the United States and the aforesaid representatives of the Jicarilla Apaches, do solemnly enter into and make the following agreement:

Art. 1st. The United States agree that the following district of country, to wit: Commencing at a point where the head water of San Juan river crosses the Southern boundary of the Territory of Colorado, following the course of said river until it intersects the Eastern boundary of the Navajo Reservation to where it intersects the Southern boundary line of the Territory of Colorado; thence due East along the said Southern boundary of the Territory of Colorado to the place of beginning, for the absolute and undisturbed use and occupation of the Jicarilla Apache Indians, and for such other friendly tribes or individual Indians, as from time to time they may be willing with the consent of the United States to admit amongst them, and the United States now solemnly agrees that no person except those herein designated and authorized so to do, and except such officers, agents and employees of the Government as may be authorized to enter upon Indian reservations in discharge of duties enjoined by law, shall ever be permitted to pass over, settle upon, or reside in the territory described in this Article for the use of said Indians.

Art. 2nd. It is agreed by the Jicarilla Apaches, parties hereto, that henceforth they will, and do hereby relinquish all claims and rights to any portion of the United States or Territories, except such as are embraced within the limits defined in the preceding Article, and that upon the ratification by Congress of these Articles of agreement, they will remove to settle upon, and reside within the limits of the above mentioned country.

Art. 3rd. The United States agrees to appropriate, for the aid and encouragement of the Jicarilla Apaches annually for and during the period of five years, the sum of ten thousand dollars to be expended by and under the direction of the President of the United States, for the benefit of the said Indians, and at the expiration of that period, they shall be entitled to an annual appropriation of three thousand dollars per year, for educational purposes, for and during the succeeding period of ten years.

Art. 4th. The United States agrees (the Utes consenting thereto) that the Jicarilla Apaches shall be attached to the Southern Ute Agency, (so soon as it may be established) and that the Agent for the said Southern Ute Agency shall exercise the same care of them and their interest, that he does of the Utes attached to his Agency; and that the said Jicarilla Apaches shall at all times have free access to the Agency, and enjoy all the benefits of it, except in the matter of appropriations for annuity goods, provisions, and special treaty appropriations for the Utes.

Art. 5th. If bad men among the whites or among other people subject to the authority of the United States, shall commit any wrong upon the person or property of the Jicarilla Apache Indians, the United States will, upon proof made to the Agent and forwarded to the Commissioner of Indian Affairs at Washington City, proceed at once to cause the offender to be arrested and punished according to the laws of the United States, and also reimburse the injured person for the loss sustained. If bad men among the said Indians shall commit a wrong or depredation upon the person or property of any one, white, black or Indian, subject to the authority of the United States and at peace therewith, the tribes herein named solemnly agree that they will, on proof made to their Agent, and notice to him, deliver up the wrong-doer to the United States, to be tried and punished according to its laws.

Art. 6th. If any individual belonging to said tribe of Indians or legally incorporated with them, being the head of a family, shall desire to commence farming, he shall have the privilege to select, in the presence and with the assistance of the Agent then in charge, by metes and bounds, a tract of land within said reservation not exceeding one hundred and sixty acres in extent, which tract, when so selected, certified, and recorded in the land book as herein directed, shall cease to be held in common but the same may be occupied and held in exclusive possession of the person selecting it and his family so long as he or they may continue to cultivate it. Any person over eighteen years of age, not being the head of a family, may, in like manner, select and cause to be certified to him or her for purposes of cultivation a quantity of land not exceeding eighty acres in extent, and thereupon be entitled to the exclusive possession of the same, as above directed.

For each tract of land so selected, a certificate containing a description thereof, and the name of the person selecting it, with a certificate endorsed thereon, that the same has been recorded, shall be delivered to the party entitled to it, by the agent, after the same shall have been recorded by him in a book, to be kept in his office, subject to inspection, which said book shall be known as the "Jicarilla Apache Land Book."

The President may at any time order a survey of the reservation, and when so surveyed, Congress shall provide for protecting the rights of such Indian settlers in their improvements, and may fix the character of the title held by each.

The United States may pass such laws on the subject of alienation and descent of property, and on all subjects connected with the government of the Indians on said reservation, and the internal police thereof as may be thought proper.

Art. 7th. In order to insure the civilization of the Indians entering into this treaty, the necessity of education is admitted, especially by such of them as are or may be engaged in either pastoral, agricultural, or other peaceful pursuits of civilized life on said reservation, and they therefore pledge themselves to induce their children, male and female, between the ages of seven and eighteen years, to attend school; and it is hereby made the duty of the Agent for said Indians to see that this stipulation is complied with to the greatest possible extent.

Art. 8th. The said Jicarilla Apache Indians agree that the Congress of the United States may authorize the passage of roads, highways and railroads through the reservation herein designated.

In case the Indian parties hereto, refuse to live upon their reservation, or engage in hostilities against the United States, then the appropriation herein provided, shall not be available for their benefit.

It is expressly understood between said Dolan and the Indians, parties hereto, that this agreement is subject to the ratification or rejection of the Congress of the United States, and by the Jicarilla Apaches in council assembled.

We, the undersigned chiefs, representative delegates of the Ute Indians do agree to the several provisions in the aforesaid Articles of convention, that mutually interest the Utes and the Jicarilla Apaches.

Thomas A. Dolan
Commissioner

Witness:
W. D. Crothers   Captains of Apaches   Agostin Vigil, his x mark
Guero Mudo, his x mark
Vicente, his x mark
Pedro Martin, his x mark
Camilo, his x mark
Guerrito Washington, his x mark
Mangus Colorado, his x mark
Apache Braves   Jose Bibian, his x mark
Vicentito Gallegos, his x mark
Jesus Luna, his x mark
Jose Ulibarri, his x mark
Antonio Embaria, his x mark

Signed this 10th day of December, 1873, in the presence of,

John Townsend
T. D. Burns

Jose Rafel, his x mark	Ute Chief	Juan Antonio, his x mark	Ute Captain
Mouse, his x mark	Ute Chief	Juan Jesus, his x mark	Ute Chief
Josetavarst, his x mark	Ute Chief	Tecota, his x mark	Ute Captain
Yeochacants, his mark	Ute Brave	Tabah, his x mark	Ute Chief
Sepereat, his x mark	Ute Brave	Carlos Traner, his x mark	Ute Captain
Arcarcunarrabitabit, his x mark	Ute Brave	Reyes, his mark	Ute Brave
Rapinash, his x mark	Ute Brave	Taos, his x mark	Ute Brave

Witness present:
    Maurice Traner
    Francisco Griego, Interpreter

San Pablo, his x mark	Apache Chief
Jose Largo, his x mark	Apache Chief
Juan Largo, his x mark	Apache Brave
Juan Julian, his x mark	Captain
Juan Pezeta, his x mark	Brave
Jesus, his x mark	Brave
Guero, his x mark	Brave
Guerito, his x mark	Brave
Jose Miguel, his x mark	Brave
Juan Largo Bonito, his x mark	Brave
Joseto, his x mark	Brave
Tisnordo, his x mark	Brave
Ramonsito, his x mark	Brave
Jose Miguel, his x mark	Brave
Lonico Valdez, his x mark	Brave
Carnocia, his x mark	Brave
Rafel, his x mark	Brave

We, the undersigned hereby certify that we were present at the signing of the foregoing names of Apache Indians, and are witnesses thereto, this 20th day of December 1873

                H. A. Simpson
                Maurice Trauer
                Francis Griego, Interpreter[8]

GLOSSARY

Abiquiu—Spanish. Abiquiu, ah-bi-que, is a *genizaro* town founded by Pueblo Indians and transplanted captives from nomadic tribes. It was famous for its 1750–1775 witch trials, a result of the mixing of cultures. Located on the Chama River, it was at the western boundary of Spanish culture. The Ute-Jicarilla Agency was here and it was a trading site where captive slaves of many nations were traded.

Acequia Madre—Spanish. The acequia madre, ah-say-key-yah mah-drey, was the mother ditch, the principal irrigation canal of a community.

Adjutant General—An adjutant general is not a general. He is a secretary and administrative officer who maintains records and writes letters and reports. Communications signed by the adjutant come from his commander and those addressed to the adjutant are intended for the adjutant's commander.

Adobe—Spanish. Adobe is a mixture of clay, sand, and hair or straw, sun dried to form bricks for construction. It also refers to buildings built of this material.

Adobe Walls—Adobe Walls is on the Canadian River in the Texas Panhandle. In 1849, William Bent sent Kit Carson to erect a fort as a trading post with the Comanche and Kiowa. Trade did not work out and the post was soon abandoned, falling into ruin to become the site of battles with the Comanche and Kiowa in 1864 and 1874.

Aguardiente—Spanish. Aguardiente, ah-whar-dee-ehn-tey, is clear brandy.

Alcalde—Spanish. Alcalde, ahl-kahl-dey, is usually translated as mayor. The office combined functions of magistrate, executive, and head of the militia. Mexican political offices combined judicial, military, and executive authority.

Ambush—In military parlance ambush describes the action of a force that conceals itself along a trail, road, or avenue of approach that the enemy must use, or to which the enemy can be lured, where they can be surprised finding themselves on unfavorable ground unable to escape while the ambushing force destroys them.

Apache—The Apache are a people speaking a single language or closely related languages of the Athapascan family of languages whose other members are found in Canada and Alaska. Thus, it is believed that they are among the last group to migrate south having arrived in the American Southwest sometime after AD 1200.

Artillery Rounds—Artillery rounds included:
- **Case Shot**—Case was like spherical shot except that a cluster of round balls surrounded the explosive core.
- **Grape**—Grape was a cluster of iron or iron balls without an explosive core that turned the cannon into a giant shotgun.
- **Shell**—Shell was a hollow iron ball filled with explosive powder that had a protruding fuse that was cut to length in accordance with how long it was desired the shell should fly before it exploded. Ignition of the propellant charge ignited the fuse. Soldiers could manually ignite the fuse and toss the shell like a hand grenade.
- **Solid Shot**—a solid iron round ball weighing six pounds in a six-pounder gun and twelve pounds in a twelve-pounder.

Atole—Spanish. Atole, ah-toh-lay, is a once common trail food made from corn. George Brewerton said, "atole is a kind of meal which when prepared forms a very nutritious dish not unlike 'mush,' both in taste and appearance."

Battalion—A battalion is a temporary formation of two or more companies usually commanded by a major or lieutenant colonel.

Beau Sabre—See *beau sabreur*. Colonel Cooke modifies the usual term to mean a "dashing cavalryman."

Beau Sabreur—A beau sabreur is a dashing adventurer.

Butcher's Bill—The butcher's bill is army slang for the casualty count.

Caballada—Spanish. Caballada, kah-bay-ah-dah, is a horse or mule herd.

Californios—Spanish. Californios are people of Mexican descent who were born in California.

Camp—See *fort*.

Canadian River—The headwaters of the Canadian River are near Raton, New Mexico. It flows south beyond Las Vegas and then east through the Texas Panhandle and Oklahoma. In the nineteenth century, it was also known as the Red River, and by its Spanish name, Colorado.

Cantle—The cantle is the upward-projecting rear portion of a saddle. In the nineteenth century, the cantle was much higher than on saddles in common use today.

Cantonment—Cantonment refers to quarters for troops or the portion of a base where the barracks are located. A camp near Taos was called Cantonment Burgwin, although it was like any other camp or fort.

Cap and Ball—Cap and Ball weapons are usually loaded through the muzzle or front of the cylinder, though some used a paper cartridge loaded through the breech. Black powder was measured and then poured down the barrel. A ball was then forced down the barrel. Finally, a fulminate of mercury percussion cap was placed on a nipple at the breech. The hammer striking the cap ignited the powder in the barrel.

Capote—A capote is a type of hooded overcoat made from a blanket.

Casualty—Casualty is often misunderstood. Casualties include killed, wounded, missing, and captured. A mortally wounded soldier may survive the battle to die later of his wound or wounds. Casualty figures can be different from different sources. Some sources will include the count of those men with minor wounds, while the official report drops them out. Wounded may become killed. Missing may become killed, wounded, deserted, or captured.

Chaparral—Spanish. Chaparral, shah-pah-ral, is shrub brush, often thorny, like mesquite.

Chimayo—Chimayo was one of the principal towns of the Rio Arriba famed as a source of Rio Grande blankets.

Chimayoso—A Chimayoso is a person from Chimayo. Many were weavers and were recognized by their braided hair.

Chronological List—The *Chronological List of Actions from January 15, 1837, to January 1891* was first published in 1891. It provides a brief description—location, date, commander's name, units involved, and casualties reported on both sides—of fights between the regular army and Native Americans. It does not include actions involving volunteer units, militia, or civilians.

Ciboleros—Spanish. Ciboleros were Mexican buffalo hunters who ventured onto the Llano Estacado. They were considered half wild and perhaps of Indian blood by their neighbors.

Cieneguilla—Spanish. Cieneguilla, see-ehn-eh-gih-yah, means the little swamp. It is the name of a tiny village on the Rio Grande about twenty miles south of Taos and the name of a battle that occurred about three miles east of the village.

Cimarron Cutoff—The Cimarron Cutoff, actually the main Santa Fe Trail, left the Arkansas River near present day Dodge City and headed southwest across the Llano Estacado meeting the Mountain Branch either at Wagon Mound north of the Turkey Mountains or at La Junta south of those mountains.

Cimarrones—Spanish. Cimarrones are wild or nomadic Indians.

Colorado River—See Canadian River. Colorado River usually refers to the Canadian River, although there is a stream north of Taos flowing into the Rio Grande sometimes known by this name.

Comancheros—Spanish. These were New Mexicans who ventured out on the Llano Estacado to trade with the Kiowa and Comanche. Since they traded weapons, powder, and shot for slaves and Indian captives, they were not well thought of.

Commons—Commons were lands held in common by the people of a town or district used for grazing and wood cutting.

Company—A company is a permanent military organization of from thirty to one hundred men commanded by a captain assisted by a first lieutenant and a second lieutenant.

Concealment—See *cover and concealment.*

Courts-Martial—The nineteenth-century military had a much higher rate of courts-martial than we have today. That was largely because there was no system of non-judicial punishment. Even minor offenses against order and discipline had to go to court-martial. Officers got to know soldiers who misbehaved. Sergeants brought men to their officers only when they found it impossible to impose discipline themselves. It was an admission of failure they tried to avoid. As a result, officers knew and wrote about the worst soldiers and we get a distorted view of military life and soldiers.

Cover and Concealment—Cover and concealment are two different and separate concepts. Cover provides protection from enemy fire, through use of a wall, a trench, a rock, or a tree. Concealment provides protection from detection as might a bush or clump of grass, or camouflage.

Covering Fire—Covering fire is weapons fire directed at the enemy to suppress and inhibit him from firing accurately, thus providing cover for your own men.

Cowboy or Cow Boy—Cowboy is a pejorative term from the nineteenth century referring to a thief, rustler, outlaw, or otherwise lawless person. People who owned cattle were stockmen and those that worked for them were drovers.

Delaware Indians—A surprising number of Delaware Indians from New Jersey and New York show up in the ranks of the mountain men. Some of them still identified as Rockaway Indians, meaning they were from Far Rockaway in Queens on Long Island.

Del Norte—Del Norte is an American corruption of Rio Grande del Norte, the Rio Grande, which is known as the Rio Bravo in Texas.

Desertion—Desertion was much more common in the nineteenth century than today. Soldiers did sign on to take advantage of an all-expense paid trip to the gold fields where they would desert, often absconding with a government horse and military weapons. The nineteenth-century military did not use the term Absent Without Leave (AWOL) as we do today. So taking "Dutch Leave" to go on a spree was counted as desertion even though the soldier soon returned to duty.

Despatches—Despatches is a common nineteenth-century spelling of dispatches. See *dispatches*.

Digger—Digger was a name used by mountain men for Paiute Indians, a desert-dwelling branch of the Ute tribe who dug for roots and other things for food. They were poor and considered untrustworthy.

Dispatches—Dispatches are official military correspondence and reports.

Don—Spanish. Don is an honorific title like colonel as it was used in Kentucky and the nineteenth-century West.

Dragoon—Dragoons are a type of cavalry trained and equipped to fight either mounted or dismounted. They were armed with saber, musketoon or carbine (a shortened musket or rifle), and pistol.

Escopeta—Spanish. An escopeta was a short, flintlock musket. See *flintlock*. See *musket*.

Eutaw—See *Ute*.

Fields of Fire—Field of fire is the area that can be seen within range of one's weapon.

Flank—The flank is a side. A frontal assault charges into the enemy's fire. A flank attack comes in from the side facing less resistance.

Flintlock—A flintlock is a black-powder weapon whose propellant charge is ignited by the striking of flint in the hammer against the steel of the frizzen pan cover. The frizzen has to open in this process and the charge may blow away or get wet.

Fort—Fort was used to describe civilian trading posts like Bent's and Barclay's as well as military settlements, which were usually ten miles square with a cantonment area in the center. In the Southwest, it was not usually a defensive structure. The dragoons and cavalry in particular established posts that were wide open with grazing for their horses. They did not intend to fight from within their forts. The infantry was more likely to build a defensive structure. There is confusion between fort and camp. A fort was paid for from the Army budget, while a camp was paid for from the regimental budget. When a camp became permanent and was picked up on the Army budget, it became a fort.

Fourth Man—When dragoons dismounted to fight, one man in four, the fourth man, would take the reins of all four horses and seek a sheltered spot near enough to the front line that the horses were available if needed. The surgeon and the pack mules usually located themselves nearby.

Fusil—A fusil was a light flintlock musket often of very cheap manufacture for the Indian trade.

Genizaro—Spanish. Genizaro, hen-is-ah-roh, evolves from the term *Janissary*. In New Mexico, they were people of nomadic tribes, taken captive, trained in Spanish/Mexican households as Christians, and then returned to border communities as a buffer against nomadic tribes. Abiquiu, Trampas, San Miguel, and Ranchos de Taos were among these protective villages.

Grape—See *artillery rounds*.

Guidon—A guidon is the split-tailed pennant that identifies a military unit. Soldiers follow the guidon of their unit in battle.

Hog Ranch—The "hog ranch" was an institution located beyond the boundaries of the military post, usually a ten-mile square, so that the ranch would be about three miles from the cantonment area (barracks and offices). The "hog ranch" provided cheap whiskey, cheap women, and cheap gambling.

Horse holders—See *fourth man*.

Howitzer—A howitzer is a type of cannon. A true cannon is fired level with the ground or nearly so, as if line of sight and the flight of the ball were the same. Howitzers have a barrel that can be raised above the horizontal to take advantage of super elevation, an arching trajectory increasing range.

Jacal—Spanish. A jacal, hah-kahl, is a structure made by setting wooden poles with the bark still on into the ground and spreading adobe mud to fill the chinks. They are dirty to live in and do not last very long before the wood rots.

Jicarilla Apache—The Jicarilla are the northernmost band of the Plains Apache. They lived in tepees and hunted buffalo. In the mid-nineteenth century they numbered between one thousand and thirteen hundred members.

Kill Zone—A kill zone is a place where an enemy stalled by obstacles can be engaged from multiple sides to great advantage.

La Junta—Spanish. La Junta, lah hoon-tah, means the union. The town of La Junta is where the Sapello and Mora Rivers come together south of the Turkey Mountains where the two branches of the Santa Fe Trail join for the last time and where Alexander Barclay built his fort. Fort Union was six miles to the north. Later the town was named Watrous after the eponymous ranch.

Land Grant—The Spanish crown made grants of land to individuals. These *patrons* would provide financial support to settlement, subdividing the land in the process. Within the grant would be individual farms, grazing commons shared by all the settlers, and forest commons where they hunted and cut lumber and firewood. More numerous grants were made by governors during the Mexican period, 1821 to 1846.

Las Vegas—Spanish. Las Vegas means the meadows. The town of Las Vegas was established in 1832 and was the first Mexican town travelers on the Santa Fe Trail encountered.

Lazy-Stitch—Beads were sewn on directly to the deer skin in sets of five forming parallel rows.

Lines of Communication—Lines of communication are the routes by which the news, the mail, reinforcements, and supplies travel.

Llanero—The Llanero, yah-nehr-roh, were the plains or red clay of the Jicarilla usually found in the Sangre de Cristo Mountains and eastward to the Canadian River. Their patron is the sun who is the keeper of animals.

Llano—Spanish. Llano, yah-noh, means a prairie.

Llano Estacado—The Llano Estacado, yah-noh es-tah-cah-doh, is the Staked Plains, an area extending eastward from the Sangre de Cristo Mountains through the Texas Panhandle and southward to the Rio Grande. It was once buffalo range. Water is scarce and the land difficult to navigate being relatively featureless.

Mangani—Jicarilla Apache. Mangani is the Jicarilla word for an Anglo.

Mechanic—Mechanic is a nineteenth-century term referring to a worker who practices a trade or handicraft, like a blacksmith or wheelwright.

Metí—Metí were mixed blood French-Canadians and Indians who had intermarried.

Mexican Land Grant—See *land grant*.

Mexicans—In the nineteenth century, those of Spanish descent in New Mexico were referred to as Mexicans although they were American citizens. There was a clear cultural divide, and so I use the term as they did.

Mora—Mora is a town founded in the 1830s by settlers from Taos. It is in the canyons east of and near the crest of the Sangre de Cristo Mountains.

Mountain Branch—The Mountain Branch of the Santa Fe Trail followed the northern bank of the Arkansas River as far as Bent's Fort and the Purgatory

River and then crossed the Arkansas River, going south across the Raton Pass to rejoin the Cimarron Cutoff near the Turkey Mountains.

Mounted Infantry—Mounted infantry is a type of infantry provided with mounts, usually mules. They would ride to the battle and then dismount to fight. Mounted infantry was not trained or equipped to fight while mounted. They carried a rifle and Bowie knife.

Musket—A musket is a weapon without rifling in the barrel, a smooth bore. It can be loaded about three times as quickly as a rifle but lacks the accuracy and range of the latter.

Musketoon—A musketoon is a shortened version of a musket as a carbine is a shortened version of a rifle. The musketoon was intended for use by mounted troops.

Nakaiyeh—Jicarilla Apache. Nakaiyeh is the Jicarilla word for a Mexican.

Ninth Military District—The Ninth Military District was redefined several times before it was finally abolished October 31, 1853, as part of a revision of the entire military geography of the United States. Generally, it included all of New Mexico, which then incorporated parts of southwestern Kansas, which later became Colorado, and Arizona. It was replaced by the Military Department of New Mexico, which consisted of the territory of New Mexico.

Ojo Caliente—Spanish. Ojo Caliente, oh-hoh kal-ih-ehn-tay, means hot spring. It is a place name and the name of the site of a battle north of Abiquiu in the San Juan Mountains.

Ollero—The Ollero, oy-yehr-oh, are the water jug, or white, clan of the Jicarilla Apache. They were usually found westward of the Sangre de Cristo Mountains and west of the Rio Grande in the San Juan Mountains northward to Mount Blanca. Their patron is the moon who is keeper of plant foods.

Pagosa Springs—Pagosa Springs was a mining community on the western slope of the San Juan Mountains about forty miles northwest of Tierra Amarilla, and forty miles northeast of Dulce and Amargo.

Paisano—Spanish. Paisano, pie-sahn-noh, means a fellow countryman. In New Mexico this is also a name for the bird called a roadrunner.

Patron—Spanish. A patron, pah-tron, is a boss or landlord with medieval overtones.

Pecos—Pecos is a very old town about thirty miles east of Santa Fe where the Santa Fe Trail enters Glorieta Pass.

Penitente—Spanish. The Penitentes were a secret society that practiced self-flagellation and other self-tortures including at Easter suspending a man from a cross. New Mexico had few priests and the Penitente Society took the place of more formal religion. The society was very powerful and members were sworn to protect each other, leading to abuses such as robbing strangers.

Peon—Spanish. A peon is a debt slave bound for a number of years to work off his debt.

Pickets—Soldiers sent out a short distance from the main body to provide early warning of the approach of enemies.

Picuris—The Picuris are a Pueblo Indian tribe who live in the Embudo Mountains near Cieneguilla. They speak the same language as the people of Taos Pueblo and have long been trading partners and sometime allies of the Jicarilla.

Pinole—Spanish. Pinole, pin-oh-lay, a once common trail food, is parched, ground corn meal, mixed with cinnamon and sugar. George Brewerton said that "this condiment is almost invaluable to the travelers in the wildernesses of the Far West; as it requires no fire to cook it, being prepared at a moment's warning by simply mixing it with cold water. It has the further advantage of occupying but little space in proportion to its weight; but when prepared for use, it swells so as nearly to double in quantity. A very small portion is there-fore sufficient to satisfy the cravings of hunger."

Placer—A placer is a deposit of gold dust or nuggets in the sediment of the bed of a water course or fossil water course. This type of deposit is worked with a sluice rather than digging underground through hard rock.

Plains Apache—The Plains Apache were Apaches who lived on the Great Plains and Llano Estacado usually in tepees hunting buffalo. Among them are the Jicarilla, Kiowa Apache, Lipan, and Mescalero. Interestingly, the Mescalero intermarried with and went to war with the eastern bands of the Chiricahua Apache.

Pueblo—Spanish. The word pueblo with a lowercase p is the Spanish word for town or village. With an uppercase P the word refers to the villages and Indian people of a number tribes who live in fixed villages. It can also refer to a tiny trading fort along the Arkansas River established in the 1840s and destroyed by the Ute and Jicarilla on Christmas Day 1854.

Ramada—Spanish. The ramada is a brush shelter with open sides providing protection from the sun in the manner of a beach umbrella.

Recruit—Recruit, as in to recruit one's horses, meant to let the animals rest, feed, and fatten. Cavalry horses could not eat enough on the trail to maintain weight and health, and so had to be allowed to recruit between missions.

Red River—See Canadian River.

Red Wall Canyon—Red Wall Canyon's lower extremity is about four miles west and north of Abiquiu. The land rises abruptly at this point to the *Piedra Lumbre*, the Rocks on Fire. It is the barrier where eighteenth-century Spanish settlement ended.

Regiment—A permanent military organization of ten companies thus having five hundred to one thousand men. It was commanded by a colonel, assisted by a lieutenant colonel and a major.

Remuda—Spanish. The remuda is a herd of horses from which those to be used for the day are chosen.

Rico—Spanish. A rico is someone who is wealthy, a property owner.

Rio Abajo—Spanish. Rio Abajo, ree-oh ah-bah-hoh, means downriver and refers to New Mexico south of Santa Fe. The culture and language are slightly different from the north. The elevation is several thousand feet lower than the

Rio Arriba, the upriver, and the climate more temperate. The Rio Arriba is home to free farmers while the Abajo is home to *ricos*, the wealthy, and their *peons*, debt slaves.

Rio Arriba—Spanish. Rio Arriba, ree-oh ah-ree-bah, means upriver and refers to New Mexico north of Santa Fe. The Rio Arriba includes Taos, Chimayo, Mora, Las Vegas, and Cimarron. *Rio Arriba*, the upriver, New Mexico north from Santa Fe, as opposed to the *Rio Abajo*, downriver, New Mexico south of Santa Fe.

Rio Colorado—Spanish. The Rio Colorado, Red River, is a common name. There is one north of Taos near Questa now called the Red River. This is also a name for the Canadian River.

Rio Puerco—The name means Filthy River and there are at least three in New Mexico. The one mentioned herein flows into the Rio Chama north of Abiquiu.

San Miguel—San Miguel was a town close to Pecos where the Santa Fe Trail turned westward to cross the Ford of the Pecos River.

Santa Cruz—Santa Cruz de la Cañada. One of the principal cities of the Rio Arriba, it was sometimes called Canada by Americans. It was the site of a battle of the Taos Rebellion of 1847.

Santa Fe—*Villa Real de Santa Fe de San Francisco de Asis.* The Royal City of the Holy Faith of St. Francis of Assisi.

Scalping—The Jicarilla Apache do not generally take scalps nor keep them as trophies. For them taking a scalp is an insult and it is soon thrown away. The Apache believe that anything a person loved in life might call him back from beyond the grave.

Shell—See *artillery rounds.*

Spanish Land Grant—See *land grant.*

Spanish Peaks—The Spanish Peaks are visible from the Arkansas River, which was the boundary between the United States and Spain and after 1821 until 1846, between the United States and Mexico.

Spies and Guides—Spies and guides is a nineteenth-century usage for scouts. They were very often hired locally and often were Indians.

Squadron—See *battalion*. Squadron refers to a cavalry formation similar to a battalion.

Staked Plains—See *Llano Estacado*.

Surprise—In military parlance, surprise means an action for which the enemy has no response, no means of defense. The frontier army often achieved surprise by attacking into a village. Men would rush to defend their families. The Indians were unable in these circumstances to form an organized defense. One sign that the enemy has been surprised is the difference in the "butcher's bill," on the opposing sides. One side may suffer overwhelming casualties while an opposing force of almost equal size suffers none.

Sutler—The sutler was the precursor to the Post Exchange, PX. He operated a store on the post under oversight by the officers, offering food and necessities to the soldiers in the manner of a general store.

Tactical Surprise—See *surprise*.

Taos—Taos is used to refer to three distinct communities. Don Fernando de Taos is the Spanish settlement usually thought of as Taos. Taos refers to the Pueblo Indian village a few miles to the north of Don Fernando de Taos. Ranchos de Taos is a *genizaro* settlement a few miles to the south of the other communities situated on the principal route over the passes from the plains.

Taos Lightning—Taos Lightning was a potent distilled whiskey made by former mountain men at Arroyo Hondo ten miles north of Taos. It was traded to Indians for beaver pelts and hides.

Troop—Troop can refer to a soldier, or, especially after the Civil War, a permanent military organization of cavalry the size of a company.

Utah—See *Ute*.

Ute—The Ute are a tribe living in western Colorado, Utah, and Nevada. There are a variety of nineteenth-century spellings for the name including: Utah, Eutaw, and Yutaw. Although they spoke different languages, they allied with and intermarried with the Jicarilla Apache.

Vecino—Spanish. A vecino is a resident, neighbor, an inhabitant of the place, a native.

Vedette—A vedette is a mounted sentinel.

Watrous—A rancher at La Junta and the modern name of La Junta.

White Clay—White clay is often used by the Jicarilla Apache as war paint to make them invisible to their enemies.

Yutaw—See *Ute*.

Zaguan—Spanish. Zaguan, zah-huan, is a covered entry, large enough to admit a wagon, to an interior courtyard or plaza.

NOTES

Introduction

1. Jicarilla Apache are Plains Apache who lived in tepees and hunted buffalo. Jicarilla is a Spanish word pronounced hick-kah-ree-yah. It is a diminutive of the word for chocolate cup and refers either to their baskets or pottery, both of which were important trade items with the Mexicans.

2. Hyslop, Stephen G. *Bound for Santa Fe: The Road to New Mexico and the American Conquest, 1806–1848*. Norman: University of Oklahoma Press, 2002.

3. *Missouri Republican*, October 24, 1834.

4. Dary, David. *The Santa Fe Trail: Its History, Legends, and Lore*. New York: Alfred A. Knopf, 2000, 181.

5. Connor, Seymour V., and Jimmy M. Skaggs. *Broadcloth and Britches: The Santa Fe Trade*. College Station: Texas A&M University Press, 1977, 75–76.

6. Hyslop, 47.

7. Neither old nor Spanish, the route was used to bring horses and mules from California to New Mexico as part of the Santa Fe trade.

8. Ebright, Malcolm. "Agent Benjamin Thomas in New Mexico, 1872–1883: Indian Agents as Advocates for Native Americans." *New Mexico Historical Review* 93/3 (Summer 2018), 304.

9. Ibid.

10. Ibid., 325.

11. An anachronism is something out of place in time. Historians endeavor to judge people in history by the standards of their own times, not ours.

12. Michno, Gregory. *Depredation and Deceit: The Making of the Jicarilla and Ute Wars in New Mexico*. Norman: University of Oklahoma Press, 2017, 8.

13. Often misspelled as Waters.

14. It was assembled from numerous grants and under the table dealings with Mexican-era governor Manuel Armijo and the assistance of Lucien Bonaparte Maxwell's father-in-law Carlos Beaubien.

15. Murphy, Lawrence. "Rayado: Pioneer Settlement in Northeastern New Mexico 1848–1857." *New Mexico Historical Review*, Vol. 46/1 (January 1971). Also see Murphy, Lawrence R. *Lucien Bonaparte Maxwell: Napoleon of the Southwest*. Norman: University of Oklahoma Press, 1983.

16. Hannum, Anna Paschall, ed. *A Quaker Forty-Niner: The Adventures of Charles Edward Pancoast on the American Frontier*. Philadelphia: University of Pennsylvania Press, 1930, 208–10.

17. La Junta means in Spanish "the junction." It is the junction of the Sapello and Mora Rivers and also one of the junctions of the Mountain and Cimarron Cutoff branches of the Santa Fe Trail. It was here that Alexander Barclay erected his adobe fort, a smaller version of Bent's Old Fort, to trade with the Indians and here as well that the Army

would eventually build Fort Union. Today the tiny town on this location is known as Watrous.

18. Eiselt, B. Sunday. *Becoming White Clay: A History and Archaeology of Jicarilla Apache Enclavement*. Salt Lake City: University of Utah Press, 2012, 7.

19. Ibid., 4.

Chapter 1

1. Brewerton, George Douglas, and Marc Simmons, introduction. *Overland with Kit Carson: A Narrative of the Old Spanish Trail in '48*. Lincoln: University of Nebraska Press, 1993, 37–38.

2. John Charles Frémont had commissioned Kit Carson as a lieutenant. Congress did not confirm his appointment.

3. Brewerton, *Overland with Kit Carson*, 37–38.

4. Ibid., 60–61.

5. The Grand River is the historic name for the Colorado River. After crossing the deserts of southern California and Utah, Carson's party crossed the river in central Utah.

6. A tree stuck fast in a streambed with its branches or roots projecting upward and bobbing up and down with the current.

7. Brewerton, *Overland with Kit Carson*, 120.

8. Ibid., 123.

9. Ibid., 131–35.

10. In his autobiography, Kit Carson noted meeting what must have been this party of soldiers under Major Reynolds pursuing the same Jicarillas. Quaife, Milo Milton, ed. *Kit Carson's Autobiography*. Lincoln: University of Nebraska Press, 1966, 124.

11. Brewerton, *Overland with Kit Carson*, 133–34.

12. Ibid., 135–36. They were referring to Lucien Maxwell's fight at Manco Burro Pass in the Raton Mountains. That affair will be discussed later. Reference to it can be found in Lecompte, Janet. "Manco Burro Pass Massacre." *New Mexico Historical Review*, Vol. 41/4 (October 1966), 305–18.

13. Eutaw, Utah, and various other nineteenth-century spellings all refer to the Ute Indians.

14. Brewerton, *Overland with Kit Carson*, 37–38.

15. Caballada is Spanish for a horse, or in this case, mule herd.

16. Thomas was an old mountain man.

17. Brewerton, *Overland with Kit Carson*, 139.

18. Ibid., 140.

19. Ibid.

20. Ibid., 141. The Indian news was probably notice of the distant approach of a battalion of the 3rd Missouri Mounted Volunteers under Major William Reynolds as Kit noted in his autobiography above.

21. Michno, Gregory, and Susan Michno. *Forgotten Fights: Little-Known Raids and Skirmishes on the Frontier, 1823 to 1890*. Missoula: Mountain Press Publishing, 2008, 96–97.

22. The weapons were what is referred to as "cap and ball." Because of the loose fit of the cap at the breech, the damp of night might penetrate and make the powder useless. The same might occur by immersion in water while crossing a stream or river.

23. Brewerton, *Overland with Kit Carson*, 66.

24. Ibid., 129.

25. Gordon-McCutchan, R.C. "'Little Chief' and the Indians," in *The Short Truth about Kit Carson and the Indians*. Taos: Kit Carson Historic Museums, 1993, 12. Those who want to know more about Kit's personal relationship with Indians can read Simmons, Marc. *Kit Carson and His Three Wives: A Family History*. Albuquerque: University of New Mexico Press, 2003.

26. Brewerton, *Overland with Kit Carson*, 83–84.

27. Simmons, Marc. "The Strange Fate of Kit Carson," in *The Short Truth about Kit Carson and the Indians*. Taos: Kit Carson Historic Museums, 1993, 5–6.

28. The Comanche were a Great Basin tribe who passed violently through the Jicarilla and Ute during the eighteenth century on their way to Texas where they settled. In the nineteenth century, American-Texans began pushing them westward where they again came into violent contact with the Jicarilla, pushing the latter off the buffalo ranges of the Llano Estacado, the Staked Plains of western Texas and eastern New Mexico. See Gunnerson, Delores A. *The Jicarilla Apaches: A Study in Survival*. Dekalb: Northern Illinois University Press, 1974.

29. Michno, Gregory. *Depredation and Deceit: The Making of the Jicarilla and Ute Wars in New Mexico*. Norman: University of Oklahoma Press, 2017, 22.

30. The people of the Rio Arriba, the lands from Santa Fe north, spoke their own dialect of Spanish, archaic with special use terms that came from their environment and many borrowed English words. See Cobos, Ruben. *Dictionary of New Mexico and Southern Colorado Spanish*. Albuquerque: Museum of New Mexico Press, 1983. As Ruben Cobos shows, this form of Spanish spread to the San Luis Valley of Colorado in the north, east onto the plains, and north from there as far as Pueblo, Colorado. This advance began after the American occupation and was held violently in check for a while by the Jicarilla and Ute.

31. Gunnerson, *Jicarilla Apaches*, 164.

32. Today we know him as a villain scalp-hunter accused of many crimes and atrocities. In 1840s New Mexico, he was viewed as a reliable and effective scout and hero. Perhaps they didn't know of his dealings in Chihuahua, though this seems unlikely. Many of his mercenaries were Delaware Indians.

33. Ranchos de Taos is a small community about ten miles south of Don Fernando de Taos, the community we think of today as Taos, which is three miles south of Taos, a Pueblo Indian community. Its beautiful church has been depicted in art and photography many times. Georgia O'Keeffe is among those who have painted it.

34. *New Orleans Picayune* (daily edition), February 28, and (weekly edition), March 2, 1840.

35. Smith, Ralph Adam. *Borderlander: The Life of James Kirker, 1793–1852*. Norman: University of Oklahoma Press, 1999, 91.

36. Ibid., 91–92.

37. Ibid., 93.
38. Many hundred may be an exaggeration and certainly does not reflect Jicarilla alone, who by 1850 may have lost one hundred or so to Kirker. Consider though that this would have been about 10 percent of their tribe, a significant number and enough that all the remaining Jicarilla would have lost a relative to him.
39. Lecompte, "Manco Burro Pass Massacre," 308.
40. Smith, *Borderlander*, 195–97.
41. French: a hostile meeting or a contest between forces or individuals.
42. Gregg, Josiah. *Commerce of the Prairies: Life on the Great Plains in the 1830's and 1840's*. Santa Barbara, CA: Narrative Press, 2001, 204.
43. Ibid., 192.
44. "On February 11, 1887 three days after the Dawes Act became law, the Jicarilla Apache Reservation was established. . . . The Jicarilla were the last Native American tribe in the United States to be permanently settled on a reservation as part of the Indian Appropriations Act of 1851." Eiselt, B. Sunday. *Becoming White Clay: A History and Archaeology of Jicarilla Apache Enclavement*. Salt Lake City: University of Utah Press, 2012, 2–3.
45. Oliva, Leo E. *Fort Union and the Frontier Army in the Southwest: A Historic Resource Study, Fort Union National Monument, Fort Union, New Mexico*, Professional Papers No. 41. Santa Fe: Southwest Cultural Resources Center, 1993, 14.
46. That is, the Jicarilla Apache.
47. John Greiner, Indian Agent, March 30, 1852, in Anonymous. *Apache Indians VII: Jicarilla Apache Tribe: Historical Materials 1540–1887*. New York: Garland Publishing, 1974, 92, quoting from Abel, Annie Heloise. "The Journal of John Greiner." *Old Santa Fe: A Magazine of History, Archaeology, Genealogy and Biography*, Vol III/11 (July 1916).
48. "The Jicarilla War. Who and What Are the Enemy?" *Santa Fe Weekly Gazette*, April 29, 1854.

Chapter 2

1. Morris Opler defines their boundaries as: "[Their] western boundary was Tierra Amarilla and Chama. Utes were between them and the Navaho. As far north as Alamosa and as far as Salida and Pueblo. The Arkansas River was the northern boundary. To the east they went as far as Sierra Grande, east of the Canadian River. They lived south of Ocate." Opler, Morris E. "Jicarilla Apache Territory, Economy, and Society in 1850." *Southwestern Journal of Anthropology* 27 (1971), 310.
2. In 1832, Charles and William Bent and their partner Ceran St. Vrain built an adobe fort at Big Timbers north of the Arkansas River as a trading post. This southern movement of the now Southern Cheyenne put pressure on the Ute (Utah) and their allies the Jicarilla. Between 1832 and 1846, this was the last point in US territory.
3. The heaviest rains come in July and August.
4. Paterek, Josephine. *Encyclopedia of American Indian Costume*. New York: W.W. Norton, 1994, 164–67.

NOTES

5. Jicarilla potter Shelden Nuñez-Velarde explained to me that the mica distributes heat evenly through the pot so that it does not crack when exposed to flame as pots made with other forms of temper, such as sand, do. He also talked about clay sources and mica sources, family secrets, some of which he was still trying to locate.
6. The flaw is also found in Navajo baskets but it is much larger. I suppose Navajo spirits are bigger, or perhaps more clumsy. Jicarilla baskets are much more tightly woven. Coated with pitch, they hold water. The pitch-covered baskets give rise to the tribe's name as they resemble a gourd or chocolate cup. See Tanner, Clara Lee. *Apache Indian Baskets*. Tucson: University of Arizona Press, 1982, 142–59.
7. The entrance to Picuris Canyon is near the Picuris Pueblo about four miles east of the Jicarilla camp.
8. The Jicarilla camp described was on Ojo Caliente Canyon in the Embudo Mountains and was the site of the March 1854 Battle of Cieneguilla. The Battle of Ojo Caliente took place about forty miles to the west of this camp in the San Juan Mountains on Vallecitos River near the hot springs.
9. Once a metal bound barrel was empty, its hoops were of little use except in trade and to Indians. The metal could be cut and formed into fine arrowheads, which soon replaced stone projectile points. Even empty tin cans were valuable. New Mexico was so metal poor that empty cans became the basis of New Mexican tinwork art. See Coulter, Lane, and Maurice Dixon, Jr. *New Mexican Tinwork: 1840–1940*. Albuquerque: University of New Mexico Press, 1990.
10. The author hasn't bothered with Jicarilla names for places. They would only lead to confusion. Point of Rocks is about sixty miles east of Cimarron on the Santa Fe Trail.
11. Josiah Gregg mentioned enmity between Americans and Jicarilla as early as 1834. Gregg, Josiah. *Commerce of the Prairies: Life on the Great Plains in the 1830's and 1840's*. Santa Barbara, CA: Narrative Press, 2001, 204. In 1839, the Jicarilla stole horses from James Kirker. See Smith, Ralph Adam. *Borderlander: The Life of James Kirker, 1793–1852*. Norman: University of Oklahoma Press, 1999, 91–93. Kit Carson expected trouble from them in 1848. Jicarilla informants tell me that in 1849, the White Wagon Train Massacre began with a demand for the "toll." Wagons on the Santa Fe Trail went four abreast in order to be instantly ready for hostile Indians. Small trains were easy targets for toll gathering and trade. Merchants had little reason to report these encounters, especially if they were concluded peacefully. There was no reason to report an encounter in what was then Mexico to American authorities and little expectation of action from Mexican authorities.
12. See Chapter 1 for information about the Jicarilla encounter with scalp hunter Kirker.

Chapter 3

1. Drawn from Gorenfeld, Will, and John Gorenfeld. *Kearny's Dragoons Out West: The Birth of the U.S. Cavalry*. Norman: University of Oklahoma Press, 2016, 222–29.
2. In the 1830s, Las Vegas was founded on the plains about fifty miles east of Santa Fe, a response to the traffic from the Santa Fe Trail. *Las Vegas* means the meadows. At the eastern foot of the Sangre de Cristo Mountains, lush green grass and water made it an

310

ideal stopping place before the last uphill pull through Glorieta Pass and Apache Canyon to Santa Fe.

3. He was overstepping bounds. There was not yet a treaty with Mexico by which she ceded her former provinces. The War Department would later declare the "Kearny Codes," along with his proclamation of conquest, illegal as unauthorized by federal law. See Gorenfeld and Gorenfeld, *Kearny's Dragoons*, 229.

4. Without a national bank since the presidency of Andrew Jackson, US finance was in chaos. Local banks were scarcely regulated and were printing and minting money. The nation depended on a common currency that came through Missouri, the 'dobe dollar or Mexican Peso. Our language preserves something of this era in phrases like "pieces of eight." To make change one cut the peso in eight pieces worth 12.5 cents each. One gave "two bits" for 25 cents and "four bits" for fifty.

5. Hughes, John Taylor. *Doniphan's Expedition*. College Station: Texas A&M University Press, 1847. (1914 edition, 1997 reprint), 68.

6. Burton, E. Bennet. "The Taos Rebellion." *Old Santa Fe*, Vol. I (1913), 191.

7. Clary, David A. *Eagles and Empire: The United States, Mexico and the Struggle for a Continent*. New York: Bantam Books, 2009, 264.

8. Sides, Hampton. *Blood and Thunder: An Epic of the American West*. Garden City, NY: Doubleday, 2006, 173–76.

9. Beck, Warren A. *New Mexico: A History of Four Centuries*. Norman: University of Oklahoma Press, 1962, 136.

10. Although I did not know it at the time and no one spoke of it, I have since learned from the descriptions of participants that the battlefield was all around McCurdy School where I attended high school. The ruined adobes at the plaza then in evidence were undoubtedly those Colonel Price reported flattened by his artillery.

11. From a report by Colonel Sterling Price to the Adjutant General, 15 February 1847, printed in McNierney, Michael. *Taos 1847: The Revolt in Contemporary Accounts*. Boulder, CO: Johnson Publishing, 1980, 47.

12. Ibid., 48.

13. Today the River Road, Highway 68, follows the Rio Grande around the west side of La Mesita and then continues northeast following the Rio and the Taos River going to the west of the Embudo Mountains. In Price's time, the River Road turned east at Embudo and went up into the mountains joining the Mountain Road at Trampas and then going east around the Embudo Mountains.

14. McNierney, *Taos 1847*, 49. Today a new road has been cut along the Rio Grande and then along the Taos River to Ranchos de Taos considerably shortening the way to Taos. Colonel Price turned east for about twenty miles going around the Embudo Mountains. He would have passed very close to Chacon's hidden camp and the Picuris Pueblo.

15. What we think of today as Taos.

16. Adobe is soft, not brittle, and absorbs the shock.

17. Gorenfeld and Gorenfeld, *Kearny's Dragoons*, 238–42.

18. McNierney, *Taos 1847*, 50–51.

19. Ibid., 51–53.

20. Garrard, Lewis H. *Wah-to-yah and the Taos Trail*. Norman: University of Oklahoma Press, 1955, 172–73.
21. Gorenfeld and Gorenfeld, *Kearny's Dragoons*, 242.

Chapter 4

1. Leroux, Antoine, mountain man (c. 1801–June 30, 1861). Born at St. Louis, he may have been part Indian. He went up the Missouri with Ashley in 1822 and came to Taos in 1824, marrying a local woman in 1833. He guided Philip St. George Cooke's battalion of road builders to California in 1846-47. He guided army expeditions against the Navajo. In 1849, along with Kit Carson, he guided Major William Grier in pursuit of the Jicarilla after the White Wagon Train Massacre. Thrapp, Dan L. *Encyclopedia of Frontier Biography*. Lincoln: University of Nebraska Press, 1988, 847–48.
2. Weaver, Paulino (Pauline), mountain man (1800–June 21, 1867); Ibid., 1525.
3. Cooke, Philip St. George, Army, 1st Dragoons (June 13, 1809–March 20, 1895). Graduated from West Point in 1827. Joined the 1st Dragoons in 1833. Promoted to major of the 2nd Dragoons in 1847. In 1854, after Lieutenant Davidson's debacle at Cieneguilla, he led the pursuit of the Jicarilla and engaged them at Ojo Caliente.
4. Maxwell, Lucien Bonaparte. Frontiersman (September 14, 1818–June 25, 1875). Maxwell married into a Hispanic family in Taos and with his father-in-law, Carlos Beaubien, put together the largest land grant in New Mexico including most of the land occupied by the Jicarilla east of the Sangre de Cristo Mountains. He was at one time the owner of the largest parcel of land in the United States. Together with his friend Kit Carson, he pioneered settlement at Rayado and Cimarron. Pete Maxwell was his son. Billy the Kid was shot to death in Maxwell's home at Fort Sumner, New Mexico. Thrapp, *Encyclopedia*, 961.
5. Frémont, John Charles. *Memoirs of My Life*. New York: Rowman & Littlefield, 2001, 586. This is Senator Benton "quoting" Kit Carson and defending his son-in-law, John Charles Frémont, who was court-martialed for refusing to obey orders from General Kearny and step down as governor of California to be replaced by the general himself as senior military officer. I'm not sure that we can trust them completely. They are quite self-serving and it would have been rather pointless for Kearny to have promised to make Frémont governor. Carson's autobiography does not suggest that he had any close rapport with General Kearny and that isn't surprising. Kearny was a somewhat rigid, formal, military disciplinarian and would have maintained a polite distance from a lieutenant. There is reason to believe that Kit Carson had a falling out with Frémont about this time. Among other things, Carson doesn't seem to have been invited on Frémont's fourth expedition, which was a disaster.
6. Davidson, John Wynn (Black Jack) (August 12, 1825–June 26, 1881). Graduated West Point and was commissioned a brevet second lieutenant of the 1st Dragoons July 1, 1845, and a second lieutenant April 21, 1846. He would have been one of the most junior officers under Kearny's command. In December 1849, in California he reported that Indians had been captured but three "were shot . . . upon attempting to escape." On May 15, 1850, men under his command killed seventy-five Indians on the Russian River, sustaining no losses of their own. Two days later, more than sixty Indians were reported

slain at Clear Lake. On March 30, 1854, he attacked a Jicarilla camp without provocation, starting a war that broke the spirit and might of the Jicarilla. Thrapp, *Encyclopedia*, 377–78.

7. Mangas Coloradas may have been as tall as 6'4", powerfully made, and in 1846 was in his prime. His name in Spanish meant Red Sleeves. It was said that they were red from the blood of his enemies, but it's more likely that it was because he wore his coat with the sleeves turned inside out exposing the red silk lining. Distinguish him from Mangas, his son. Mangas Coloradas was the father-in-law of Cochise. He was killed by soldiers in early 1863 while their prisoner.

8. Gorenfeld, Will, and John Gorenfeld. *Kearny's Dragoons Out West: The Birth of the U.S. Cavalry*. Norman: University of Oklahoma Press, 2016, 243.

9. Ibid.

10. Ibid., 243–44.

11. Ibid., 247.

12. Gorenfeld, *Kearny's Dragoons*, 265–72, provides an excellent discussion of the tactics. His discussion of the battle is also more complete and accurate than anything found elsewhere. He draws on more primary sources, as well as excellent background material, than any other writer.

13. Carter, Harvey Lewis. *"Dear Old Kit": The Historical Christopher Carson*. Norman: University of Oklahoma Press, 1990, 113. I almost wonder if these were the same animals Emory reported having captured on the Colorado. There is a difference in date and a difference in the names of the officers involved that leads me to think it is two distinct events. In any case, the important point here is that half of the command was mounted on gentle horses not trained to war. "Davidson's raid probably added a good twenty-five adequate riding animals to those the dragoons acquired from the horse-thieves on the Colorado River, yielding, conservatively, a total of seventy-five reasonably well-conditioned, but not well-trained, horses and mules. Thus slightly fewer than half of the command was mounted on restive but healthy stock." Gorenfeld and Gorenfeld, *Kearny's Dragoons*, 250.

14. Ibid., 249–50.

15. Norris, L. David, James C. Milligan, and Odie B. Faulk. *William H. Emory: Soldier-Scientist*. Tucson: University of Arizona Press, 1998, 25.

16. The Bear Flaggers included Americans then living in California as well as some of the forty-five mountain men who had come to California with Frémont.

17. Gillespie, Archibald H. (October 10, 1812–August 16, 1873) was an officer in the US Marine Corps during the Mexican-American War. On October 30, 1845, Lieutenant Gillespie was sent by President James Polk with secret messages to the US consul Thomas O. Larkin in Monterey, California, Commodore John D. Sloat in command of the Pacific Squadron, and John C. Frémont. He assisted Frémont in the Bear Flag Revolt of June 14, 1846. Put in charge of Los Angeles, the largest city in California with about three thousand residents, things might have remained peaceful, except that Captain Gillespie placed the town under martial law, greatly angering some of the Californios. On September 23, 1846, about two- to three hundred Californios staged a revolt.

18. Gorenfeld says seventy-five. Gorenfeld and Gorenfeld, *Kearny's Dragoons*, 254. Kit Carson estimated one hundred. Carter, *"Dear Old Kit,"* 112.

19. Gorenfeld and Gorenfeld, *Kearny's Dragoons*, 253. Gorenfeld notes that "On the eve of battle, in an instance of honesty rare for the man forced to resign from the Marine Corps in 1854 for pilfering his ship's funds, Gillespie bluntly appraised Kearny's troops as 'physically and morally depleted.'" I would never accept at face value any marine's assessment of an army unit. The dragoons were worn and in bad physical condition, the battle would not go well for them, but I doubt the marine assessment that "strength and spirits seemed to be entirely gone." Kit Carson describes them differently as men anxious for battle.

20. Gillespie said the night was moonlit bright as day. Others say drizzle and fog limited visibility and it was "too dark to commence an attack." Gorenfeld and Gorenfeld, *Kearny's Dragoons*, 260–61.Gorenfeld says: "Finally, no analyst of this debacle should underestimate the pervasive power of alcohol. Sources strongly suggest that drunkenness played a role at San Pasqual. In an article for the November 13, 1868, edition of the *California Daily Alta*, correspondent Charles Pickett squarely blamed the defeat at San Pasqual upon the officers' consumption of wine on the eve of battle, and Archibald Gillespie's fiery denial in the next day's paper only fanned the flames of rumor." Gorenfeld and Gorenfeld, *Kearny's Dragoons*, 256. The accusation comes twenty years after the event from a secondary source. Gillespie, who was there, and who had occasion to criticize Kearny for the general's brush off of the marines and Bear Flaggers under his command, denied the accusation. The evidence is clear that the officers of Kearny's command were drinking on the evening of December 5. That they were still inebriated in the morning is possible but unlikely.

21. Ibid., 261.

22. What Carson calls spies were vedettes, that is, sentries, a cavalry sentry or outpost, mounted soldiers stationed some distance from the main body to give early warning of an enemy approach. In the nineteenth century, scouts and vedettes were often referred to as spies and scout companies as spies and guides.

23. Carter, *"Dear Old Kit,"* 112.

24. Ibid.

25. Gathered together to form compact lines of defense or offense.

26. "To execute the charge as foragers, all the troopers of the squadron disperse, and direct themselves in couples upon the point each wishes to attack, observing not to lose sight of their officers, who charge with them." Cooke, Philip St. George. *Cavalry Tactics or Regulations for the Instruction, Formations, and Movements of the Cavalry of the Army and Volunteers of the United States, Vol. I.* Washington, DC: Department of War, 1861, 208. In other words, instead of acting en masse the dragoons would pair off in the attack. This was a form of attack used in pursuit of a disorganized enemy.

27. Carter, *"Dear Old Kit,"* 113.

28. Ibid.

29. According to Dr. Griffin and Lieutenant Emory, he was the only dragoon to die of gunfire. Gorenfeld and Gorenfeld, *Kearny's Dragoons*, 264.

30. Norris, Milligan, and Faulk, *William H. Emory*, 27.

31. A normal complement would have been six men to a gun. Davidson may have had less. Two or three can handle the guns with less success. Nonetheless, the casualty count does not seem to be high enough to include nine men killed at the guns, though it may have appeared so to Carson. Gorenfeld says that all of the privates killed and wounded were from Moore's Company C. Lieutenant Hammond died of his injuries later. Perhaps the killed and wounded among the Bear Flaggers, marines, and sailors were not included in the reported total and perhaps some of Moore's men were tending the guns. Norris, Milligan, and Faulk say that Captain Johnston, four non-commissioned officers, and twelve privates were dead. The wounded included the general, Gillespie, Warner, and twelve others. Ibid.

32. Carter, *"Dear Old Kit,"* 114.

33. "Ten dragoons officers and seven noncommissioned officers were either killed or wounded, while nine privates, entirely from Moore's Company C, were reported killed, missing or seriously wounded." Gorenfeld speculates that the rank and file got a case of "the slows." The overwhelming majority of killed and wounded were among the officers and sergeants. The morale of the dragoons may have been down after their long, arduous journey. On the other hand, other factors could easily account for the discrepancy. The officers were better mounted having their choice in a force riding largely untrained livestock. They arrived in the battle ahead of their men. The heavy woolen clothing and overcoats of the dragoons saved many, like Lieutenant Davidson, from injury, as the lancers had difficulty piercing the heavy wool. Gorenfeld and Gorenfeld, *Kearny's Dragoons,* 269.

34. Carter, *"Dear Old Kit,"* 114.

Chapter 5

1. In 1844, Gregg originally published *Commerce of the Prairies* in two volumes. It covers the period 1831 to 1840. Gregg, Josiah. *Commerce of the Prairies: Life on the Great Plains in the 1830's and 1840's.* Santa Barbara: Narrative Press, 2001, 204.

2. Tom Otobus is the name Webb gives him. He is probably Tom Autobees, a noted mountain man of the Taos–Arkansas River area.

3. Ute and Jicarilla range overlapped in this area. The Ute seem to have been "peaceful" at this time. The Ute who had killed a herder might have been a Jicarilla.

4. Webb, James Josiah, and Ralph P. Bieber, ed. *Adventures in the Santa Fe Trade 1844–1847.* Lincoln: University of Nebraska Press, 1995, 134–36.

5. Lecompte, Janet. *Pueblo, Hardscrabble, Greenhorn: Society on the High Plains, 1832–1856.* Norman: University of Oklahoma Press, 1978, 208.

6. The story of the traveler at Embudo having his belly slashed comes from the writings of Charles Bent. Lecompte, Janet. "Manco Burro Pass Massacre." *New Mexico Historical Review,* Vol. 41/4 (October 1966), 308. Bent to Alvarez, Taos, March 2 and 4, 1846.

7. Webb, *Adventures in the Santa Fe Trade,* 287.

8. Donaciano Vigil was born in Santa Fe in 1802, perhaps at Christmas time since his name means "the gift." He grew to be 6'2". Vigil helped smooth the transition from Mexican to American rule. He assumed office after the death of Governor Charles Bent proclaiming: "The term of my administration is purely transitory. Neither my

qualifications nor the ad interim character, according to the organic law in which I take the reins of government, encourage me to continue in so difficult and thorny a post, the duties of which are intended for individuals of greater enterprise and talents; but I protest to you, in the utmost fervor of my heart that I will devote myself exclusively to endeavouring to secure you all the prosperity so much desired by your fellow-citizen and friend. Donaciano Vigil. January 22, 1847." Donaciano Vigil, Wikipedia, https://en.wikipedia.org/wiki/Donaciano_Vigil.

9. Padre Martínez was the first New Mexican ever ordained. When the government in Mexico sent all the Spanish monks, no longer trusted after the revolution of 1821, back to Spain, New Mexico had only two remaining priests. Padre Martínez opened the first schools and obtained permission to train and ordain priests. He was also rumored to be the head of the Penitentes. The Penitentes were and are a lay brotherhood who took over the role of religious leadership in priest-poor New Mexico. They practiced self-flagellation and suspended a man from a cross at Easter. They were rumored to take advantage of strangers. It would be difficult to exaggerate the power held by the Padre. It was both religious and political, and his family was one of the wealthiest in the Rio Arriba.

In the New Mexican tradition, civil leaders such as the *alcalde*, usually translated as mayor, and governor combined the functions of judge, civil administrator, and leader of the army or militia. Law was not administered in letter or in spirit. It was manipulated to preserve order and maintain the status quo. Outsiders found themselves at a severe disadvantage since the object of decisions was to appease the local population.

10. Tiller, Veronica E. Velarde. *The Jicarilla Apache Tribe*. Lincoln: University of Nebraska Press, 1992, 33.

11. In New Mexico, before 1830, there were usually only two secular priests. The land was a mission field and the Spanish Crown paid to send missionary Franciscan Friars to the Pueblo Indians. Priests for the people were an afterthought. The area was poor and no one wanted the job. The upside of this was that the people didn't have to tithe. On the other hand, if one wanted a sacrament performed, the stole fees were high. Occasionally, priests would provide schooling to village children. Only the *ricos*, the wealthy, could afford tutors for their children. As already mentioned above, Padre Antonio José Martínez had founded the first school in New Mexico. Very few people could read. Nonetheless, in 1834, stout souls with high hopes imported a printing press and began to publish a newspaper, *El Crepusculo de la Libertad*—The Twilight of Liberty. It lasted four editions. Thereafter, Padre Martínez acquired the press and up through the 1850s most of the printing done in New Mexico was done on his press. See Hocking, Doug. "New Mexico's Reviled Heroic Padre." *Wild West Magazine*, December 2013, 46–51.

12. *Santa Fe Republican*, September 17, 1847; Lenderman, Gary D. *The Santa Fe Republican: New Mexico Territory's First Newspaper 1847–1849*. San Bernardino, CA: Createspace, 2011.

13. Lecompte, "Manco Burro," 308. Letter of Thos. Fitzpatrick, Bent's Fort, December 18, 1847.

14. Fountain that boils, so named "for a pair of bubbling mineral springs on its banks where it debouches from the mountains at the present site of Manitou, Colorado" (near Colorado Springs). Lecompte, *Pueblo, Hardscrabble, Greenhorn*, 8.

15. The Beaubien referred to could be one of the nine children of Judge Carlos Beaubien.

16. G. Bent is George Bent, who died October 27, 1847, at Bent's Fort of a fever. He was a younger brother of Charles and William. A nephew, son of William and Owl Woman, was named George Bent as well and grew up as a Cheyenne (1843 to 1918). Thrapp, *Encyclopedia of Frontier Biography*, 97–98.

17. Gantt's Fort was an adobe trading post six miles east of Fountain Creek. Lecompte, *Pueblo, Hardscrabble, Greenhorn*, 8.

18. Hammond, George P. *The Adventures of Alexander Barclay, Mountain Man*. Denver: Old West Publishing, 1976, 151.

19. Major William W. Reynolds was third in the line of command of the 3rd Regiment of Missouri Mounted Volunteers behind Colonel John Ralls, and Lieutenant Colonel Richard H. Lane. The regiment arrived in New Mexico in July 1847 and replaced a regiment whose men's enlistments had expired. Lenderman, *The* Santa Fe Republican, 163.

20. *Santa Fe Republican*, November 13, 1847; Lenderman, *The* Santa Fe Republican. By October 1847, the post at Don Fernando de Taos included companies G, H, and K of the 3rd Missouri Mounted Volunteers under the command of Major W. W. Reynolds. Murphy, Lawrence. "The United States Army in Taos, 1847–1852." *New Mexico Historical Review*, Vol. 47/1, January 1972.

21. Manco Burro, Lame Donkey Pass, was one of the routes across the Raton Mountains from the Arkansas River to the eastern plains of New Mexico. Today known as San Francisco Pass, it cut through the series of high mesas that stretch at right angles from the Sangre de Cristo Mountains eastward along the Colorado–New Mexico state line. The top of the pass is in Colorado, two or three miles north of the New Mexico line and 8,250 feet above sea level. Lecompte, "Manco Burro," 305.

22. *Santa Fe Republican*, April 2, 1848; Lenderman, *The* Santa Fe Republican.

Chapter 6

1. Lecompte, Janet. "Manco Burro Pass Massacre." *New Mexico Historical Review*, October 1966, 308.

2. I've left Charles Bent's spelling as I found it without using [*sic*] at every error, concluding that so many interruptions would have made it even harder to read. Lecompte, "Manco Burro," 306–7.

3. Lecompte, Janet. *Pueblo, Hardscrabble, Greenhorn: Society on the High Plains, 1832–1856*. Norman: University of Oklahoma Press, 1978, 207.

4. *Santa Fe Republican*, May 13, 1848, Lenderman. *The* Santa Fe Republican.

5. Lecompte, *Pueblo, Hardscrabble, Greenhorn*, 207.

6. Ibid., 315n4.

7. Ibid., 209.

8. Ibid., 208–9; "Claims for Indian Depredations in New Mexico," 35th Cong., 1st. Sess., House Exec. Doc. 122 (Ser. 929), 11. Maxwell's claim was for thirty mules, fifty horses, and six hundred buckskins stolen by Jicarilla Apaches on June 12, 1848, though it was not filed until 1854 and was not allowed. On June 4, when he wrote to his father-in-law, Beaubien, from Greenhorn about the June 1 event, he claimed he had lost sixty

horses and four hundred deerskins. A further loss during the June 6 event seems to have resulted in an additional loss. Either that or Maxwell exaggerated or the seed of the memory had sprouted in his mind. Either way, a claim filed six years after the event would not have affected the bloody events of 1849. Maxwell was operating on the very edge of the frontier. It is not surprising that he, Beaubien, Doyle, Barclay, and others suffered frequent losses.

9. Lecompte, "Manco Burro," 309–10.

10. The *Santa Fe Republican* reports news of this misadventure and illness in its August 1, 1848, edition naming Captain Samuel Boake as "Capt. Hoane, of Mo. Mounted Regt." The copy of the newspaper used was partly illegible and this may explain the error.

11. Lenderman, Gary D. *The* Santa Fe Republican: *New Mexico's Territory's First Newspaper 1847–1849.* San Bernardino, CA: Createspace, 2011, 163.

12. Near modern Trinidad, Colorado.

13. Favour, Alpheus H. *Old Bill Williams, Mountain Man.* Norman: University of Oklahoma Press, 1962, 163; Lecompte, "Manco Burro," 310; Lecompte, *Pueblo, Hardscrabble, Greenhorn,* 209.

14. Their mother was unwilling or unable to care for them at Pueblo. Lecompte, "Manco Burro," 310.

15. Bent's Fort on the Arkansas is about seventy miles northeast of Raton Pass. Manco Burro Pass, now known as San Francisco Pass, is east of Raton Pass across Fisher Peak from the Raton. With the Jicarilla camped near the northern entrance to Raton Pass, this approach would have kept the party about five miles away from the Apaches.

16. The *Santa Fe Republican* reported their numbers in this passage: "Mr. L. Maxwell, in company with some fourteen Americans, and two Mexicans, while encamped at midday on the head of red river (or the Canadian Fork) were attacked by a large party of Apaches." *Santa Fe Republican,* June 27, 1848; Lenderman, Santa Fe Republican.

17. Lodo Moro, New Mexico, July 19th, 1848.

On the 19th ultimo, a party of us, fourteen in number, were attacked by about 150 Indians, on the head waters of Red River, and near the Ratoan [*sic*] mountains. We had been encamped about one hour, and just in the act of eating our dinner, when we were alarmed by the yells of the Indians, while they were in the act of running off our animals, which were grazing a short distance from us. As they passed us, we fired on them; but they were so far off that our shots had no effect. In about twenty minutes they all returned, surrounded our camp, and set fire to the grass around us, with the view of driving us from our position, which we were inclined to keep, with a view of saving our baggage, or a portion of it. But in this we were foiled! We however, defended ourselves for about four hours, firing at the enemy every opportunity we had. Our position not being a good one, they had the decided advantage of us. We defended ourselves until five of our party were slightly wounded, and one killed. We now determined to retreat to the mountains, as the last and only alternative. On retreating, I received two shots,—one in the left thigh, the ball passing though the thigh though fortunately, not breaking the bone; the other on the middle finger of the left hand. Charles Town, who was ahead of me, receive a shot in one of his legs, which broke it. He, of course, fell, and not being able to walk, was left to the mercy of the Indians. That was the last I saw of him. There was a Spaniard who was shot in the kidneys, before we left camp, who also was left. Our number now consisted of eleven, eight of us wounded, all of whom succeeded in making our escape. Night came on, we traveled until we came to water, when we huddled ourselves as near together as possible, for the purpose of resting and trying to sleep. Having lost everything save what we had on our backs, we suffered much from cold, and could not sleep. The next day we moved off up the mountain when we cached ourselves till night, being afraid to travel in the day time. On the night of the 20th we all put out for Taos, distant 80 miles. Those of the party that were wounded, were slightly so, and generally in the arms and body, with the exception of myself and one man, whose ankle was slightly injured. My wound being in the thigh, rendered it very difficult to walk. Consequently, the party had to wait for me to come up, frequently. We had traveled but a short distance, when they left me. I hailed them, but could receive no answer, so I was left within two miles of the battle ground, and in sight of the fires of the Indian village. I determined not to give up, but pursued my journey, keeping near the water course until I struck the Bent's Fort road, leading to Santa Fe. On the third day out, I fortunately came to an Indian camp, which from all appearances, must have been deserted but a very short time. Their fires were still burning, and part of an antelope was left on the ground, which I helped myself to, not having eaten anything for four days. I filled my shot pouch with meat, and again pursued my journey, traveling at day and night in the best way I possibly could for I was very lame, and could not make more than a mile an hour. Some times I crawled, and in fact got along any way and every way I could. The seventh day I came to fresh wagon tracks, and, to my astonishment, for I had no expectation that any of the trade would think of leaving the Santa Fe road. This so much elated me that I spurred up, and, in a short time, came in sight of the trail consisting of four wagons, a company of Miners, the Messrs. Jackson and Mr. Thos. O. Boggs, who had left the main road with a view of going to Taos. So soon as they discovered me, they sent a horse and man to me, who aided me to the train, when I received every attention that was in their power to bestow on me. The next day we started in the direction of Taos, but were induced to change our route, from having discovered a party of Indians, and it was thought advisable not to attempt to cross the mountains with so small a force; whereupon, we came to this point.

I am happy to say to you that I am, in a manner, well, and will proceed on to Santa Fe tomorrow. The other men of our defeated party arrived in Taos in a worse condition, as I informed them, than I was when I was picked up; one of whom, a Spaniard has since died of his wounds. They reported me as most unquestionably dead. Indeed it was very natural, for I think, in a thousand trials of the same kind, in not one could a person escape.

Respectfully, your obedient servant, Elliot Lee.

P.S. Every letter that was entrusted to my care, has been lost. The distance I traveled in the seven days, is said, by those who know, to be 80 miles.

—Lecompte, "Manco Burro," 311–13.

18. Richens (Uncle Dick) Wootton (May 6, 1816–August 22, 1893) was born in Virginia. He hired out to Bent, St. Vrain, & Company. Wootton engaged in a number of pioneering activities. He was a trapper, Indian trader, and rancher most closely associated with Bent's Fort and Pueblo in Colorado. He built a toll road over Raton Pass in 1865.

19. Lecompte, *Pueblo, Hardscrabble, Greenhorn*, 209.

20. Lecompte, "Manco Burro," 314.

21. *Santa Fe Republican*, June 27, 1848; Lenderman, *The* Santa Fe Republican.

22. "A state of mild hostility among the people of New Mexico continued throughout the late 1840s. Indian depredations increased along the Santa Fe Trail. The Jicarillas were willing participants and they were considered especially menacing because of their position on the Cimarron Cutoff." Tiller, Veronica E. Velarde. *The Jicarilla Apache Tribe*. Lincoln: University of Nebraska Press, 1992, 33.

23. William (Old Bill) Williams (June 3, 1787–March 21, 1849) was born in North Carolina. He served as a sergeant in the War of 1812, married an Osage woman, and lived among them. In 1824, he headed for the Rocky Mountains and worked with Jedediah Smith. In 1825, he signed on with a government expedition to chart the Santa Fe Trail. Thrapp, Dan L. *Encyclopedia of Frontier Biography*. Lincoln: University of Nebraska Press, 1988, 1573–74.

24. Levin Mitchell (ca. 1809–post-1854), born in Ohio. He reached the Rocky Mountains as a trapper by 1830 perhaps with William Sublette and trapped with Joe Meek. He was a trader at Pueblo and a deputy sheriff under Wootton in 1848. Ibid., 995–96.

25. Robert Fisher (1807–1852) was born in Virginia. He reached Santa Fe in 1824. He joined Bent and St. Vrain as a trusted employee and mountaineer. Ibid., 494.

26. In the nineteenth century scouts and guides were referred to as spies.

27. A low-quality, muzzle-loading rifle or musket.

28. Smith, Ralph Adam. *Borderlander: The Life of James Kirker, 1793–1852*. Norman: University of Oklahoma Press, 1999, 196–97; *Santa Fe Republican,* August 1, 1848; Michno, Gregory, and Susan Michno. *Forgotten Fights: Little-Known Raids and Skirmishes on the Frontier, 1823 to 1890*. Missoula, MT: Mountain Press Publishing, 2008, 96–97.

29. *Santa Fe Republican*, September 6, 1848.

30. Ibid.

31. Rodenbough, Theophilus F. *From Everglade to Cañon with the Second Dragoons*. Norman: University of Oklahoma Press, 2000, 162–63.

32. *Santa Fe Republican*, August 30, 1848.

33. Dunlay, Thomas W. *Kit Carson and the Indians*. Lincoln: University of Nebraska Press, 2000, 133–34.

34. Ibid., 134.

35. Anonymous. *Apache Indians VII: Jicarilla Apache Tribe: Historical Materials 1540–1887*. New York: Garland Publishing, 1974, 85.
36. Kit Carson may just have wanted to settle down. In his autobiography he gives no indication of a break with Frémont. At least publicly, Kit remains the loyal friend:

> I was with Fremont [from] 1842 to 1847. The hardships through which we passed I find it impossible to describe, and the credit which he deserves I am incapable to do him justice in writing. But his services to his country have been left to the judgment of impartial freemen, and all agree in saying that his services were great and have redounded to his honor and that of his country.
>
> I have heard that he is enormously rich. I wish to God that he may be worth ten times as much more. All that he has or may ever receive, he deserves. I can never forget his treatment of me while in his employ and how cheerfully he suffered with his men when undergoing the severest of hardships. His perseverance and willingness to participate in all that was undertaken, no matter whether the duty was rough or easy is the main cause of his success. And I say without fear of contradiction, that none but him could have surmounted and succeeded through as many difficult services, as his was.
> —Carter, Harvey Lewis. *'Dear Old Kit': The Historical Christopher Carson*. Norman: University of Oklahoma Press, 1990, 121–22.

In 1849, on his ill-fated fourth expedition, without Kit Carson, Frémont headed into the winter mountains against advice. When the expedition failed and he was forced back, he left many men behind, both dead and alive, continuing on to Taos and California before all had been rescued. He didn't live up to the picture of him that Carson paints. Carson was loyal to a fault. Indeed it was his principle fault.

Chapter 7

1. Lawrence R. Murphy. "The United States Army in Taos 1847–1852." *New Mexico Historical Review* 47 (January 1972), 35–36. Dunlay, Thomas W. *Kit Carson and the Indians*. Lincoln: University of Nebraska Press, 2000, 133–34.
2. Lecompte, Janet. *Pueblo, Hardscrabble, Greenhorn: Society on the High Plains, 1832–1856*. Norman: University of Oklahoma Press, 1978, 238.
3. No eyewitness accounts put them there. Ibid.
4. *Cerro de la Olla*, say-roh de lah oi-yah, the Hill of the Water Jug, is west of Questa, New Mexico.
5. Parkhill, Forbes. *The Blazed Trail of Antoine Leroux*. Los Angeles: Westernlore Publications, 1965, 115–16.
6. Ibid., 117.
7. Cooke, Philip St. George. *Cavalry Tactics or Regulations for the Instruction, Formations, and Movements of the Cavalry of the Army and Volunteers of the United States, Vol. I*. Washington, DC: Department of War, 1861, 152–65. Although his book was not published until 1861, Cooke served with the 1st Dragoons up through the Mexican War and

afterward was with the 2nd Dragoons. The tactics used in the Civil War are very close to those used in this period.

8. Parkhill, *Blazed Trail*, 117.

9. Ibid.

10. Ibid., 118–19.

11. I've taken a few liberties to bring this to life based on knowledge of soldiers and the tactics that they used. Accounts of the Battle of Cerro de la Olla come from Lecompte, *Pueblo, Hardscrabble, Greenhorn*, 238; Michno, Gregory, and Susan Michno, *Forgotten Fights: Little-Known Raids and Skirmishes on the Frontier, 1823 to 1890*. Missoula, MT: Mountain Press Publishing, 2008, 99; and Webb, George W. *Chronological List of Engagements between the Regular Army of the United States and Various Tribes of Hostile Indians*. New York: Old Army Press, 1979 (1891), 13, listed as El Cetro del Oya.

12. The Rio Colorado, now called the Red River, flows through Questa north of Taos near Cerro de la Olla.

13. Murphy, Lawrence. "The United States Army in Taos, 1847–1852." *New Mexico Historical Review*, Vol. 47/1, January 1972, 37.

14. Chapman to Judd, April 10, 1849, LR, 9MD, USAC, RG 393, NA, Fort Union Collection, Highlands University, Las Vegas, NM, Vol. 47, 58.

15. New Mexico was still under a military governor and had not yet been organized as a territory, so that the military court would have handled the case of an alcalde who was trading illegally with the Utes.

16. Judd to Dickerson (Departmental Adjutant), April 25, 1849, LR, 9MD, USAC, RG 393, NA, Fort Union Collection, Highlands University, Las Vegas, NM, Vol. 47, 60.

17. "Maxwell was developing the vast estate of his father-in-law, Judge Charles Beaubien. The estate comprised the celebrated 'Beaubien and Miranda Grant': a sheer gift, in 1841, from Governor Manuel Armijo to his friends Don Carlos Beaubien and Don Guadalupe Miranda and expanded to more than 1,700,000 acres—a principality larger than the state of Delaware. Don Carlos bought out Don Guadalupe's interest; and when in this spring of 1849 (according to Carson's memory) Lucien Maxwell moved over from Taos to the valley of the Rayado tributary of the Cimarroncito, about fifty miles eastward of Taos, to act as resident manager of the great rancho, there was plenty of room and opportunity for his rancher friend Kit. . . . The Mountain Branch of the Santa Fe Trail —that from Bent's Fort southwest over Raton Mountain and thence southward to join with the main Trail for Santa Fe—passed through the Grant by way of the Rayado. Encouraged by the presence of both Maxwell and Carson in that region which Ute and Comanche, Apache and Southern Cheyenne made perilous, other pioneers entered and squatted, to form a nucleous [sic] of Indian fighters." Sabin, Edwin L. *Kit Carson Days, 1809–1868: Adventures in the Path of Empire*, 2 Volumes. Lincoln: University of Nebraska Press, 1995 (1935), 617.

18. Ibid., 618.

19. Carter, Harvey Lewis. *"Dear Old Kit": The Historical Christopher Carson*. Norman: University of Oklahoma Press, 1990, 123–24.

20. Hannum, Anna Paschall, ed. *A Quaker Forty-Niner: The Adventures of Charles Edward Pancoast on the American Frontier.* Philadelphia: University of Pennsylvania Press, 1930, 208–10.

21. Murphy, Lawrence R. *Lucien Bonaparte Maxwell: Napoleon of the Southwest.* Norman: University of Oklahoma Press, 1983, 111; Dunlay, Thomas W. *Kit Carson and the Indians.* Lincoln: University of Nebraska Press, 2000, 137.

22. Col. J. M. Washington to Major General Jones, Adjutant General, Fort Union Collection, Highlands University, Las Vegas, NM, Vol. 47, 62.

23. Sen. Ex. Doc. No. 1—31st Cong., 1st sess. 1849. Part 1 of 2 Parts—Report of the Secretary of War— 108–9, Fort Union Collection, Highlands University, Las Vegas, NM, Vol. 47, 62.

24. Some sources say that the Ninth Military District established Cantonment Burgwin on August 14, 1852. Sergeant Bally is clear that he rode out from Cantonment Burgwin; the military post at Taos may already have been referred to by this name. Burgwin is about ten miles southeast of Don Fernando de Taos.

25. The Embudo Mountains are south of Taos, and east of the Rio Grande. Chapman's fight took place nearby but on the other side of the river, making it likely that these were peaceful Olleros. There might have been more alarm when Bally approached if they had been the people who so recently had fought Captain Chapman. Julyan, Robert. *The Place Names of New Mexico.* Albuquerque: University of New Mexico Press, 1996, 249.

26. The sergeant says that this was on the Rio Pablo about twenty-five miles south of Taos. Santa Barbara was three miles east of Peñasco. This is also quite near Picuris Pueblo. These Pueblo Indians were friends of the Jicarilla who often camped near their village. The Jicarilla would often be encountered in this area.

27. Chacon is often mentioned in the Embudo Mountains, at Abiquiu, and at Anton Chico as a "peace chief."

28. Flache Vayada is not quite a Spanish name. More likely the name is *Fleche Rayado,* Striped Arrow.

29. Bally to Lt. John Adams, May 22, 1849, LR, 9MD, USAC, RG 393, NA; Judd to Dickerson, June 1, 1849, LR, 9MD, USAC, RG 393, NA.

30. It is unclear what place he is referring to.

31. Bally to Lt. John Adams, May 22, 1849, LR, 9MD, USAC, RG 393, NA; Judd to Dickerson, June 1, 1849, LR, 9MD, USAC, RG 393, NA; Oliva, Leo E. *Fort Union and the Frontier Army in the Southwest: A Historic Resource Study, Fort Union National Monument, Fort Union, New Mexico,* Professional Papers No. 41. Santa Fe: Southwest Cultural Resources Center, 1993, 22.

32. Rio Grande del Norte.

33. Also known as *Lobo Blanco,* White Wolf. Whittlesey says that as a result of the death of Jose Antonio, Lobo remained the principal chief of the Apache Nation. He's usually counted as third in line behind Chacon, who was considered principal chief. Chieftainship was a matter of personal influence. It would be difficult to gauge who was the principal chief and the arrangement might change at any time. It would be better to say that both were important leaders. However, the Army found it convenient to have

someone to deal with who would speak for the whole tribe. Nonetheless, when making treaties, the Army realistically got as many individuals to sign as possible.

34. Whittlesey to Dickinson, June 18, 1849, LR, 9MD, USAC, RG 393, NA. New Mexico State Library, Santa Fe.

35. Murphy, "Army in Taos," 37.

36. This is a lengthy report and will be referred to again below. Whittlesey to Dickerson (adjutant at Santa Fe), June 18, 1849, LR, 9MD, USAC, RG 393, NA, Fort Union Collection, Highlands University, Las Vegas, NM, Vol. 50, 18.

37. August 8, 1849, *Santa Fe Republican*, Lenderman. *The* Santa Fe Republican.

38. That is, the area north of Taos to the Sangre de Cristo Pass.

39. Whittlesey to Dickerson (adjutant at Santa Fe), June 18, 1849, LR, 9MD, USAC, RG 393, NA, Fort Union Collection, Highlands University, Las Vegas, NM, Vol. 50, 18; Whittlesey to Dickinson, June 18, 1849, LR, 9MD, USAC, RG 393, NA. New Mexico State Library, Santa Fe. It is unclear if the adjutant's name was Dickinson or Dickerson. Even the same correspondents alternated in their spelling.

40. Rodenbough writes that Steen was leading troopers of Company H, 2nd Dragoons, which he was chronicling. Floyd in the *Chronological List* (Floyd, Dale E., introduction. *Chronological List of Actions from January 15, 1837 to January 1891*, Washington, DC: Old Army Press, 1979, 13) says G & H, 1st Dragoons. Steen was the commander of Company H, 1st Dragoons. The Chronological List is drawn from official reports.

41. Presumably somewhere near the San Pedro Mountains.

42. Apparently, this was Sierra Blanca Peak (White Mountain) near Alamogordo.

43. The *Chronological List* says only one trooper was wounded and does not record any Apache killed. Rodenbough, Theophilus F. *From Everglade to Cañon with the Second Dragoons*. Norman: University of Oklahoma Press, 2000, 163.

44. Michno, Gregory. *Depredation and Deceit: The Making of the Jicarilla and Ute Wars in New Mexico*. Norman: University of Oklahoma Press, 2017, 257–58.

45. Field artillery units were supplied with many horses to pull their guns. The mountain howitzer was attached to a limber chest on wheels atop which two artillerymen rode. The combination was drawn by four horses each mounted by an artilleryman for a crew of six gunners. That meant that there were at least four horses for every six men and thus in the West, the artillery was more useful than the infantry, as they could be employed as cavalry.

46. Judd to Dickerson, August 16, 1849, LR, 9MD, USAC, RG 393, NA, Vol. 51, No. 272, Fort Union Collection, Highlands University, Las Vegas, NM.

47. Judd to Dickerson, August 16, 1849, LR, 9MD, USAC, RG 393, NA reported in Tiller, Veronica E. Velarde. *The Jicarilla Apache Tribe*. Lincoln: University of Nebraska Press, 1992, 34.

48. Tiller, *Jicarilla Apache Tribe*, 34.

49. Oliva, *Fort Union*, 23.

50. Ball, Durwood. *Army Regulars on the Western Frontier, 1848–1861*. Norman: University of Oklahoma Press, 2001, xi–xii.

51. Ibid., xii.

52. Oliva, *Fort Union*, 23. Remarkably, the *Chronological List* does not include this action. Nonetheless, Captain Judd's report is in the record. Judd to Dickerson, August 16, 1849, LR, 9MD, USAC, RG 393, NA.

53. Tiller, *Jicarilla Apache Tribe*, 34.

54. Not all sources include mention of Lobo Blanco's daughter. The information comes from later reports as a reason for the attack on the White Wagon Train near Point of Rocks. Tiller does not include it. This suggests that this was of no great importance to the Jicarilla. In November, an attempt was made to exchange her for Mrs. Ann White with horrific results.

55. Judd to Dickerson, September 10, 1849, LR, 9MD, USAC, RG 393, NA, Fort Union Collection, Highlands University, Las Vegas, NM, Vol. 51, No. 274.

56. Oliva, *Fort Union*, 23.

57. Tiller, *Jicarilla Apache Tribe*, 34.

58. Judd to Dickerson, September 29, 1849, LR 9MD, USAC, RG 393, NA, Fort Union Collection, Highlands University, Las Vegas, NM, Vol. 50, No. 22.

Chapter 8

1. Chaput, Donald. *François X. Aubry: Trader, Trailmaker and Voyageur in the Southwest 1846–1854*. Glendale, CA: Arthur H. Clark, 1975, 83–86.

2. Meline, James F. *Two Thousand Miles on Horseback: Santa Fe and Back: A Summer Tour through Kansas, Nebraska, Colorado, and New Mexico in the Year 1866*. Albuquerque: Horn & Wallace, 1966, 267–68.

3. Chaput, *Aubry*, 83.

4. Carter, Harvey Lewis. *"Dear Old Kit": The Historical Christopher Carson*. Norman: University of Oklahoma Press, 1990, 250.

5. Chaput, *Aubry*, 83.

6. Ibid., 83–86: "Why White left the train in advance is not clear. A biographer of Kit Carson maintains that Aubry gave the family permission to go ahead, thinking that any danger of Indian attack had passed. There is no precedent in Aubry's career for such a rash judgment; he, more than once, had been attacked on the outskirts of Las Vegas and Santa Fe. A more plausible explanation was that White made the decision, 'as the weather was becoming cold and disagreeable for Mrs. White and child.' One of Aubry's trail companions, P. A. Senecal, later reported that White believed the danger was past, 'and in spite of the warnings of Aubry, set out in front of the convoy.' This version is not only a firsthand account, but is more consistent with Aubry's code for survival." Also see Barry, Louise. *The Beginning of the West: Annals of the Kansas Gateway to the American West 1540–1854*. Topeka: Kansas State Historical Society, 1972, 885. Barry provides the most complete list of who was in the party.

7. Barry, *Beginning*, 885. Barry provides the dates here and below; Hammond, George P. *The Adventures of Alexander Barclay, Mountain Man*. Denver: Old West Publishing, 1976, 176 and 221n209.

8. Oliva, Leo E. *Fort Union and the Frontier Army in the Southwest: A Historic Resource Study, Fort Union National Monument, Fort Union, New Mexico*, Professional Papers No. 41. Santa Fe: Southwest Cultural Resources Center, 1993, 24–25 provides the

information that there were two wagons and that they had just crossed Palo Blanco Creek.

9. Tiller, Veronica E. Velarde. *The Jicarilla Apache Tribe*. Lincoln: University of Nebraska Press, 1992, 23: "Jicarillas hunted during the fall season from September to November and some of the women went along."

10. Calhoun to Brown, No. 18, November 2, 1849, Vol. 47, No. 87, Fort Union Collection, Highlands University, Las Vegas, NM. Orlando Brown was the commissioner of Indian Affairs from 1849 to 1850. William Medill (1845 to 1849) preceded him in office. Calhoun quoted several people who came upon the scene and wrote several letters. His first, No. 15, went to Medill on October 29.

11. Since New Mexico was not yet a territory, Smith's status was ambiguous at best. He was duly elected, but in no way official.

12. Calhoun to Brown, No. 18, November 2, 1849.

13. Dearborn wagon, a light, four-wheeled vehicle with a top and sometimes side curtains, usually pulled by one horse. Long-standing tradition, dating back to 1821, attributes its design to General Henry Dearborn. It usually had one seat but sometimes as many as two or three, and they often rested on wooden springs. The station wagon of its day, from 1819 to 1850. Encyclopedia.com, https://www.encyclopedia.com/history/dictionaries-thesauruses-pictures-and-press-releases/dearborn-wagon.

14. A barouche is a heavy and luxurious, open, four-wheeled carriage, drawn by two horses.

15. Barry, *Beginning*, 885.

16. Calhoun to Medill, No. 15, October 29, 1849, Vol. 47, No. 82, Fort Union Collection, Highlands University, Las Vegas, NM.

17. Meline, *Two Thousand Miles*, 268.

18. There is reason to believe that among Sioux and Cheyenne she might have been "passed over the prairie." This might also be more of a horror story made up by whites. If she was claimed by one of the men as a wife or slave, this would probably not have happened. There is little evidence that the Apache exhibited this sort of misbehavior anywhere except in the movies.

19. That is to say, the Canadian River of modern maps.

20. Calhoun to Brown, November 2, 1849.

21. Chaput, *Aubry*, 84.

22. Calhoun to Medill, No. 15, October 29, 1849.

23. Colonel John Munroe became military and civilian governor on October 23, 1849, replacing Colonel John Washington. James S. Calhoun was superintendent of Indian affairs and would become governor on March 3, 1851.

24. Chaput, *Aubry*, 84.

25. Calhoun to Medill, No. 15, October 29, 1849.

26. McLaws (Adjutant, Ninth Military District, Santa Fe) to Grier, October 29, 1849, LR, 9MD, USAC, RG 393, NA, New Mexico State Library and Archive, Santa Fe, NM.

27. Major William N. Grier, West Point, 1835, of the First US Dragoons, was in command. He was stationed at Taos at this time, and saw several years' service in the

Southwest. Like Carson, he was brevetted brigadier general during the Civil War. Carter, *"Dear Old Kit,"* 125.

28. Antoine Leroux (about 1801 to June 30, 1861) was also known as Joaquin Leroux and Watkins Leroux. He was born in St. Louis. He had some education before reaching Taos in 1824. He trapped the Southwest, married a Mexican woman, and obtained a Mexican land grant. In 1846, he guided Colonel Philip St. George Cooke and his battalion to California, building the southern emigrant road as they went. He guided military expeditions against the Navajo and Ute. Although never as well-known as Kit Carson, he was considered Kit's equal. Dan L. Thrapp, *Encyclopedia of Frontier Biography*. Lincoln: University of Nebraska Press, 1988, 847–48; "Carson's biographer, Colonel Peters, was disappointed that Kit was subordinate to Leroux, and wrote: "Leroux was an old and famous trapper and mountaineer whose reputation and skill as a guide in the Far West was second only to Kit Carson's. A few of his warm partisans, who were ever very warm in their praise of their friend, at one time considered him superior even to Kit Carson; but when the skill of the two men came to be tried in the same cause, the palm was yielded to Kit Carson." Parkhill, Forbes. *The Blazed Trail of Antoine Leroux*. Los Angeles: Westernlore Publications, 1965, 134–35.

29. Robert Fisher (1807 to 1852) was born in Virginia. He reached Santa Fe in 1824 and worked with Bent and St. Vrain. He operated as a free trapper and helped to build the Adobe Walls trading post in the Texas Panhandle for Bent. He was active in the suppression of the Taos Rebellion in 1847 and was involved in the Cumbres Pass fight against the Jicarilla. Thrapp, *Encyclopedia*, 494.

30. Parkhill, *Blazed Trail*, 135, says that Grier had five companies of dragoons in the expedition. This is highly unlikely as there were barely that many companies in all of New Mexico and they were scattered. The Chronological List says: "November 17, Too Koon Kurre Butte on Red River, N.M. Co. I, 1st Dragoons, Capt. W.N. Grier, one enlisted man wounded, Apache Indians." Floyd, Dale E., introduction. *Chronological List of Actions from January 15, 1837 to January 1891*. Washington, DC: Old Army Press, 1979, 13. Grier was a brevet major.

31. The exact size of Major Grier's force is unclear. Perhaps there were only eight or ten mountain men along. There had been companies of locally recruited men operating out of Taos and Abiquiu. Captain Quinn commanded one of these companies. Alexander Barclay wrote in the aftermath of the attack on the Jicarilla village at Tucumcari Butte, "24th Quinn & party here with all the Apache plunder passing—some of his men slept in the courtyard." This indicates that Quinn's "mercenaries" were present at the battle. Hammond, George P. *The Adventures of Alexander Barclay, Mountain Man*. Denver: Old West Publishing, 1976, 179.

32. Richens Lacy "Uncle Dick" Wootton (May 6, 1816, to August 22, 1893) was born in Mecklenburg County, VA. He hired on with Bent and St. Vrain in 1836. He trapped the Rockies.

33. Tom Toben (about 1823 to May 16, 1904) was born in St. Louis and reached Taos in 1837. He was nearly killed in the Taos Rebellion of 1847.

34. Both quotes are from Parkhill, *Blazed Trail*, 134. Peters and Carson would later quarrel in part over Peters's florid language in describing Kit, over inaccuracies in the

biography, and over the lack of proceeds of the sale thereof that found their way to Kit. Bennett got dates and other information wrong in his text to such an extent that I sometimes wonder if he was actually in New Mexico. He said that he enlisted under a name other than his own. Some of his stories verge on the fantastic. Consider that Grier, who graduated from West Point in 1835, would have been born about 1813 and thus would have been thirty-six in 1849; that's hardly a "fatherly old man."

35. Peters, DeWitt C. *The Life and Adventures of Kit Carson, the Nestor of the Rocky Mountains, from Facts Narrated by Himself.* Middlesex: Echo Library, 2006, 176.

36. Carter, *"Dear Old Kit,"* 124.

37. Plains Indians lashed tepee poles to the back of a horse forming a long triangle behind the animal. Cargo was then lashed between the two poles. This would have left a distinctive track of two parallel lines.

38. Carter, *"Dear Old Kit,"* 124.

39. Kit wanted to charge in and rescue the woman before any ill could befall her; he felt certain, from experience, that they would slay her when attacked. Major Grier and one presumes Leroux (Carson thought so) thought that a parley would be more appropriate. In any event, Carson thought the soldiers would follow him and was surprised when they didn't. Carter, Harvey Lewis, and LeRoy R. Hafen, ed. "Robert Fisher," in *Mountain Men and Fur Traders of the Far West*. Lincoln: University of Nebraska Press, 1982 (1965), 183. See also Parkhill, *Blazed Trail*, 134–42.

40. Oliva, *Fort Union*, 24–25.

41. Carter, *"Dear Old Kit,"* 124–25.

42. Undoubtedly this was a "spent" round, that is, one still moving beyond its maximum range lacking the force of penetration in the target. The ball probably wasn't aimed at the major; it was just a lucky shot.

43. Carter, *"Dear Old Kit,"* 125–26; Peters, *Life and Adventures*, 177.

44. Peters, *Life and Adventures*, 178.

45. The book was probably Charles Averill's *Kit Carson, Prince of the Gold Hunters*. Published in 1849, it is thought to have been the first of many thrillers explaining the real and imaginary adventures of Carson. Carson did not participate in the California Gold Rush. Carter, "Robert Fisher," 183.

46. Peters, *Life and Adventures*, 178.

47. Meline, *Two Thousand Miles*, 267–68.

48. Carter, *"Dear Old Kit,"* 125–26.

49. Sabin, Edwin L. *Kit Carson Days, 1809–1868: Adventures in the Path of Empire*, 2 Volumes. Lincoln: University of Nebraska Press, 1995 (1935), 621. The offer was fifteen hundred dollars for her delivery.

50. Comancheros were people, mostly New Mexicans, who took trade goods to the Comanche.

51. Ann White died on November 17, 1849. Bennett said that he arrived in New Mexico in 1850 and records Mrs. White's death and this incident as occurring on April 10, 1851. Bennett reports that "[a]s we came in view of the Indians, they were so taken by surprise that they fled in dismay. Their shrill shrieks were echoed by the exultant yells of the soldiers who fired a volley after the fleeing foe. Indian horses were stampeded, dogs

barked, and mothers left their children regardless of danger or destruction to jump into the river in efforts to gain safety." Bennett claims they found "8 bodies lying dead on the ground and at least 3 more were shot in the water." Other sources say only one Indian was slain and that this occurred as he swam the river. Floyd, *Chronological List*, 14, does not show any Indian casualties. It should be abundantly clear that Bennett was not there and had only the vaguest idea of what had occurred. The 1st Dragoons do not need a black eye over this product of Bennett's fertile imagination. Bennett, James A., and Clinton E. Brooks, ed. *Forts and Forays: A Dragoon in New Mexico, 1850–1856*. Albuquerque: University of New Mexico Press, 1995, 24–25.

52. Apparently Barclay made insertions in his diary a few days after the event.

53. Hammond, *Adventures of Alexander Barclay*, 179.

54. Carter, *"Dear Old Kit,"* 125–26.

55. South of present-day Ulysses, Kansas.

56. Hell hath no fury like a Jicarilla woman. We can only speculate on what might have set her off. Did the soldiers "try it on" with her? Did someone suggest that they were setting a trap for Jicarillas who came to parley?

57. There are two versions of the story. One comes from Chief Chacon and the other from Agent John Greiner. They are similar in all but the reason she was escorted or asked to be escorted to the top of Wagon Mound. Simmons, Marc. "The Wagon Mound Massacre," in Mark L. Gardner, ed., *The Mexican Road: Trade, Travel, and Confrontation on the Santa Fe Trail*. Manhattan, KS: Sunflower University Press, 1989, 48–49.

58. Oliva, *Fort Union*, 25.

Chapter 9

1. Oliva, Leo E. *Fort Union and the Frontier Army in the Southwest: A Historic Resource Study, Fort Union National Monument, Fort Union, New Mexico*, Professional Papers No. 41. Santa Fe: Southwest Cultural Resources Center, 1993, 30. "Each light artillery company was authorized to contain 64 privates. . . . Each infantry company was to have 42 privates, the dragoons were authorized 50 privates; and the mounted riflemen were assigned 64. . . . Almost 10% of the army in 1850 was stationed among the eleven posts of the Ninth Military Department. There were two companies of Second Artillery, ten companies (the entire regiment) of Third Infantry, three companies of First Dragoons, and four companies of Second Dragoons. The total authorized strength of these units was 1,603 officers and men, but only 987 were actually present in the department." Oliva, *Fort Union*, 37. Soldiers in training depots, in transit, on leave, on detail came out of unit strength so a company of fifty dragoon privates was lucky to muster twenty-three such as Major Grier found himself with at Rayado in June.

2. Ibid., 25.

3. This is the figure given by Oliva and is the figure reported at the time. It is undoubtedly an exaggeration. The Jicarilla would have had great difficulty caring for this many sheep.

4. Anonymous, *Jicarilla Apache Tribe: Historical Materials 1540–1887*. New York: Garland Publishing, 1974, 93.

5. Simmons, Marc. "The Wagon Mound Massacre," in Mark L. Gardner, ed., *The Mexican Road: Trade, Travel, and Confrontation on the Santa Fe Trail*. Manhattan, KS: Sunflower University Press, 1989, 48.

6. Oliva, *Fort Union*, 25.

7. Simmons, "Wagon Mound," 45.

8. Ibid., 46.

9. Leigh Holbrook was actually named Sergeant William Holbrook according to military records. It is uncertain why Carson knew him as Leigh.

10. William New was "the trapper with whom Carson had come out to Bent's Fort a dozen years back." Sabin, Edwin L. *Kit Carson Days, 1809–1868: Adventures in the Path of Empire*, 2 Volumes. Lincoln: University of Nebraska Press, 1995 (1935), 623; Carter, Harvey Lewis. *"Dear Old Kit": The Historical Christopher Carson*. Norman: University of Oklahoma Press, 1990, 126.

11. Peters, DeWitt C. *The Life and Adventures of Kit Carson, the Nestor of the Rocky Mountains, from Facts Narrated by Himself*. Middlesex: Echo Library, 2006, 181. In his autobiography Kit Carson said, "took the trail of the animals that was driven off, followed it at a gallop for 25 miles and discovered, at a distance, the Indians. During the pursuit, some of our animals gave out and were left on the trail." Carter, *"Dear Old Kit,"* 126–27.

12. Canadian, the name implying in Spanish that it's in a canyon. Oliva, *Fort Union*, 26.

13. Dunlay, Thomas W. *Kit Carson and the Indians*. Lincoln: University of Nebraska Press, 2000, 140–41.

14. "April 6, Near Rayado, N.M. Det. Co. I, 1st Drag. Under Sgt. W.C. Holbrook, 5 Indians killed, 2 wounded, Apache Indians. Sgt. And 10 enl. men." Floyd, Dale E., introduction. *Chronological List of Actions from January 15, 1837 to January 1891*. Washington, DC: Old Army Press, 1979, 14.

15. Dunlay, *Kit Carson*, 140–141.

16. East bank of the Canadian.

17. The correct name is New not Newell. Holbrook to McLaws, April 7, 1850, LR, 9MD, USAC, RG 393, NA, New Mexico State Library and Archive, Santa Fe, NM.

18. Munroe to Jones, April 15, 1850, LS, 9MD, USAC, RG 393, NA, New Mexico State Library and Archive, Santa Fe, NM.

19. Calhoun to Brown, No. 56, April 20, 1850, Vol. 47, No. 164, Fort Union Collection, Highlands University, Las Vegas, NM.

20. Simmons, "Wagon Mound," 45.

21. Ibid., 46.

22. Ibid., 49; Barry, Louise. *The Beginning of the West: Annals of the Kansas Gateway to the American West 1540–1854*. Topeka: Kansas State Historical Society, 1972, 916.

23. Burnside to Ward (Post Adjutant), May 23, 1850. Vol. 51, No. 300-301, Fort Union Collection, Highlands University, Las Vegas, NM. Burnside stated in his report after viewing the Wagon Mound site on May 22, that the "track of the wagon could not be discerned." He concluded that the mail party arrived at Wagon Mound "either before the snow fell on the third of this month or, whilst the snow was still on the ground." Simmons says that the men died about May 7, but I don't see what he based this on.

Simmons, "Wagon Mound," 49. Barry also provides "about May 7" as the date of the attack. Barry, *Beginning*, 916.

24. Simmons, "Wagon Mound," 50.

25. Santa Clara Mesa on modern maps.

26. William W. H. Davis, US attorney, appears to have acquired information from Apache informants. He related that "the first attack was made in the morning, and the fight lasted all day, without much damage being done, only a man or two wounded." The Apaches were working alone on the first day conducting a "flying skirmish" that lasted all day. Davis claimed a war party of Utes joined the Jicarilla but told the Apache that they did not know how to fight Americans. The Apache would show them. Simmons, "Wagon Mound," 50–51.

27. Burnside to Ward (Post Adjutant), May 23, 1850. Vol. 51, No. 300-301, Fort Union Collection, Highlands University, Las Vegas, NM. Also see Stanley, F. *The Wagon Mound, New Mexico Story*. Pep, TX: Stanley, 1968.

28. The soil in the West can be very hard and rocky and graves very shallow. In many places the grave would have had no depth at all. Large stones would have been piled on top of the bodies to discourage scavengers. The wolves referred to were probably prairie wolves, i.e., coyotes, but there were still Mexican lobos in the area at that time.

29. Simmons, "Wagon Mound," 51.

30. The picture was forwarded along with the report, but has since been lost. Burnside to Plympton (Post Adjutant), June 12, 1850. Vol. 51, No. 304, Fort Union Collection, Highlands University, Las Vegas, NM.

31. There were only twenty-three Topographical Engineers, all officers, under Colonel Abert. They did more than any others to open the West. Their corps was separate from the Corps of Engineers until the Civil War when it was absorbed. There were no enlisted men. If escorts were needed they applied to the dragoons and infantry. If additional labor was needed they hired artists, scientists, and survey teams. They mapped the West and its rivers and ports, cataloged its flora and fauna, and described its geography, topography, trails, waters, peoples, and minerals. They painted pictures so people could see the look of the West and told people what was there and why they should come west to settle.

32. It's very unlikely that they would have been working together. This was probably Jicarilla and possibly Ute.

33. Oliva, *Fort Union*, 28n99.

34. Floyd, *Chronological List*, 14.

35. Oliva, *Fort Union*, 28.

36. Grier to McLaws, June 26, 1850, Vol. 54, No. 8, Fort Union Collection, Highlands University, Las Vegas, NM.

37. Anonymous, *Jicarilla Apache Tribe*, 94.

38. There were six cylinders on a Colt, but one was left unloaded with the hammer resting on its nipple. A percussion cap under the resting hammer might accidentally set the weapon off without a trigger pull or being cocked. Thus it was usually carried empty.

39. Anonymous, *Jicarilla Apache Tribe*, 94.

40. Floyd, *Chronological List*, 14.

41. Oliva, *Fort Union*, 28; Anonymous, *Jicarilla Apache Tribe*, 94.

42. Anonymous, *Jicarilla Apache Tribe*, 94–99. "July 25, Headwaters of Canadian River or Red River, N.M. Cos. C & I 1st Drag. & K 2nd Dragoons. 1 enlisted man killed. Wounded and died of wounds. Surprised a camp of 150 lodges." Floyd, *Chronological List*, 14.

43. Calhoun to Brown, No. 81, September 20, 1850; Abel, Annie Heloise. *The Official Correspondence of James S. Calhoun: While Indian Agent at Santa Fe and Superintendent of Indian Affairs in New Mexico*. Washington, DC: Government Printing Office (Forgotten Books Reprint), 1915, 259–60.

44. The report of Lucien Maxwell's death had apparently been much exaggerated.

45. Calhoun to Brown, No. 82. October 12, 1850. Abel, *Correspondence*, 262–63.

46. Calhoun to Lea, No. 2, March 31, 1851. Abel, *Correspondence*, 308.

47. Luke Lea replaced Orlando Brown as commissioner of Indian Affairs in 1850.

48. Lea to Calhoun, November 18, 1850. Abel, *Correspondence*, 269.

49. "In the 1840's there was a small settlement of trappers and their squaws and children about twenty-five miles south of Pueblo, Colorado, where the Taos Trail crossed Greenhorn Creek. The creek took its name from the Comanche chief, Guerno Verde, who was killed in battle there with Governor Anza of New Mexico in 1779. The creek flows into the St. Charles or San Carlos River a few miles before that stream joins the Arkansas River." Carter, *"Dear Old Kit,"* 128n264.

50. Elias Brevoort, born in 1822, had been an Indian trader for seven years and at twenty-eight years old was quite well to do. In 1856, he would travel with four companies of dragoons to Tucson to take possession of the Gadsden Purchase, and afterward he would be the sutler for Fort Buchanan and would there be associated with Captain Richard Ewell. In 1870, he partnered with Tom Jeffords as Indian trader at the Canada Alamosa Reservation.

51. Carter, *"Dear Old Kit,"* 128–30.

Chapter 10

1. Choice to Calhoun, January 29, 1850. Abel, Annie Heloise. *The Official Correspondence of James S. Calhoun: While Indian Agent at Santa Fe and Superintendent of Indian Affairs in New Mexico*. Washington, DC: Government Printing Office (Forgotten Books Reprint), 1915, 121.

2. Anonymous. *Apache Indians VII: Jicarilla Apache Tribe: Historical Materials 1540–1887*. New York: Garland Publishing, 1974, 95–99.

3. Lea to Calhoun, April 5, 1851. Abel, *Correspondence*, 392.

4. Calhoun to Lea, No. 6, May 28, 1851. Ibid., 354–55.

5. Adjutant General is only a general in the sense of "in general." The adjutant is a military position equivalent to a secretary who sends and receives letters and does the filing. In this case, the position was held by Lieutenant McLaws, 7th Infantry.

6. Munroe to Calhoun, May 24, 1851. Abel, *Correspondence*, 352.

7. Munroe to Jones, March 30, 1851. Ibid., 310–11.

8. Anonymous. *Jicarilla Apache Tribe*, 95–99.

9. Manzana, or more correctly Manzano, is southeast of Albuquerque on the eastern slope of the Manzano Mountains.

10. It is unclear what is meant by "Smoky mountains." There are no mountains sixty miles ESE of Manzano. In that direction and somewhat closer is Mesa del los Jumanos. J is pronounced like an English h, and humo in Spanish is smoke. SSE of Manzano about sixty miles are the Jicarilla Mountains. Jicarilla Apache Tribe Historical Materials identifies the Smoky mountains as the Oscura, in Spanish dark or obscured, which are south of Manzano. Anonymous. *Jicarilla Apache Tribe*, 95–99.

11. Calhoun to Lea, March 31, 1851. Abel, *Correspondence*, 307–8.

12. Calhoun to Stuart (Sec. Dept. of Interior), April 2, 1851. Abel, *Correspondence*, 313–16.

13. Only very late in the century did the government consider allowing the Jicarilla and Navajo to become herdsmen. There was an inherent distrust of herdsmen. Herding cultures around the world are violent, from American cowboys and Plains Indians to Mongols of the steppe or the Riding Clans of the Scots-English border. Perhaps it has something to do with the allure of so much highly mobile wealth.

14. Carson, William G. B., ed. "William Carr Lane, Diary, Part I." *New Mexico Historical Review*, Vol. 39/3 (July 1964), 187–88.

15. Ward to Alexander, May 26, 1851, quoted in Tiller, Veronica E. Velarde. *The Jicarilla Apache Tribe*. Lincoln: University of Nebraska Press, 1992, 38.

16. Lea to Calhoun, April 12, 1851. Abel, *Correspondence*, 325–26.

17. Calhoun to ____, April 18, 1851. Ibid., 327–28.

18. "Chacon was anxious to keep true to the treaty. In evidence of this see letter from McLaws to Alexander, p 330." Ibid.

19. Munroe to Jones, June 29, 1851. Ibid., 358–59.

20. Tiller, *Jicarilla Apache Tribe*, 39.

21. Anonymous. *Jicarilla Apache Tribe*, 95–99.

22. Oliva, Leo E. *Fort Union and the Frontier Army in the Southwest: A Historic Resource Study, Fort Union National Monument, Fort Union, New Mexico*, Professional Papers No. 41. Santa Fe: Southwest Cultural Resources Center, 1993, 25.

23. Abel, Annie Heloise. "The Journal of John Greiner." *Old Santa Fe: A Magazine of History, Archaeology, Genealogy and Biography*, Vol III/11 (July 1916), 194.

24. Carter, Harvey Lewis. *"Dear Old Kit": The Historical Christopher Carson*. Norman: University of Oklahoma Press, 1990, 130n275.

25. Ibid., 129–30.

26. Ibid., 130.

27. Ibid., 131.

28. Ibid., 132. Also Dunlay, Thomas W. *Kit Carson and the Indians*. Lincoln: University of Nebraska Press, 2000, 142–44.

29. Conrad (Sec. of War) to Sumner, April 1, 1851, Vol. 1, No. 35, Fort Union Collection, Highlands University, Las Vegas, NM.

30. Michno, Gregory. *Depredation and Deceit: The Making of the Jicarilla and Ute Wars in New Mexico*. Norman: University of Oklahoma Press, 2017, 126.

31. Either because a bullet was said to have bounced off his thick skull or because of his bullheadedness, or perhaps both.

32. Michno, *Depredation*, 124–25.

33. When established in 1852, the post north of Taos would be named Fort Massachusetts. Munroe to Jones, January 27, 1851. Vol. 1, No. 3, Fort Union Collection, Highlands University, Las Vegas, NM.

34. Michno, *Depredation*, 123.

35. Hog ranch is an old term for the bordellos and gambling dens that surrounded military posts.

36. Sumner to Calhoun, November 10, 1851, quoted in Michno, *Depredation*, 134.

37. Michno, *Depredation*, 147.

38. Truchas, NM, the trout, is a community on the western slope of the Sangre de Cristo about twenty-five miles north of Santa Fe.

39. The Rio Pecos has its headwaters fifteen miles northeast of Santa Fe and flows from there through the communities of Pecos, San Miguel, and Anton Chico before turning south to Bosque Redondo and eventually flowing into the Rio Grande east of El Paso. Near Anton Chico, the Pecos and the Canadian (Red) River are only forty miles apart. The Canadian turns eastward to flow across the Texas Panhandle and Oklahoma to join the Arkansas River and flow into the Mississippi River.

40. *Tinaja* means a water jug. What is referred to is the micaceous pottery made by the Jicarilla.

41. Abel, "Journal," 202–3.

42. Greiner to Lea, June 30, 1852, quoted in Michno, *Depredation*, 146.

43. Tribes or bands of Apaches were named by their special habits or more often for where they were encountered. The names don't necessarily reflect any political organization that the people so named would recognize. At this time, since the border with Mexico was along the Gila River, as the Gadsden Purchase had not yet been made, Americans were not in contact with the Western Apache bands. The Gila and Mimbres Apaches seem to correspond to the Chihenne and Bedonkohe Bands of the Chiricahua, though some of the eastern Coyotero or White Mountain Apache might also be included.

44. Abel, "Journal," 220.

45. Claims for reparations were allowed under the Treaty of July 1, 1852, which was the only early treaty ratified by the US Senate. In 1853 Juan de Jesus Mares of Taos County was allowed $2,530 in reparation for cattle, horses, and other property taken by the Jicarilla. In 1854 Pablo Trujillo of Mora County was allowed $470, while Juan Antonio Borrego of Rio Arriba County was allowed $315, Jose Anastacio Trujillo of Mora County was allowed $370, and Francisco Lopez of San Miguel County was allowed $470. Michno, *Depredation and Deceit*, 262–264.

46. Kappler, Charles J., LLM, Clerk to the Senate Committee on Indian Affairs, Compiled and Edited. *Indian Affairs: Laws and Treaties, Vol. II (Treaties).* Washington, DC: Government Printing Office, 1904, http://avalon.law.yale.edu/19th_century/apa1852.asp.

47. Carson, William G. B., ed. "William Carr Lane, Diary, Part I." *New Mexico Historical Review*, Vol. 39/3 (July 1964), 187.

48. Emmett, Chris. *Fort Union and the Winning of the Southwest.* Norman: University of Oklahoma Press, 1965, 151–52.

49. Carson, "William Carr Lane," 189.

50. Fort Webster was near the Santa Rita Copper Mines east of modern day Silver City in the south of New Mexico.

51. *Acequia* is an irrigation ditch, and an *acequia madre* is a mother ditch that feeds smaller ditches.

52. "The Indians of New Mexico," *Santa Fe Weekly Gazette*, May 21, 1853.

53. Bender, Averam B. *The March of Empire: Frontier Defense in the Southwest, 1848–1860*. Lawrence: University of Kansas Press, 1952, 156.

54. David Meriwether (October 30, 1800–April 4, 1893) had served in the Kentucky legislature and in the US Congress.

55. Report of Superintendent in New Mexico, David Meriwether to Manypenny, No. 79, August 31, 1853.

56. Michno, *Depredation*, 167–68.

57. Ibid., 168–69.

58. Ibid., 169–70.

59. Graves to Meriwether, No. 80, August 31, 1853.

60. On October 31, 1853, the Army reorganized its military districts. The Ninth Military District was eliminated and the Department of New Mexico created.

61. Kit Carson is supposed to have said: "The head chief, Lobo Blanco or White Wolf, to whom the woman [Ann White] had been prize, came into a treaty camp (as Carson wrathfully asserted) wearing a necklace made up of the teeth of the late merchant White." Sabin, Edwin L. *Kit Carson Days, 1809–1868: Adventures in the Path of Empire*, 2 Volumes. Lincoln: University of Nebraska Press, 1995 (1935), 622. Sabin does not provide a citation for this statement and so far I have not found it anywhere else. Moreover, Carson does not appear to have been present at any of the several treaty negotiations that took place before Lobo Blanco's death and thus could not have observed this personally.

62. James Bennett claimed that he had been a dragoon serving under an assumed name in the 1st Regiment and that he kept a diary. The "diary" includes many fantastic events not found elsewhere along with accounts of events he could not possibly have witnessed. The presumed diary has events in the wrong months, seasons, and years. In short, whatever it is, it is not a diary or based on a diary.

Chapter 11

1. Cooke to Nichols, January 29, 1854, Vol. 2, No. 94, Fort Union Collection, Highlands University, Las Vegas, NM. Major W. A. Nichols was General Garland's adjutant at Albuquerque. The account is difficult to follow as Cooke is responding to a letter Nichols had written.

2. Cooke to Bell, March 1, 1854, Vol. 2, No. 99, Fort Union Collection, Highlands University, Las Vegas, NM.

3. Frazer, Robert W. *Forts and Supplies: The Role of the Army in the Economy of the Southwest: 1846–1861*. Albuquerque: University of New Mexico Press, 1983, 88. In 1863, the 109th degree of west longitude became the dividing line between the territories of New Mexico and Arizona.

4. Oliva, Leo E. *Fort Union and the Frontier Army in the Southwest: A Historic Resource Study, Fort Union National Monument, Fort Union, New Mexico*, Professional Papers No. 41. Santa Fe: Southwest Cultural Resources Center, 1993, 81.

5. Nichols to Cooke, March 2, 1854, Vol. 2, No. 100, Fort Union Collection, Highlands University, Las Vegas, NM.

6. Cooke to Nichols, March 8, 1854, Vol. 2, No. 101, Fort Union Collection, Highlands University, Las Vegas, NM.

7. Crass, David C., and Deborah L. Wallsmith. "Where's the Beef? Food Supply at an Antebellum Frontier Post." *Historical Archaeology* 26 (1992).

8. The Canadian River.

9. William Tipton, Samuel Watrous's son-in-law.

10. The correct spelling is Samuel Watrous. His ranch can still be seen at Watrous, New Mexico, on I-25. Watrous was the beef contractor for Fort Union and a close neighbor of Alexander Barclay and Doyle at Barclay's Fort where the Mora and Sapello come together. Watrous made frequent complaints of depredations. He ranched in an exposed position in Jicarilla country. It seems likely that Watrous was one of the people Kit Carson referred to in 1849 when he said that some people didn't make gifts of a few beeves to the Indians and suffered for it.

11. Lieutenant Colonel Philip St. George Cooke had come up through the officer ranks of the 1st Dragoons under General Kearny. Kearny had maintained peace on the Great Plains for many years by the show of force without actually having to engage in combat. Cooke was one of his most promising protégés. See Gorenfeld, Will, and John Gorenfeld. *Kearny's Dragoons Out West: The Birth of the U.S. Cavalry.* Norman: University of Oklahoma Press, 2016. He led the Mormon Battalion during the Mexican War and was transferred to the 2nd Dragoons in order to accept a promotion. He was the commander of Fort Union at this time.

12. Cooke to Bell, February 13, 1854, Vol. 2, No. 97, Fort Union Collection, Highlands University, Las Vegas, NM.

13. Dunlay, Thomas W. *Kit Carson and the Indians.* Lincoln: University of Nebraska Press, 2000, 162.

14. Ibid., 162–63.

15. The Jicarilla had made a treaty with the government in March 1853. As the Jicarilla would have seen it, the treaty was binding especially since both sides had begun to fulfill their treaty obligations. Kit Carson, Graves, Governor Meriwether, and figures in the military all thought that once the Jicarilla began to starve they would have no choice but to depredate. It would appear that with a very small raid on Watrous and a few insults to settlers, the Jicarilla, even the 750 who were not involved in the Rio Puerco project, kept up their end. Given that government figures were saying that failure to ratify the treaty, which allowed for modification by the Senate, would lead to war, the reasonable and rational thing for Congress to do was to ratify and the reasonable thing for Graves and Meriwether to do would have been to beg for rapid ratification rather than simply blaming the coming war on their predecessors.

16. It seems likely that three cattle had been taken from Watrous, a reasonable number for a starving band. A few months later, in conference with Governor Meriwether, Chief

Chacon said, "At the beginning of the war, don't know what caused it. I was away with the Utahs. Had heard it was about three cattle (Lieutenant Bell's expedition)—We were ready to return the cattle, but the Americans wanted three chiefs." Quoted in Johnson, David M., and Chris Adams. *Final Report on the Battle of Cieneguilla: A Jicarilla Apache Victory Over the U.S. Dragoons, March 30, 1854*. Santa Fe: Southwestern Region, 2009, 20.

17. Watrous. The February 10 incident is still the only issue.

18. Cooke to Bell, March 1, 1854, Vol. 2, No. 99, Fort Union Collection, Highlands University, Las Vegas, NM.

19. David Bell (ca. 1826–December 2, 1860) graduated from West Point and was commissioned a brevet second lieutenant July 1, 1851, in the 2nd Regiment of Dragoons. He was twenty-eight years old at this time and had the equivalent time in service to company commanders of the present day.

20. I dislike using this source. Rodenbough embellishes in the interest of telling a good story. His details cannot always be trusted. Rodenbough, Theophilus F. *From Everglade to Cañon with the Second Dragoons*. Norman: University of Oklahoma Press, 2000, 176–78.

21. The primary sources say the Congillon River in a variety of spellings but the name no longer has any meaning nor does "Cinto Mountains." The distance described could have put them close to the Conchas River and Michno says near Conchas, New Mexico. Michno, Gregory. *Encyclopedia of the Indian Wars: Western Battles and Skirmishes 1850–1890*. Missoula, MT: Mountain Press Publishing, 2003, 23. They were about forty miles southeast of Fort Union.

22. Various primary and secondary sources now recall that Lobo Blanco had massacred the White Wagon Train in 1849 and captured Ann White and go on to implicate him in the Wagon Mound Massacre. In the years between 1850 and 1854, Lobo Blanco had kept the peace, had attended peace conferences, and had been described as a peace chief and as trustworthy and reliable. Governor Meriwether and Colonel Cooke had to go back five years to find a crime for which he was clearly responsible.

23. Rodenbough says it was a "mounted interview." From his wording I understand the Apache to have been on foot. The old dragoon is not entirely trustworthy but his description is within the realm of the possible. Rodenbough, *Second Dragoons*, 176–78. The Jicarilla had been in contact with the Spanish for hundreds of years. Many bore Spanish surnames. This may have been the result of having been raised in Spanish families as *genizaros*. Given the nature of Bell's instructions and his belief that Lobo was responsible for a number of outrages, the author assumes that his accusations were made roughly and rudely.

24. The dragoon carried horse pistol, saber, and musketoon, a shortened, smoothbore musket. This latter muzzle-loading weapon had a slide-mounted ramrod (so it couldn't be dropped while riding) and was short enough to facilitate loading from the saddle. The downside was that its effective range was about fifty yards.

25. Bell wrote in his report: "succeeded in escaping to impracticable ground, which was near, taking with them a number wounded, leaving five killed." Emmett, Chris. *Fort Union and the Winning of the Southwest*. Norman: University of Oklahoma Press, 1965, 170.

26. I've followed Rodenbough, *Second Dragoons*, 176–78, and his account of the battle. The names of the wounded and dead come from Oliva, *Fort Union*, 124.

27. Rodenbough, *Second Dragoons*, 176–78.

28. Cooke to Nichols, March 8, 1854, Vol. 2, No. 101, Fort Union Collection, Highlands University, Las Vegas, NM.

29. The number is incredible. If the entire tribe numbered twelve hundred, one in five would have been of appropriate age and sex to be a warrior, meaning there could have been no more than 240 warriors. No one ever counted more than eight hundred in one place during these years, meaning there would be no more than 160 warriors, but that suggests the consolidation of the tribe from Rio Puerco, the San Luis Valley, along the Arkansas and Canadian. One hundred warriors are possible but still improbable. The number in the opposing force tends to grow when they're shooting at you. Dividing the estimate by ten usually yields the most probable figure. The Jicarilla had only had a day to gather, so thirty warriors seems likely.

30. Goddard, Pliny Earle. *Jicarilla Apache Texts*. Charleston, SC: BiblioBazaar, 2008, 121. This book was originally published in 1911 based on fieldwork done in 1909. At the time of the fight, Casa Maria would have been a teenager. Casa Maria was probably with the group at Mora. The demand for four chiefs is repeated in Chief Chacon's version of the story, though he says three, so there might be something to it. In my experience, the Apache are likely to recall as significant the detail of the bell on the cow. They may not have understood its purpose and thus thought the cow especially significant.

31. Cooke to Nichols, March 8, 1854, Vol. 2, No. 101, Fort Union Collection, Highlands University, Las Vegas, NM.

32. Cooke to Blake, March 11, 1854, Vol. 2, No. 104, Fort Union Collection, Highlands University, Las Vegas, NM. Major George Blake was the commander at Don Fernandez de Taos and Cantonment Burgwin.

33. Nichols to Cooke, March 12, 1854, Vol. 2, No. 105, Fort Union Collection, Highlands University, Las Vegas, NM.

34. Two warriors per lodge would have been normal and what the military usually estimated. Later he would get an actual count of 107 warriors.

35. Cooke to Blake, March 19, 1854, Vol. 2, No. 108, Fort Union Collection, Highlands University, Las Vegas, NM.

36. Bell wrote this letter on December 27, 1854, giving permission to Williams, the recipient, to show it to Davidson as he did not wish to say anything behind his back. It led to a court of inquiry demanded by Davidson to clear his name. Johnson and Adams, *Final Report*, 120–24.

37. "Davidson's detachment attacked a rancheria (in Scotts Valley) killing 4 and taking the chief. Early on the morning of the 15th, the landing on the island was affected under strong opposition from the Indians, who took flight in every direction, plunging into the water among the heavy growth of tule that surrounds the island. I saw no alternative but to pursue them into the tule . . . with most gratifying results; the number killed . . . not less than 60 and doubt little, extended to 100 and upwards. The Indians were supposed to number about 400. No injury to the command occurred. The village was burned along with a large amount of stores. . . ." The dead included men, women, and children. John

Parker. *The Kelsey Brothers: A California Disaster*, Talk presented at the 2012 November meeting of the Lake County Historical Society. https://www.academia.edu/5539505/The_Kelsey_Brothers_A_California_Disaster.

38. Johnson and Adams, *Final Report*, 146.

39. Oliva, *Fort Union*, 125.

40. Johnson and Adams, *Final Report*, 146.

41. Oliva says that Chacon was included. Oliva, *Fort Union*, 125. Johnson has Chacon with the Ute Chief Chico Velasquez near Fort Massachusetts (ninety miles north of Taos) at the time of the March 30 battle in the Embudo Mountains (Cieneguilla). Fleche Rayada (also given as Flechas Rayadas, Striped Arrow) would then have been the Jicarilla leader and one of those who spoke to Carson. Johnson and Adams, *Final Report*, 21.

42. Johnson and Adams, *Final Report*, 98.

43. The military accounts place them near Peñasco, on the road from Fort Union to Cantonment Burgwin. They move to the westward. Picuris is near and their final camp only five miles beyond that near an old trail from Cieneguilla to Picuris. The Jicarilla would undoubtedly have seen themselves as obeying Kit Carson's instructions to stay put at Picuris. Later Kit would indicate that military officers goaded the Apache into war. This is a sign that he saw them as complying with his instructions where others have suggested they did not. The Jicarilla said they had been there for four days making pottery when the soldiers attacked on the 30th. Goddard, *Jicarilla Apache Texts*, 121.

44. James Bennett serving under the name James A. Bronson was assigned to Davidson's I Troop. He gives the following account of March 1854:

> March 6 - In company with Lieut. Davidson and 60 men, started to watch the movements of a party of Apache Indians. Met 150 Indians. Talked with them. The chiefs agreed to come into our Fort and treat (or make a treaty) when we returned. Arrived at Mora.
>
> March 7 - Lieut. Davidson went to Fort Union to report to Col. Cooke. Spent the day in town. At night a dance took place. A man of Company F, 1st Dragoons, had difficulty with some Mexicans and got five pistol balls through different parts of his body. He was picked up insensible and sent to Fort Union Hospital.
>
> March 9 - Started for home yesterday. At dusk arrived at Picirise, where we learned the Indians we met two days ago had gone on to join another tribe instead of going to our fort as they had agreed. We saddled up our horses, started across the mountains, got lost, and scattered. It was the darkest night I ever saw. Men were shouting to each other. Riding under trees, we lost nearly all our hats. The sleet and wind made it a terrible night. This morning at daylight, I got home. The other men came stringing in by ones and twos. 8 o'clock in the morning we started anew, having heard that the Indians were a few miles off. We traced them to Taos Rancho. Surrounded the Rancho and found 10 Indians. Took them prisoners to the fort, where we held a council. Three

chiefs agreed to accompany Major Blake to Fort Union to conclude a treaty with Col. Cooke.

March 11 - Major Blake with 12 men and the three Indian Chiefs started for Fort Union.

March 29 - Major Blake came galloping into our fort with the news that the Indians would not come to terms but had run away from him. We were, 60 of us, to saddle up immediately and pursue the band to prevent them from crossing the Rio Grande and joining the Chachon band of Apaches. At the same time that Major Blake came in a Mexican also came riding in saying that 1500 head of cattle were driven off by the Indians and two herders were killed. We mounted and left at 11 o'clock that night. Encamped on the banks of the Rio Grande at Cienequilla, where there are five mud houses. Heard of Indians.

—Bennett, James A., and Clinton E. Brooks, ed.
Forts and Forays: A Dragoon in New Mexico, 1850–1856.
Albuquerque: University of New Mexico Press, 1995, 52–55.

45. Jicarilla accounts say that there were four hostages at this point. Goddard, *Jicarilla Apache Texts*, 121.

46. The signature on the original is obscured but to all appearances this is a note from Colonel Cooke at Fort Union to Major Blake at Cantonment Burgwin. Johnson and Adams, *Final Report*, 99.

47. Johnson and Adams, *Final Report*, 146. Tiller gives a slightly different account. "Carson had obtained prior assurances from the friendly Jicarilla that they would remain near Picuris until he returned from Santa Fe but the band fled. They encountered Major Phillip R. Thompson's detachment of dragoons en route from Fort Union to Taos. Major Thompson demanded that four of them accompany him to Cantonment Burgwin and remain there as hostage to ensure the good conduct of the whole band. They consented and proceeded to Taos; but the following morning they all fled, including the prisoners." Tiller, Veronica E. Velarde. *The Jicarilla Apache Tribe*. Lincoln: University of Nebraska Press, 1992, 44.

48. Johnson and Adams, *Final Report*, 146.

49. According to Lieutenant Bell: "I was present. Lt. D. left Cant. B. on the 29th inst under orders from Major Blake to follow and watch the movement of the Apaches, but to avoid if possible bringing on an action." Johnson and Adams, *Final Report*, 120–24. Two years later, speaking in retrospect with Davidson attempting to clear himself of wrongdoing, Blake said of his orders that "I directed Lt Davidson according to my instructions from Col. Cooke, to take out his Company to proceed on their trail and watch and control their movements." Johnson and Adams, 146. He's left out the part about avoiding bringing on an action. Still one does not need to attack a stationary enemy in order to "control their movements." Davidson violated his orders. Also left out is the concern of Blake in controlling their movements that they not be allowed to cross the Rio Grande to the westward. It is clear from their subsequent actions that this was what Blake meant by controlling their movements. Why he was concerned is not clear. There was nothing west of the Rio Grande. Abiquiu and El Rito were farther south. The

San Juan Mountains were Ute and Jicarilla country. No settlements would have been endangered by a movement across the river. Embudo, where Davidson headed, was the closest ford. Moving to the ford, instead of heading to Peüasco to follow their trail, was an attempt to head them off.

50. This is from Weldon's account at the hearing. He is the only one that mentions F Troop's leadership. Johnson and Adams, *Final Report*, 164.

51. It was just a collection of a few huts. Cieneguilla means the little swamp. Today the village is known as Pilar. From there a trail led to Embudo and the River Road to Santa Fe.

52. This is the same Sergeant Holbrook who had been at Rayado with Kit Carson and fought the Jicarilla alongside of the scout in 1849 and 1850. At the court of inquiry, Edward Maher testified that he was one of those who went with Silva. Johnson and Adams, *Final Report*, 160–61.

53. Ibid., 164.

54. Bronson and Strowbridge report the return of the scout and the discovery of tracks. Ibid., 149, 155. Bronson is the name under which James Bennett served in the dragoons. While his accounts of other battles are clearly fictionalized, he was wounded at Cieneguilla. His testimony is much more complete and perhaps more accurate than what appears in *Forts and Forays* where he wrote:

> March 30 - At sunrise this morning started, found the body of a white man who was killed by the Indians. Followed their trail; found ourselves at 8 o'clock A.M. in ambush, surrounded by about 400 Indians; fought hard until 12 noon when we started to retreat. I was wounded shortly after by a rifle ball through both thighs. I then ran about a mile; found I was not able to walk alone any farther; got between two horses, seized their stirrups. The horses dragged me one half mile when I managed to mount my horse. In riding under low trees I lost my hat. Blood flowed freely. I got weak and such pain I can not describe. At sundown the Indians left us after fighting with us all day. At 11 o'clock arrived at Rancho de Taos. I was taken off my horse, having ridden 25 miles after being wounded. I was placed in a wagon; taken to the fort (Cantonment Burgwin); and put to bed in the hospital."
>
> —Bennett, *Forts*, 55

Strangely, no one else recalls finding the body of the man killed by Apaches.

55. Chief Chacon said: "At the time the fight began, the Indians were making clay pottery and that some of the Indians were even on their knees begging for peace. The Americans killed a chief Pacheco, and a ball cut out the entrails of a woman, who survived." Johnson and Adams, *Final Report*, 20.

56. This is from Bronson's recollection. Ibid., 149.

57. Strowbridge recalled the war whoop and an old soldier telling him to cap his piece. Ibid., 155. They carried muzzle-loading musketoons, horse pistols, and a proud few had revolving .44-caliber Colt Dragoon pistols. All required a percussion cap whose loading

armed the weapon. It fitted over a nipple at the rear of the chamber, or six at the rear of the cylinder on the revolvers. On the move, a cap riding under the hammer might accidentally discharge the weapon with disastrous effect. The soldier carried two pouches on his belt. One held paper cartridges, a premeasured charge of powder and ball wrapped in paper. The military load for musketoon was "buck and ball," a .69-caliber ball topped by four .31-caliber buckshot. The other held percussion caps. Ibid., 42–43.

58. This is from Maher's testimony at Davidson's hearing. On that heavily wooded hillside, Maher would have had great difficulty seeing anyone more than thirty paces away. If Lieutenant Davidson could see the man, Maher, some distance back in the column probably couldn't have. Ibid., 160–61. Davidson had a different recollection and Lt. Bell, who picked up the story from Davidson's report, survivors, and speaking with Davidson, had a different version. In his combined accounts, Johnson summarized this event as follows:

> At some point, either as the troops entered the narrow canyon or as they advanced up the slopes, the Indians let out a war whoop (Davidson, in United States Government 1856b) or someone from the Apache speaking in plain English (Pvt. Maher in United States Government 1856b), broken English (Pvt. Weldon in United States Government 1856b) or Spanish (Lt. Bell in United States Government 1854aa) called out to them to come on if they wanted a fight. At that point, Davidson felt he had no choice but to attack.
> —Ibid., 25

Bronson didn't mention this at all. Those that do say he spoke good English, broken English, or Spanish. They'd have had great difficulty seeing a man in the Indian camp at all. There is no record of a white man with the Jicarilla in this period. The episode is doubtful, but it is crucial to Lieutenant Davidson. This was his sole cause for launching an attack. It isn't much of a cause in any event even by the standards of the time.

59. The dismounting and advancing as two platoons under Kent and Holbrook is documented in almost all of the accounts.

60. The ridge where the Jicarilla camp lay was above eight thousand feet elevation and the climb, through loose pine needles, very steep indeed.

61. Strowbridge recalled: "We had moved out about 15 or 20 paces when the firing commenced, I can not say from which side first, from us or from the Indians. We charged the hill and took it, driving the Indians from it." This is to say, that when the first firing occurred at least some of his platoon was still on the hill below the camp. Johnson and Adams, *Final Report*, 155. Bronson recalled: "After advancing some hundred and fifty yards, I heard shots fired from the Indian Camp. The command then increased their gait and charged on the Indian Camp, and drove the Indians from it." Johnson and Adams, *Final Report*, 149. Maher recalled: "and when we moved on the camp after dismounting, the Indians fired on us first killing one man and wounding another." Johnson and Adams, *Final Report*, 160–61.

62. The Picuris tell the story of the battle saying that the soldiers shot and killed the two old people. "This made the Apaches who were hiding very mad and they came out of

their hiding places to attack the soldiers." Johnson and Adams, *Final Report*, 22. Chief Chacon mentioned that Chief Pacheco was killed and one woman wounded. Johnson and Adams, *Final Report*, 20. Today the Jicarilla say that no Jicarilla died. Immediately after the battle they claimed that two warriors had been killed. That makes the Picuris account improbable but it gives some idea of how the battle began and conveys Chacon's message that the Jicarilla did not want a fight.

63. At his court of inquiry, Davidson spent much effort in demonstrating that no wounded or dead had been left behind to be tortured or mutilated (scalped) by the Jicarilla until they were in extremis. It was a matter of honor. The court of inquiry from which many of these accounts are drawn was an interesting affair. In December 1854, Lieutenant Bell wrote a letter from Fort Leavenworth, KST, claiming that the battle had been conducted in an incompetent manner and otherwise casting doubt on Davidson's fitness and honor. Two years after the battle, in 1856, Davidson demanded a court of inquiry into his behavior. There was no "prosecution." Bell's letter made the accusations. Davidson called the witnesses and asked the questions. Although many of the witnesses denied that Davidson had asked about their testimony ahead of time, many were in his company and it was clear he knew what they would say. He ran the entire affair.

64. Sergeant Kent's body was found the next day in the Jicarilla camp. Four more soldiers were found between the camp and the horse-holders' position. Johnson and Adams, *Final Report*, 25.

65. Matson, Daniel S., and Albert H. Schroeder. "Cordero's Description of the Apache—1796." *New Mexico Historical Review*, Vol. 32/4 (October 1957), 345.

66. Johnson and Adams, *Final Report*, 120–24.

67. Ibid.

68. Archaeological evidence, the ratio of dropped percussion caps to caps that had been fired, suggests that the troops were at this point disciplined and in control. Ibid., 67.

69. Strowbridge mentions an exchange between the doctor and the lieutenant. Bronson points to Davidson's courage and to his calming the troops. On the stand, one soldier after another denied that such an order had been given. All praised the lieutenant's courage and leadership. On the other hand, Davidson selected who would speak and he asked the questions.

70. In his letter, that led to the court of inquiry, Lieutenant Bell said:

> and now the command is given "mount men and save yourselves." This Lt. does not or at least did not deny. This order was calculated to strike terror to the heart of the bravest soldier, for he would know that nothing but the utmost exertion could prevent his falling a prey to the merciless savage. This order was alone sufficient to ruin a command. The consequence was a disorderly flight over ground of the difficulties of which the Indians well knew how to take advantage. Every other consideration was forgotten in that of personal safety and hence the entire abandonment of arms etc.
> —Johnson and Adams, *Final Report*, 120–24

71. Bronson reported: "I saw Capt Davidson run back from front to rear and the Indians were driven back by himself and a few men with him." Ibid., 149.

72. Bronson reports this consultation. Ibid.

73. Strowbridge recalled:

> We got about halfway up the hill, when Capt. Davidson gave the order to halt. Dr. Magruder was in advance of the men going up the hill. Capt Davidson gave the command a second time, to halt in front, the third time, he said Dr. Magruder for God's sake halt. He then halted & the men halted. Capt Davidson then asked the Doctor to help him to take charge of the men. Dr. Magruder said he would. We rested there a minute or two and saw the Indians crossing the ravine to get to the top of the mountain to head us off."
> —Ibid., 156–57

74. Strowbridge's names for soldiers killed and wounded don't match the names on the official list. He was recorded at the Court of Inquiry two years after the event. He gives a feel for the action that agrees in general with other accounts, adding more details than most.

75. Official sources say twenty-three were wounded. It seems probable that thirty-six were wounded since a wounded man was sent as express rider. The official count may not include those who were less severely wounded.

76. Michno, *Encyclopedia*, 24. "With 36 wounded out of the remaining 40." Sabin, Edwin L. *Kit Carson Days, 1809–1868: Adventures in the Path of Empire*, 2 Volumes. Lincoln: University of Nebraska Press, 1995 (1935), 661.

77. Anonymous. *Apache Indians VII: Jicarilla Apache Tribe: Historical Materials 1540–1887*. New York: Garland Publishing, 1974, 140.

78. Moody, Marshall D. "Kit Carson, Agent to the Indians in New Mexico 1853–1861." *New Mexico Historical Review*, Vol. 28/1 (January 1953), 4.

79. Dunlay, *Kit Carson*, 157.

80. Johnson and Adams, *Final Report*, 120–24.

81. Bell accused Davidson of cowardice and of panicking when he called for withdrawal from the horse-holders' position that he had held for an hour or two, though perhaps not the three that Davidson claimed. Davidson lost one man, Sergeant Kent, in the Apache village, and four on the way down the hill. He did not lose any more at the horse-holders' site although he was there for some time and suffered wounded men and horses. The archaeology shows that his men remained calm. Nothing seems to have occurred to induce a sudden panic. Evidence suggests that he remained calm and in control later in the battle when his unit suffered seventeen dead and when order began to disintegrate. A unit on the move cannot defend itself effectively. Reloading becomes problematic. Carrying equipment and assisting the wounded leaves men unable to use their weapons effectively. The description of the battle says they moved and stopped to defend and moved again. Classic military tactics would have had half of the effectives—that is, those still able to fight—hold and fire while the other half moved, leapfrogging past each other as they went. With so many wounded and dead, and with the enemy attacking from all

sides, this would have been very difficult. The lieutenant intended to seek a new defensive position but on arriving found it indefensible and had to continue the withdrawal. Meline wrote: "Kit Carson, in speaking of the affair says; 'Nearly every person engaged in, and who survived that day's bloody battle, has since told me that his commanding officer never once sought shelter, but stood manfully exposed to the aim of the Indians, encouraging his men, and apparently unmindful of his own life. In the retreat, he was as cool and collected as if under the guns of his fort. The only anxiety he exhibited was for the safety of his remaining men.'" Meline, James F. *Two Thousand Miles on Horseback: Santa Fe and Back: A Summer Tour through Kansas, Nebraska, Colorado, and New Mexico in the Year 1866*. Albuquerque: Horn & Wallace, 1966, 104.

82. Murphy, Lawrence. "The United States Army in Taos, 1847–1852." *New Mexico Historical Review*, Vol. 47/1 (January 1972), 11–12.

83. Gorenfeld, Will. "The Taos Mutiny of 1855." *New Mexico Historical Review*, Vol. 88/3 (Summer 2013).

84. Johnson and Adams, *Final Report*, 12.

85. Ibid., 72.

86. Ibid., 123.

87. Haley, James L. *Apaches: A History and Culture Portrait*. Norman: University of Oklahoma Press, 1981, 210.

Chapter 12

1. Both villages are near Ojo Caliente.

2. Conejos is in the San Luis Valley between Taos and Fort Massachusetts. Casa Maria, 1908. Goddard, Pliny Earle. *Jicarilla Apache Texts*. Charleston, SC: BiblioBazaar, 2008, 122.

3. Rodenbough, Theophilus F. *From Everglade to Cañon with the Second Dragoons*. Norman: University of Oklahoma Press, 2000, 178.

4. James H. Quinn was a merchant of Taos and sometime partner of Lucien Maxwell.

5. John Mostin served as Carson's "interpreter" from January 1854 to October 1859, when he died. Carson did not require an interpreter, but was authorized one. He needed a clerk, since he was illiterate, but a clerk was not authorized. Governor Meriwether gave Kit grief over listing a clerk on the payroll.

6. Carter, Harvey Lewis. *"Dear Old Kit": The Historical Christopher Carson*. Norman: University of Oklahoma Press, 1990, 135–36.

7. Garland to Cooke, April 7, 1854, tense changed, quoted in Haley, James L. *Apaches: A History and Culture Portrait*. Norman: University of Oklahoma Press, 1981, 210.

8. "Proclamation," *Santa Fe Weekly Gazette*, April 22, 1854.

9. The country they were passing through is over six thousand feet elevation, much of it over seven thousand. Colonel Cooke mentions the snow, over and over, and snowstorms as well, as does Kit Carson. Cooke to Nichols, May 24, 1854, Vol. 2, No. 175-180, Fort Union Collection, Highlands University, Las Vegas, NM.

10. *Arroyo Hondo* means deep dry streambed. The town and the arroyo is one of the places where a stream has cut an approach to the Rio Grande Gorge.

11. Cooke mentions the cattle in his account.

12. Carter, *"Dear Old Kit,"* 136.

13. Cooke to Nichols, May 24, 1854, Vol. 2, No. 175-180, Fort Union Collection, Highlands University, Las Vegas, NM.

14. Carter, *"Dear Old Kit,"* 137.

15. Quinn, James H., May 2, 1854, Vol. 2, No. 126-129, Fort Union Collection, Highlands University, Las Vegas, NM.

16. Ibid.

17. Cooke, Vol. 2, No. 175-180.

18. Rodenbough, *Second Dragoons*, 178–80.

19. Carson to Messervy, April 19, 1854, Vol. 2, No. 147, Fort Union Collection, Highlands University, Las Vegas, NM; Anonymous, *Jicarilla Apache Tribe: Historical Materials 1540–1887.* New York: Garland Publishing, 1974, 131–33.

20. Quinn, Vol. 2, No. 126-129.

21. Cooke, Vol. 2, No. 175-180.

22. Abiquiu.

23. Carson to Messervy, April 19, 1854, Vol. 2, No. 147-148, Fort Union Collection, Highlands University, Las Vegas, NM; Anonymous, *Jicarilla Apache Tribe*, 131–33.

24. It is possible that Chacon, the peace chief, who had been so recently reported near Fort Massachusetts with the Ute, was the leader. The army counted two warriors per lodge and thus seventy-seven lodges indicated 140 warriors. The force of one hundred that had fought Davidson had grown perhaps by an addition from Chacon's immediate band. This also demonstrates again that the Apache loss at Cieneguilla was limited to from two to four warriors.

25. The author admires Philip St. George Cooke, who was one of the greatest soldiers in the West. He led a long and distinguished career and had no lack of either courage or battle cunning. He also knew how to present his accomplishments in the very best light, not without justification in this case. This was the enemy force that had handed Davidson a severe defeat at little cost to themselves.

26. Cooke, Vol. 2, No. 175-180.

27. Dunn to Messervy, April 14, 1854, Vol. 2, No. 141, Fort Union Collection, Highlands University, Las Vegas, NM. Kit Carson was in the field with Colonel Cooke. Dunn was acting as Indian agent in his absence just as Messervy was acting governor.

28. Cooke, Vol. 2, No. 175-180.

29. Rodenbough, *Second Dragoons*, 178–80; Cooke to Nichols, May 24, 1854, Vol. 2, No. 175-180, Fort Union Collection, Highlands University, Las Vegas, NM; The Chronological List recalls the actions of April 8 as follows: "April 8, 1854, Ojo Caliente, Co d 2nd Art, H & G 1st Dragoons, H 2nd Dragoons. Ltc. Cooke, 1 enlisted killed, 1 wounded." Floyd, Dale E., introduction. *Chronological List of Actions from January 15, 1837 to January 1891.* Washington, DC: Old Army Press, 1979, 15.

30. The word *provisions* above is my guess. The person who transcribed the original letter had written *suspicions*, which in this context doesn't make any sense.

31. Carson to Messervy, April 12, 1854, Vol. 2, No. 138, Fort Union Collection, Highlands University, Las Vegas, NM.

32. Moody, Marshall D. "Kit Carson, Agent to the Indians in New Mexico 1853–1861." *New Mexico Historical Review*, Vol. 28/1 (January 1953), 4.

33. Dunn to Messervy, Vol. 2, No. 141, Fort Union Collection, Highlands University, Las Vegas, NM.

34. Garland to Thomas, April 30, 1854, Vol. 2, No. 161, Fort Union Collection, Highlands University, Las Vegas, NM; Anonymous, *Jicarilla Apache Tribe*, 133–34.

35. The author's high school roommate and lifelong friend, Richard Valdez, owns a ranch at Tusas where his family has lived since the nineteenth century. There is no electric power and the road to Tusas closes in the winter. The probability is strong that he is related to Captain Valdez.

36. Brooks expedition, May 1854, Vol. 2, No. 165-166, Fort Union Collection, Highlands University, Las Vegas, NM.

37. The Red River is north of Taos and now known as Questa. The Canadian River was also known as the Rio Colorado, which translates to Red River, but is east of the Sangre de Cristo.

38. Carter, *"Dear Old Kit,"* 139–40.

39. Casa Maria seems to be describing Fisher's Peak and the subsequent joining with the Ute. Surviving Mexicans identified a few Jicarilla among the one hundred or so Ute who attacked Pueblo. The military had a tendency to claim as members of Indian bands they attacked anyone that was "needful," that is, politically expedient to name among those they had just attacked. Probably, they honestly believed the claims, but supporting evidence is often scarce. Throughout the campaign of 1855, Jicarilla are always said, almost vaguely, as having been among the Ute attackers. There is evidence that a party of twenty-five warriors operated with the Ute during this period. Casa Maria seems to be recalling the destruction of Pueblo and the subsequent movement of the Utes being pursued by the army. This makes a case that he and his family were among the Ute. Goddard, *Jicarilla Apache Texts*, 122. We will get to the story of the Pueblo Christmas Massacre in a few pages. The two Sandoval brothers and Chepita Miera were taken captive by the Ute-Jicarilla war party. Confirming Casa Maria's story of dancing with the scalp, we have the recollection of one of the brothers: "She turned around and saw an Indian with bow and arrow in his hands. As she started to run away, the Indian shot another arrow, which struck her in the back and came out through her breast. Seizing the head of the arrow in her hands, she fell to the ground, and the Indian children, who had been standing around watching, stoned her to death with small rocks. The Indians told Felix Sandoval that Chepita had to die because she was down-hearted and refused to be comforted. A month after the massacre, soldiers from Taos discovered Chepita Miera's scalp hanging from a tree in the Wet Mountain Valley. The scalp had long black hair with ribbons on it." Lecompte, Janet. *Pueblo, Hardscrabble, Greenhorn: Society on the High Plains, 1832–1856*. Norman: University of Oklahoma Press, 1978, 250.

40. Carleton and Carson met in 1851 when Carson was returning from making purchases for Maxwell in St. Louis and was accosted by Cheyenne.

41. Michno, Gregory. *Encyclopedia of the Indian Wars: Western Battles and Skirmishes 1850–1890*. Missoula, MT: Mountain Press Publishing, 2003, 26–27.

42. Carson to Messervy, June 12, 1854, Vol. 2, No. 192-193, Fort Union Collection, Highlands University, Las Vegas, NM.

43. The Spanish Peaks.

44. Carson to Messervy, June 12, 1854.

45. Carter, *"Dear Old Kit,"* 140–42.

46. Quaife, Milo Milton, ed. *Kit Carson's Autobiography*. Lincoln: University of Nebraska Press, 1935.

47. Quinn's Report, June 1854, Vol. 2, No. 167-168, Fort Union Collection, Highlands University, Las Vegas, NM.

48. Ibid.

49. Ibid.

50. Carson to Messervy, June 12, 1854.

51. Macrae to Nichols, June 29, 1854, Vol. 2, No. 199, Fort Union Collection, Highlands University, Las Vegas, NM.

52. A squadron is akin to a battalion, two or more companies but less than a full regiment of ten companies.

53. Macrae to Sykes, June 29, 1854, Vol. 2, No. 198, Fort Union Collection, Highlands University, Las Vegas, NM.

54. Michno, *Encyclopedia*, 27; Floyd, *Chronological List*, 15.

55. Rodenbough, *Second Dragoons*, 526.

56. Richard Stoddard Ewell (1817–1872) went on to be second in command under General Thomas "Stonewall" Jackson and to command a corps at the Battle of Gettysburg. In southern New Mexico (Arizona), he was the first military officer to confront Cochise. Carter notes that Ewell was a very successful company commander of the 1st Dragoons and would later win renown in fighting Mescaleros, Western, and Chiricahua Apaches. Carter, *"Dear Old Kit,"* 142.

57. Garland to Thomas, June 30, 1854, Vol. 2, No. 196, Fort Union Collection, Highlands University, Las Vegas, NM.

58. Rio Arriba County, the Up River, north of Santa Fe. The four northern counties at the time were Taos, Rio Arriba, Santa Fe, and San Miguel.

59. Garland to Thomas, June 30, 1854, Vol. 2, No. 204, Fort Union Collection, Highlands University, Las Vegas, NM.

60. Garland to Thomas, July 30, 1854, Vol. 2, No. 211, Fort Union Collection, Highlands University, Las Vegas, NM.

61. Utley, Robert M. *Frontiersmen in Blue: The United States Army and the Indian, 1848–1865*. New York: Macmillan, 1967, 146.

62. Garland to Thomas, September 30, 1854, Vol. 2, No. 219, Fort Union Collection, Highlands University, Las Vegas, NM.

63. Dunlay, Thomas W. *Kit Carson and the Indians*. Lincoln: University of Nebraska Press, 2000, 169.

64. Cheyenne and Arapaho spoke the same language as the two tribes only divided from each other around 1800. They would have been difficult to distinguish from one another.

65. Dunlay, *Kit Carson*, 170.

66. Sabin, Edwin L. *Kit Carson Days, 1809–1868: Adventures in the Path of Empire*, 2 Volumes. Lincoln: University of Nebraska Press, 1995 (1935), 666. Utley speculated that the clothing given the Ute may have been infected with smallpox. Michno, *Encyclopedia*, 30; Utley, *Frontiersmen*, 146.

67. Taylor, Morris F. "Campaigns against the Jicarillas, 1855." *New Mexico Historical Review*, Vol. 45 (1970), 121.

Chapter 13

1. Mahan, Bill. "Fort Massachusetts." *San Luis Valley Historian*, Vol. 15/2 (Spring 1983), 4.

2. It is known as Mount Blanca because its peak was perpetually snow covered. It is one of the sacred mountains of the Jicarilla and a boundary of their range.

3. Burgwin.

4. Peters, Dr. DeWitt Clinton, DeWitt Clinton Peters Papers, Bancroft Library, Berkeley, CA, March 3, 1855.

5. Ibid., December 20, 1854.

6. Lecompte, Janet. *Pueblo, Hardscrabble, Greenhorn: Society on the High Plains, 1832–1856*. Norman: University of Oklahoma Press, 1978, 271; Utley (Utley, Robert M., *Frontiersmen in Blue: The United States Army and the Indian, 1848–1865*. New York: Macmillan, 1967, 146), and Sabin (Sabin, Edwin L., *Kit Carson Days, 1809–1868: Adventures in the Path of Empire*, 2 Volumes. Lincoln: University of Nebraska Press, 1995 [1935], 666), say: "On Christmas Day, a Ute and Jicarilla Apache war party of 100 attacked the small settlement of Pueblo, on the Arkansas River. They killed 15 men and wounded 2, carried off a woman and 2 children, and stole 200 horses."

7. Fauntleroy to Nichols, December 10, 1854, Vol. 2, No. 237, Fort Union Collection, Highlands University, Las Vegas, NM.

8. Unfortunately, the actions of irregulars, volunteers, and militia are not recorded in the *Chronological List* (Floyd, Dale E., introduction. *Chronological List of Actions from January 15, 1837 to January 1891*. Washington, DC: Old Army Press, 1979). Fauntleroy was already preparing to go north to the San Luis Valley to engage the Ute and he made no report of the outcome of this pursuit.

9. Fauntleroy to Nichols, February 9, 1854, Vol. 3, No. 30, Fort Union Collection, Highlands University, Las Vegas, NM.

10. Canadian River.

11. Canyon Largo. Largo is Spanish for long or tall.

12. Chacon, Eusebio, trans. Rafael Chacon. "Campaign Against Utes and Apaches in Southern Colorado, 1855." *Colorado Magazine*, Vol. 11 (May 1934), 108.

13. Floyd, *Chronological List*, 16; Peters, DeWitt C. *The Life and Adventures of Kit Carson, the Nestor of the Rocky Mountains, from Facts Narrated by Himself*. Middlesex: Echo Library, 2006, 253. Dr. Peters was assigned as surgeon at Fort Massachusetts. He wrote the first biography of Kit Carson. He and Kit fell out perhaps over profits to be shared that were not forthcoming. The book did not sell well. Then again, Kit may have disliked the writing style, which is positively florid.

14. Peters, DeWitt Clinton Peters Papers, March 3, 1855.

15. Peters, *Kit Carson,* 253.

16. Ibid., 254.

17. Taylor, Morris F. "Campaigns against the Jicarillas, 1855." *New Mexico Historical Review,* Vol. 45 (1970), 124. The Ute went to war because they were upset over the "poisoned" blankets given to their chiefs, but they were also deeply disturbed by the invasion of the San Luis Valley.

18. Peters, *Kit Carson,* 254.

19. The *Chronological List* says: "Mar 19, 1855, Cochotope Pass, NM Cos D & F 1st Dragoons, Co D 2nd Arty, Capt H. Brooks, 2 wounded, 100 Apache and Utah Indians engaged by Col. Fauntleroy's command." Floyd, *Chronological List,* 16. On May 5, Colonel Fauntleroy wrote: "I take this opportunity to correct a mistake made in my report of the fight of the 19th of March, in which I called the pass where it took place the Coochetopa. It was the Chowatache Pass, and is the spot almost identical with our last affair, as related above." Fauntleroy to Sturgis, May 5, 1855, Vol. 3, No. 66, Fort Union Collection, Highlands University, Las Vegas, NM. Working from his phonetic attempt at the name, I take Chowatche to be Saguache.

20. Peters, *Kit Carson,* 254.

21. Taylor, Morris F. "Action at Fort Massachusetts: The Indian Campaign of 1855." *Colorado Magazine,* Vol. 42/4 (1965), 298–300.

22. Dunlay, Thomas W. *Kit Carson and the Indians.* Lincoln: University of Nebraska Press, 2000, 171.

23. Ibid.

24. Taylor, "Fort Massachusetts," 299.

25. Carter says this was reported by Lucien Stewart, although the flanking attack is not mentioned in other sources. It is likely to have occurred as reported. It is not uncommon for different participants to see the battle in a different light. Carter, Harvey Lewis. *"Dear Old Kit": The Historical Christopher Carson.* Norman: University of Oklahoma Press, 1990, 145n311.

26. Chacon, "Campaign," 109.

27. Taylor, "Fort Massachusetts," 299.

28. Corrected on May 5 to Saguache.

29. Taylor, "Fort Massachusetts," 300.

30. Taylor, "Campaigns 1855," 125.

31. Carter says that the encounter was near modern Salida, Colorado. Carter, *"Dear Old Kit,"* 146n313.

32. Chacon, "Campaign," 109–11.

33. Taylor, "Campaigns 1855," 125. The *Chronological List* records: "March 21-23, Poncha Pass, Arkansas River, Cos B & F 1st Drag, Co D 2nd Arty, Capt H. Brooks, 1 enlisted soldier wounded." Floyd, *Chronological List,* 16.

34. Chacon, "Campaign," 109–12.

35. Carter, *"Dear Old Kit,"* 146.

36. Whittlesey to Sturgis, May 1, 1855, Vol. 3, No. 69, Fort Union Collection, Highlands University, Las Vegas, NM; Taylor, "Campaigns," 126.

37. Poncha Pass (9,011 feet) separates the Rio Grande drainage basin from that of the Arkansas. Carter, *"Dear Old Kit,"* 146n315.

38. Peters, DeWitt Clinton Peters Papers, May 10, 1855; Carter, *"Dear Old Kit,"* 146.

39. Garland to Thomas, May 31, 1855, Vol. 3, No. 84, Fort Union Collection, Highlands University, Las Vegas, NM.

40. Taylor, "Campaigns 1855," 127–28.

41. Garland to Thomas, May 31, 1855, Vol. 3, No. 84, Fort Union Collection, Highlands University, Las Vegas, NM.

42. Carter, *"Dear Old Kit,"* 146.

43. Easton to Commander at Abiquiu, June 17, 1855, Vol. 3, No. 92, Fort Union Collection, Highlands University, Las Vegas, NM.

44. Carter, *"Dear Old Kit,"* 146.

45. "A Friend to Truth," *Santa Fe Weekly Gazette*, March 17, 1855.

46. Carson, C. to *Santa Fe Weekly Gazette*, September 5, 1855, *Santa Fe Weekly Gazette*, September 15, 1855.

47. "Return of Gov. Meriwether from Abiquiu," *Santa Fe Weekly Gazette*, September 15, 1855.

48. "Tierra Amarilla, New Mexico." *Wikipedia*, https://en.wikipedia.org/wiki/Tierra_Amarilla_New_Mexico. I find Wikipedia useful for basic and undisputed facts that can be verified elsewhere. In this case, Torrez, Robert J., and Robert Trapp, ed. *Rio Arriba: A New Mexico County*. Los Ranchos, NM: Rio Grande Books, 2010.

49. The Padre was unbelievably powerful. New Mexico had been a mission field and its priests were brothers of the Franciscan order and Spaniards. Martínez was the first New Mexican ever elevated to the priesthood. After 1830, when the Mexican state, distrusting Spaniards, expelled the brothers he was one of only two priests in New Mexico. He obtained the unusual permission to open a seminary and ordain priests. By 1853 most of the priests in New Mexico were his former pupils. He was also probably the leader of the powerful Penitente secret society. In addition, he had been a member of the legislature under Mexico and served in the new American legislature. His family was from Abiquiu and owned vast tracts of land. He was one of the richest men in New Mexico. See Hocking, Doug. "New Mexico's Reviled Heroic Padre." *Wild West Magazine*, December 2013, 46–51.

50. "Memorial to the President," *Santa Fe Weekly Gazette*, May 3, 1856.

51. "Tierra Amarilla," *Wikipedia*. The grant belonged to a Martínez from Abiquiu, a close relative of the Padre.

52. It seems this proposal would have put the reservation in the fertile land of Death Valley. The thinking here is unclear, but it's likely that this "fertile" western paradise was probably a figment of a poor understanding of geography.

53. Murphy, Lawrence R. *Lucien Bonaparte Maxwell: Napoleon of the Southwest*. Norman: University of Oklahoma Press, 1983, 122.

54. Carter, *"Dear Old Kit,"* 147.

55. Ibid., 144.

56. Dunlay, *Kit Carson*, 171.

57. Carter, *"Dear Old Kit,"* 147.

58. Dunlay, *Kit Carson*, 184.

59. Santiago, Mark. *A Bad Peace and a Good War: Spain and the Mescalero Apache Uprising of 1795–1799*. Norman: University of Oklahoma Press, 2018.

60. Dunlay, *Kit Carson*, 184.

61. The author has to wonder if Davidson, whose experience involved slaughtering Pomo Indians in the Bloody Island Massacre, thought he could get away with the same kind of aggression against Apaches. The remarks attributed to him by Lieutenant David Bell certainly indicate that Davidson thought the Jicarilla an easy target.

Chapter 14

1. This is the same Bonneville made famous by Washington Irving in *The Adventures of Captain Bonneville*.

2. Johnson, David M., and Chris Adams. *Final Report on the Battle of Cieneguilla: A Jicarilla Apache Victory Over the U.S. Dragoons, March 30, 1854*. Santa Fe, NM: Southwestern Region, 2009, 130.

3. Ibid., 130.

4. Ibid., 132.

5. Dunlay, Thomas W. *Kit Carson and the Indians*. Lincoln: University of Nebraska Press, 2000, 184.

6. Moody, Marshall D. "Kit Carson, Agent to the Indians in New Mexico, 1853." *New Mexico Historical Review*, Vol. 28/1 (January 1953), 19–20.

7. Carter, Harvey Lewis. *"Dear Old Kit": The Historical Christopher Carson*. Norman: University of Oklahoma Press, 1990, 147.

8. Dunlay, *Kit Carson*, 175.

9. Abiquiu is on the Chama River. This appears to refer to the treaty negotiations of September 1855.

10. Dunlay ponders by what authority the dragoon officer might have arrested a civilian.

11. Dunlay, *Kit Carson*, 176. My presentation is drawn from Dunlay and Carter. Meriwether, David. *My Life in the Mountains and on the Plains. The Newly Discovered Autobiography*. Norman: University of Oklahoma Press, 1965, 226–32. It does not mention the attempt upon his life by the disgruntled Tabeguache Ute.

12. Carter, *"Dear Old Kit,"* 148n320.

13. Ibid., 147–49.

14. Pueblo in Spanish means village. Kit was talking about permanent, adobe homes, much like those of the Pueblo Indians.

15. Mechanic is an old term for people like blacksmiths with the skills to make and mend tools.

16. Dunlay, *Kit Carson*, 185.

17. Ibid., 186.

Chapter 15

1. Works consulted include: Frazier, Donald S. *Blood & Treasure: Confederate Empire in the Southwest*. College Station: Texas A&M University Press, 1997; Taylor, John M.

Bloody Valverde: A Civil War Battle on the Rio Grande, February 21, 1862. Albuquerque: University of New Mexico Press, 1999; Hocking, Doug. *Black Legend: George Bascom, Cochise, and the Start of the Apache Wars.* Guilford, CT: TwoDot, 2018; Thompson, Jerry D. *Civil War in the Southwest: Recollections of the Sibley Brigade.* College Station: Texas A&M University Press, 2001; Windham, William T. "The Problem of Supply in the Trans-Mississippi Confederacy." *Journal of Southern History* 27/2 (May 1961).

2. Mesilla is today a suburb of Las Cruces, New Mexico. On the Rio Grande, it was the county seat of Doña Ana County, which stretched all the way to the Colorado River and included Tubac and Tucson, the only towns then occupied in what became Arizona.

3. Overland Mail is the correct name for the organization assembled by John Butterfield, which never bore his name.

4. Mail, the Pony Express, and emigrants ran over the Oregon-California Trail far to the north, through South Pass in what became Wyoming.

5. Murphy, Lawrence R. *Lucien Bonaparte Maxwell: Napoleon of the Southwest.* Norman: University of Oklahoma Press, 1983, 122; Carson to William Dole, October 17, 1862.

6. Murphy, *Maxwell*, 122.

7. Ibid., 77. Opler, Morris E. "Jicarilla Apache Territory, Economy, and Society in 1850." *Southwestern Journal of Anthropology* 27 (1971), 309–29.

8. Bender, Averam B. *Apache Indians IX: A Study of Jicarilla Apache Indians 1846–1887.* New York: Garland Publishing, 1974 (1959), 76–79.

9. "Shooting Scrape Graydon," *Weekly Arizonian*, April 21, 1859.

10. Fort Buchanan was about fifty miles southeast of Tucson at the headwaters of Sonoita Creek, three miles west of the modern town of Sonoita.

11. Ake, Jeff, and James B. O'Neil, ed. *They Die but Once: The Story of a Tejano.* New York: Knight Publications, 1935, 40. Sarah Bowman was an army wife and laundress, red haired and over six feet tall. She was nicknamed after the largest ship of the time, the Great Western. She won distinction for her courage in the Mexican War at Fort Brown.

12. Paddy rode with Surgeon Bernard John Dowling Irwin, the Fighting Surgeon, with twelve men, all for which the 7th Infantry had riding mules, to break a cordon of five hundred Apaches under Cochise and relieve Lieutenant George Bascom and the sixty-six men with him. Surgeon Irwin received the Medal of Honor for this action. Paddy was along as civilian interpreter.

13. Fort Stanton is about ten miles from Lincoln, which was not there at this time. The Sacramento Mountains were home to the Mescalero Apache.

14. He was promoted to general in 1862.

15. Sabin, Edwin L. *Kit Carson Days, 1809–1868: Adventures in the Path of Empire*, 2 Volumes. Lincoln: University of Nebraska Press, 1995 (1935), 702.

16. Part of the mission of Fort Stanton was to patrol the Pecos River guarding against another Confederate invasion. Any such invasion would either have to come up the Rio Grande or up the Pecos River as these provided water.

17. We are forced to rely on Graydon's report. Clearly there was mutual suspicion between the two sides.

18. Thompson, Jerry D. *Desert Tiger: Captain Paddy Graydon and the Civil War in the Far Southwest.* El Paso: Western Press, University of Texas at El Paso, 1992, 54–61.

19. Sabin, *Kit Carson*, 704–5.
20. Bender provides the following head counts of Jicarilla at various agencies (Bender, Averam B. *Apache Indians IX: A Study of Jicarilla Apache Indians 1846–1887*. New York: Garland Publishing, 1974 (1959), 147–51). At times the tribe was divided between agencies, i.e., Abiquiu, Taos, and Cimarron. In theory these counts should be added together, but some Apache may have visited more than one agency; they weren't confined. They came in to receive presents. In other cases, the count is lumped together with Utes. While eight hundred were at Mescalero, still others may have been roaming the Llano Estacado. Bosque Redondo/Fort Sumner did not report issuing supplies to any Jicarilla. Here are Bender's figures:

Nov 10, 1846	Gov. Bent	500	100 lodges	
Mar 31, 1851	LT J.P. Holliday	200	60 warriors	near Smoky Mtns 60 miles east of Manzano Mountains; led by Chacon
Feb 7, 1853	Michael Steck	400–500	100 lodges	
May 30, 1853	Gov. Lane	600		
Aug 31, 1853	Gov. Meriwether	250	150 warriors	vicinity Rio Puerco
Sep 15, 1855	Gov. Meriwether	200–300	100 warriors	west of Rio Grande
Sep 30, 1857	Diego Archuleta	1,000	300 warriors	
Aug 29, 1860	Kit Carson	950		vicinity Taos Agency
Sep 24, 1860	Gov. Collins	1,000	including a few Mescaleros	
Sep 1, 1862	WFM Arny	960	at Cimarron actual count	
Sep 3, 1862	Jose Manzanares	1,300	Cimarron & Abiquiu	
Sep 10, 1865	Felipe Delgado	900 or 1,000	Cimarron	
Sep 30, 1865	Labadi	987	Cimarron actual count	
Jan 9, 1866	Delgado	900		
Nov 18, 1866	Norton	800	Cimarron	
1867	Dr. William Bell	500	on Maxwell Res Cimarron & Taos	
Jun 24, 1867	WFM Arny	1,000		
Jan 29, 1868	WFM Arny	814		
Nov 19, 1868	John Ward	400	a portion roaming	
Sep 15, 1868	NM Davis	1150	Moache Utes & Jicarillas	
Dec 12, 1868	Thomas Kearns	300	with 1000 Wememutche & 300 Capote	
Jan 11, 1869	Sec War Schofield	800	200 warriors	
Jul 19, 1870	Arny	960	by actual count	
Sep 2, 1870	Arny	600 + 280	600 at Cimarron, 280 west of Rio Grande	
Nov, 1870	Arny	864		
Sep 25, 1882		747	by actual count Amargo	
Aug 1, 1887		800	returned from Mescalero to Amargo	

Carson's and Arny's figures are most likely to be correct. Some Ute and Mescalero may have been reported as Jicarilla and vice versa. Some may have been roaming until after 1887. The actual count lies somewhere between 960 and not more than 1200.

21. Murphy, *Maxwell*, 130–31.

22. Sabin, *Kit Carson*, 707.

23. Ibid.

24. Ibid., 708.

25. Ibid., 711.

26. Canyon de Chelly is pronounced deh shay. It is a corruption of a Navajo word rendered into Spanish and then English, *Tsegi*, which means something like "rock canyon" or "in a canyon." The name appears in other forms all over Navajo country. Grant, Campbell. *Canyon de Chelly: Its People and Rock Art.* Tucson: University of Arizona Press, 1978, 3.

27. Sabin, *Kit Carson*, 717.

28. Dunlay, Thomas W. *Kit Carson and the Indians.* Lincoln: University of Nebraska Press, 2000, 295.

29. Sabin, *Kit Carson*, 721. Carson's report of January 23, 1864.

30. Sabin, *Kit Carson*, 718.

31. Sides, Hampton. *Blood and Thunder: An Epic of the American West.* Garden City, NY: Doubleday, 2006, 358.

32. Dunlay, *Kit Carson*, 302–3.

33. Sides, *Blood and Thunder*, 360.

34. Ibid., 363.

35. Ibid., 364.

36. Bender, *Apache Indians*, 88.

37. Hyde, George E., and Svoie Lottinville, ed. *Life of George Bent: Written from his Letters.* Norman: University of Oklahoma Press, 1968, 110–11. Parole meant that a captured soldier was released on his promise not to take up arms again in the current conflict until "exchanged." Exchanged meant that officers by name and enlisted men by unit who were prisoners or paroled men were traded between the opposing forces allowing them to go back into service as fighting men. This meant that officers, who were gentlemen good to their word, did not languish in prisoner of war camps and that enlisted men did not stay in camps for long. The practice was abandoned during the Civil War with horrifying consequences. In this modern age, US soldiers swear not to give their parole.

38. Comancheros may have been hated by Texans, but they do not come close to the image Hollywood has created. They were predominantly New Mexicans who traded with the Comanche and Kiowa on the Llano Estacado. Comanches for their part divided Americans into two distinct categories: Americans and Texans.

39. George Bent recalled the fort having been constructed before 1840 and thus before he was born. Other sources make 1842 or 1843 more likely. Hyde, *George Bent*, 355–56. Lynn believes that most evidence points to Bent constructing the adobe fort in 1845, and having constructed a wooden fort somewhere nearby (nine miles? I guess that's close by West Texas standards) in 1843. Lynn, Alvin R. *Kit Carson and the First*

Battle of Adobe Walls: A Tale of Two Journeys. Lubbock: Texas Tech University Press, 2014, 70. In note 36 to page 70 he cites: "David Lavender, *Bent's Fort* (Garden City: Doubleday and Company, Inc., 1954), 264. Lavender states that Bent and St. Vrain followed soon behind Lt. Abert with adobe brick makers to establish the adobe fort. Abert camped south of there in September 1845 so the adobe building probably was constructed in the fall or winter of that year: see Galvin, *Through the Country of the Comanche Indians*, 17, 71."

40. "The sequence of events preceding the destruction of Fort Adobe is surmised. Carson's biographies do not mention Kit's trip, but George Bent had the story of it from both Carson and John Smith. (Grinnell Papers, Southwest Museum Los Angeles. Enough is known of Kit's whereabouts to ascribe the fall of 1848 as about the only time the adventure could have occurred.)" Lavender, David. *Bent's Fort.* Lincoln: University of Nebraska Press, 1954, 331.

41. Fort Bascom was about ten miles north of modern Tucumcari, New Mexico, on the Canadian River. It was named for Captain George Bascom, who had been killed at Valverde in February 1862, while commanding a company of the 7th US Infantry in the hottest part of the battle against the invading Texans. You can read about his life in Doug Hocking's *Black Legend.*

42. At the start of the Civil War, enlistments were as short as ninety days, although six months and one year were more common. Very few were recruited for the duration and many did not care to reenlist after having done their bit and seen battle and hardship. There were a great many veterans at home during the latter part of the war. Many from the California Column stayed on in New Mexico and Arizona.

43. Who had been exchanged after his capture by Confederates in Arizona in 1862.

44. Dunlay, *Kit Carson*, 324–28.

45. Goddard, Pliny Earle. *Jicarilla Apache Texts.* Charleston, SC: BiblioBazaar, 2008, 135. Goddard recorded Casa Maria's account in 1908 and published it the next year.

46. Lynn, *Adobe Walls*, 6–7.

47. Pettis, George H. *Kit Carson's Fight with the Comanche and Kiowa Indians, at the Adobe Walls on the Canadian River, November 25th, 1864.* Miami: Hard Press Publishing (Kindle), 1878, 9.

48. Ibid., 11.

49. Ibid., 13.

50. Lynn, *Adobe Walls*, 59.

51. Ibid., 60.

52. Ibid., 62.

53. Pettis, *Adobe Walls*, 17.

54. Lynn, *Adobe Walls*, 67–68. There is disagreement as to whether this person was actually the captive child, Millie Durgan, who had been adopted by Kiowa parents. Lynn provides a discussion.

55. Lynn, *Adobe Walls*, 68.

56. Pettis, *Adobe Walls*, 22–23.

57. Lynn, *Adobe Walls*, 74. Pettis estimated that there were three thousand Indians opposing them coming from several villages.
58. Pettis, *Adobe Walls*, 29.
59. Lynn, *Adobe Walls*, 75–84.
60. Dunlay, *Kit Carson*, 333.
61. Ibid., 336.
62. Lynn, *Adobe Walls*, 85.

Epilogue: The Forgotten Warriors

1. Simmons, Marc. *Kit Carson and His Three Wives: A Family History*. Albuquerque: University of New Mexico Press, 2003, 132, 141, 144.
2. Simmons, Marc. "The Strange Fate of Kit Carson," in *The Short Truth about Kit Carson and the Indians*. Taos: Kit Carson Historic Museums, 1993, 5–6.
3. Getty to McKeever, June 25, 1868, Vol. 22, No. 234, Fort Union Collection, Highlands University, Las Vegas, NM.
4. Murphy, Lawrence R. *Lucien Bonaparte Maxwell: Napoleon of the Southwest*. Norman: University of Oklahoma Press, 1983, 123.
5. Ibid., 126.
6. Bender, Averam B. *Apache Indians IX: A Study of Jicarilla Apache Indians 1846–1887*. New York: Garland Publishing, 1974 (1959), 104.
7. Averam Bender wrote that in 1867 Indian agents visiting the Jicarilla at Cañon del Oso were told that in 1846 Colonel Washington had told the Indians they could live there. Colonel Washington was not in New Mexico in 1846, however, Colonel Stephen Watts Kearny met with them near Abiquiu in September 1846, and made a treaty of peace and friendship with them and this is undoubtedly what the Jicarilla were relying on.
8. Bender, *Apache Indians*, 105.
9. Ibid., 110.
10. Brooks to Hunter, June 29, 1868, Vol. 22, No. 242, Fort Union Collection, Highlands University, Las Vegas, NM.
11. Inman, Colonel Henry. *The Old Santa Fe Trail, the Story of a Great Highway*. Kindle: CreateSpace, 2016 (1897).
12. In their early stages, before farms and stock ranches grew up around them, mining towns often subsisted on the efforts of game hunters. Deer, elk, and buffalo were on the menu.
13. Murphy, *Maxwell*, 188.
14. Gregg to A.A.G., Department of the Missouri, March 30, 1871, Vol. 25, No. 93, Fort Union Collection, Highlands University, Las Vegas, NM.
15. Tiller, Veronica E. Velarde. *The Jicarilla Apache Tribe*. Lincoln: University of Nebraska Press, 1992, 74.
16. Abiquiu was the location of the agency where the Jicarilla reported and drew rations. It may refer to anything from Abiquiu on the Chama to Cañon del Oso closer to the Rio Grande, to Tierra Amarilla many miles to the north where eventually there

was a sub-agency to the area around Ojo Caliente. The agents wrote from Abiquiu and this was not where the Apache were camped.

17. Tiller, *Jicarilla Apache Tribe*, 69–70.

18. Torrez, Robert J., and Robert Trapp, ed. *Rio Arriba: A New Mexico County*. Los Ranchos, NM: Rio Grande Books, 2010, 122.

19. Camp Plummer (1866–1869) was established by Civil War volunteer military. When the regular army, Company C, 37th Infantry, replaced the volunteers the name was changed to Fort Lowell. Giese, Dale F. *Forts of New Mexico, Echoes of the Bugle*. Silver City, NM: Phelps Dodge, 1991, 13. When a sub-agency of the Abiquiu Agency was established at Tierra Amarilla, the site was actually Las Nutrias, and was frequently referred to as Abiquiu.

20. Tiller, *Jicarilla Apache Tribe*, 78.

21. Chief Ouray (1820–1880), acknowledged chief of the Ute, was born in Taos of a Ute father and Jicarilla Apache mother. He learned to speak several languages, which made him instrumental in negotiations with the United States. The Ute recognize him as a great chief. Thrapp, Dan L. *Encyclopedia of Frontier Biography*. Lincoln: University of Nebraska Press, 1988, 1094. Tiller says that Ouray was Huero Mundo's half-brother. Tiller, *Jicarilla Apache Tribe*, 14.

22. Tiller, *Jicarilla Apache Tribe*, 76–80.

23. Tiller, *Jicarilla Apache Tribe*, 82.

24. Hatch is referring to the Mescalero Reservation in southern New Mexico. The Jicarilla would soon make the excuse that they couldn't go there because of the Lincoln County War and rustlers might steal their horses. The town of Lincoln is just a few miles away. The rustlers included Billy the Kid. The Llanero at times favored moving in with the Mescalero, while the Ollero generally opposed such a move.

25. Hatch to AAG Department of the Missouri, April 13, 1876, Vol. 30, No. 72, Fort Union Collection, Highlands University, Las Vegas, NM.

26. Hatch to AAG Department of Missouri, February 14, 1878, Vol. 32, No. 48, Fort Union Collection, Highlands University, Las Vegas, NM.

27. Tiller, *Jicarilla Apache Tribe*, 77.

28. Ibid., 77.

29. Ibid., 81.

30. Hatch to Commanding Officer, Fort Stanton, July 19, 1878, Vol. 32, No. 255, Fort Union Collection, Highlands University, Las Vegas, NM.

31. Hatch to Rucker, July 24, 1878, Vol. 32, No. 266, Fort Union Collection, Highlands University, Las Vegas, NM.

32. Loud, AAG, to Rucker, August 3, 1878, Vol. 32, No. 275, Fort Union Collection, Highlands University, Las Vegas, NM.

33. Loud to AAG Department of Missouri, September 10, 1878, Vol. 32, No. 330, Fort Union Collection, Highlands University, Las Vegas, NM.

34. Loud to Parker, 9th Cav., Cimarron, August 30, 1879, Vol. 33, No. 302, Fort Union Collection, Highlands University, Las Vegas, NM.

35. Hatch to AAG Department of Missouri, October 1, 1879, Vol. 34, No. 72, Fort Union Collection, Highlands University, Las Vegas, NM.

36. Augustin Vigil at age 104 was still alive on the reservation when the author was a child there.

37. Nothing remains today of Amargo. It was about four miles east of Dulce, near the ghost town Monero, which was occupied originally in the 1880s to mine coal for the Denver Rio Grande Railroad that ran from Durango, Colorado, to Chama, New Mexico, and on to Antonito, Colorado. In the 1880s, logging operations were conducted in the area. The tracks were pulled up in the 1970s and only the section from Chama to Antonito remains as a tourist train over the Cumbres Pass where Jicarilla fought the army in the 1840s.

38. Tiller, *Jicarilla Apache Tribe*, 83–84.

39. Ibid., 88.

40. This was blurred beyond recognition in the original report, which was corrected in a subsequent report which said Chino was actually Santiago Largo.

41. Whittamore to AAG District of New Mexico, February 3, 1881, Vol. 37, No. 56, Fort Union Collection, Highlands University, Las Vegas, NM.

42. Whittamore to AAG District of New Mexico, February 5, 1881, Vol. 37, No. 61, Fort Union Collection, Highlands University, Las Vegas, NM.

43. Ranald Mackenzie (July 27, 1840–January 19, 1889) was recognized as one of the greatest Indian fighters the US Army ever produced. In 1873, he took the 4th Cavalry Regiment deep into Mexico to punish Kickapoo Indians. His orders were secret and his action would have been disavowed if the Mexicans had caught him. The John Wayne movie *Rio Grande*, part of the cavalry trilogy, loosely follows this adventure. Thrapp, *Encyclopedia*, 927–28.

44. Mackenzie to AAG Department of Missouri, May 29, 1882, Vol. 38, No. 217, Fort Union Collection, Highlands University, Las Vegas, NM.

45. Mackenzie to Brady, July 31, 1882, Vol. 38, No. 278, Fort Union Collection, Highlands University, Las Vegas, NM.

46. Brady to AAG District of New Mexico, August 2, 1882, Vol. 38, No. 283, Fort Union Collection, Highlands University, Las Vegas, NM.

47. Mackenzie to AAG Department of Missouri, August 9, 1882, Vol. 38, No. 293, Fort Union Collection, Highlands University, Las Vegas, NM.

48. Pagosa Springs, Colorado, is about forty miles north of Amargo and is in a mining area.

49. Fort Lewis is at Durango, Colorado.

50. Mackenzie to Commander Fort Lewis, May 19, 1883, Vol. 39, No. 86, Fort Union Collection, Highlands University, Las Vegas, NM.

51. In 1861, the temperature dropped beyond 40 degrees F below zero. The temperature stayed below zero and didn't come up again for two months, never failing to go below minus 20 each night. People were living in tents, and a few froze to death while many others suffered from pneumonia.

52. Tiller, *Jicarilla Apache Tribe*, 88.

53. Ibid., 90.

54. Colonel Mackenzie held brevet rank as a general.

55. Mackenzie to Commander Fort Lewis, July 16, 1883, Vol. 39, No. 127, Fort Union Collection, Highlands University, Las Vegas, NM.
56. Stanley to AAG District of New Mexico, August 11, 1883, Vol. 39, No. 136, Fort Union Collection, Highlands University, Las Vegas, NM.
57. It would seem likely that a few hundred had faded away into the mountains and prairies declining the walk to Mescalero.
58. Farmer, W. Michael. *Apacheria: True Stories of Apache Culture: 1860–1920*. Guilford, CT: TwoDot, 2017.
59. Bradley to Commander Fort Stanton, July 7, 1885, Vol. 40, No. 133, Fort Union Collection, Highlands University, Las Vegas, NM.
60. And here you thought that government shutdowns and Congress failing to pass a budget were something new.
61. Lines had been strung from Mescalero to Fort Stanton and elsewhere. In some of the messages we catch the reference "the telephone, when it works," suggesting that phone service is almost as good as it was in my childhood on the Jicarilla Reservation.
62. Augustin Velarde and Augustin Pedillo.
63. Some of these messages originated as telegrams and the styling and wording are less than literary. Vance to AAG District of New Mexico, August 25, 1886, Vol. 41, No. 133, Fort Union Collection, Highlands University, Las Vegas, NM.
64. Bradley to Vance, August 26, 1886, Vol. 41, No. 116, Fort Union Collection, Highlands University, Las Vegas, NM.
65. The telephone wasn't working.
66. Pedillo and Velarde.
67. Vance to AAG District of New Mexico, September 27, 1886, Vol. 41, No. 142, Fort Union Collection, Highlands University, Las Vegas, NM.
68. Miles to Bradley, October 6, 1886, Vol. 41, No. 156, Fort Union Collection, Highlands University, Las Vegas, NM.
69. Wint to Commander, District of New Mexico, November 18, 1886, Vol. 41, No. 170, Fort Union Collection, Highlands University, Las Vegas, NM.
70. Grierson, Benjamin Henry (July 8, 1826–September 1, 1911) in April/May 1863 led a raid from Vicksburg to Baton Rouge, six hundred miles, behind Confederate lines to destroy southern railroads and divert troops. The story is loosely recounted in the John Wayne movie *The Horse Soldiers*.
71. The 10th Cavalry Regiment was one of two all-black cavalry regiments known as Buffalo Soldiers.
72. Grierson to AAG Whipple Barracks, Dept. of Arizona, November 19, 1886, Vol. 41, No. 171, Fort Union Collection, Highlands University, Las Vegas, NM.
73. Grierson to AAG Whipple Barracks, Dept. of Arizona, November 24, 1886, Vol. 41, No. 175, Fort Union Collection, Highlands University, Las Vegas, NM.
74. "The Dawes Act of 1887 (also known as the General Allotment Act or the Dawes Severalty Act of 1887), authorized the President of the United States to survey Native American tribal land and divide it into allotments for individual Native Americans. Those who accepted allotments and lived separately from the tribe would be granted United States citizenship. . . . The objectives of the Dawes Act were to abolish tribal

and communal land ownership of the tribes into individual land ownership rights in order to . . . stimulate assimilation of [Native Americans] into mainstream American society, and thereby lift individual Native Americans out of poverty. Individual household ownership of land and subsistence farming on the European-American model was seen as an essential step. The act provided that the government would classify as "excess" those Indian reservation lands remaining after allotments, and sell those lands on the open market, allowing purchase and settlement by non-Native Americans." https://en.wikipedia.org/wiki/Dawes_Act.

75. The Allotment Acts are hated by most Indians because they were used to cheat Indians out of much of their land and to limit tribal sovereignty. Indians were allotted a portion of land from their reservation and the surplus was sold off for the general welfare of the tribe. Amazingly, all of the desirable land seems to have fallen into white hands. The reservations you see today on maps are largely owned by whites. With whites on tribal land, tribal sovereignty was limited. By taking up US citizenship, the Indian was giving up his place in the tribe. Very few accepted the offer. The money raised by sale of land for the general good of the tribe seems to have gone mostly into the general fund, the annual budget of the Bureau of Indian Affairs. Not being a citizen had advantages for the Indian. In an outbreak he was usually treated as an enemy belligerent and prisoner of war rather than as a murderer or traitor. All Indians were made citizens by Congress in 1924. Duthu, N. Bruce. *American Indians and the Law.* New York: Penguin Books, 2009, 138.

76. Grierson to AAG Department of Arizona, February 1, 1887, Vol. 41, No. 180-181, Fort Union Collection, Highlands University, Las Vegas, NM.

77. Tiller, *Jicarilla Apache Tribe*, 96.

78. Tiller, *Jicarilla Apache Tribe*, 95.

79. Grierson to Lieutenant Glass, 6th Cavalry, October 21, 1887, Vol. 41, No. 260, Fort Union Collection, Highlands University, Las Vegas, NM.

80. Grierson to AAG Department of Arizona, May 25, 1888, Vol. 41, No. 293, Fort Union Collection, Highlands University, Las Vegas, NM.

Appendix B: Treaties with the Jicarilla

1. Hughes, John Taylor. *Doniphan's Expedition.* College Station: Texas A&M University Press, 1847 (1914 edition, 1997 reprint), 68.

2. Anonymous. *Jicarilla Apache Tribe: Historical Materials 1540–1887.* New York: Garland Publishing, 1974, 101–3.

3. Kappler, Charles J., LLM, Clerk to the Senate Committee on Indian Affairs, Compiled and Edited. *Indian Affairs: Laws and Treaties, Vol II (Treaties).* Washington, DC: Government Printing Office, 1904, http://avalon.law.yale.edu/19th_century/apa1852.asp.

4. Senate Executive Documents, 33 Cong, 1 Sess, No. 1, Pt. 1, 432; ibid., 33 Cong, 2 Sess, No. 1, Pt. 1, 374; Lane to Manypenny, May 28, 1853, and Treaty, MSS, LR. IAO New Mexico, NA.

5. Bender, Averam B. *The March of Empire: Frontier Defense in the Southwest, 1848–1860.* Lawrence: University of Kansas Press, 1952, 156.

6. Anonymous. *Jicarilla Apache Tribe: Historical Materials 1540–1887*. New York: Garland Publishing, 1974, 154–58. Meriwether, Sept 12, 1855: Unratified Treaty with Jicarillas, 274A, NM, OIA; Meriwether to Manypenny, Sept 15, 1855, N535/1855 NM LR OIA Sen Ex Docs. 34 Cong 1&2 see I No. 1, Pt. 1, 507–9.

7. OIA-LR, New Mexico Superintendency, doc. Y26-I858, M234, roll 549.

8. Misc. Records, Indian Collections, New Mexico State Records Center and Archives, Santa Fe.

Bibliography

Archival Sources

Fort Union Collection, Highlands University, Las Vegas, NM
New Mexico State Library and Archive, Santa Fe, NM
Peters, Dr. DeWitt Clinton, DeWitt Clinton Peters Papers, Bancroft Library, Berkeley, CA

Newspapers

Denver Post
New Orleans Picayune
Santa Fe Republican
Santa Fe Weekly Gazette

Articles/Chapters

Abel, Annie Heloise. "The Journal of John Greiner." *Old Santa Fe: A Magazine of History, Archaeology, Genealogy and Biography*, Vol. III/11 (July 1916).

Altshuler, Constance Wynn. "Arizona in 1861: A Contemporary Account by Samuel Robinson." *Journal of Arizona History* 25/1 (Spring 1984), 21–76.

Bender, Averam B. "Frontier Defense in the Territory of New Mexico, 1846–1853." *New Mexico Historical Review*, Vol. 9 (July 1934), 249–72.

Brooks, Clinton E., and Frank D. Reeve, ed. "A Dragoon in New Mexico, 1850–1856." *New Mexico Historical Review*, Vol. 22 (January and April 1947).

Burton, E. Bennet. "The Taos Rebellion." *Old Santa Fe*, Vol. I (1913), 186–209.

Carson, William G. B., ed. "William Carr Lane, Diary, Part I." *New Mexico Historical Review*, Vol. 39/3 (July 1964), 169–234.

———"William Carr Lane, Diary, Part II." *New Mexico Historical Review*, Vol. 39/4 (October 1964), 274–332.

Carter, Harvey Lewis, and LeRoy R. Hafen, ed. "Robert Fisher." In *Mountain Men and Fur Traders of the Far West*. Lincoln: University of Nebraska Press, 1982 (1965), 97–102.

Chacon, Eusebio, trans. Rafael Chacon. "Campaign Against Utes and Apaches in Southern Colorado, 1855." *Colorado Magazine*, Vol. 11 (May 1934), 108–12.

Crass, David C., and Deborah L. Wallsmith. "Where's the Beef? Food Supply at an Antebellum Frontier Post." *Historical Archaeology* 26 (1992), 3–23.

Ebright, Malcolm. "Agent Benjamin Thomas in New Mexico, 1872–1883: Indian Agents as Advocates for Native Americans." *New Mexico Historical Review*, Vol. 93/3 (Summer 2018), 303–38.

Gardner, Hamilton. "Philip St. George Cooke and the Apache, 1854." *New Mexico Historical Review*, Vol. 28 (April 1954), 115–32.

Goodrich, James. "Revolt at Mora, 1847." *New Mexico Historical Review*, Vol. 47/1 (Winter 1972), 49–60.

Gordon-McCutchan, R. C. "'Little Chief' and the Indians," in *The Short Truth about Kit Carson and the Indians.* Taos: Kit Carson Historic Museums, 1993.

Gorenfeld, Will. "The Battle of Cieneguilla: Dragoons vs. Jicarilla Apaches." *Wild West* 20/5 (February 2008).

———. "The Taos Mutiny of 1855." *New Mexico Historical Review*, Vol. 88/3 (Summer 2013).

Hocking, Doug. "New Mexico's Reviled Heroic Padre." *Wild West Magazine*, December 2013, 46–51.

Johnson, David M. "Apache Victory against the U.S. Dragoons, the Battle of Cieneguilla, New Mexico." In *Fields of Conflict, Battlefield Archaeology from the Roman Empire to the Korean War*, Douglas Scott et al. ed. Washington, DC: Potomac Books, 2009, 235–55.

Lecompte, Janet. "Manco Burro Pass Massacre." *New Mexico Historical Review*, Vol. 41/4 (October 1966), 305–18.

Mahan, Bill. "Fort Massachusetts." *San Luis Valley Historian*, Vol. 15/2 (Spring 1983).

Matson, Daniel S., and Albert H. Schroeder. "Codero's Description of the Apache—1796." *New Mexico Historical Review*, Vol. 32/4 (October 1957).

Moody, Marshall D. "Kit Carson, Agent to the Indians in New Mexico 1853–1861." *New Mexico Historical Review*, Vol. 28/1 (January 1953).

Murphy, Lawrence. "Rayado: Pioneer Settlement in Northeastern New Mexico 1848–1857." *New Mexico Historical Review*, Vol. 46/1, January 1971.

———. "The United States Army in Taos, 1847–1852." *New Mexico Historical Review*, Vol. 47/1, January 1972.

Opler, Morris E. "Jicarilla Apache Territory, Economy, and Society in 1850." *Southwestern Journal of Anthropology* 27 (1971): 309–29.

Parker, John. "The Kelsey Brothers: A California Disaster." Lake County Historical Society, 2012, https://www.academia.edu/5539505/The_Kelsey_Brothers_A_California_Disaster.

Simmons, Marc. "The Strange Fate of Kit Carson," in *The Short Truth about Kit Carson and the Indians.* Taos: Kit Carson Historic Museums, 1993.

———. "The Wagon Mound Massacre," in Mark L. Gardner, ed., *The Mexican Road: Trade, Travel, and Confrontation on the Santa Fe Trail.* Manhattan, KS: Sunflower University Press, 1989.

Taylor, Morris F. "Action at Fort Massachusetts: The Indian Campaign of 1855." *Colorado Magazine*, Vol. 42/4 (1965), 292–310.

———. "Campaigns against the Jicarillas, 1854." *New Mexico Historical Review*, Vol. 44/4 (1969).

———. "Campaigns against the Jicarillas, 1855." *New Mexico Historical Review*, Vol. 45/2 (1970).

Windham, William T. "The Problem of Supply in the Trans-Mississippi Confederacy." *Journal of Southern History* 27/2 (May 1961).

Woodward, Arthur. "Lances at San Pascual." *California Historical Society Quarterly* XXV/4 (December 1946), 289–308.

———. "Lances at San Pascual." *California Historical Society Quarterly* XXVI/1 (March 1947), 21–62.

BIBLIOGRAPHY

Books

Abel, Annie Heloise. *The Official Correspondence of James S. Calhoun: While Indian Agent at Santa Fe and Superintendent of Indian Affairs in New Mexico.* Washington, DC: Government Printing Office (Forgotten Books Reprint), 1915.

Ahnert, Gerald T. *The Butterfield Trail and Overland Mail Company in Arizona, 1858–1861.* Canastota, NY: Canastota Publishing, 2011.

Ake, Jeff, and James B. O'Neil, ed. *They Die but Once: The Story of a Tejano.* New York: Knight Publications, 1935.

Alexander, David V., and Daniel C. B. Rathbun. *New Mexico Frontier Military Place Names.* Las Cruces, NM: Yucca Tree Press, 2003.

Anonymous. *Apache Indians VII: Jicarilla Apache Tribe: Historical Materials 1540–1887.* New York: Garland Publishing, 1974.

Ball, Durwood. *Army Regulars on the Western Frontier, 1848–1861.* Norman: University of Oklahoma Press, 2001.

Barry, Louise. *The Beginning of the West: Annals of the Kansas Gateway to the American West 1540–1854.* Topeka: Kansas State Historical Society, 1972.

Beck, Warren A. *New Mexico: A History of Four Centuries.* Norman: University of Oklahoma Press, 1962.

Bender, Averam B. *Apache Indians IX: A Study of Jicarilla Apache Indians 1846–1887.* New York: Garland Publishing, 1974 (1959).

———. *The March of Empire: Frontier Defense in the Southwest, 1848–1860.* Lawrence: University of Kansas Press, 1952.

Bennett, James A., and Clinton E. Brooks, ed. *Forts and Forays: A Dragoon in New Mexico, 1850–1856.* Albuquerque: University of New Mexico Press, 1995.

Bison, George Rutledge, and Ralph P. Bieber, ed. *Journal of a Soldier Under Kearny and Doniphan, 1846.* Philadelphia: Porcupine Press, 1974.

Brewerton, George Douglas, and Marc Simmons, introduction. *Overland with Kit Carson: A Narrative of the Old Spanish Trail in '48.* Lincoln: University of Nebraska Press, 1993.

Carter, Harvey Lewis. *"Dear Old Kit": The Historical Christopher Carson.* Norman: University of Oklahoma Press, 1990.

Chaput, Donald. *François X. Aubry: Trader, Trailmaker and Voyageur in the Southwest 1846–1854.* Glendale, CA: Arthur H. Clark, 1975.

Chavez, Fray Angelico. *Origins of New Mexico Families: A Genealogy of the Spanish Colonial Period.* Santa Fe: Museum of New Mexico Press, 1992 (1954).

Chronic, Halka. *Roadside Geology of Arizona.* Missoula, MT: Mountain Press Publishing, 1983.

Clarke, Dwight L. *The Original Journals of Henry Smith Turner: With Stephen Watts Kearny to New Mexico and California 1846-1847.* Norman: University of Oklahoma Press, 1966.

Clary, David A. *Eagles and Empire: The United States, Mexico and the Struggle for a Continent.* New York: Bantam Books, 2009.

365

Cobos, Ruben. *Dictionary of New Mexico and Southern Colorado Spanish*. Albuquerque: Museum of New Mexico Press, 1983.

Coffman, Edward M. *The Old Army: A Portrait of the American Army in Peacetime 1784–1898*. New York: Oxford University Press, 1986.

Connor, Seymour V., and Jimmy M. Skaggs. *Broadcloth and Britches: The Santa Fe Trade*. College Station: Texas A&M University Press, 1977.

Cook, Mary J. Straw. *Dona Tules: Santa Fe's Courtesan and Gambler*. Albuquerque: University of New Mexico Press, 2007.

Cooke, Philip St. George. *Cavalry Tactics or Regulations for the Instruction, Formations, and Movements of the Cavalry of the Army and Volunteers of the United States, Vol. I*. Washington, DC: Department of War, 1861.

———. *Scenes & Adventures in the Army, or Romance of Military Life*. Santa Barbara, CA: Narrative Press, 2004.

Coulter, Lane, and Maurice Dixon, Jr. *New Mexican Tinwork: 1840–1940*. Albuquerque: University of New Mexico Press, 1990.

Coy, Owne C. *The Battle of San Pasqual*. Sacramento: California State Printing Office, 1921.

Dary, David. *The Santa Fe Trail: Its History, Legends, and Lore*. New York: Alfred A. Knopf, 2000.

Davidson, Homer K. *Black Jack Davidson, A Cavalry Commander on the Western Frontier: The Life of General John W. Davidson*. Glendale, CA: Arthur H. Clark, 1974.

Decker, Peter R. *"The Utes Must Go!" American Expansion and the Removal of a People*. Golden, CO: Fulcrum Publishing, 2004.

Dunlay, Thomas W. *Kit Carson and the Indians*. Lincoln: University of Nebraska Press, 2000.

Duthu, N. Bruce. *American Indians and the Law*. New York: Penguin Books, 2009.

Ebright, Malcolm, and Rick Hendricks. *The Witches of Abiquiu: The Governor, the Priest, the Genizaro Indians, and the Devil*. Albuquerque: University of New Mexico Press, 2006.

Eiselt, B. Sunday. *Becoming White Clay: A History and Archaeology of Jicarilla Apache Enclavement*. Salt Lake City: University of Utah Press, 2012.

Eisenhower, John S. D. *So Far from God: The U.S. War with Mexico, 1846–1848*. Norman: University of Oklahoma Press, 2000.

Emmett, Chris. *Fort Union and the Winning of the Southwest*. Norman: University of Oklahoma Press, 1965.

Farmer, W. Michael. *Apacheria: True Stories of Apache Culture: 1860–1920*. Guilford, CT: TwoDot, 2017.

Favour, Alpheus H. *Old Bill Williams, Mountain Man*. Norman: University of Oklahoma Press, 1962.

Field, Matthew C., and John E. Sunder, ed. *Matt Field on the Santa Fe Trail*. Norman: University of Oklahoma Press, 1960.

Field, Ron. *Forts of the American Frontier: 1820–1891*. New York: Osprey, 2006.

Floyd, Dale E., introduction. *Chronological List of Actions from January 15, 1837 to January 1891.* Washington, DC: Old Army Press, 1979.

Frazer, Robert W. *Forts and Supplies: The Role of the Army in the Economy of the Southwest, 1846–1861.* Albuquerque: University of New Mexico Press, 1983.

Frazier, Donald S. *Blood & Treasure: Confederate Empire in the Southwest.* College Station: Texas A&M University Press, 1997.

Frémont, John Charles. *John Charles Frémont: Explorer of the American West, Memoirs of My Life.* New York: Cooper Square Press, 2001 (1887).

Garrard, Lewis H. *Wah-to-yah and the Taos Trail.* Norman: University of Oklahoma Press, 1955.

Giese, Dale F. *Forts of New Mexico, Echoes of the Bugle.* Silver City, NM: Phelps Dodge, 1991.

Goddard, Pliny Earle. *Jicarilla Apache Texts.* Charleston, SC: BiblioBazaar, 2008.

Gorenfeld, Will, and John Gorenfeld. *Kearny's Dragoons Out West: The Birth of the U.S. Cavalry.* Norman: University of Oklahoma Press, 2016.

Grant, Campbell. *Canyon de Chelly: Its People and Rock Art.* Tucson: University of Arizona Press, 1978.

Gregg, Josiah. *Commerce of the Prairies: Life on the Great Plains in the 1830's and 1840's.* Santa Barbara, CA: Narrative Press, 2001.

Groom, Winston. *Kearny's March: The Epic Creation of the American West.* New York: Alfred A. Knopf, 2011.

Guild, Thema S., and Harvey L. Carter. *Kit Carson: A Pattern for Heroes.* Lincoln: University of Nebraska Press, 1984.

Gunnerson, Delores A. *The Jicarilla Apaches: A Study in Survival.* Dekalb: Northern Illinois University Press, 1974.

Haley, James L. *Apaches: A History and Culture Portrait.* Norman: University of Oklahoma Press, 1981.

Hammond, George P. *The Adventures of Alexander Barclay, Mountain Man.* Denver: Old West Publishing, 1976.

Hannum, Anna Paschall, ed. *A Quaker Forty-Niner: The Adventures of Charles Edward Pancoast on the American Frontier.* Philadelphia: University of Pennsylvania Press, 1930.

Hocking, Doug. *Black Legend: George Bascom, Cochise, and the Start of the Apache Wars.* Guilford, CT: TwoDot, 2018.

———. *Tom Jeffords: Friend of Cochise.* Guilford, CT: TwoDot, 2017.

Hughes, John Taylor. *Doniphan's Expedition.* College Station: Texas A&M University Press, 1847 (1914 edition, 1997 reprint).

Hyde, George E., and Svoie Lottinville, ed. *Life of George Bent: Written from his Letters.* Norman: University of Oklahoma Press, 1968.

Hyslop, Stephen G. *Bound for Santa Fe: The Road to New Mexico and the American Conquest, 1806–1848.* Norman: University of Oklahoma Press, 2002.

Inman, Colonel Henry. *The Old Santa Fe Trail, the Story of a Great Highway.* Kindle: CreateSpace, 2016 (1897).

Jackson, Hal, and Marc Simmons. *The Santa Fe Trail, a Guide*. Woodston, KS: Trails Press, 2015.

Johnson, David M., and Chris Adams. *Final Report on the Battle of Cieneguilla: A Jicarilla Apache Victory Over the U.S. Dragoons, March 30, 1854*. Santa Fe: Southwestern Region, 2009.

Julyan, Robert. *The Place Names of New Mexico*. Albuquerque: University of New Mexico Press, 1996.

Kappler, Charles J., LLM, Clerk to the Senate Committee on Indian Affairs, Compiled and Edited. *Indian Affairs: Laws and Treaties, Vol. II (Treaties)*. Washington, DC: Government Printing Office, 1904, http://avalon.law.yale.edu/19th_century/apa1852.asp.

Katcher, Philip. *U.S. Cavalry on the Plains, 1850–1890*. New York: Osprey, 1985.

Langellier, John P. *Bluecoats: U.S. Army in the West, 1848–1897*. Mechanicsburg, PA: Stackpole, 1995.

Langellier, John P., and Bill Younghusband. *U.S. Dragoons: 1833–1855*. New York: Osprey, 1995.

Lauritzen, Jonreed. *The Battle of San Pasqual*. New York: G.P. Putnam's Sons, 1968.

Lavender, David. *Bent's Fort*. Lincoln: University of Nebraska Press, 1954.

Leckie, Shirley A., and William H. Leckie. *Unlikely Warriors: General Benjamin Grierson and His Family*. Norman: University of Oklahoma Press, 1984.

Lecompte, Janet. *Pueblo, Hardscrabble, Greenhorn: Society on the High Plains, 1832–1856*. Norman: University of Oklahoma Press, 1978.

Lenderman, Gary D. *The* Santa Fe Republican*: New Mexico Territory's First Newspaper 1847–1849*. San Bernardino, CA: Createspace, 2011.

Lowe, Percival. *Five Years a Dragoon: '49 to '54, and Other Adventures on the Great Plains*. Norman: University of Oklahoma Press, 1965.

Lynn, Alvin R. *Kit Carson and the First Battle of Adobe Walls: A Tale of Two Journeys*. Lubbock: Texas Tech University Press, 2014.

Magoffin, Susan Shelby, and Stella M. Drumm, ed. *Down the Santa Fe Trail and into Mexico: The Diary of Susan Shelby Magoffin, 1846-1847*. Lincoln: University of Nebraska Press, 1926, 1962.

Mails, Thomas E. *The People Called Apache*. Englewood Cliffs, NJ: Routledge/Prentice-Hall, 1974.

McChristian, Douglas C. *Regular Army O! Soldiering on the Western Frontier, 1865–1891*. Norman: University of Oklahoma Press, 2017.

McLachlan, Sean. *Combat Apache Warrior versus U.S. Cavalryman 1846–1886*. Oxford: Osprey, 2016.

McNierney, Michael. *Taos 1847: The Revolt in Contemporary Accounts*. Boulder, CO: Johnson Publishing, 1980.

Meline, James F. *Two Thousand Miles on Horseback: Santa Fe and Back: A Summer Tour through Kansas, Nebraska, Colorado, and New Mexico in the Year 1866*. Albuquerque: Horn & Wallace, 1966.

Meriwether, David. *My Life in the Mountains and on the Plains. The Newly Discovered Autobiography*. Norman: University of Oklahoma Press, 1965.

Michno, Gregory. *Depredation and Deceit: The Making of the Jicarilla and Ute Wars in New Mexico.* Norman: University of Oklahoma Press, 2017.

———. *Encyclopedia of the Indian Wars: Western Battles and Skirmishes 1850–1890.* Missoula, MT: Mountain Press Publishing, 2003.

Michno, Gregory, and Susan Michno. *A Fate Worse Than Death: Indian Captivities in the West, 1830–1885.* Caldwell, ID: Caxton Press, 2007.

———. *Forgotten Fights: Little-Known Raids and Skirmishes on the Frontier, 1823 to 1890.* Missoula, MT: Mountain Press Publishing, 2008.

Miller, Darlis A., ed. *Above a Common Soldier: Frank and Mary Clarke in the American West and Civil War.* Albuquerque: University of New Mexico Press, 1997.

Morgan, Dale, ed. *Overland in 1846: Diaries and Letters of the California-Oregon Trail,* Volumes 1 and 2. Lincoln: University of Nebraska Press, 1993.

Murphy, Lawrence R. *Lucien Bonaparte Maxwell: Napoleon of the Southwest.* Norman: University of Oklahoma Press, 1983.

Norris, L. David, James C. Milligan, and Odie B. Faulk. *William H. Emory: Soldier-Scientist.* Tucson: University of Arizona Press, 1998.

Oliva, Leo E. *Fort Union and the Frontier Army in the Southwest: A Historic Resource Study, Fort Union National Monument, Fort Union, New Mexico.* Professional Papers No. 41. Santa Fe: Southwest Cultural Resources Center, 1993.

Opler, Morris Edward. *Childhood and Youth in Jicarilla Apache Society.* Los Angeles: Southwest Museum, 1946.

———. *Myths and Tales of the Jicarilla Apache Indians.* New York: Dover Publications, 1995 (1938).

Parkhill, Forbes. *The Blazed Trail of Antoine Leroux.* Los Angeles: Westernlore Publications, 1965.

Paterek, Josephine. *Encyclopedia of American Indian Costume.* New York: W.W. Norton, 1994.

Peters, DeWitt C. *The Life and Adventures of Kit Carson, the Nestor of the Rocky Mountains, from Facts Narrated by Himself.* Middlesex, UK: Echo Library, 2006.

Pettis, George H. *Kit Carson's Fight with the Comanche and Kiowa Indians, at the Adobe Walls on the Canadian River, November 25th, 1864.* Miami: Hard Press Publishing (Kindle), 1878.

Phone, Wilhelmina, Maureen Olson, and Matilda Martinez. *Dictionary of Apache: Abáachi Mizaa Iłkeé Siijai.* Albuquerque: University of New Mexico Press, 2007.

Poling-Kempes, Leslie. *Valley of the Shining Stone: The Story of Abiquiu.* Tucson: University of Arizona Press, 1997.

Porter, Clyde, and Mae Reed Porter, John E. Sunder, ed. *Matt Field on the Santa Fe Trail.* Norman: University of Oklahoma Press, 1960.

Quaife, Milo Milton, ed. *Kit Carson's Autobiography.* Lincoln: University of Nebraska Press, 1966.

Rickey, Don, Jr. *Forty Miles a Day on Beans and Hay: The Enlisted Soldier Fighting the Indian Wars.* Norman: University of Oklahoma Press, 1963.

Riddle, Kenyon, John Riddle, and Nancy Riddle Madden, ed. *Records and Maps of the Old Santa Fe Trail*, Revised and Enlarged Edition. Stuart, FL: Southeastern Printing, 1963.

Roberts, David. *A Newer World: Kit Carson, John C. Fremont, and the Claiming of the American West*. New York: Touchstone by Simon & Schuster, 2001.

Roberts, Robert B. *Encyclopedia of Historic Forts: The Military, Pioneer, and Trading Posts of the United States*. New York: Macmillan, 1988.

Rodenbough, Theophilus F. *From Everglade to Cañon with the Second Dragoons*. Norman: University of Oklahoma Press, 2000.

Sabin, Edwin L. *Kit Carson Days, 1809–1868: Adventures in the Path of Empire*, 2 Volumes. Lincoln: University of Nebraska Press, 1995 (1935).

Sanchez, Pedro. *Recollections of the Life of the Priest Don Antonio José Martínez.* Santa Fe: Sunstone, 2006.

Santiago, Mark. *A Bad Peace and a Good War: Spain and the Mescalero Apache Uprising of 1795–1799*. Norman: University of Oklahoma Press, 2018.

Schaafsma, Curtis F. *Apaches de Navajo: Seventeenth-Century Navajos in the Chama Valley of New Mexico*. Salt Lake City: University of Utah Press, 2002.

Scott, Douglas, Lawrence Babits, and Charles Haecker, ed. *Fields of Conflict: Battlefield Archaeology from the Roman Empire to the Korean War*. Lincoln, NE: Potomac Books, 2009.

Sides, Hampton. *Blood and Thunder: An Epic of the American West.* Garden City, NY: Doubleday, 2006.

Simmons, Marc. *Kit Carson and His Three Wives: A Family History*. Albuquerque: University of New Mexico Press, 2003.

Smith, Ralph Adam. *Borderlander: The Life of James Kirker, 1793–1852*. Norman: University of Oklahoma Press, 1999.

Sperry, T. J. *Fort Union, A Photo History*. Tucson: Southwest Parks and Monuments Association, 1991.

Spicer, Edward H. *Cycles of Conquest: The Impact of Spain, Mexico, and the United States on the Indians of the Southwest, 1533–1960*. Tucson: University of Arizona Press, 1962.

Stanley, F. *Jicarilla Apache*. Pampa, TX: Pampa Print Shop, 1967.

———. *The Wagon Mound, New Mexico Story*. Pep, TX: Stanley, 1968.

Steffen, Randy. *The Horse Soldier 1776–1943: The United States Cavalryman: His Uniforms, Arms, Accoutrements, and Equipments, Volume 1—The Revolution, the War of 1812, the Early Frontier 1776–1850.* Norman: University of Oklahoma Press, 1977.

Stevens, T. Rorie. *The Death of a Governor*. Jacksonville, TX: Jayroe Graphic Arts, 1971.

Sunseri, Jun U. *Situational Identities along the Raiding Frontier of Colonial New Mexico*. Lincoln: University of Nebraska Press, 2017.

Tanner, Clara Lee. *Apache Indian Baskets*. Tucson: University of Arizona Press, 1982.

Taylor, John M. *Bloody Valverde: A Civil War Battle on the Rio Grande, February 21, 1862*. Albuquerque: University of New Mexico Press, 1999.

Terrell, John Upton. *Apache Chronicle: The Story of the People*. New York: Thomas Y. Crowell, 1974.

Tevis, Captain James Henry, Betty Barr, and William Kelly, ed. *Arizona in the 50s*. Albuquerque: University of New Mexico Press, 1954.

Thompson, Jerry D. *Civil War in the Southwest: Recollections of the Sibley Brigade*. College Station: Texas A&M University Press, 2001.

———. *Desert Tiger: Captain Paddy Graydon and the Civil War in the Far Southwest*. El Paso: Western Press, University of Texas at El Paso, 1992.

Thrapp, Dan L. *Encyclopedia of Frontier Biography*. Lincoln: University of Nebraska Press, 1988.

Tiller, Veronica E. Velarde. *The Jicarilla Apache Tribe*. Lincoln: University of Nebraska Press, 1992.

Torrez, Robert J., and Robert Trapp, ed. *Rio Arriba: A New Mexico County*. Los Ranchos, NM: Rio Grande Books, 2010.

Twitchell, Ralph Emerson. *The History of the Military Occupation of the Territory of New Mexico from 1846 to 1851*. Chicago: Rio Grande Press, 1983 (1909).

Utley, Robert M. *Frontiersmen in Blue: The United States Army and the Indian, 1848–1865*. New York: Macmillan, 1967.

Utley, Robert M., and Wilcomb E. Washburn. *Indian Wars*. New York: Houghton Mifflin, 2002 (1977).

Van Roekel, Gertrude. *Jicarilla Apaches*. San Antonio: Naylor Press, 1971.

Webb, George W. *Chronological List of Engagements between the Regular Army of the United States and Various Tribes of Hostile Indians*. New York: Old Army Press, 1979 (1891).

Webb, James Josiah, and Ralph P. Bieber, ed. *Adventures in the Santa Fe Trade 1844–1847*. Lincoln: University of Nebraska Press, 1995.

Wetherington, Ronald K. *Ceran St. Vrain: American Frontier Entrepreneur*. Santa Fe: Sunstone, 2012.

INDEX

About the Author

In 2018, Doug Hocking's biography *Tom Jeffords: Friend of Cochise* (think Jimmy Stewart in *Broken Arrow* riding alone into Cochise's Stronghold to make the peace) was honored with a Spur Award from Western Writers of America and a Co-Founders Award from Westerners International. Award-winning author and speaker Doug Hocking is an independent scholar who has completed advanced studies in American history, ethnology, and historical archaeology. He is a retired armored cavalry officer who also worked in military intelligence. He grew up among the Jicarilla Apache and *paisanos* of the Rio Arriba (Northern New Mexico). *True West Magazine* named *Black Legend: George Bascom, Cochise, and the Start of the Apache Wars* Best Indian History of 2018. His work has appeared in *True West*, *Wild West*, *Desert Tracks*, and the *Journal of Arizona History*. Doug is a gubernatorial appointee to the board of the Arizona Historical Society.